PSYCHOSOCIAL DYNAMICS OF CYBER SECURITY

This new volume, edited by industrial and organizational psychologists, looks at the important topic of cyber security work in the United States and around the world. With contributions from experts in the fields of industrial and organizational psychology, human factors, computer science, economics, and applied anthropology, the book takes the position that employees in cyber security professions must maintain attention over long periods of time, must make decisions with imperfect information with the potential to exceed their cognitive capacity, may often need to contend with stress and fatigue, and must frequently interact with others in team settings and multiteam systems. Consequently, psychosocial dynamics become a critical driver of cyber security effectiveness. Chapters in the book reflect a multilevel perspective (individuals, teams, multiteam systems) and describe cognitive, affective, and behavioral inputs, processes, and outcomes that operate at each level. The book chapters also include contributions from both research scientists and cyber security policy makers/professionals to promote a strong scientist–practitioner dynamic. The intent of the book editors is to inform both theory and practice regarding the psychosocial dynamics of cyber security work.

Stephen J. Zaccaro is professor of psychology at George Mason University.

Reeshad S. Dalal is chair of the Department of Psychology and associate professor of industrial/organizational psychology at George Mason University.

Lois E. Tetrick is professor in the industrial/organizational psychology program at George Mason University.

Julie A. Steinke is a Lead Social and Behavioral Scientist with The MITRE Corporation.

SERIES IN APPLIED PSYCHOLOGY

Jeanette N. Cleveland, Colorado State University
Kevin R. Murphy, Landy Litigation and Colorado State University

Series Editors
Edwin A. Fleishman, Founding series editor (1987-2010)

Winfred Arthur, Jr., Eric Anthony Day, Winston Bennett, Jr., and Antoinette M. Portrey
Individual and Team Skill Decay: The Science and Implications for Practice

Gregory Bedny and David Meister
The Russian Theory of Activity: Current Applications to Design and Learning

Winston Bennett, Jr., Charles E. Lance, and David J. Woehr
Performance Measurement: Current Perspectives and Future Challenges

Michael T. Brannick, Eduardo Salas, and Carolyn Prince
Team Performance Assessment and Measurement: Theory, Methods, and Applications

Zinta S. Byrne
Understanding Employee Engagement: Theory, Research, and Practice

Neil D. Christiansen and Robert P. Tett
Handbook of Personality at Work

Jeanette N. Cleveland, Margaret Stockdale, and Kevin R. Murphy
Women and Men in Organizations: Sex and Gender Issues at Work

Aaron Cohen
Multiple Commitments in the Workplace: An Integrative Approach

Russell Cropanzano
Justice in the Workplace: Approaching Fairness in Human Resource Management, Volume 1

Russell Cropanzano
Justice in the Workplace: From Theory to Practice, Volume 2

David V. Day, Stephen J. Zaccaro, and Stanley M. Halpin
Leader Development for Transforming Organizations: Growing Leaders for Tomorrow

Stewart I. Donaldson, Mihaly Csikszentmihalyi and Jeanne Nakamura
Applied Positive Psychology: Improving Everyday Life, Health, Schools, Work, and Safety.

James E. Driskell and Eduardo Salas
Stress and Human Performance

Sidney A. Fine and Steven F. Cronshaw
Functional Job Analysis: A Foundation for Human Resources Management

Sidney A. Fine and Maury Getkate
Benchmark Tasks for Job Analysis: A Guide for Functional Job Analysis (FJA) Scales

J. Kevin Ford, Steve W. J. Kozlowski, Kurt Kraiger, Eduardo Salas, and Mark S. Teachout
Improving Training Effectiveness in Work Organizations

Jerald Greenberg
Organizational Behavior: The State of the Science, Second Edition

Jerald Greenberg
Insidious Workplace Behavior

Itzhak Harpaz and Raphael Snir
Heavy Work Investment: Its Nature, Sources, Outcomes and Future Directions

Edwin Hollander
Inclusive Leadership: The Essential Leader-Follower Relationship

Ann Hergatt Huffman and Stephanie R. Klein
Green Organizations: Driving Change with I-O Psychology

Jack Kitaeff
Handbook of Police Psychology

Uwe E. Kleinbeck, Hans-Henning Quast, Henk Thierry, and Hartmut Häcker
Work Motivation

Laura L. Koppes
Historical Perspectives in Industrial and Organizational Psychology

Ellen Kossek and Susan Lambert
Work and Life Integration: Organizational, Cultural, and Individual Perspectives

Martin I. Kurke and Ellen M. Scrivner
Police Psychology into the 21st Century

Joel Lefkowitz
Ethics and Values in Industrial and Organizational Psychology

John Lipinski and Laura M. Crothers
Bullying in the Workplace: Causes, Symptoms, and Remedies

Manuel London
Job Feedback: Giving, Seeking, and Using Feedback for Performance Improvement, Second Edition

Manuel London
How People Evaluate Others in Organizations

Manuel London
Leadership Development: Paths to Self-Insight and Professional Growth

Manuel London
The Power of Feedback: Giving, Seeking, and Using Feedback for Performance Improvement

Robert F. Morrison and Jerome Adams
Contemporary Career Development Issues

Michael D. Mumford
Pathways to Outstanding Leadership: A Comparative Analysis of Charismatic, Ideological, and Pragmatic Leaders

Michael D. Mumford, Garnett Stokes, and William A. Owens
Patterns of Life History: The Ecology of Human Individuality

Kevin Murphy
A Critique of Emotional Intelligence: What Are the Problems and How Can They Be Fixed?

Kevin R. Murphy
Validity Generalization: A Critical Review

Kevin R. Murphy and Frank E. Saal
Psychology in Organizations: Integrating Science and Practice

Susan E. Murphy and Rebecca J. Reichard
Early Development and Leadership: Building the Next Generation of Leaders

Susan Elaine Murphy and Ronald E. Riggio
The Future of Leadership Development

Margaret B. Neal and Leslie B. Hammer
Working Couples Caring for Children and Aging Parents: Effects on Work and Well-Being

Robert E. Ployhart, Benjamin Schneider, and Neal Schmitt
Staffing Organizations: Contemporary Practice and Theory, Third Edition

Steven A.Y. Poelmans
Work and Family: An International Research Perspective

Erich P. Prien, Jeffery S. Schippmann, and Kristin O. Prien
Individual Assessment: As Practiced in Industry and Consulting

Robert D. Pritchard, Sallie J. Weaver, and Elissa L. Ashwood
Evidence-Based Productivity Improvement: A Practical Guide to the Productivity Measurement and Enhancement System (Pr.Mes)

Ned Rosen
Teamwork and the Bottom Line: Groups Make a Difference

Eduardo Salas, Stephen M. Fiore, and Michael P. Letsky
Theories of Team Cognition: Cross-Disciplinary Perspectives

Heinz Schuler, James L. Farr, and Mike Smith
Personnel Selection and Assessment: Individual and Organizational Perspectives

John W. Senders and Neville P. Moray
Human Error: Cause, Prediction, and Reduction

Lynn Shore, Jacqueline A.M. Coyle-Shapiro and Lois E. Tetrick
The Employee–Organization Relationship: Applications for the 21st Century

Kenneth S. Shultz and Gary A. Adams
Aging and Work in the 21st Century

Frank J. Smith
Organizational Surveys: The Diagnosis and Betterment of Organizations Through Their Members

Dianna L. Stone and Eugene F. Stone-Romero
The Influence of Culture on Human Resource Management Processes and Practices

Kecia M. Thomas
Diversity Resistance in Organizations

Kecia M. Thomas, Victoria C. Plaut, and Ny Mia Tran
Diversity Ideologies in Organizations

George C. Thornton III and Rose Mueller-Hanson
Developing Organizational Simulations: A Guide for Practitioners and Students

George C. Thornton III and Deborah E. Rupp
Assessment Centers in Human Resource Management: Strategies for Prediction, Diagnosis, and Development

Yoav Vardi and Ely Weitz
Misbehavior in Organizations: Theory, Research, and Management

Patricia Voydanoff
Work, Family, and Community: Exploring Interconnections

Mo Wang, Deborah A. Olson, and Kenneth S. Shultz
Mid and Late Career Issues: An Integrative Perspective

Mark Alan Wilson, Winston Bennett, Shanan Gwaltney Gibson and George Michael Alliger
The Handbook of Work Analysis: Methods, Systems, Applications and Science of Work Measurement in Organizations

Stephen J. Zaccaro, Reeshad S. Dalal, Lois E. Tetrick, and Julie A. Steinke
Psychosocial Dynamics in Cyber Security

PSYCHOSOCIAL DYNAMICS OF CYBER SECURITY

Edited by
Stephen J. Zaccaro, Reeshad S. Dalal,
Lois E. Tetrick, and Julie A. Steinke

NEW YORK AND LONDON

First published 2016
by Routledge
711 Third Avenue, New York, NY 10017

and by Routledge
27 Church Road, Hove, East Sussex BN3 2FA

Routledge is an imprint of the Taylor & Francis Group, an Informa business

© 2016 Taylor & Francis

The right of the editors to be identified as the authors of the editorial material, and of the authors for their individual chapters, has been asserted in accordance with sections 77 and 78 of the Copyright, Designs and Patents Act 1988.

All rights reserved. No part of this book may be reprinted or reproduced or utilised in any form or by any electronic, mechanical, or other means, now known or hereafter invented, including photocopying and recording, or in any information storage or retrieval system, without permission in writing from the publishers.

Trademark notice: Product or corporate names may be trademarks or registered trademarks, and are used only for identification and explanation without intent to infringe.

Library of Congress Cataloging-in-Publication Data
Psychosocial dynamics of cyber security / edited by Stephen J. Zaccaro, Reeshad S. Dalal, Lois E. Tetrick, and Julie Steinke.
pages cm. – (Applied psychology)
Includes index.
ISBN 978-1-84872-565-2 (hbk) – ISBN 978-1-84872-566-9 (pbk) – ISBN 978-1-315-79635-2 (ebk)
1. Computer programmers–Job stress. 2. Electronic data processing personnel–Job stress. 3. Data protection. 4. Computer security. 5. Computer networks–Security measures. 6. Information technology–Security measures. 7. Psychology, Industrial. I. Zaccaro, Stephen J., editor.
HD8039.D37P79 2016
658.4'78–dc23
2015023244

ISBN: 978-1-84872-565-2 (hbk)
ISBN: 978-1-84872-566-9 (pbk)
ISBN: 978-1-31579-635-2 (ebk)

Typeset in Bembo
by Cenveo Publisher Services

CONTENTS

About the Editors   *xi*
About the Contributors   *xiv*
List of Figures   *xxi*
List of Tables   *xxiii*
Series Foreword   *xxiv*
Kevin R. Murphy and Jeanette N. Cleveland
Foreword: The Need for a Psychosocial Look at Cyber Security   *xxvi*
Shari Lawrence Pfleeger

1   The Psychosocial Dynamics of Cyber Security: An Overview   1
Stephen J. Zaccaro, Reeshad S. Dalal, Lois E. Tetrick, and Julie A. Steinke

2   A Comprehensive Multilevel Taxonomy of Cyber Security Incident Response Performance   13
Stephen J. Zaccaro, Amber K. Hargrove, Tiffani R. Chen, Kristin M. Repchick, and Tracy McCausland

3   The Role of Processes in Security Operations Centers   56
Sandeep Bhatt, William Horne, Sathya Sundaramurthy, and Loai Zomlot

4   Escalation: An Understudied Team Decision-Making Structure   74
Reeshad S. Dalal, Balca Bolunmez, Alan J. Tomassetti, and Zitong Sheng

5	Insider Threat in Cyber Security: What the Organizational Psychology Literature on Counterproductive Work Behavior Can and Cannot (Yet) Tell Us *Reeshad S. Dalal and Aiva K. Gorab*	92
6	Creativity and Innovation in Cyber Security Work *Julie A. Steinke, Laura Fletcher, Qikun Niu, and Lois E. Tetrick*	111
7	Cyber Security Executive Leadership *Richard Klimoski and James Murray*	135
8	Requisite Attributes for Cyber Security Personnel and Teams: Cyber Risk Mitigation through Talent Management *Irwin Jose, Kate LaPort, and D. Matthew Trippe*	167
9	Selection and Staffing of Cyber Security Positions *Rose Mueller-Hanson and Maya Garza*	194
10	Training Cyber Security Personnel *Bradley J. Brummel, John Hale, and Matthew J. Mol*	217
11	Designing Meaningful, Healthy, and Effective Cyber Security Work *Sharon K. Parker, Carolyn J. Winslow, and Lois E. Tetrick*	240
12	Factors Influencing the Human–Technology Interface for Effective Cyber Security Performance *Michael D. Coovert, Rachel Dreibelbis, and Randy Borum*	267
13	Technological Solutions for Improving Performance of Cyber Security Analysts *Massimiliano Albanese and Sushil Jajodia*	291
14	Conclusions and Directions for Future Research *Lois E. Tetrick, Reeshad S. Dalal, Stephen J. Zaccaro, and Julie A. Steinke*	305
Index		*312*

ABOUT THE EDITORS

Stephen J. Zaccaro is a professor of psychology at George Mason University, Fairfax, Virginia. He is also an experienced leadership development consultant. He has written over 125 journal articles, book chapters, and technical reports on leadership, group dynamics, team performance, and work attitudes. He has authored a book titled *The Nature of Executive Leadership: A Conceptual and Empirical Analysis of Success* and has co-edited four other books on the topics of organizational leadership, leader development, multiteam systems, and occupational stress. He has worked with executives and managers from private industry as well as from the public and military sectors. He has served as a principal investigator, co-principal investigator, or consultant on multiple projects in the areas of leadership and executive assessment, leadership and team training, leader adaptability, executive coaching, multiteam systems, and cyber security team performance. He serves on the editorial board of *The Leadership Quarterly*, and he is an associate editor for the *Journal of Business and Psychology* and for *Military Psychology*. He is a Fellow of the Association for Psychological Science and of the American Psychological Association, Divisions 14 (Society for Industrial and Organizational Psychology) and 19 (Military Psychology).

Reeshad S. Dalal is chair of the Department of Psychology and an associate professor of industrial/organizational psychology at George Mason University in Fairfax, Virginia. He received his MA in social psychology and his PhD in industrial and organizational psychology from the University of Illinois at Urbana–Champaign (in 2001 and 2003, respectively). His research interests are in the areas of personality and its interactions with features of the work situation (primarily the "strength" of the situation), employee performance (primarily deviant/counterproductive behavior, citizenship behavior, safety behavior, and within-person variability in performance across time and situations), work motivation (primarily within-person changes in motivation), decision making (primarily decision making in the workplace, decision-making competence/skill, and the giving and taking of advice during decision making), job attitudes (primarily job satisfaction, employee engagement, and employee moods/emotions), industrial and organizational psychology approaches to the study of cyber security, and research methods (primarily policy-capturing designs and ecological momentary assessment). He currently serves on the editorial board of the *Academy of Management Journal*, and he formerly served on the editorial board of, among others, the *Journal of Applied Psychology*. In addition to his academic work, he has been involved in applied projects related to job attitudes, work experiences, cyber security incident response teams, job analysis (including cognitive task analysis), standard setting, program evaluation, content validity, and forecasting.

Lois E. Tetrick is a university professor in the industrial/organizational psychology program at George Mason University. She is a former president of the Society for Industrial and Organizational Psychology and a founding member of the Society for Occupational Health Psychology. Dr. Tetrick is a fellow of the European Academy of Occupational Health Psychology, the American Psychological Association, the Society for Industrial and Organizational Psychology, and the Association for Psychological Science. She is a past editor of the *Journal of Occupational Health Psychology* and is currently the editor of the *Journal of Managerial Psychology*. Dr. Tetrick has edited several books and has published numerous chapters and journal articles on topics related to her research interests in occupational health and safety, occupational stress, the work–family interface, psychological contracts, social exchange theory and reciprocity, organizational commitment, and organizational change and development.

Julie A. Steinke is a Lead Social and Behavioral Scientist with The MITRE Corporation. Previous to joining MITRE, she completed a Postdoctoral Research Fellowship in the Industrial/Organizational Psychology Program at George Mason University where she was extensively involved in an interdisciplinary research project of international scope on the effectiveness of cyber security incident response teams. She earned her PhD in industrial and organizational psychology from Wright State University. Her research interests include ways that individuals, teams, and multiteam systems (MTSs) function under stress and adversity, such as the role of competition, cooperation, and conflict in individual, team, and MTS performance; resilience; and the extent to which individuals seek out and engage in difficult and challenging situations. In her research, she has investigated numerous populations including athletes, emergency response teams, cyber security response teams, and nonprofit organizations, and has conducted research for NASA on astronaut selection. Prior to entering the field of industrial and organizational psychology, she graduated from Saint Mary's College in Notre

Dame, Indiana, and studied kinesiology with a concentration in sport psychology at Indiana University, Bloomington. She previously worked in college athletics administration and has taught a variety of courses at both the undergraduate and graduate levels at several universities.

Note: The author's affiliation with The MITRE Corporation is provided for identification purposes only, and is not intended to convey or imply MITRE's concurrence with, or support for, the positions, opinions, or viewpoints expressed by the author.

ABOUT THE CONTRIBUTORS

Massimiliano Albanese is an assistant professor in the Department of Information Sciences and Technology at George Mason University, the associate director of the Center for Secure Information Systems, and the codirector of the Laboratory for IT Entrepreneurship. Dr. Albanese received his PhD degree in computer science and engineering in 2005 from the University of Naples Federico II and joined George Mason University in 2011 after serving as a postdoctoral researcher at the University of Maryland. His research interests are in the areas of modeling and detection of cyber attack, network hardening, moving target defense, and cyber physical systems. He has participated in sponsored research projects totaling $7.7 million and has coauthored over 60 publications in peer-reviewed journals and conference proceedings. Dr. Albanese is a recipient of the 2014 Mason Emerging Researcher/Scholar/Creator Award, one of the most prestigious honors at George Mason University.

Sandeep Bhatt is a researcher in the Security and Manageability Laboratory, Hewlett-Packard (HP) Labs, where he has worked on firewall analysis, end-to-end access control in enterprise networks, and algorithms to detect anomalous behavior from distributed log data. Before joining HP Labs, Dr. Bhatt was director of systems performance at Akamai Technologies, where he led performance studies for Internet content delivery. Previously, he was director of network algorithms at Telcordia Technologies, which he joined after serving on the faculty of computer science at Yale University, with appointments at the California Institute of Technology and Rutgers University. His research interests have included parallel computation, network communication, and very-large-scale integration layout. His pioneering research in the theory of graph embeddings influenced the design of the "fat tree" communications systems now used in data center networking.

Dr. Bhatt has PhD, SM, and SB degrees in computer science from the Massachusetts Institute of Technology.

Balca Bolunmez is a doctoral student in the industrial/organizational psychology program at George Mason University in Fairfax, Virginia. Bolunmez received her MS in textile engineering from Dokuz Eylül University in Turkey, where she conducted research on performance improvement in apparel production. She received her MBA from the New Jersey Institute of Technology, where she conducted research on decision support systems. Prior to attending George Mason University, Bolunmez taught in academia and worked in the apparel sourcing field. Her primary research interests include individual and team decision-making processes, decision quality, advice taking, and advice networks. Her other research interests include invisible stigmas, job performance, and research methods.

Randy Borum is a professor and coordinator for strategy and intelligence studies in the School of Information at the University of South Florida.

Bradley J. Brummel is an associate professor of psychology at the University of Tulsa. He is also an affiliate faculty member in the University of Tulsa's Institute for Information Security. Dr. Brummel conducts research on organizational training and development, focusing on coaching and simulation-based delivery methods for professional ethics and cyber security content areas. He is a member of the Society for Industrial and Organizational Psychology, the Academy of Management, and the Association for Research in Personality. Dr. Brummel's research has been published in *Personnel Psychology*, the *Journal of Applied Psychology*, the *Journal of Management*, and *Human Relations*.

Tiffani Rose Chen, PhD, is a consultant on a U.S. Department of Homeland Security-sponsored research project to study the effectiveness of cyber security incident response teams. She owns her own consulting company focused on helping public- and private-sector organizations develop effective leaders, teams, and multiteam systems. Her research interests include teams, shared leadership, and personality. In her research, she has looked at the combinations of personality variables that encourage the development of shared leadership and the relationship between shared leadership and other positive team emergent states. Dr. Chen received her PhD in industrial/organizational psychology from George Mason University and her BA in psychology from Princeton University.

Michael D. Coovert, PhD, is professor of psychology at the University of South Florida. Dr. Coovert is author/coauthor of numerous articles on quantitative methods, performance measurement, teams, and human factors. Dr. Coovert publishes and consults in the areas of performance measurement, teams, quantitative methods, human–computer interaction, and computer-supported cooperative work. For the past few years, his research has addressed issues related to cyber security; multimodal visual, auditory, and tactile displays; and human performance (e.g., workload, human–robot interaction, human-systems integration, and work teams). Dr. Coovert has completed projects for many sponsors, including the U.S. Air Force (Human Performance Wing), the U.S. Navy (Naval Air Warfare Center/Training Systems Division), and the U.S. Army (Human Effectiveness Directorate, Army Research Laboratory). He is a member of several professional societies, including the Society for Multivariate Experimental Psychology, and a fellow of the Society of Industrial and Organizational Psychology, the American Psychological Society, and the American Psychological Association. Dr. Coovert recently received an appointment from the National Research Council.

Rachel Dreibelbis is a third-year doctoral student in industrial and organizational psychology at the University of South Florida, working under Dr. Michael Coovert. Her main research stream involves the nature and antecedents of cyber security behaviors and how the human–technology interface affects cyber security performance.

Laura Fletcher is a doctoral student in George Mason University's industrial/organizational psychology program. Before entering the program, she had spent three years working in Beijing, China, as a leadership and talent assessment consultant for Hay Group, an American human resources management consulting firm, specializing in issues with multinational corporations in northeastern China. Her work focused primarily on leader and talent assessment and development programs, competency modeling, and training. Prior to her time spent as a consultant, she received a Fulbright grant to evaluate perceptions of mental health counseling in China for a year, for which she was also primarily located in Beijing. Fletcher holds a BA in psychology and Asian studies from Vassar College, with minors in cultural anthropology and Chinese language. Her research primarily focuses on cross-cultural issues, teams and multiteam systems, networks, and creativity.

Maya Garza has ten years of experience providing human capital consulting to private and public organizations, leading and contributing to innovative client solutions. For several years, Garza worked with numerous federal government agencies and industry and academic partners on the National Initiative for Cybersecurity Education, specifically on workforce planning and professional development efforts. She led the design and development of the National Cybersecurity Workforce Framework for cyber security professionals (http://csrc.nist.gov/nice/framework/). Garza is a member of the Society for Industrial and Organization Psychology, the Association for Psychological Science, and the Personnel Testing Council of Metropolitan Washington. She has published and presented on the topics of decision making, job stress, and leadership development. She has also been invited to present and write on the topic of workforce development and training for cyber security. Her articles have appeared in such outlets as AOL Government and HR.BLR.com.

Aiva K. Gorab is a graduate research assistant in the industrial/organizational psychology program at George Mason University.

John Hale is a professor in the Tandy School of Computer Science at the University of Tulsa (TU). He is a founding member of TU's Institute for Information Security, where he pursues research on attack modeling, cyber trust, and security of cyber physical systems. His research in these areas has been funded the National Science Foundation, the Defense Advanced Research Projects Agency, the National Security Agency, and the National Institute of Justice. He served as director of TU's Institute for Information Security from 1999 to 2009, overseeing the development its cyber security curricula.

Amber K. Hargrove is a doctoral student in the industrial/organizational psychology program at George Mason University. Her research interests include workplace well-being; emotions and emotion regulation in organizational contexts; and individual, team, and multiteam system motivation and performance. She recently served as a project manager and research lead on a large-scale project examining the effectiveness of cyber security teams. She received both her MA and BS in psychology from George Mason University.

William Horne is the director of security research for Hewlett-Packard (HP) Labs, where he directs research on systems and network security, cryptography, privacy, and risk management and is responsible for transferring security technology developed in HP Labs to customers and business units. He is currently an associate editor for *IEEE Security & Privacy Magazine*. Prior to joining HP, he held industrial research positions at InterTrust Technologies and NEC Research Institute. Horne has an MSEE and PhD in electrical engineering from the University of New Mexico and a BS in electrical engineering from the University of Delaware.

Sushil Jajodia is university professor, BDM International Professor, and the founding director of Center for Secure Information Systems at George Mason University. He is also the founding site director of the National Science Foundation Industry/University Cooperative Research Program Center for Configuration Analytics and Automation at George Mason. He has authored or coauthored seven books, edited 44 books and conference proceedings, and published more than 450 technical papers in the refereed journals and conference proceedings. Dr. Jajodia received the 1996 International Federation for Information Processing (IFIP) Technical Committee 11 Kristian Beckman Award, the 2000 Volgenau School of Engineering Outstanding Research Faculty Award, the 2008 Association for Computing Machinery Special Interest Group on Security, Audit and Control Outstanding Contributions Award, and the 2011

IFIP Working Group 11.3 Outstanding Research Contributions Award. He was elected a fellow of the Institute of Electrical and Electronics Engineers in January 2013. He is the founding consulting editor of the Springer International Series on Advances in Information Security and SpringerBriefs in Computer Science. He was the founding editor-in-chief of the *Journal of Computer Security* and a past editor of *ACM Transactions on Information and Systems Security*, *IET Information Security*, the *International Journal of Cooperative Information Systems*, *IEEE Concurrency*, and *IEEE Transactions on Knowledge and Data Engineering*.

Irwin Jose is a graduate student at George Mason University.

Richard Klimoski is a professor of psychology and management at George Mason University. His research explores the dynamics of senior organizational leadership, with a special focus on how these play out in teams of leaders. He also has done work on the development of the capacities that promote effectiveness in senior leadership roles. He is the author or coauthor of several books, the most recent of which is *Advancing Human Resource Project Management* (Wiley, 2014). Examples of his work can also be found in the major journals publishing on the most recent findings of organizational science.

Kate LaPort is associate assessment consultant at Aon Human Capital Services. She obtained her PhD from George Mason University.

Tracy McCausland is associate behavioral scientist at the RAND Corporation. She obtained her PhD from George Mason University.

Matthew J. Mol is an industrial/organizational psychology doctoral student at the University of Tulsa. He currently works as a research assistant examining factors that influence trust decisions in cyber space as part of the University of Tulsa's Institute for Information Security. His research interests include personality development, training and development, and scale development.

Rose Mueller-Hanson leads the performance impact solutions group at PDRI, a CEB Company. She is the coauthor of several recent articles, including "Building a High-Performance Culture: A Fresh Look at Performance Management," published by the Society for Human Resources Management Foundation. She is also coauthor of the book *Developing Organizational Simulations: A Guide for Practitioners and Students*. Mueller-Hanson is a co-recipient of the M. Scott Myers Award for Applied Research in the Workplace (with colleagues from PDRI), awarded by the Society for Industrial and Organizational Psychology (SIOP). In 2014, she was elected a fellow of SIOP, and she currently serves as the chair of its Continuing Education Committee. She has presented her work at numerous national conferences and in technical reports, test manuals, and other publications. She is the past president of the Personnel Testing Council of Metropolitan Washington, DC, and the current president of the board of directors for Community Interface Services, a nonprofit organization serving adults with developmental disabilities. Prior to joining PDRI in 2002, Mueller-Hanson worked as a human resources manager and served in the U.S. Air Force.

James Murray is a practicing management and cyber security subject matter expert serving U.S. federal government agencies and commercial industry. He leads research and application enhancements to cyber security management, operations, and incident response. Murray has advanced cyber security management approaches at Fortune 50 companies, federal agencies, and universities over the past 40 years.

Qikun Niu is an industrial/organizational psychology doctoral student at George Mason University. As a supervisee of Dr. Lois E. Tetrick, his research interests include occupational health psychology (self-regulation and stress recovery), team cohesion, survey methodology, and computational modeling.

Sharon K. Parker is professor in the industrial/organizational psychology program at the University of Western Australia.

Shari Lawrence Pfleeger is the editor-in-chief of *IEEE Security & Privacy* magazine and the author of 15 books and dozens of articles on software engineering, software quality, and computer security. In the last 20 years, as a scientist at the RAND Corporation and then as research director of a U.S. consortium of universities, national laboratories, and research centers, she defined and led multidisciplinary, multinational projects aimed at understanding and improving cyber security.

Kristin M. Repchick is a doctoral candidate in the industrial/organizational psychology program at George Mason University. Her research interests include team processes, cyber security incident response team effectiveness, and multiteam systems. Repchick received an MA in industrial and organizational psychology from George Mason University.

Zitong Sheng is currently a doctorate student in the Industrial/Organizational Psychology Program at George Mason University. Her main research interests include methodology issues, leadership, creativity, organizational citizenship behavior, counterproductive work behavior, and work–family issues. She received her BS in psychology from Peking University (Beijing, China) in 2012 and her MA in industrial/organizational psychology from George Mason University in 2014.

Sathya Sundaramurthy is a fourth-year PhD student in computing and information sciences at Kansas State University.

Alan J. Tomassetti is a doctoral candidate in George Mason University's industrial/organizational psychology program. He earned his master's degree from George Mason University in 2012. His research interests include judgment and decision making, policy capturing, leadership, team effectiveness, and situational strength.

D. Matthew Trippe is a senior staff scientist at the Human Resources Research Organization (HumRRO). He received his PhD in industrial–organizational psychology from Virginia Tech. Dr. Trippe's research interests lie in personnel selection, test development, test validation, and psychometrics. Early in his career at HumRRO, he became involved in a U.S. Air Force-funded project to develop an information and communications technology literacy-based aptitude assessment. This early project has led to a decade-long research program with the U.S. Air Force, the U.S. Army, and the U.S. Navy. Dr. Trippe continues to work with Department of Defense clients to improve personnel selection and classification within cyber-related occupational families.

Carolyn J. Winslow is currently a doctoral student in the industrial/organizational psychology program at George Mason University. Her primary research interest is understanding and improving employee emotions and psychological well-being, with a special interest in the efficacy of workplace well-being interventions that incorporate self-guided activities for enhancing positive aspects of emotional well-being. In addition, Winslow is interested in the role of personality and other individual-difference variables in organizational contexts.

Loai Zomlot is a principal software engineer at ArcSight, Hewlett-Packard (HP). Previously, he was a postdoctoral fellow in the Cloud and Security Laboratory, HP Labs, researching the dynamics and processes of cyber security incident response teams with the aim of providing better automated support to analysts. Dr. Zomlot received a Fulbright scholarship to study for a master's in software engineering at Kansas State University, where he received his PhD in computer science. He received a BS in computer engineering from the Islamic University of Gaza, Palestine. Dr. Zomlot's professional interests lie in the general field of cyber security, with a special focus on enterprise network security.

FIGURES

1.1	A Model for Enhancing Cyber Security Effectiveness	6
2.1	Generic Performance Processes of Cyber Security Work	17
2.2	Cyber Security Incident Response Team Goal Hierarchy Example	23
3.1	Escalation Swim Lane Diagram	60
3.2	High-Level Process Diagram as Described in Figure 3.1	66
4.1	Individual, Team, and Judge–Advisor System Decision-Making Structures	77
4.2	Escalation Decision-Making Structure	78
6.1	Model Depicting the Interactive Cycle between Cyber Security Workers and Hackers	115
6.2	Creative Problem-Solving Applied to Incident Response	123
7.1	Deloitte Risk Intelligence Enterprise Framework	140
7.2	PricewaterhouseCoopers Cyber Security Risk Management Model	143
7.3	National Institute of Standards and Technology Risk Management Framework	144
7.4	Information Security Title Related to Outcomes	147
7.5	IT Spending per Employee by Industry	149
7.6	Cyber Security Maturity by Industry	149
7.7	Personal Characteristics and Organizational Awareness Traits of Security Leadership	153
7.8	Evolution of Chief Information Security Officer Capabilities	154
7.9	Cyber Security Transformational Interest versus Technology Investment Ratio	156

7.10	Recapping the Themes of the Chapter	163
8.1	A Multistage Model of Cyber Security Personnel Performance	172
9.1	Hypothesized Predictors of Individual Cyber Security Job Performance	202
13.1	Example of Attack Graph	298

TABLES

2.1	A Preliminary Taxonomy of Cyber Security Incident Response Performance	26
2.2	Incident Response Performance Outcomes	46
8.1	Categories from the National Initiative for Cybersecurity Education Framework	170
8.2	National Initiative for Cybersecurity Education Framework for Cyber Security Workload and Workforce Requirements	171
8.3	Sample of Cyber Security Job Tasks and Knowledge, Skills, and Abilities (KSAs)	175
9.1	Selection Approaches for Cyber Security Predictors	203
10.1	Cyber Security Training by Organizational Role	220
10.2	Checklist for Cyber Security Training Design	227
11.1	Evidence-Based Work Design Principles and Their Potential Application within Cyber Security Work	250
11.2	Principles for the Process of Work Design and/or Work Redesign	261
12.1	Recommendations for Achieving Balance between Individuals and Technology	279

SERIES FOREWORD

The goal of the Applied Psychology series is to create books that exemplify the use of scientific research, theory, and findings to help solve real problems in organizations and society. Zaccaro, Dalal, Tetrick, and Steinke's *Psychosocial Dynamics of Cyber Security* exemplifies this approach. Cyber security is usually approached as a software problem, in which the solutions to the security of the computer systems that are at the heart of a modern economy lie mainly in the domain of computer science. Zaccaro, Dalal, Tetrick, and Steinke make the important point that human behavior, and the limits of human capabilities, are at the heart of many cyber security problems and solutions.

The human side of cyber security involves issues ranging from resistance to implementation of security measures (e.g., many people use simple, easily guessed passwords and resist changing them) to explorations of the limits of human capacity (e.g., there are limits on people's capacity to maintain vigilance against potential security threats), and this book examines this entire range. The book explores three main themes for understanding how the interaction between human capabilities and computerized systems play out to create and to address vulnerabilities. First, Chapters 2–7 examine the ways cyber security systems operate, with special attention to the interplay between computer systems and individuals and organizations. Next, Chapters 8–11 tackle the problem of staffing, training, and supporting a cyber security workforce. These chapters make the point that this workforce is unique in terms of both its technological and its psychological demands (e.g., vigilance) and that both dimensions need to be considered in developing and maintaining an effective workforce. Finally, Chapters 12 and 13 consider in more depth the technological issues in cyber security and the implications of evolving technologies for the human–computer interactions that cybser security demands.

The topics this book covers are timely and important. The National Research Council recently released a report titled *Professionalization of the Nation's Cybersecurity Workforce? Criteria for Decision-Making* (National Academies Press, 2013) that highlighted the critical challenges this country faces in building a workforce that can protect critical computer systems. *Psychosocial Dynamics of Cyber Security* lays out in detail how the application of psychological research can help to address these challenges. We are happy to add *Psychosocial Dynamics of Cyber Security* to the Applied Psychology series.

Kevin R. Murphy
Jeanette N. Cleveland

FOREWORD

The Need for a Psychosocial Look at Cyber Security

Shari Lawrence Pfleeger

Our technology—and our need for it—change every day. Years ago, it was *de rigeur* to wear a watch on your wrist; these days, "for many in the cellphone generation, watches now seem about as relevant as grandfather clocks" (Earnest, 2006, Paragraph 5). And where the old-fashioned watch posed no threats to security or privacy, today's watches pose significant threats. For instance, the newly announced Apple Watch

> includes a heart rate sensor and a sensor for tracking movement.... It has a chip that helps it make wireless payments. The watch also includes Digital Touch, an application that enables a new method of communication between watch users. (B. X. Chen, 2015, Paragraphs 27–28)

Indeed, many devices in the ever larger Internet of Things capture data, store data, communicate data, and analyze data—supporting judgments about your identity, needs, location, health, and intentions.

At the same time, the threat environment keeps changing. Attacks and intrusions that once were rare are now commonplace, so manufacturers rush to provide updates and patches to fix known problems and to anticipate likely ones. But "the changing nature of both technology and the threat environment makes the risks to information and infrastructure difficult to anticipate and quantify" (Pfleeger & Caputo, 2012, p. 598).

Traditionally, technologists have responded to this dynamic environment by "improving" devices so that they constrain our behavior, on the basis of the notion that technology itself will encourage secure behavior while discouraging or even preventing bad behavior. But this approach has had many flaws, and it has sometimes resulted in the opposite of its intention; by circumventing security mechanisms, users have actually made their environments less secure.

To see why, consider what happens when users perceive security technology as an obstacle to getting their work done. Sometimes this behavior derives from feeling overwhelmed by difficulties in security implementation, understanding, installation, or use. For example, France Bélanger and her colleagues at Virginia Tech (Bélanger, Collignon, Enget, & Negangard, 2011) studied the "resistance behavior" exhibited when people are faced with a mandatory password change. For many of the several hundred study respondents, even when passwords were changed as required, changes were intentionally delayed; the request to change a password was often perceived as an unnecessary interruption of more important tasks. These findings reinforce what Anne Adams and Martina Angela Sasse (1999) pointed out more than a decade earlier: that users concentrate on performing their primary tasks, and they view security as a disruptive secondary effort. Indeed, from a security point of view, Adams and Sasse insisted that users are not the enemy and that, in fact, users can be helpful participants in efforts to provide good cyber security.

Neither technological constraint nor repeated education and training have been particularly successful at improving cyber security. But recent studies suggest that blending the two can lead to effective results. For example, in U.K. schools teaching online safety,

> [w]here the provision for e-safety was outstanding, the schools had managed rather than locked down systems. In the best practice seen, pupils were helped, from a very early age, to assess the risk of accessing sites and therefore gradually to acquire skills which would help them adopt safe practices even when they were not supervised. (Office for Standards in Education, Children's Services and Skills, 2010, p. 8)

In other words, teaching appropriate behaviors and then trusting users to behave responsibly led to a successful blend of technology, risk awareness, and secure behavior.

Deanna Caputo and I (Pfleeger & Caputo, 2012) have investigated many areas in which taking a psychosocial approach to cyber security can lead to more secure behavior and outcomes, pointing out that

> if humans using computer systems are given the tools and information they need, taught the meaning of responsible use, and then trusted to behave appropriately with respect to cyber security, desired outcomes may be obtained without security's being perceived as onerous or burdensome. (p. 598)

In other words, "[b]y both understanding the role of human behavior and leveraging behavioral science findings, the designers, developers and maintainers of information infrastructure can address real and perceived obstacles to productivity and provide more effective security" (Pfleeger & Caputo, 2012, p. 598).

But we are not the only researchers investigating ways to improve cyber security using psychosocial methods. The box presents a few examples of successful applications of social science techniques in this area. For instance, Alessandro Acquisti and his colleagues have applied behavioral economics to security and privacy issues, yielding a rich body of work on when, whether, and how users value their privacy. Denise Anthony has explored the privacy of medical data from a sociologist's point of view. Deanna Caputo's groundbreaking work on insider threat and spear phishing has involved her expertise in behavioral psychology, and I have worked with Martina Angela Sasse to study security behavior from a social psychology perspective. In each such research instance that has shed important light on cyber security issues, cyber security experts and social scientists have combined forces to break new ground.

EXAMPLE PUBLICATIONS THAT SUCCESSFULLY APPLY BEHAVIORAL SCIENCE TO COMPUTER SECURITY AND PRIVACY

Acquisti, A., Brandimarte, L., & Loewenstein, G. (2015). Privacy and human behavior in the age of information. *Science, 347*, 509–514.

Anthony, D., & Campos-Castillo, C. (2015). A looming digital divide? Group differences in the perceived importance of electronic health records. *Information, Communication, & Society.* Advance online publication. http://dx.doi.org/10.1080/1369118X.2015.1006657

Campos-Castillo, C., & Anthony, D. (2014). The double-edged sword of electronic health records: Implications for patient disclosure. *Journal of American Medical Informatics Association.* Advance online publication. http://doi:10.1136/amiajnl-2014-002804

Caputo, D. D., Maloof, M. A., & Stephens, G. D. (2009, November/December). Detecting insider theft of trade secrets. *IEEE Security & Privacy, 7*(6), 14–21.

Caputo, D., & Pfleeger, S. L., & Freeman, J. D., & Johnson, M. E. (2014, January/February). Going spear phishing: Exploring embedded training and awareness. *IEEE Security & Privacy, 12*(1), 28–38.

Castelfranchi, C., & Falcone, R. (2010). Trust and technology. In *Trust theory: A socio-cognitive and computational model* (pp. 343–357). Chichester, UK: Wiley.

Davis, M. A., Anthony, D. L., & Pauls, S. D. (2015). Seeking and receiving social support on Facebook for surgery. *Social Science and Medicine, 131*, 40–47.

Pfleeger, S. L., Sasse, M. A., & Furnham, A. (2014). From weakest link to security hero: Transforming staff security behavior. *Journal of Homeland Security and Emergency Management, 11*, 489–510.

Predd, J., Pfleeger, S. L., Hunker, J., & Bulford, C (2008, July/August). Insiders behaving badly. *IEEE Security & Privacy, 6*(4), 66–70.

What is clear from this research is that providing human-centered security requires technologists to understand a host of behavioral science implications as they design, develop, and use technology. In fact, Sasse and Flechais (2005) explicitly characterized secure systems as *socio-technical systems*; by doing so, we can use an understanding of behavioral science to "prevent users from being the 'weakest link'" (p. 14). For example, some behavioral scientists have investigated how trust mechanisms affect and can strengthen cyber security. Castelfranchi and Falcone (2010) have viewed trust as having several components, including beliefs that must be held to develop trust (the social context) and relationships with previous experience (the temporal context). They combined these perspectives with psychological factors to model trust in multiagent systems.

Each of these results can be extended by incorporating useful aspects of human behavior. For instance, in addition to social and temporal concerns, we can add expectations of fulfillment, in which someone trusts someone or something else only because of an expectation of something in return. These behavioral perspectives shed light not only on a user's expectation of the technology but also on the user's perception of whether to trust technology-mediated interactions. In turn, we can close the technology–behavior loop: This understanding can then inform the design of protective systems and processes.

The editors of this book have taken the next great leap forward by viewing how technology works as part of a psychosocial system: when designed, built, or used by individuals as well as groups. Their work on cyber security incident response teams (T. R. Chen et al., 2014) has examined individual and team responsibilities and interactions from an organizational psychologist's perspective: the knowledge, skills, and abilities needed to do the job effectively. This book is both a broader and deeper look at those teams: how they are trained, how they work together, how their work can be modeled, how technology can support them, and how they can be encouraged to be more effective. The editors and contributors lay out what we know now and what might be the next steps for research and practice. In doing so, they help us all to move away from a "more technology is better" mindset to one in which both process and technology are based on understanding of the entire psychosocial system: problems, perceptions, personal interactions, and the flows among technologies and people. This shift is significant: a move from the art of building technology to the science of creating more effective means for us to live with technology and use it to improve our world.

References

Adams A., & Sasse, M. A. (1999, December). Users are not the enemy. *Communications of the ACM, 42*(12), 40–46.

Bélanger, F., Collignon, S., Enget, K., & Negangard, E. (2011). User resistance to mandatory security implementation. In *Proceedings of the 2011 Dewald Roode Workshop on Information Systems Security Research, IFIP WG8.11/WG11.13* (Paper 5). Retrieved from http://ifip.byu.edu/ifip2011.html

Castelfranchi, C., & Falcone, R. (2010). Trust and technology. In *Trust theory: A sociocognitive and computational model* (pp. 343–357), Chichester, England: Wiley.

Chen, B. X. (2015, March 9). Apple Watch success will hinge on apps. *The New York Times*. Retrieved from http://www.nytimes.com/2015/03/10/technology/apple-watch-event.html?rref=technology&module=Ribbon&version=context&region=Header&action=click&contentCollection=Technology&pgtype=Blogs

Chen, T. R., Shore, D. B., Zaccaro, S. J., Dalal, R. S., Tetrick, L. E., & Gorab, A. K. (2014, September/October). An organizational psychology perspective to examining computer security incident response teams. *IEEE Security & Privacy*, *12*(5), 61–67.

Earnest, L. (2006, April 16). Wrist watches get the back of the hand. *The Los Angeles Times*. Retrieved from http://articles.latimes.com/2006/apr/16/business/fi-watch16

Office for Standards in Education, Children's Services and Skills. (2010). *The safe use of new technologies* (Report No. 090231). Manchester: Ofsted.

Pfleeger, S. L. & Caputo, D. D. (2012). Leveraging behavioral science to mitigate cyber-security risk. *Computers and Security*, *31*, 597–611.

Sasse, M. A., Flechais, I. (2005). Usable security: Why do we need it? How do we get it? In L. F. Cranor & S. Garfinkel (Eds.), *Security and usability: Designing secure systems that people can use* (pp. 13–30). Sebastopol, CA: O'Reilly Media.

1
THE PSYCHOSOCIAL DYNAMICS OF CYBER SECURITY

An Overview

Stephen J. Zaccaro, Reeshad S. Dalal, Lois E. Tetrick, and Julie A. Steinke

To state the very obvious, computers and computerized systems reside at the core of work in organizations today. Such systems are the primary conduit for information flow and exchange in organizations. They are used to organize, regulate, and in many instances synchronize work, particularly "knowledge work" (Davenport, 2005; Davenport, Jarvenpaa, & Beers, 1996; Reinhardt, Schmidt, Sloep, & Drachsler, 2011), among organizational members. Moreover, access to the Internet has exponentially increased connectivity across organizational boundaries. Accordingly, specialists in computer systems and information technology (IT) have become critical to organizational functioning.

The ubiquity of computer-based information systems in organizations, and the greater connectivity they foster, has also increased organizations' vulnerability to external intrusion into information infrastructures. Accordingly, cyber crime has soared, increasing 96 percent over the last five years (Ponemon Institute, 2010, 2014), and has become very costly to organizations (e.g., Sony Corporation, 2015). This heightened vulnerability has increased the number and importance of personnel in organizations who have the responsibility for increasing the security posture of their firms and, when attacks do occur, providing the comprehensive detection, remediation, and recovery responses necessary to restore that posture (Alberts, Dorofee, Killcrece, Ruefle, & Zajicek, 2004; Cichonski, Millar, Grance, & Scafone, 2012; West-Brown et al., 2003). Indeed, as Zaccaro, Hargrove, Chen, Repchick, and McCausland note in Chapter 2 of this volume:

> As one indicator of this surge, the membership of incident response teams in the professional organization Forum of Incident Response and Security Teams ... has nearly doubled in the last five years.... Moreover, the Federal Bureau of Investigation has newly created a division dedicated to cyber

crime and has elevated the cyber threat to the number three national priority. (p. 14)

Given the centrality of information systems in organizational work and the costs of cyber attacks to organizations, maximizing the work effectiveness of cyber security personnel should be a critical organizational priority. Improvement of cyber security performance can take place along two broad avenues. One involves using automated and technological strategies to increase the strength of infrastructure security and facilitate cyber incident handling. The complexity of information systems and the unmanageable onslaught of data that cyber professionals need to monitor mandate the use of such strategies. For example, millions of events can come across the screen of a network monitor on a typical day (Grance, Kent, & Kim, 2004; NRI Secure Technologies, 2014). Software such as ARCSIGHT (http://www8.hp.com/us/en/software-solutions/arcsight-esm-enterprise-security-management/index.html) is used to sift through these numbers, pulling out the suspicious events whose signatures suggest that more extensive review is needed. Such systems reduce the cognitive load on the incident monitor to a level where the task of incident detection can be reasonably and successfully performed.

The promise of automated strategies in maximizing efficiency and reducing errors often makes them the dominant and preferred approach to cyber security performance enhancement. However, such strategies need to be integrated with those defining a second avenue of performance improvement—psychosocial strategies that target the human element of cyber security. These strategies seek to maximize the human capital organizations can deploy to protect against cyber attacks and to improve their information infrastructures. Such capital can take, for example, the form of knowledge, skills, and abilities (KSAs) that contribute to effective cyber security performance. Psychosocial strategies can also include management and team enhancement tools that facilitate not only individual performance but also the collaboration activities often required by the complexity of cyber work (Osorno, Millar, & Rager, 2011; see also Zaccaro et al., this volume). These strategies also include establishing functional work designs and calibrating organizational structures to align them more closely with the changing cyber security operating environment. Taken together, these strategies are a necessary complement to the technology and automation strategies used to enhance cyber security performance. Indeed, one long-established premise in organizational psychology is that changes in technological systems must be carefully integrated with changes in social systems; failure to do so can result in the impairment and collapse of both systems (Trist & Bamforth, 1951).

Research on cyber security performance, however, has generally favored technical over psychosocial approaches. For example, Ahmad, Hadgkiss, and Ruighaver (2012) noted recently that much incident response literature consists of industry white papers that outline recommended (technical) practices for implementing an incident response capability in organisations....The fact that incident response research focuses on a technical view and gives relatively less attention to holistic socio-organisational perspectives is consistent with trends in information security research as a whole. (p. 643)

Pfleeger and Caputo (2012) pointed to the negative consequences of implementing technological solutions to enhance cyber security without considering the social and behavioral dimensions of such solutions. For example, they noted how users can perceive security technology more as an "obstacle" when requests are made for behavior changes (e.g., mandatory password changes) and often "may mistrust, misinterpret, or override the security" (Pfleeger & Caputo, 2012, p. 598). Other researchers have noted the failure to understand the link between technology and human capacities. For example, Parasuraman and Manzey (2010) indicated that "research has shown that automation does not simply supplant human activity but rather changes it, often in ways unintended and unanticipated by the designers of automation" (p. 381). In Chapter 12 of this volume, Coovert, Dreibelbis, and Borum speak to similar themes. These researchers point to how the strong and growing role of technology in the cyber security domain is fundamentally changing the roles of humans in this same domain without systematic attention being devoted to understanding these role shifts.

At the team and organizational levels, efforts to enhance cyber security performance are also heavily weighted toward technological considerations. Researchers have established a set of technical skills and procedures that contribute to effective performance and developed process models of how such performance should occur (e.g., Alberts et al., 2004; Cichonski et al., 2012). However, relatively less attention has been devoted to socio-organizational aspects of cyber security work. For example, whereas process models can elucidate the flow of incident response work, such work processes involve a considerable number of judgment and decision points that are susceptible to a range of biases (Tversky & Kahneman, 1974). Effective incident handling also utilizes a number of cognitive processes—such as situational awareness, complex problem-solving, divergent thinking and creativity, and adaptation (Mumford, Mobley, Uhlman, Reiter-Palmon, & Doares, 1991; Mumford, Schultz, & Van Doorn, 2001)—that would also not be fully reflected in incident response process models. Cyber security performance may also be influenced by an array of nontechnical KSAs and other attributes as well as team dynamics and a number of other contextual variables (see Jose, LaPort, & Trippe, Chapter 8, this volume).

This lack of balance between technical and psychosocial perspectives suggests a need for greater understanding of how these two perspectives can be better integrated and aligned to produce a more comprehensive approach to cyber security. That is the purpose of this book. We have drawn on the science of industrial and organizational (I/O) psychology to (a) understand the unique challenges of cyber security work, (b) provide insight into work processes and dynamics specific to cyber security, (c) elucidate drivers of effective performance in this domain, and (d) provide the basis for enhancing such performance. Our overall goal is to help maximize the human element in the integrated sociotechnical system that comprises the cyber security domain in all organizations.

One might ask, why not simply and directly apply what is already known about work enhancement from the I/O psychology literature? Why does the domain or context of cyber security need special coverage? We believe that cyber security work contains aspects that mark it as somewhat different from other types of work. These aspects are noted in several chapters in this book, so we only summarize them here. First, cyber security work perhaps integrates technological and human elements more than many other forms of work. IT systems represent both the tools and the focus of such work. This greater entwinement of human and technological systems creates different kinds of performance requirements, as noted in the aforementioned chapters. Second, cyber security, particularly incident response and handling, entails a threat-oriented reactive posture (Bronk, Thorbruegge, & Hakkaja, 2007; West-Brown et al., 2003). This posture emphasizes particular work characteristics—such as monitoring and vigilance, threat handling, and complex problem-solving—with successful performance defined as recovery to a secure status quo (rather than enhancement of a particular process or outcome, although these too can be elements of cyber security performance). Also, the consequences of failed performance can be widespread and/or devastating. Such characteristics are characteristic of other work domains, including the military, nuclear system regulation, air traffic control, fire and rescue, police, and emergency medicine as well as jobs related to natural and man-made disaster preparation and response (Steinke et al., in press). However, in most of these work domains, the ratio of action-oriented to knowledge work is higher than it is in cyber security. In the latter, the work to be completed is mostly knowledge work, in which cognitive loads may be relatively higher, requiring greater deployment of different cognitive resources in response to threats.

This difference points to a third separation between cyber security work and other work domains. Most of the aforementioned domains entail some level of *performance adaptation*, defined as "cognitive, affective, motivational, and behavioral modifications made in response to the demands of a new or changing environment, or situational demands" (Baard, Rench, & Kozlowski, 2014, p. 50). Given the high turbulence in the cyber security operating environment, with the constant evolution and novelty of both technology and the nature of incoming threats, we would argue that the adaptation requirements may be even higher in this work domain than in most others. Zaccaro, Weis, Chen, and Matthews (2014) argued that adaptive performance requirements can also vary in terms of their cognitive, social, and emotional loads, with significant implications for the particular KSAs required for effective performance, along with the requisite training strategies to foster these KSAs. They argued that *adaptive readiness*, or an "individual's readiness to adapt to changing operational and environmental contingencies" (p. 94), depends upon identification of the right load balance among cognitive, social, and emotional performance requirements and implementation of training regimens that match this balance. We have noted that the typical or "routine" work of cyber security carries a higher cognitive load in general; we would add on the basis of these arguments that adaptation in this domain imposes higher cognitive demands than are characteristic of other domains.

There are other unique aspects of cyber security work that differentiate it from other forms of work; however, the combination of high person–technology work interface, threat-focused knowledge work, and the need for high adaptive cognitive-oriented readiness suggests that work performance models in this domain will vary significantly from those in most other work domains. The chapters in this book were invited to provide some insight into these models. Our authors include a mix of scientists who are well versed in either cyber security technology, I/O psychology, or both. Their contributions provide an integrated framework for understanding the work of cyber security.

Overview of the Chapters

One means of approaching this book as a whole and its chapters is to consider a traditional performance enhancement model widely used in I/O psychology (e.g., Campbell, Dunnette, Lawler, & Weick, 1970; Dunnette, 1963; Ghiselli, Campbell, & Zedeck, 1981; Zaccaro, 2001). This model, shown in Figure 1.1, indicates that the environmental context of cyber security—with its constantly changing threat profiles, evolving technology, and shifting national and international priorities—influences (a) cyber security technological requirements; (b) cyber security performance requirements; and (c) organizational contexts, particularly in terms of decisions about cyber security infrastructure, functional structure and departments within an organization, and cyber security policies. Technology requirements also influence, in turn, cyber security performance requirements and elements of the organizational context. The decisions made by organizations regarding their cyber security posture also influence the performance requirements to be addressed by cyber security personnel.

This combination of environmental factors, technological and performance requirements, and organizational context provides the foundation for specification of the attributes and performance processes that lead to performances outcomes. The model in Figure 1.1 depicts these links between attributes, processes, and outcomes as occurring at three levels within the cyber security infrastructure—individuals, teams, and systems. At the individual level, attributes are KSAs and other personal qualities that contribute to effective enactment of performance processes. Processes are those cognitive and behavioral activities enacted to meet performance requirements and produce outcomes (Campbell, McCloy, Oppler, &

6 Stephen J. Zaccaro et al.

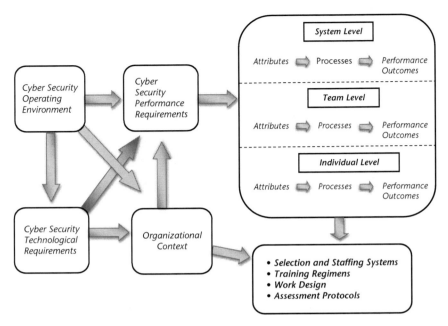

FIGURE 1.1 A Model for Enhancing Cyber Security Effectiveness

Sager, 1993). At the team level, attributes include team composition (Mathieu, Tannenbaum, Donsbach, & Alliger, 2014) and team emergent states (e.g., trust, cohesion, collective efficacy; Marks, Mathieu, & Zaccaro, 2001) that influence the collaboration and interaction processes used to accomplish team-level work and produce team-level outcomes. Systems can refer to multiteam systems (Mathieu, Marks, & Zaccaro, 2001) or to other collectives larger than single teams. System attributes are compositional and emergent states at the larger system level and the relationships among different component teams and elements. As at lower levels, such attributes influence system-level processes and performance outcomes.

The attributes, processes, and performance outcomes at multiple levels provide the basis for strategies and interventions to improve performance (Goldstein & Ford, 2002). All three components could be represented in a variety of assessments and metrics to measure cyber security effectiveness. Performance outcomes evaluated as below desired standards could spark new and targeted training efforts. Individual, team, and system attributes would contribute learning objectives to such efforts, whereas processes might provide the basis for evaluation of skill gains. Likewise, below-standard performance might prompt reevaluation of existing selection and staffing systems, with the intent of revising them. Finally, if training and selection were not appropriate strategies, or at least not ones likely to boost performance, work design interventions might become the strategy of choice to improve overall effectiveness.

Each chapter in this book addresses specific aspects of the model in Figure 1.1. Some are written by authors with a primary background in I/O psychology, whereas a few come from a primarily computer science background. However, they all share the overall purpose of the book of integrating psychosocial and technical approaches to improving cyber security.

Chapters 2–7 provide multiple perspectives on the processes of cyber security operations. Chapter 2 (by Zaccaro et al.) describes a taxonomy of the processes that define effective incident response performance. The authors also include a classification of outcomes that can accrue from the enactment of these processes. They base their classification on performance requirements for incident responders. Their taxonomy contains three dimensions, including reactive and proactive processes and cognitive (planning) and behavioral (execution) activities. Moreover, they specify these processes and activities at three levels of action—individual, team, and multiteam system. Outcomes described in this chapter include a range of objective and subjective metrics at these three levels. Because the taxonomy captures incident handling performance processes along these three dimensions, the authors note that it is more comprehensive than prior classifications of such performance. As such, it provides a stronger basis than had been available for future research and efforts to improve cyber security performance.

Chapter 3 (by Bhatt, Horne, Sundaramurthy, & Zomlot) offers an examination of cyber security processes from the perspective of computer scientists. The authors also note the relatively lower utility of prior process models and describe in some detail the activities of security operations centers. They also elucidate the performance challenges confronting analysts in such centers. Both of these contributions provide a useful complement to the model in Chapter 2. Bhatt et al. summarize efforts to develop process models and process management strategies to improve operational efficiency. However, they note as detriments of such approaches an orientation toward rigidity and a bias away from creative thinking. They offer adaptive case management as a way to address these limitations of traditional process models.

A key element in incident response is the decision about when to escalate handling of an event to a higher organizational level. Although a common phenomenon in the cyber security domain, such decision making has not received much coverage in the I/O psychology literature or in other decision-making literatures. Chapter 4 (by Dalal, Bolunmez, Tomassetti, and Sheng) provides a framework for approaching and understanding this decision-making structure. In essence, Dalal et al. examine incident escalation from the perspectives of the person who escalates, the recipient of escalated incidents, the content of escalation reports, when such escalation is likely to occur, and the results of such escalation. Given the paucity of research and models on this decision phenomenon, this chapter demonstrates a nice cross-fertilization between the cyber security practice domain and research on decision making.

In Chapter 5, Dalal and Gorab examine another phenomenon, insider threat, which is a common theme in the cyber security domain but, as they point out is not well addressed in the I/O psychology literature. Insider threats reflect behaviors that have the consequence of degrading cyber security performance. Accordingly, this chapter represents a shift from the functional perspectives in Chapters 2–4 to one that focuses on dysfunctional performance activities. The authors apply research on counterproductive work behavior (CWB) to this phenomenon and point out how existing CWB models and findings can inform thinking about insider threat. However, they also indicate several holes in current CWB frameworks that limit their application to the understanding of insider threats. This chapter provides a way forward for research on CWB to provide insight on such threats. As does Chapter 4, this chapter fosters a nice cross-fertilization between the cyber security and organizational psychology domains, as practical problems in the former raise important new research questions in the latter.

Chapter 6 (by Steinke, Fletcher, Niu, & Tetrick) addresses performance elements posed by the dynamic nature of cyber security and the need to constantly confront new and evolving threats. This aspect of the cyber security environment requires creativity and innovation from its personnel. The authors describe the iterative dynamic of creative hackers sparking creative responses by incident handlers, which then push more innovative hacking. Thus, creativity and innovation are ingrained as markers of effective cyber security performance. Steinke et al. apply research on models of creative problem-solving to show how these processes infuse several stages of incident response and management. They also note the downsides of creativity in this domain, pointing to the need to balance the kinds of routine processes described early in Chapter 3 by Bhatt et al. with the processes of creative incident handling presented in this chapter.

Chapter 7 (by Klimoski and Murray) captures both the leadership performance processes that contribute to cyber security effectiveness and the contextual influences of executive leadership within the cyber security environment. The authors describe the responsibilities of leaders to help provide the social structures for successful actions by cyber security personnel. They list the functional requirements for executives in the cyber security domain and indicate the leadership competencies needed to meet these requirements. Executive leadership is presented not only as a process but also as a key element of the organizational structure providing the context for cyber defense. Klimoski and Murray describe cyber executives as responsible for making strategic decisions that reflect both the dynamics of the cyber security environment outside of the organization and the evolving technological requirements raised by these dynamics. These decisions set the framework for more specific performance requirements that need to be confronted by cyber security personnel within the organization. Thus, in Figure 1.1, executive leadership is reflected not only in system-level processes but also as central in the overall context for organizational cyber security.

As suggested in Figure 1.1, cyber security performance requirements determine the necessary attributes at different levels that contribute to cyber security effectiveness. Whereas Chapters 6 and 7 elucidate some of these attributes, Chapter 8 provides more comprehensive coverage of them. Jose et al. propose a multistage and multilevel framework that includes cognitive, motivational and personality qualities as distal attributes that drive the development and enactment of proximal attributes such as technical knowledge, problem-solving skills, and social skills. They also examine the composition of teams and multiteam systems and their respective emergent states (e.g., cohesion, trust) that influence the display of effective performance processes. This chapter, then, is an important bridge between prior chapters focusing primarily on these processes and the next several chapters, which concern strategies for enhancing cyber security performance.

Chapter 9 (by Mueller-Hanson & Garza) examines issues related to selection for cyber security positions. The authors note that the rapidly shifting technological environment causes a similar churn in the knowledge and skills necessary for effective performance. Accordingly, they argue that selection approaches for these positions need to include not only the critical attributes necessary for effectiveness "at the moment" but also the ability to gain new skills and adapt quickly. This chapter provides another summary of the performance challenges facing cyber security professionals and the baseline personal qualities needed to meet those challenges. Thus, it nicely complements other chapters in the book. The authors describe a variety of methods that can be used for selection of cyber security personnel. They also take a multilevel perspective consistent with the one offered in Chapter 2 by considering issues related to the staffing of teams and multiteam systems.

Selection reflects one broad set of strategies to increase human capital and capacity in cyber security domains. A second set, training, is the focus of Chapter 10 (by Brummel, Hale, & Mol). This chapter provides a summary of training practices and methods that can be used to develop cyber security personnel. It also examines individual differences such as gender, age, personality, attitudes, and values that can determine how to differentiate and target training for different personnel. The authors offer a brief summary of system tools that can be implemented when training fails, providing a bridge to Chapters 12 and 13, which focus more on technical approaches to cyber security performance.

Selection and training are not the only approaches to enhancing cyber security human capital. Another approach is to design or structure the work environment to foster those factors that facilitate better performance, and minimize those factors that inhibit or degrade performance. Chapter 11 (by Parker, Winslow, & Tetrick) describes this approach, focusing on three outcomes—motivation and performance, health and safety, and learning and development. They note that although cyber security jobs are high in some motivating features, such as task significance, they may be lower in others. Moreover, these jobs carry high cognitive and physical loads that can harm worker well-being. Finally, the authors point to the need for cyber security work to be designed in ways that foster continual learning and development, a key concern given the highly turbulent nature of technological environments and the issue raised in Chapter 9 by Mueller-Hanson and Garza that selection for such work typically targets competencies for the current job profile that may quickly become obsolete. A healthy learning environment can provide a means of priming positive changes in current capacities.

Chapters 2–11 reflect primarily applications of tools and models from the organizational science domain to improve cyber security effectiveness. Chapters 12 and 13 deal more directly with technological aspects of the cyber security socio-technical systems. In Chapter 12, Coovert, Dreibelbis, and Borum address the themes mentioned earlier in this overview regarding the balance between human and technological approaches to cyber security. They note how efforts to combat cyber attacks by increasing the complexity of IT systems within organizations can be counterproductive. Employees may respond by becoming frustrated with the compounding security policies and procedures and failing to follow them in prescribed ways. Alternatively, the creation of complex systems may create a perception in organizational employees that their own security risk behaviors are really not harmful as in-place systems will neutralize the potential effects of these behaviors. The authors define trust as a key element in these dynamics and use current models of trust to elucidate how to understand end users' connections to technology and their display of security risk behaviors. Coovert et al. describe other behaviors, motives, and cognitive states that can influence human–technology interface and conclude with a number of recommendations for improving that interface.

Chapter 13 focuses more directly on the technology side of the human–technology interface. Albanese and Jajodia examine how automation and technological systems can improve incident discovery and cyber situational awareness. In Chapter 2, these activities are defined as key reactive performance processes in incident handling. Albanese and Jajodia describe tools that work in partnership with humans to accomplish several of the cognitive processes described in that earlier chapter. This chapter provides an interesting complement to the organizational solutions suggested in Chapters 9–11.

In the final chapter, we provide a summary of the issues raised across the chapters and point to several directions for future research. In doing so, we seek to integrate themes that we encountered in our reading of the chapters as the book editors. We invited the chapters in this book in hopes of stimulating two audiences—organizational scientists and cyber security personnel. We note that for the former, some chapters pose new research questions driven by relatively unique challenges and dynamics in the cyber security operating environment. Other chapters provide the basis for applications and human resource management strategies that should be useful to cyber personnel seeking to enhance cyber security performance. Our intent is to foster a greater understanding of the human, social, and technical forces that are entwined in the cyber security environment and how they combine to drive successful cyber defense. Such understanding will become increasingly vital as more complex cyber threats emerge on the horizon.

REFERENCES

Ahmad, A., Hadgkiss, J., & Ruighaver, A. B. (2012). Incident response teams—Challenges in supporting the organizational security function. *Computers & Security, 31*, 643–652.

Alberts, C., Dorofee, A., Killcrece, G., Ruefle, R., & Zajicek, M. (2004, October). *Defining incident management processes for CSIRTs: A work in progress* (CMU/SEI-2004-TR-015). Retrieved from http://www.dtic.mil/dtic/tr/fulltext/u2/a453378.pdf

Baard, S. K., Rench, T. A., & Kozlowski, S. W. (2014). Performance adaptation: A theoretical integration and review. *Journal of Management, 40*, 48–99.

Bronk, H., Thorbruegge, M., & Hakkaja, M. (2007, December 22). *A basic collection of good practices for running a CSIRT*. Retrieved from https://www.enisa.europa.eu/activities/cert/support/guide2/files/a-collection-of-good-practice-for-cert-quality-assurance

Campbell, J. P., Dunnette, M. D., Lawler, E. E., & Weick, K. E. (1970). *Managerial behavior, performance and effectiveness.* New York: McGraw-Hill.

Campbell, J. P., McCloy, R. A., Oppler, S. H., & Sager, C. E. (1993). A theory of performance. In N. Schmitt & W. C. Borman (Eds.), *Personnel selection in organizations* (pp. 35–70). San Francisco: Jossey-Bass.

Cichonski, P., Millar, T., Grance, T., & Scarfone, K. (2012, August). *Computer security incident handling guide: Recommendations of the National Institute of Standards and Technology* (Special Publication No. 800-61, Rev. 2). Gaithersburg, MD: National Institute of Standards and Technology, U.S. Department of Commerce.

Davenport, T. H. (2005). *Thinking for a living: How to get better performance and results from knowledge workers.* Boston: Harvard Business School Press.

Davenport, T. H., Jarvenpaa, S. L., & Beers, M. C. (1996). Improving knowledge work processes. *Sloan Management Review, 37*, 53–65.

Dunnette, M. D. (1963). A modified model for selection research. *Journal of Applied Psychology, 47*, 317–323.

Ghiselli, E. E., Campbell, J. P., & Zedeck, S. (1981). *Measurement theory for the behavioral sciences.* New York: W. H. Freeman.

Goldstein, I. L., & Ford, J. K. (2002). *Training in organizations* (4th ed.). Belmont, CA: Wadsworth.

Grance, T., Kent, K., & Kim, B. (2004). *Computer security incident handling guide: Recommendations of the National Institute of Standards and Technology* (Special Publication No. 800-61). Washington, DC: U.S. Government Printing Office.

Marks, M. A., Mathieu, J. E., & Zaccaro, S. J. (2001). A temporally based framework and taxonomy of team processes. *Academy of Management Review, 26*, 356–376.

Mathieu, J. E., Marks, M. A., & Zaccaro, S. J. (2001). Multiteam systems. In N. Anderson, D. S. Ones, H. Kepir Sinangil, & C. Viswesvaran (Eds.), *Handbook of industrial, work, and organizational psychology: Vol. 2. Organizational psychology* (pp. 289–312). London: Sage.

Mathieu, J. E., Tannenbaum, S. I., Donsbach, J. S., Alliger, G. M. (2014). A review and integration of team composition models: Moving toward a dynamic and temporal framework. *Journal of Management, 40*, 130–160.

Mumford, M. D., Mobley, M. I., Reiter-Palmonc, R., Uhlmand, C. E., & Doarese, L. M. (1991). Process analytic models of creative capacities. *Creativity Research Journal, 4*, 91–122.

Mumford, M. D., Schultz, R., & Van Doorn, J. A. (2001). Performance in planning: Processes, requirements, and errors. *Review of General Psychology, 5*, 213–240.

NRI Secure Technologies. (2014). *Cyber security trend—Annual review 2014*. Retrieved from http://www.nri-secure.com/pdf/cyber_security_trend_report_2014.pdf

Osorno, M., Millar, T., & Rager, D. (2011, June). Coordinated cybersecurity incident handling: Roles, processes, and coordination networks for crosscutting incidents. In *Proceedings of the 16th International Command and Control Technology Symposium*. Retrieved from http://www.dtic.mil/dtic/tr/fulltext/u2/a547075.pdf

Parasuraman, R., & Manzey, D. H. (2010). Complacency and bias in human use of automation: An attentional integration. *Human Factors, 52*, 381–410.

Pfleeger, S. L., & Caputo, D. D. (2012). Leveraging behavioral science to mitigate cybersecurity risk. *Computers and Security, 31*, 597–611.

Ponemon Institute. (2010, July). *First annual cost of cyber crime study: Benchmark study of U.S. companies*. Retrieved from http://www.greycastlesecurity.com/resources/documents/Ponemon_Cost_of_CyberCrime_Study_07-10.pdf

Ponemon Institute. (2014, October). *2014 global report on the cost of cyber crime*. Retrieved from http://h20195.www2.hp.com/v2/getpdf.aspx/4AA5-5207ENW.pdf?ver=1.0

Reinhardt, W., Schmidt, B., Sloep, P., & Drachsler, H. (2011). Knowledge worker roles and actions—Results of two empirical studies. *Knowledge and Process Management, 18*, 150–174.

Sony Corporation. (2015). *Consolidated financial results forecast for the third quarter ended December 31, 2014, and revision of consolidated forecast for the fiscal year ending March 31, 2015*. Retrieved from http://www.sony.net/SonyInfo/IR/financial/fr/150204_sony.pdf

Steinke, J., Bolunmez, B., Fletcher, L., Wang, V., Tomassetti, A. J., Repchick, K., ... Tetrick, L. E. (in press). Improving cyber security incident response team effectiveness using teams-based research. *IEEE Security and Privacy*.

Trist, E. L., & Bamforth, K. W. (1951). Some social and psychological consequences of the longwall method of coal-getting. *Human Relations, 4*, 3–38.

Tversky, A., & Kahneman, D. (1974). Judgment under uncertainty: Heuristics and biases. *Science, 185*, 1124–1131.

West-Brown, M. J., Stikvoort, D., Kossakowski, K.-P., Killcrece, G., Ruefle, R., & Zajicek, M. (2003, April). *Handbook for computer security incident response teams (CSIRTs)* (CMU/SEI-2003-HB-002). Retrieved from http://resources.sei.cmu.edu/library/asset-view.cfm?assetid=6305

Zaccaro, S. J. (2001). *The nature of executive leadership: A conceptual and empirical analysis of success*. Washington, DC: American Psychological Association.

Zaccaro, S. J., Weis, E., Chen, T. R., & Matthews, M. D. (2014). Situational load and personal attributes: Implications for adaptive readiness and training. In H. F. O'Neil, R. S. Perez, & E. L. Baker (Eds.), *Teaching and measuring cognitive readiness* (pp. 93–115). New York: Springer.

2

A COMPREHENSIVE MULTILEVEL TAXONOMY OF CYBER SECURITY INCIDENT RESPONSE PERFORMANCE[1]

Stephen J. Zaccaro, Amber K. Hargrove, Tiffani R. Chen, Kristin M. Repchick, and Tracy McCausland

Highly damaging intrusions and attacks on our cyber network have become practically daily constants. Many organizations have experienced such attacks in one form or another, including insurance, retail, entertainment, educational, and government institutions. Other organizations that are vulnerable to such attacks include those in critical infrastructure sectors (e.g., financial services, information technology, energy, water, emergency services, transportation systems, the defense industrial base) where damage or breakdown could create devastating effects for our nation's economy and security. The costs of responding to cyber threats have increased exponentially year after year. The *2014 Global Report on the Cost of Cyber Crime* found that, in the United States alone, costs had increased from $3.8 million to $12.7 million in the previous five years, up 96 percent (Ponemon Institute, 2010, 2014). Cyber attacks can be financially devastating, even ruinous, to single companies. For example, in a recent financial results forecast report, Sony estimated that costs related to the investigation and remediation of a cyber attack might be $15 million (Sony Corporation, 2015). Likewise, Jervis (2014), summarizing a study from the National Cyber Security Alliance in a recent news report, noted that "60% of small companies are unable to sustain their business within six months of a cyber crime attack" (para. 11). NSA Director General Keith Alexander cautioned that "the ongoing cyber-thefts from the networks of public and private organizations, including Fortune 500 companies, represent the greatest transfer of wealth in human history" (Alexander, 2012). Indeed, President Obama recently declared that cyber threats represent "one of the most serious economic and national security challenges we face as a nation" (Obama, 2015).

Such challenges have magnified the importance for organizations to develop highly effective cyber security incident response processes and systems.

Accordingly, cyber security incident response teams (CSIRTs) have grown in size and visibility across increasing numbers of organizations. As one indicator of this surge, the membership of incident response teams in the professional organization, Forum of Incident Response and Security Teams (FIRST), has nearly doubled in the last five years (Forum of Incident Response and Security Teams, n.d.). Moreover, the Federal Bureau of Investigation has newly created a division dedicated to cyber crime and has elevated the cyber threat to number three in national priorities (McFeely, 2013).

Unfortunately, this rate of expansion has outpaced efforts to understand and develop best practices designed for maximizing the effectiveness of SIRTs. Although there is a substantial literature in the general organizational psychology domain on team effectiveness (e.g., see reviews by Kozlowski & Ilgen, 2006; Mathieu, Maynard, Rapp, & Gilson, 2008), little of it has been applied to CSIRTs. Although the general literature on team effectiveness can certainly inform an examination of what factors maximize the success of CSIRTs, research needs to consider how the particular nature of CSIRT work influences the drivers of their performance. For example, the knowledge- and information-based activities and adaptation requirements of such work mean that certain member knowledge, skills, and abilities (KSAs) and particular forms of shared knowledge will likely be more prominent predictors of team performance in CSIRTs than in other types of teams.

Likewise, although the literature on performance and its facets is also quite large (e.g., Campbell, McCloy, Oppler, & Sager, 1993; Sackett, 2002; Wildman, Bedwell, Salas, & Smith-Jentsch, 2011), few, if any, studies have examined the particular performance requirements confronting CSIRTs and their members, the performance processes they engage in to address these requirements, and the domain-specific outcomes of these processes. Moreover, there has been little systematic research in the cyber security field specifically examining the facets of performance in response to cyber threat and, in particular, the behavioral and human drivers of such performance. In regard to computer systems users, Pfleeger and Caputo (2012) argued that "by both understanding the role of human behavior and leveraging behavioral science findings, the designers, developers and maintainers of information infrastructure can address real and perceived obstacles to productivity and provide more effective security" (p. 598). The same is true for cyber security responders: By understanding the human elements of successful performance by incident responders, organizations can create more effective cyber security threat response infrastructures and systems.

Such understanding needs to start from a well-articulated and validated classification of the CSIRT performance domain that captures the activities comprised within this domain and the range of outcomes that result from these activities. Researchers in cyber security have offered a number of classifications of CSIRT work (e.g., Alberts, Dorofee, Killcrece, Ruefle, & Zajicek, 2004; Cichonski, Millar, Grance, & Scarfone, 2012; Grance, Kent, & Kim, 2004; Killcrece, Kossakowski, Ruefle, & Zajicek, 2003; Kossakowski et al., 1999;

Maj, Reijers, & Stikvoort, 2010; National Institute of Standards and Technology [NIST], National Initiative for Cybersecurity Education, 2013; Werlinger, Muldner, Hawkey, & Beznosov, 2010; West-Brown et al., 2003). Most of these have been elaborations of the four basic CSIRT functions defined by West-Brown et al. (2003): *triage, handling, feedback*, and *announcement* (see Chapter 3, this volume, for additional explanation of CSIRT functions). Although these prior classifications have been quite useful in defining CSIRT tasks, they generally place lower emphasis—or miss altogether—three important distinctions. The first is a separate delineation of the set of cognitive and behavioral activities that define task completion. Most classifications have conflated these processes as single sets or categories (e.g., triage). The second distinction is a distinguishing of performance processes from performance outcomes. Most of the aforementioned classifications have focused exclusively on defining CSIRT work tasks or activities. However, a comprehensive classification of the CSIRT performance domain should include not only cognitive and behavioral processes that contribute to effective cyber security incident response, but also the markers and outcomes of effectiveness.

The third distinction refers to the level at which work is performed, either by a single individual, a team of responders, or multiple teams of responders and analysts. Prior classifications have simply delineated tasks and left open the issue of their accomplishment by individuals working either alone or with others. However, task accomplishment can change in fundamental ways across such levels. At the individual level, responders engage cognitive resources to diagnose incidents and events, generate explanations, and derive and implement solutions. There is little or no reliance on others to accomplish such tasks. When incidents require the intervention of multiple responders, processes of externalized cognition, or macrocognition, occur as multiple individuals work together as a team to diagnose and resolve incidents (Fiore, Rosen, et al., 2010). These processes transpire as individual team members offer ideas, other members use these ideas as prompts or inspirations for further ideas, members converge on shared cognitive representations of a problem and its solution, and a team collectively implements the solution (Fiore, Smith-Jentsch, Salas, Warner, & Letsky, 2010; Kennedy & McComb, 2010). Moreover, these processes can also occur in multiteam systems, in which teams work in close collaboration with other teams to resolve more complex cyber security incidents that influence multiple stakeholders. Classifications of CSIRT work need to capture how task accomplishment changes as processes move from the individual to the team and system levels.

In this chapter, we describe a taxonomy of cyber security incident response performance that includes the fundamental work functions described in prior classifications but also makes the three aforementioned distinctions (see Table 2.1 later in this chapter). Thus, it delineates cognitive and behavioral activities that define CSIRT performance, it defines several outcomes of such processes, and it specifies how these processes and outcomes change at multiple levels of aggregation. This taxonomy follows from a conceptual framing of CSIRT performance requirements. It also derives from other models of team performance processes and collective complex problem-solving (e.g., Burke, Stagl, Salas, Pierce, & Kendall, 2006; Hinsz, Tindale, & Vollrath, 1997; Marks, Mathieu, & Zaccaro, 2001). In the next section, we offer distinctions about the concept of work performance that are represented in the taxonomy.

Some Principles and Concepts that Guided Development of the Taxonomy

A full description of the principles of taxonomy development and validation are beyond the scope of this chapter. We refer interested readers to Fleishman and Quaintance (1984) and Bailey (1994). However, we do reference some basic principles that characterized the development of the taxonomy of cyber security incident response performance presented here. The fundamental purpose of a taxonomic classification is to provide a structure to a class of phenomena that allows some generalizations about relationships both among similar objects within a set and between different but related object sets (Fleishman & Quaintance, 1984). Once established, this structure can provide the basis for subsequent classification of other encountered related objects. Thus, a taxonomy of cyber security incident response performance would group similar response activities (e.g., triage, diagnosis, generation of corrective solution) into separate sets while also denoting how these sets are related.

Fleishman and Quaintance (1984) argued that the construction of a taxonomy entails three basic steps (see also Fleishman, Mumford, Zaccaro, Levin, & Hein, 1991). The first is to define the essential elements of the phenomena targeted in the taxonomy. Such a definition provides the conceptual underpinning of the taxonomy and helps delineate both the distinctions between and similarities among taxa in the taxonomy. The structure of the taxonomy offered here rests fundamentally on the performance requirements of cyber security incident response and the processes these requirements engender.

The next step in taxonomic classification, according to Fleishman and Quaintance (1984), is to specify the causal relationships that connect different classes of objects within the taxonomy. Prior classifications of cyber security work have suggested a causal process similar to the much simplified one in Figure 2.1, in which incidents are detected and analyzed, possible corrective actions are generated and planned, and best-fitting or selected solutions are implemented (e.g., Cichonski et al., 2012; Kossakowski et al., 1999; Orsono, Millar, & Rager, 2011; West-Brown et al., 2003). These represent the generic performance processes of cyber security work. To these, we have added performance outcomes to fully capture the performance domain. A similar causal process served as part of the framework for the taxonomy offered in this chapter.

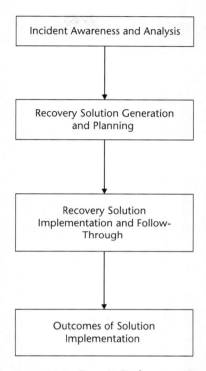

FIGURE 2.1 Generic Performance Processes of Cyber Security Work

The third step is to gather evidence for the validity and utility of the proposed taxonomy. Part of this evaluation entails demonstration of its content construct validity; that is, in this case, does it include the full range of the cyber security work activities that contribute to effective incident response performance? Another aspect of this evaluation is to determine whether the underlying structure captures the conceptual relationships among taxonomic dimensions and taxa.

In the remainder of this chapter, we describe how we implemented each of these steps to develop a comprehensive taxonomy of cyber security incident response performance. In the next section, we describe the conceptual bases for the structure of the proposed taxonomy. We then describe the taxonomy, including its overarching relational structure and each taxon with its corresponding member objects. We follow this with a description of a preliminary effort to provide validation for the taxonomy. Finally, our intent for the taxonomy is to provide a tool that can be useful in applications to improve the effectiveness and performance of cyber security incident response systems. Accordingly, we conclude with a description of the various possible uses of the proposed taxonomy.

Performance Requirements of CSIRT Work

Bronk, Thorbruegge, and Hakkaja (2007) defined a *CSIRT* as,

> a team that responds to computer security incidents by providing all necessary services to solve the problem(s) or to support the resolution of them. In order to mitigate risks and minimize the number of required responses, most CSIRTs also provide preventative and educational services for their constituency. (p. 12)

This definition, a common one in the CSIRT literature (e.g., West-Brown, Stikvoort, & Kossakowski, 1998; West-Brown et al., 2003), indicates that the core function of cyber security incident response is cyber threat detection and mitigation. This primary focus means that central performance processes include threat vigilance, incident awareness, incident analysis, and development and implementation of mitigating responses. Accordingly, as noted earlier in this chapter, all prior classifications of CSIRT work have included these basic functions. Most have also included another set of preparatory functions pertaining to reducing the effectiveness of an attack and developing tools to intercept possible incidents (e.g., Alberts et al., 2004; Cichonski et al., 2012; Killcrece et al., 2003; Maj et al., 2010). In essence, part of CSIRT work is engaging in anticipatory thinking and behavior designed to ward off attacks and reduce the damage caused by unavoidable incidents. Such preparation may include contingency planning to establish normative response protocols for different categories of incidents. Given the fundamentally threat-focused nature of CSIRT work, we have retained these two sets of activities in the taxonomy proposed here. We delineate them as sets of proactive and reactive performance processes (see Table 2.1).

Knowledge Work

Cyber security incident response reflects what organizational researchers define as *knowledge work*. Reinhardt, Schmidt, Sloep, and Drachsler (2011) argued that

> the main feature differentiating knowledge work from other conventional work is that the basic task of knowledge work is thinking. Although all types of jobs entail a mix of physical, social, and mental work, it is the perennial processing of non-routine problems that require non-linear and creative thinking that characterizes knowledge work. (p. 150)

The categorization of incident response as knowledge work informed the structure of the proposed taxonomy in several ways. First, incident response work is cognitively demanding, requiring high use of a range of cognitive resources. Accordingly, we have delineated a set of cognitive performance processes that are distinct from behavioral processes. Most prior classifications have conflated these two sets of processes. However, cognitive performance processes entail different activities from behavioral processes and, accordingly, have different influential drivers. Also, cognitive processes act as both causal antecedents and consequences of behavioral activities. As we noted earlier, an effective taxonomic structure provides a depiction of how different sets of objects are related causally to one another (Fleishman & Quaintance, 1984), a research feature that allows for the generation of testable hypotheses. For the present taxonomy, this implied causal structure has a practical benefit as well; the delineation of causal antecedents to behavioral activities can contribute to more fine-grained and internally valid performance training systems (Fleishman & Quaintance, 1984).

As noted in Reinhardt et al.'s (2011) definition, the nature of knowledge work entails "the perennial processing of non-routine problems" (p. 150). This emphasis points to another key feature of cyber security incident response that has informed the proposed taxonomy. The resolution of cyber security events entails a form of complex and often creative problem-solving that utilizes a number of different cognitive processes. These can include environmental monitoring, problem detection, problem construction and categorization, generation of solution parameters, generation of candidate solutions, evaluation and selection of a solution path, planning of solution implementation, and execution of a solution (Mumford, Mobley, Uhlman, Reiter-Palmon, & Doares, 1991; Mumford, Schultz, & Van Doorn, 2001). Note that these processes entail a planning or solution-generation-evaluation phase and an execution or solution-implementation phase. This division is similar to one that has appeared in other team performance taxonomies (e.g., Fleishman & Zaccaro, 1992; Marks et al., 2001).

Most prior classifications of cyber security incident response work have alluded to these processes at a very broad level. This abbreviated approach does provide a valuable parsimony to classification that increases its utility to both researchers and practitioners. However, such an approach can obscure distinct subordinate processes that are critical for effective performance. To create an appropriate balance between parsimony and comprehensiveness, the proposed taxonomy includes superordinate and subordinate taxa that vary in their levels of detail about specific performance processes. The superordinate dimensions provide parsimony, whereas the subordinate dimensions offer a more comprehensive perspective (see Table 2.1).

Another aspect of cyber security incident response as knowledge work that informed the development of the proposed taxonomy is that it includes high levels of adaptive performance requirements. As incident responders derive solutions to particular types of incidents, hackers adapt the nature of their attacks. Thus, over time, incident responders have to confront new and different types of events that do not conform to prior solution strategies. Baard, Rench, and Kozlowski (2013) defined *performance adaptation* as "cognitive, affective, motivational, and behavioral modifications made in response to the demands of a new or changing environment, or situational demands" (p. 3). Adaptation occurs when performers need to switch from existing solution protocols to qualitatively different strategies that correspond to fundamentally different problems (Ely, Zaccaro, & Conjar, 2009). Pulakos, Arad, Donovan, and Plamondon (2000) defined several task requirements that call for adaptation and that are highly descriptive of cyber security incident response, including "handling emergencies or crisis situations"; "handling work stress"; "solving problems creatively"; "dealing with uncertain and unpredictable work situations"; and "learning work tasks, technologies, and procedures" (p. 617).

This quality of cyber security incident response work means that complex problem-solving processes may include some that reflect a focus on noting differences in problem structures and being aware of how particular incidents and events require fundamental shifts in solutions strategies. The latter processes pertain to the use of adaptive expertise when engaging in problem awareness, problem construction, and solution generation (Smith, Ford, & Kozlowski, 1997).

Multilevel Cyber Security Incident Response

Most prior cyber security performance taxonomies have simply listed generic tasks without reference to whether they are completed by individuals, teams, or larger organizational systems. However, performance processes and outcomes do change significantly as task accomplishment moves from the individual to the collective level. These multilevel changes matter greatly for cyber security incident response training, selection, and staffing. Moreover, CSIRT managers need to attend not only to individual performance drivers but also to those factors that promote team and system performance. Accordingly, the proposed taxonomy includes three distinct levels of task performance: individual, team, and multiteam system (see Table 2.1).

Individual performance processes include those activities completed by single persons with little or no active engagement with other team members. Thus, actions or processes related to incident awareness and identification, triage, incident handling, feedback, and solution announcement that individuals accomplish alone reflect this level of performance. While handling an incident, an individual analyst may choose to escalate the issue to a higher level analyst (e.g., transferring an incident from a Level 1 analyst to a Level 2 analyst) or hand off an incident to another group. Likewise, the analyst may engage in knowledge distribution by posting information about particular threats, attacks, malware, and other types of incidents to a central knowledge repository, such as a wiki or virtual whiteboard. The act of sharing information in this manner does not raise the performance act from an individual one to a collective one; the analyst is simply passing along information for use by other analysts.

Incident response performance becomes team action when two or more analysts collaborate to identify, define, triage, solve, and provide information about cyber incidents. In many CSIRTs, such collaboration is typically instigated by an individual analyst who encounters an incident that is outside of his or her area of expertise, prior experience, or general knowledge; or the incident maybe novel or complex enough to require a collaborative solution. In essence, the decision often belongs to the individual analyst to establish or set up a team of analysts to resolve a particular incident (Chen et al., 2014). Such "discretionary collaboration" is hallmark of most responder teams, in which members may call for backup when incidents require the input of more than one person.

According to Kozlowski and Ilgen (2006),

> A team can be defined as (a) two or more individuals who (b) socially interact (face-to-face, or, increasingly, virtual[ly]); (c) possess one or more common goals; (d) are brought together to perform organizationally relevant tasks; (e) exhibit interdependencies with respect to workflow, goals, and outcomes; (f) have a different roles and responsibilities; and (g) are together embedded in an encompassing organizational system, with boundaries and linkages to the broader system context and task environment. (p. 79)

Although all of these elements are present in CSIRTs, the key to incident response moving from individual-level to team-level performance is increasing interdependence between two or more analysts as they work together to resolve a malicious cyber event. Thus, handoffs, escalations to other analysts (without the continued involvement of the original analyst), and information or knowledge postings are not necessarily "team-level" events, because they typically involve little or no wou interdependence between analysts. Cyber team performance occurs when multiple analysts interact closely to resolve a cyber incident.

We have noted that cyber security incident response is knowledge work, in which "the basic task … is thinking" (Reinhardt et al., 2011, p. 150), which means that cognitive processes play an integral role in CSIRT performance. At the team level, such work, then, involves "thinking together." Several researchers of team dynamics have noted processes of team cognition that contribute to the production of shared knowledge and to collective problem-solving. For example, Hinsz et al. (1997) noted that "the processing of information in groups involves activities that occur within as well as among the minds of group members" (p. 43). Fiore, Rosen, et al. (2010) elaborated on such collective or externalized cognition further by describing phases of collaborative problem-solving that include "knowledge construction, problem model development, team consensus, and outcome evaluation and revision" (p. 215). These phases entail the communication of individual ideas and the collective consideration and refinement of these ideas by other team members. Salazar, Lant, Fiore, and Salas (2012) described similar processes in diverse science teams in which members contribute unique knowledge to team conversations, and other members either assimilate such information into their existing understanding of a problem or accommodate the knowledge from different members into a new mental representation (Piaget, 1952). As a whole, this body of work emphasizes how individual team members can contribute to a collective understanding of a problem space and the subsequent utilization of this understanding to collectively solve team problems. Such collective understanding then becomes utilized in the processes of collaborative problem-solving. Accordingly, the proposed taxonomy includes not only individual-level cognitive and behavioral activities associated with incident response and resolution but also the externalized cognitive and behavioral activities that occur when team members think together about an incident and coordinate their actions to resolve it.

Mathieu, Marks, and Zaccaro (2001) argued that the forms of interdependence and interactions that can occur within teams may also occur between teams as they collaborate to solve complex problems. Calling such collectives *multiteam systems* (MTSs), they defined them as

> Two or more teams that interface directly and interdependently in response to environmental contingencies toward the accomplishment of collective goals. MTS boundaries are defined by virtue of the fact that all teams within the system, while pursuing different proximal goals, share at least one common distal goal; and in doing so exhibit input, process and outcome interdependence with at least one other team in the system.
> (Mathieu et al., 2001, p. 290)

Note that an MTS is not simply an amalgamation of teams coexisting within an organization—most organizations are composed of collectives of teams. Instead, an MTS is an integrated system of teams in which at least two or more teams are collaborating closely around the accomplishment of a proximal goal while all of the teams in the MTS work toward achievement of the same distal goal.

Figure 2.2 illustrates a simplified task goal hierarchy of a hypothetical cyber security incident response MTS. This MTS includes five distinct teams—network monitoring, forensics and malware analysis, operations, threat intelligence, and communications. Each team works closely with at least one other team on a particular goal-related task. For example, the monitoring team collaborates with the forensics team and the threat intelligence team to determine the nature of a particular event. The forensics teams then works with operations to develop a solution and mitigate or eradicate the threat. Finally, the threat intelligence and communications teams work together to share information and knowledge about the threat with other relevant stakeholders. Whereas team-level performance processes entail individual team members thinking and working together, MTS-level performance processes involve representatives of different teams thinking and working together. Accordingly, the proposed taxonomy

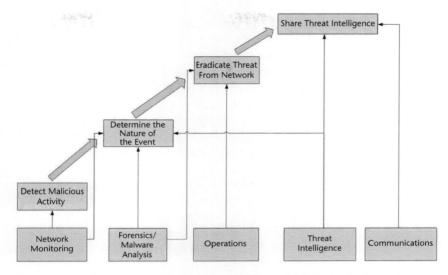

FIGURE 2.2 Cyber Security Incident Response Team Goal Hierarchy Example

includes similar collaborative activities occurring both within and between teams in a cyber security incident response MTS (see Table 2.1).

Summary

Conceptually, the proposed taxonomy rests on a foundation of several performance requirements for effective cyber security incident response. These are (a) a proactive or contingency focus, (b) a reactive or threat focus, (c) knowledge work, (d) complex problem-solving, (e) adaptation, and (f) multilevel collaboration. These requirements suggest two sets of cognitive and behavioral performance activities. The accomplishment of these activities drives levels of various multilevel performance outcomes. In the next section, we describe the development and structure of the proposed taxonomy. We call this a "preliminary" taxonomy to reflect the need for subsequent and multiple validations and revisions (e.g., see Fleishman & Zaccaro, 1992, for an example of an iterative taxonomy).

A Preliminary Taxonomy of Cyber Security Incident Response Performance

Taxonomy Construction

A first step in taxonomic development entails the definition of the entity of interest. Most prior definitions of CSIRTs have either excluded a specific reference to team-level processes (e.g., NIST, National Initiative for Cybersecurity

Education, 2013) or included, in limited ways, a team and MTS focus (e.g., Alberts et al., 2004). Thus, although Cichonski et al. (2012) noted that CSIRT "plans, policies, and procedures should reflect the team's interactions with other teams within the organization as well as with outside parties" (p. 6), there were few specifications of the particular team and MTS processes denoting such interactions. The dynamic collaboration of individual incident responders with other responders and of teams of responders with other stakeholders is, therefore, a key element of the proposed taxonomy. Accordingly, its construction reflected the following definition of *cyber security incident response MTSs*:

> A cyber security MTS is a collection of two or more teams, each of which is composed of two or more individuals interacting with each other, information technology (IT) infrastructure, IT personnel, end users, management, and other component teams to provide proactive and reactive cyber security services to support the mission of a defined constituency. (adpted from Steinke, Bolunmez, Fletcher, Wang, Tomassetti, Repchick, Zaccaro, Dalal, & Tetrick, 2015, p. 2).

Note that this definition emphasizes (a) individuals (b) working in teams, (c) which are also working closely with multiple stakeholder teams, (d) to provide a range of contingency- and threat-focused services, (e) with all teams focused on a central mission. Performance, then, is defined in terms of individual, team, and multiteam activities and outcomes that drive overall mission accomplishment.

The next step in the construction of the proposed taxonomy was a review of existing performance taxonomies that reflected one or more of the aforementioned performance requirements. Included in this review were classifications of generic task performance (e.g., Borman & Brush 1993, Borman, Bryant, & Dorio, 2010; Campbell et al., 1993; Peterson, Mumford, Borman, Jeanneret, & Fleishman, 1999; Viswesvaran, 1993), cyber security incident response performance (e.g., Alberts et al., 2004; Cichonski et al., 2012; Maj et al., 2010), complex problem-solving processes (Mumford, et al., 1991, 2001), team information processing (Hinsz et al., 1997), team performance (Fleishman & Zaccaro, 1992; Ilgen, Hollenbeck, Johnson, & Jundt, 2005; Marks et al., 2001), MTS performance (DeChurch et al., 2011; Zaccaro, Marks, & DeChurch, 2012), and adaptive performance (Burke et al., 2006; Ely et al., 2009; Pulakos et al., 2000). This review led to the establishment of several structural elements in the proposed taxonomy. First, in line with the contingency-focused and threat-focus performance requirements noted in Figure 2.2, the taxonomy delineates a separate set of proactive and reactive performance processes. This delineation corresponds to other incident response performance classifications (e.g., Alberts et al., 2004; Cichonski et al., 2012; Killcrece et al., 2003; Maj et al., 2010). Proactive performance processes include those activities that focus on establishing the mission, goals, organizational structures, protocols, and standard operating procedures that create the framework for future incident responses. These processes also include a contingency approach to detecting possible system vulnerabilities and anticipating possible future threats. Reactive performance processes include activities that occur in response to incoming threats and incidents, such as triage, deeper incident analysis, documentation and reporting of incident-handling activities, and incident mitigation. These processes are specified as performed by individuals, teams, and MTSs.

Multiple taxonomies of individual and collective problem-solving emphasize (a) a planning phase that generally entails processes such as situation assessment, problem construction, and solution generation as well as (b) an execution phase that involves solution implementation, monitoring, feedback, and after-action review. For example, Mumford et al. (1991) defined *complex problem-solving* as involving processes related to problem detection, problem construction and categorization, solution generation and evaluation, and the planning and execution of solution implementation. Marks et al.'s (2001) taxonomic model of team processes specifies a transition phase within a problem episode that includes processes such as mission analysis and planning, goal specification, and strategy formulation. That model also specifies an action phase that includes coordination and execution of member activities and various monitoring and backup behaviors. Burke et al.'s (2006) model of adaptive performance contains four phases—situation assessment, plan formulation, plan execution, and team learning. DeChurch et al., (2011) and Zaccaro and DeChurch (2012) specify similar transition and action processes in MTSs. On the basis of these models, the proposed taxonomy includes planning and execution activities as part of both proactive and reactive incident response performance. These activities are also specified as performed by individuals, teams, and MTSs. Thus, the basic structure of the preliminary taxonomy of cyber security incident response performance processes contains three dimensions: (a) proactive and reactive performance processes; (b) planning and execution activities; and (c) individual, team, and multiteam levels of action. Table 2.1 displays an abbreviated version of the preliminary taxonomy. Both for the sake of parsimony and because of chapter space limitations, we have combined planning and execution activities into one column (see Column 1 in Table 2.1). For example, "Define and formalize mission, tasks, and services" includes the planning functions of defining cyber security incident response MTS purposes and goals as well as the execution functions of formalizing these plans, sharing them with stakeholders, and obtaining senior management support. Likewise, more specific planning and execution activities have been grouped under individual, team, and MTS levels.[2] In the next sections, we describe these taxa and their incorporated activities in more detail.

Reactive Performance Processes

Reactive cyber security incident response performance processes include several taxa that are recognizable from most other cyber incident response classifications (e.g., Alberts et al., 2004; Cichonski et al., 2012; Killcrece et al., 2003; Osorno,

TABLE 2.1 A Preliminary Taxonomy of Cyber Security Incident Response Performance

Reactive performance: Planning and execution processes

Detect, gather information, and alert others about security incidents	Individual • (p) Attend to intrusion-detection alerts • (p) Gather additional information about the nature of the attack • (p) Assess for false positives • (p) Select cases for triage and further response • (e) Send out initial incident alerts • (e) Prepare incident ticket Team • (p) Collectively focus team attention on intrusion-detection alerts • (p) Exchange information and ideas with other team members about nature of attack • (p) Gather evaluations and obtain concurrence from other team members on assessments of false positives • (e) Coordinate distribution of initial alerts Multiteam system (MTS) • (p) Collectively attend to intrusions detected by other component teams in the MTS • (p) Coordinate and consult with possibly affected component teams to gather and exchange information about the nature of the attack • (p) Gather evaluations and obtain concurrence from appropriate component teams on assessments of false positives • (e) Coordinate distribution of initial alerts to stakeholders and possibly affected clients outside of the MTS
Triage incoming incidents and communicate assessments	Individual • (p) Assess and categorize potential incidents (new/old, level of typicality, level of potential harm, etc.) • (p) Define and prioritize problem parameters posed by the nature of the event • (e) Update case file on the basis of assessment, prioritization, and categorization • (e) Communicate with other responders or affected constituency when incident is determined to reach level of immediate notification Team • (p) Share assessments of identified threats; exchange information and reach agreement about how to categorize identified incidents (new/old, level of typicality, level of potential harm, etc.) within team • (p) Exchange information and reach agreement about problem parameters posed by the nature of the event • (e) Coordinate on updating of case file (i.e., ticket) • (e) Engage in workload sharing to complete triage assessment

(*Continued*)

TABLE 2.1 A Preliminary Taxonomy of Cyber Security Incident Response Performance (Continued)

Reactive performance: Planning and execution processes

	• (e) Collaborate on when and how to communicate with other responders or affected constituency when incident is determined to reach level of immediate notification • (e) Collaborate on report preparation and system updating MTS • (p) Share assessments of identified threats across relevant component teams; exchange information and reach agreement across affected component teams about how to categorize identified incidents (new/old, level of typicality, level of potential harm, etc.) • (p) Exchange information and reach agreement across affected component teams about problem parameters posed by the nature of the event • (e) Coordinate across component teams on updating of case file • (e) Engage in workload sharing between component teams to complete triage assessment • (e) Collaborate across component teams on when and how to communicate with other responders or affected constituency when incident is determined to reach level of immediate notification • (e) Collaborate across component teams on report preparation and system updating
Analyze incidents	Individual • (p) Forecast potential damage from incident • (p) Identify constituents affected by incident • (p) Gather and examine evidence and artifacts related to the incident • (p) Determine the incident cause • (e) Prepare analysis report • (e) Hand off and/or escalate incident to other responders as needed Team • (p) Exchange relevant information within the team to forecast potential incident damage • (p) Exchange relevant information within the team to identify constituents affected by incident • (p) Gather and examine evidence and artifacts related to the incident • (p) Exchange relevant information and reach consensus within the team on the cause of the incident • (e) Coordinate team member roles and responsibilities for incident analysis • (e) Collaborate on when to hand off and/or escalate incident to other responders, affected constituency members • (e) Collaborate on preparation of analysis report

(Continued)

TABLE 2.1 A Preliminary Taxonomy of Cyber Security Incident Response Performance (Continued)

Reactive performance: Planning and execution processes

	MTS • (p) Exchange relevant information between teams to forecast potential incident damage • (p) Exchange relevant information between teams to identify constituents affected by incident • (p) Gather and examine evidence and artifacts related to the incident from multiple component teams • (p) Exchange relevant information and reach consensus across component teams on the cause of the incident • (e) Coordinate component team roles and responsibilities for incident analysis • (e) Collaborate with other component teams on when to hand off and/or escalate incident to other responders, affected constituency members • (e) Collaborate with component teams to create analysis report
Develop and implement comprehensive mitigation solutions	Individual • (p) Define specifications of potential best-fitting solutions • (p) Generate and research potential solutions that match desired specifications • (p) Simulate potential best-fitting solutions • (p) Evaluate and select best-fitting solution • (p) Develop solution-implementation plan • (e) Use selected security tools, applications, and/or procedures to mitigate incident Team • (p) Exchange information among team members and collaborate on specifications for potential best-fitting solutions; reach consensus on desired solution specifications • (p) Exchange ideas about candidate solutions; exchange information about members' expertise and experiences with candidate solutions • (p) Conduct team-wide simulation of potential best-fitting solutions • (p) Exchange evaluations and reach consensus on best-fitting solutions • (p) Determine team members roles in solution implementation plans • (e) Coordinate team members' actions in executing implementation and utilization of selected security solutions MTS • (p) Exchange information among component teams on specifications for potential solutions; reach consensus across component teams • (p) Exchange ideas among component teams about potential solutions • (p) Conduct simulation with multiple component teams of potential best-fitting solutions • (p) Reach consensus among multiple component teams about best-fitting solutions

(Continued)

TABLE 2.1 A Preliminary Taxonomy of Cyber Security Incident Response Performance (Continued)

Reactive performance: Planning and execution processes

	• (p) Determine roles of each component team in solution-implementation plans • (e) Coordinate across component teams in executing implementation of selected security solutions
Document and report action logs	Individual • (e) Complete and file written analysis and summary of incident handling case (i.e., close ticket) • (e) Post related incident handling information and new threat information to internal source (i.e., wiki, blog, etc.) Team • (e) Integrate contributions from participating team members into case summary MTS • (e) Integrate contributions from participating component teams into case summary
Conduct after-action review and implement necessary after-action adaptation	Individual • (p) Gather information and evaluate completed incident handling cases, including the following phases: threat assessment, solution generation, solution implementation, and solution effectiveness • (p) Assess and evaluate necessary revisions to policies, procedures, tools, applications, and/or infrastructure • (e) Implement necessary changes in incident handling policies, procedures, tools, applications, and/or infrastructure Team • (p) Exchange information and evaluate team interactions and collective activities during all phases of completed incident handling cases • (p) Assess and evaluate necessary revisions to team policies, interaction protocols, and member roles • (e) Coordinate implementation of necessary changes to team incident handling interaction protocols and member roles MTS • (p) Exchange information and evaluate interactions and activities across all component teams involved in incident handling cases • (p) Assess and evaluate necessary revisions to component teams' goals, roles, policies, and interaction protocols • (e) Coordinate implementation of necessary changes to component teams' roles and interaction protocols
Manage component team members' interpersonal interactions	Team • (e) Monitor and facilitate team communication protocols • (e) Manage conflict among team members • (e) Monitor and maintain cohesion among team members • (e) Address morale issues arising among team members

(Continued)

TABLE 2.1 A Preliminary Taxonomy of Cyber Security Incident Response Performance (Continued)

Reactive performance: Planning and execution processes

	MTS • (e) Monitor and facilitate communication protocols and interactions among component teams • (e) Manage conflicts among component teams • (e) Monitor and maintain cohesion between component team members and across the incident response MTS • (e) Address morale issues between component team members and across the incident response MTS
Manage component team members' interpersonal interactions	Team • (e) Monitor and facilitate team communication protocols • (e) Manage conflict among team members • (e) Monitor and maintain cohesion among team members • (e) Address morale issues arising among team members
	MTS • (e) Monitor and facilitate communication protocols and interactions among component teams • (e) Manage conflicts among component teams • (e) Monitor and maintain cohesion between component team members and across the incident response MTS • (e) Address morale issues between component team members and across the incident response MTS

Proactive performance: Planning and execution processes

Define and formalize mission, tasks, and services	Individual • (p) Identify main mission, tasks, environmental conditions, practical constraints, and necessary resources • (e) Consult with relevant stakeholders about mission parameters and stakeholder requirements • (e) Obtain management support and appropriate funding to carry out mission and services • (e) Establish and communicate formal mission statements and services
	Team • (p) Exchange and evaluate ideas about mission priorities • (p) Develop a shared understanding of the team's mission • (p) Determine team procedures and strategies to best accomplish team goals and mission • (e) Establish and implement standard team interaction protocols to synchronize team members' actions around goal accomplishment
	MTS • (p) Exchange and evaluate mission-related ideas and goals from different component teams

(Continued)

TABLE 2.1 A Preliminary Taxonomy of Cyber Security Incident Response Performance (Continued)

Proactive performance: Planning and execution processes

	• (p) Develop a shared understanding among component teams of overall incident response mission and plan • (p) Determine multiteam procedures and strategies to accomplish overall incident response goals • (e) Establish and implement standard between-team interaction protocols to synchronize component team actions around MTS goal accomplishment
Determine and implement necessary security tools, applications, and infrastructure	Individual • (p) Identify and specify infrastructure requirements • (p) Generate potential tools, programs, and methods that meet infrastructure requirements • (p) Evaluate and select potential security enhancement interventions • (e) Establish and implement selected security tools, applications, and infrastructure Team • (p) Exchange relevant information and ideas to develop a shared understanding about infrastructure requirements for the team • (p) Generate and evaluate members' ideas and proposals about necessary, viable, and innovative security measures, tools, and applications • (p) Garner collective endorsement and support for most appropriate security measures, tools, and applications • (e) Coordinate implementation of security measures, tools, and applications across team members to ensure the most appropriate system configuration • (e) Engage in collective monitoring and backup behavior of team members to ensure that all incident responders within the team implement security measures, tools, and applications to the same level of effectiveness and efficiency MTS • (p) Exchange information and ideas among component teams to develop an integrated understanding about the infrastructure requirements of each separate team • (p) Generate and evaluate ideas and proposals from different component teams about potential security measures, tools, and applications that can address the needs of all component teams • (p) Garner collective endorsement and support from all component teams for the most appropriate security measures, tools, and applications

(Continued)

TABLE 2.1 A Preliminary Taxonomy of Cyber Security Incident Response Performance (Continued)

Proactive performance: Planning and execution processes

	• (e) Coordinate implementation of security measures, tools, and applications across members of different component teams to ensure the most appropriate system configuration • (e) Engage in collective monitoring and backup behavior across component teams to ensure all incident responders within the MTS implement security measures, tools, and applications to the same level of effectiveness and efficiency
Plan and execute procedures for maintenance of security tools, applications, and infrastructure	Individual • (p) Design necessary procedures for maintaining effectiveness of existing security tools, applications, and infrastructure • (e) Implement and complete scheduled maintenance activities • (e) Monitor operating conditions of existing security tools, applications, and infrastructure Team • (p) Exchange relevant information to develop a shared understanding of necessary maintenance procedures • (p) Share information with team members about operating conditions of existing security tools, applications, and infrastructure • (e) Coordinate maintenance activities and engage in workload sharing with team members to accomplish maintenance procedures MTS • (p) Exchange relevant information between component teams to determine maintenance requirements for each team's security tools, applications, and infrastructure • (p) Integrate maintenance requirements for the security tools, applications, and infrastructure of different component teams • (p) Share information with component teams about operating conditions of existing security tools, applications, and infrastructure • (e) Coordinate maintenance activities across component teams; engage in workload sharing across component teams to accomplish maintenance procedures
Identify and test for potential security vulnerabilities and threats	Individual • (p) Scan and monitor information systems for emerging trends and potential weaknesses, deteriorations, and obsolescence • (p) Identify emerging security vulnerabilities and possible threats • (p) Forecast criticality of vulnerabilities and potential threats • (e) Test existing information systems for potential weaknesses, deteriorations, and obsolescence • (e) Post/publicize information about potential threats and system weaknesses, deteriorations, and obsolescence

(Continued)

TABLE 2.1 A Preliminary Taxonomy of Cyber Security Incident Response Performance (Continued)

Proactive performance: Planning and execution processes

	Team • (p) Exchange information and brainstorm ideas with team members about emerging trends and potential weaknesses, deteriorations, and obsolescence • (p) Reach consensus on and a shared understanding of the veracity and probability of potential vulnerabilities and threats • (e) Coordinate member actions in conducting multiple and different tests of existing information systems for potential weaknesses, deteriorations, and obsolescence • (e) Exchange data and reach consensus on information to be posted/publicized about potential threats and system weaknesses, deteriorations, and obsolescence MTS • (p) Exchange information and brainstorm ideas across component teams about emerging threats and trends for each component team • (p) Reach consensus and a shared understanding across component teams on the veracity and probability of potential vulnerabilities and threats • (e) Coordinate actions of component teams in conducting multiple and different tests of existing information systems for potential weaknesses, deteriorations, and obsolescence • (e) Exchange data and reach consensus across component teams on information to be posted/publicized about potential threats and system weaknesses, deteriorations and obsolescence
Determine and implement proactive security tools, applications, and solutions	Individual • (p) Generate, evaluate, and research software, tools, and other solutions for potential and emerging threats • (p) Assess and develop system capabilities to integrate possible candidate solutions • (p) Select best-fitting solutions • (p) Develop plans for implementing proactive security tools, applications, and solutions • (e) Implement and update necessary infrastructure programming, software revisions, and new applications to counter potential and emerging threats • (e) Inform cyber security personnel and constituencies of new software and proactive security applications Team • (p) Exchange information and brainstorm ideas among team members about software, tools, and other solutions for potential and emerging threats

(Continued)

TABLE 2.1 A Preliminary Taxonomy of Cyber Security Incident Response Performance (Continued)

Proactive performance: Planning and execution processes

	• (p) Exchange information and expertise about system capabilities relative to candidate solutions • (p) Select best-fitting software, tools, and other solutions for potential and emerging threats • (e) Assign member roles and coordinate implementation of necessary infrastructure programming, software revisions, and new applications to counter potential and emerging threats MTS • (p) Exchange information and brainstorm ideas among component teams about how new software, tools, and other solutions for potential and emerging threats fit each team's mission requirements • (p) Exchange information and expertise across component teams about system capabilities relative to candidate solutions • (p) Reach consensus and collective endorsement across component teams of best-fitting software, tools, and other solutions for potential and emerging threats • (e) Assign component team roles and coordinate implementation of necessary infrastructure programming, software revisions, and new applications to counter potential and emerging threats
Plan and establish team and MTS structures	Team • (p) Identify team member roles and role requirements • (e) Staff the team/train team members to match role requirements • (p) Establish and (e) foster acceptance of team norms • (p) Determine and (e) implement team reward structures • (p) Determine within team performance criteria and feedback structures • (e) Facilitate team confidence, motivation, and task-based cohesion MTS • (p) Identify component teams that need to work together within an MTS • (p) Define component team roles and proximal goals/tasks • (p) Establish and (e) foster acceptance of MTS norms • (p) Determine and (e) implement MTS reward structures • (p) Determine MTS level performance criteria and feedback structures • (e) Facilitate between-team and MTS confidence, motivation, and task-based cohesion

Note: p = planning process; e = execution process.

Maj et al., 2010; Millar, & Rager, 2011; Werlinger et al., 2010). Thus, they reflect the fundamental activities of detect, triage, and respond (Alberts et al., 2004). As we noted earlier, three significant additions to prior classifications are (a) a multilevel perspective that differentiates noncollaborative and collaborative team- and MTS-level reactions, (b) an elaboration of after-incident learning processes, and (c) activities related to managing team and MTS interpersonal processes. The reactive performance processes also highlight in greater detail than do previous classifications the cognitive and planning processes that contribute to effective incident response performance.

Detect, Gather Information, and Alert Others about Security Incidents

The first three reactive performance taxa reflect acquisition of a situational awareness of potential incoming threats. Endsley (1995) and her colleagues (Bolstad, Endsley, Costello, & Howell, 2010) have defined *situational awareness* as including three processes: environmental scanning and perception, sense-making and understanding, and forecasting and predicting. Planning processes in this first taxon reflect their scanning and initial sense-making activities. They include the initial assessment of an event's nature and the decision of whether further attention is required. Accordingly, cognitive processes in this taxon reflect initial phases of complex problem-solving—problem definition, information gathering, and initial *meaning making*, or understanding or interpreting the information being gathered (Mumford, Medeiros, & Partlow, 2012; Mumford et al., 1991).

At the individual level, cognitive activities include monitoring threat environments, attending to anomalous events, gathering information about the event, and using existing knowledge to frame the event and provide an initial awareness of the problem posed by the event (cf. Mumford et al., 1991). Individual responders then decide which events merit further analysis (or can be classified as false positives). Behavioral processes include communicating an initial alert and creating a ticket for the incident. For example, Alberts et al. (2004) described such activities as "forward any suspicious or notable event information to the Triage process" and "reassign events to areas outside of the incident management process" (p. 17). Likewise, Osorno et al. (2011) noted that at this stage, "the fundamental action is to report the information to the relevant CSIRT or organizational response elements" (p. 7). At the team level, collective information processing entails members working together, often at the instigation of the individual incident responder, to provide an initial assessment of an event. Team members share their unique expertise about potential events and develop a shared awareness and concurrence about the event's nature and its threat potential. Behavioral processes may include coordination of the distribution of alerts by different members to other partnering teams and external stakeholders.

Detection activities at the MTS level may involve consulting with members of other teams (e.g., malware analysis, engineering) to determine initial threat potential. Component teams engaged in this determination develop a shared, cross-team awareness and concurrence about an event's nature and its threat potential. In some MTSs, networking monitoring teams may work closely with communication teams to send out possible initial alerts to notify stakeholders (Osorno et al., 2011).

Triage Incoming Incidents and Communicate Assessments

Once an event is detected and evaluated as having significant threat potential, further analysis is conducted to determine the type of event and what problem parameters are posed by the threat (severity of the event). According to Endsley's (1995) model of situational awareness (see also Bolstad et al., 2010), this process reflects generation of an understanding of environmental events. The information gathered from this process informs the further analysis and forecasting indicated in the next taxon (Osorno et al., 2011). These processes also correspond to the information-organization and conceptual-combination activities in complex problem-solving (Mumford et al., 1991, 2012). At the individual level, cognitive activities include the use of personal incident responder's experience and ascertain what type of threat is attacking the system and determine the problem elements of the attack. Thus, the event is "conceptualized" into a particular category that provides indicators of the problems posed (and, therefore, the parameters of potential solutions). Behavioral activities include updating case files and communicating findings to other stakeholders.

Events may be outside the incident responder's experience or have many complex elements. Such events are likely to engender collaborative (i.e., team and/or multiteam) analysis. At the team level, such analysis entails the use of collective expertise or the unique experiences of multiple team members to develop a shared awareness and understanding of how to categorize an event. Team members may also reach concurrence on how to define the problems caused by the event. Such concurrence results from the communication, discussion, and integration of ideas from multiple team members. For example, team members may discuss the event to ensure that critical information about its nature is not missed, to ensure that an analyst has come to the correct conclusion about the severity of the event, or to determine whether any team members in the group have seen a similar event before and can offer their insights. Behavioral activities at the team level include coordinating on updating case files, communicating with stakeholders, and preparing reports.

Similar collective assessment can occur between teams, because the categorization of an event may require the input and perspectives of different teams. For example, the network monitoring team may work with malware analysis and threat intelligence teams to develop a better sense of the nature of novel or unknown incidents and gain a more accurate understanding of threats posed. Note that the processes of such collaboration necessitate the communication and integration of unique ideas from different teams. The behavioral activities at this level are similar to those at the team level, except they entail coordination between teams.

Analyze Incidents

This taxon reflects primarily the third of Endsley's (1995) three cognitive processes in acquiring situational awareness—*forecasting*, which refers, in this context, to projecting or predicting the likely consequences of an incident or a threat for targeted systems. Forecasting potential damage includes identification of potentially affected clients, constituents, and other stakeholders. At the individual level, very experienced incident responders may engage in such forecasting and analysis on their own. However, the complexity of infrastructure systems and the ranges of possible affected stakeholders suggest that such analysis is more likely to occur collaboratively within and between incident response teams. For example, different members of a network monitoring or incident response team may have varying experience with a particular threat that can inform the forecasting of likely consequences. Likewise, members of incident response, forensics, and threat intelligence teams may work together to uncover and understand implications for different stakeholders. In this collective analysis, team and MTS members provide their own forecasts, discuss and evaluate them, and come up with a shared understanding of threat implications. This understanding contributes to the parameters necessary for determining appropriate threat-mitigation solutions (Endsley, 1995). Behavioral activities at each of these levels include additional case assignment, report writing, case escalation, and notification of affected constituencies. At the team level, such activities occur collaboratively among team members, whereas at the MTS level, they occur collaboratively between teams.

Develop and Implement Comprehensive Mitigation Solutions

The previous three taxa reflect planning activities intended to set the stage for the generation, evaluation, and implementation of threat-mitigation solutions. This next taxon contains individual, team, and MTS activities focused on the development and implementation of incident-resolution strategies. Models of complex problem-solving suggest a number of cognitive steps in solution generation, including the definition of solution specifications, generation of potential solutions that fit these specifications, simulation and evaluation of potential solutions, selection of the best solution, development of a solution-generation plan, and coordinated implementation of this plan.

Forecasting is also critical in this phase of incident response. In the previous taxon, forecasting processes were used to determine the likely consequences of detected threats; in this taxon, *forecasting* refers to "envisioning multiple different outcomes of alternative actions" (Byrne, Shipman, & Mumford, 2010, p. 120). Byrne et al. described two functions of such forecasting. The first occurs in the idea-evaluation phase in which responders predict likely outcomes of different solution pathways. The second occurs during the development of a solution-implementation plan; forecasting processes are used to determine resources that are needed and constituencies that need to be involved in solution implementation. Also, according to Byrne et al., forecasting solution implementation helps to uncover potential problems and fosters backup planning.

For relatively minor and common incidents, individuals can engage in these activities on their own. However, for more novel and complex threats that involve multiple stakeholders, collective solution generation, evaluation, and implementation become necessary. Although an individual may offer an idea or potential solution, the vetting and evaluation of the idea becomes the province of the team and the MTS as a whole (Hunter & Cushenbery, 2011). When team and MTS members have different types of expertise, experience, and perspectives, collectively, they can provide a greater cognitive capacity for such evaluation (Bantel & Jackson, 1989; Joshi & Roh, 2009).

At the team level, solution implementation involves defining roles for different members and coordinating different execution actions. Members may also engage in monitoring and backup behavior to ensure that all actions occur at appropriate times and to help any member who falters on an implementation task (Marks et al., 2001). The same processes of role assignment, coordinated execution, and monitoring/backup occur among different teams in an incident-response MTS. Thus, as shown in Figure 2.2, forensics, operations, threat intelligence, and communications teams may all coordinate their activities at different stages of threat eradication and the sharing/communication of threat intelligence.

Document and Report Action Logs

This taxon and the next one contain performance processes related to preparing summary reports about how an incident was handled. The completion of such reports provides the basis for future incident analysis. At the individual level, this activity may entail preparing and filing an incident case report. At the team and MTS levels, different team members and different teams, respectively, may contribute parts of this report such that it integrates different actions and perspectives from different stakeholders.

Conduct After-Action Review and Implement Necessary After-Action Adaptation

We noted earlier that one of the critical performance requirements of cyber security incident response is *adaptation*, or the necessity to constantly evolve performance strategies in response to environmental change. Accordingly, effective performance entails review of how incident responders handled events, with an eye toward implementing improved procedures, policies, and infrastructure tools. At the individual level, these processes include (a) gathering information about each phase of the case; (b) identifying those elements that need revision or adaptation; and (c) generating, evaluating, and implementing necessary improvements. At the team and MTS levels, multiple members work together to provide such assessments and evaluations and to generate and implement changes.

Manage Component Team Members' Interpersonal Interactions

The final taxon under reactive performance contains activities that pertain to the management and maintenance of team and MTS interpersonal interactions (Marks et al., 2001; Zaccaro et al., 2012). Marks et al. (2001) argued that team performance entails three sets of activities that occur through both transition and action phases of performance episodes: conflict management, affect management, and motivation/confidence building. As team members interact in various phases of incident response, the analysis of information and the vetting and evaluation of ideas can lead to interpersonal conflict. Accordingly, effective incident response performance involves using "reactive conflict management" (Marks et al., 2001, p. 368) strategies. These include compromising, perspective taking, and working through differing ideas to prevent affective conflict (Marks et al., 2001; Sessa, 1996; Thomas, 1992).

The context of incident response can be stressful and frustrating. The costs of failure can be quite high. Accordingly, effective incident response performance also entails activities related to affect management. These include emotion-regulation processes that help members maintain composure, deal with different stressors, and maintain team morale in the face of difficult challenges and working conditions (Amason & Sapienza, 1997; Hargrove, Winslow, & Kaplan, 2013; Marks et al., 2001). Related to affect management are those processes that focus on maintaining and managing team motivation. Effective incident response requires that team members be willing to exert strong effort on behalf of the team's mission. Team states that foster such willingness include trust, cohesion, and confidence that the team can effectively accomplish its mission (Marks et al., 2001; Zaccaro, Rittman, & Marks, 2001). Thus, to maintain these states, team leaders and members may engage in team-bonding experiences, celebrations of team success, and social activities that enhance team cohesion (Marks et al., 2001; Zaccaro et al., 2001; Zaccaro, Weis, Hilton, & Jeffries, 2011).

At the MTS level, similar activities are used in conflict management, affect management, and motivation building between component teams and throughout the MTS as a whole (Zaccaro et al., 2012). Just as individuals within teams can come into conflict, teams can also clash with one another. The stress and failure that can bring down team morale can also affect a network of teams. Likewise, MTS motivation building means fostering a sense of trust, cohesion, and confidence between teams. Each component team needs to believe that it can trust the other teams in the MTS. Accordingly, effective incident response performance involves enhancement of each team's willingness to work hard in close collaboration with other teams to achieve the overall MTS mission.

Proactive Performance Processes

The proposed taxonomy includes several proactive performance taxa that encompass processes focused on establishing the fundamental mission, purpose, and goals of the CSIRT. They also concern establishing and maintaining the security infrastructure and anticipating and hunting for potential security vulnerabilities and threats. Finally, one taxa refers specifically to team/MTS structuring.

Define and Formalize Missions, Tasks, and Services

This set of activities pertains to planning and execution processes that involve defining and establishing the overall mandate and purpose of an incident response team and MTS within a defined organizational structure. Individual-level activities, usually performed by those in leadership positions (DeChurch et al., 2011; Morgeson, DeRue, & Karam, 2010; Zaccaro, Heinen, & Shuffler, 2009), entail environmental scanning and sense-making activities to determine conditions, constraints, and necessary resources for primary missions; boundary spanning with key stakeholders to inform mission parameters; and working with senior management to obtain mission support and resources. At the team level, mission definition and formalization involves idea exchanges among team members regarding mission priorities, interactions tailored to create a shared understanding of the mission, determination of how mission parameters and goals are to be accomplished through team interactions, and development of a shared sense of how team members will typically interact to accomplish the mission. Similar processes occur for incident response MTSs, except they occur between component teams. At this level, members of component teams are interacting across team boundaries to share mission-related ideas and develop a shared sense of the mission across teams. Likewise, they are determining how component teams will work together to accomplish the mission, establishing goal-interaction protocols similar to the one noted in Figure 2.2. The effective outcomes of these sets of activities should be a clear and shared understanding of the incident response mission and goals and collective agreement about how individual responders will typically coordinate their actions within and across teams in an incident response MTS, and with external stakeholders.

Determine and Implement Necessary Security Tools, Applications, and Infrastructure

This set of activities entails planning and establishing the generic infrastructure and software tools that incident responders will use to handle future events.

At the individual level, this involves identifying and developing specifications for security infrastructure; generating candidate software, tools, and programs to fit within this infrastructure; choosing the most appropriate or best-fitting tools and programs; and, finally, putting into place for active use the selected elements of the infrastructure. At the team and MTS levels, activities entail interaction and exchange of ideas among team members and component teams, respectively, about infrastructure requirements and about possible security programs, tools, and software. Different members may have unique experiences with candidate programs; likewise, different component teams may vary in terms of what they need from the security infrastructure and any possible candidate tools. Information exchanges among team members and members of different component teams in an effective incident response MTS occur with an intent to ensure collective endorsement and support for an integrated security infrastructure across the MTS. Team and MTS execution processes are geared to making sure that within- and between-team configurations are appropriate and operating at the same levels of effectiveness and efficiency. Backup and monitoring behavior means stepping in to help team members and component teams respond to shifting and unexpected challenges that arise as they build the infrastructure (Marks et al., 2001).

Plan and Execute Procedures for Maintenance of Security Tools, Applications, and Infrastructure

Once the security infrastructure has been established, effective incident response performance requires the continued routine maintenance of this infrastructure and its elements. At the individual level, this entails planning and designing the procedures required to maintain infrastructure effectiveness and responsiveness, implementing the planned procedures, and continuing to watch for infrastructure breakdowns and disruptions. At the team level, activities in this set entail interactions and exchanges of information among team members to develop a shared understanding of routine maintenance requirements. Members also need to exchange information about system status, alerting relevant team members regarding any infrastructure malfunctions. Likewise, team members need to coordinate maintenance activities, which include engaging in workload sharing to account for periodic variations in member schedules and availability. At the MTS level, different component teams may (a) use different tools, systems, and/or infrastructure or (b) use the same infrastructure as other component teams but in different ways. Accordingly, well-performing incident response MTSs exchange information about the infrastructure maintenance requirements of different component teams, and integrate that information into an overall maintenance protocol. Component teams also coordinate in the completion of this protocol and alert relevant teams regarding any infrastructure breakdowns.

Identify and Test for Potential Security Vulnerabilities and Threats

The foregoing taxa concern the development of standard operating procedures and protocols for incident responders, their teams, and the overall incident response MTS. These performance processes establish the technology structures and protocols to enable incident response MTSs and their members to respond effectively to known and anticipated threats. However, an additional proactive performance aspect of effective incident response concerns the consideration of emerging and potential cyber security threats and vulnerabilities, sometimes called the "hunter" element of cyber security performance (Lemos, 2013). Thus, some incident response systems may employ "black hat" operatives who probe the existing security infrastructure for potential vulnerabilities. Other incident responders who are typically in research and/or engineering component teams may have the responsibility of searching out and identifying potential and emerging new threats that have not yet attacked their infrastructure (Alberts et al., 2004; Maj et al., 2010). These kinds of performance activities compose a separate taxon in the proposed taxonomy.

Individual-level activities in this set include the scanning and monitoring of cyber security information sources (e.g., websites, blogs, information boards, personal communications) for possible vulnerabilities in existing infrastructures (e.g., information about possible ways to hack into systems) or news of emerging threats and viruses that have not yet hit the incident responder's system. Likewise, incident responders may research attacks made on other systems. After identifying possible threats, they may forecast the criticality of any vulnerabilities and begin testing the level of possible threat to their own infrastructure. Finally, incident responders may then post or communicate potential threats and vulnerabilities to relevant stakeholders in order to initiate proactive corrections.

Similar processes happen at the team and MTS levels, except the scanning, identification, and forecasting of possible threats occurs through collective information processing. Team members may bring different expertise and experiences to interactions and conversations about such threats. Members benefit from each other's contributions to come to a collective understanding about the likelihood and severity of possible infrastructure vulnerabilities and potential threats. They may coordinate testing of different aspects of the infrastructure and integrate their data to produce a comprehensive assessment of system vulnerability to new threats. At the MTS level, component teams bring different perspectives to such assessments. Some teams may be tasked with researching potential vulnerabilities, providing data and information that are collectively considered by other component teams. Other teams may be responsible for providing the tools and software used to determine infrastructure vulnerability, and still others may be tasked with running system tests and analyzing their results. Finally, a separate team may have the task of communicating vulnerabilities and emerging threats to clients and stakeholders. Thus, in teams and MTSs, multiple types of incident responders work together to identify and assess emerging threats and system vulnerabilities.

Determine and Implement Proactive Security Tools, Applications, and Solutions

The prior set of activities concerns the identification and assessment of emerging security infrastructure vulnerabilities. Another set of performance processes reflects the identification, selection, and implementation of new security tools, applications, and solutions to counter possible threats. At the individual level, these processes include activities related to the generation, analysis, evaluation, and selection of new software tools, applications, and other solutions that can address infrastructure vulnerability. They also include the development of plans for the implementation of infrastructure improvements and the execution of those plans. Finally, new security procedures require the training of others in their use.

At the team and MTS levels, performance processes center on the collective consideration, evaluation, and endorsement of candidate solutions to infrastructure vulnerabilities. As with the assessment of potential new threats and vulnerabilities, team members can bring different expertise and experiences to the analysis and selection of new solutions. When implementing chosen solutions, team members may have different but connected roles in installing, testing, and adapting these solutions. At the MTS level, each component team may have different team mission requirements with alternate implications for new tools and solutions. Thus, for example, to understand a threat across incidents, a common database could be developed requiring input from a network monitoring team, a malware analysis team, and a digital forensics team to define the contents of the database on the basis of the unique threat data that they each produce. Further, a fourth team might provide query and reporting requirements to use the database to identify trends. Thus, members of different component teams may work together to select and implement a set of tools and solutions that meet the needs of all teams with a stake in the solution.

Plan and Establish Team and MTS Structures

The proactive performance functions defined in the earlier taxa all refer to the establishment of the technological infrastructure to uncover and resolve anticipated and emerging threats. This next taxon refers to the establishment of social structures—that is, those of the incident response teams and MTSs—to respond collectively with little process loss (Steiner, 1972) to future events. Effective team performance derives from a team being composed of the right individuals and the establishment of appropriate roles and role requirements for those individuals. However, identifying the best individuals to work together is not enough; the team also needs to facilitate the emergence of collective states that are conducive to high performance. Such emergent states refer to shared cognitive, motivational, and behavioral beliefs and expectations about the team (Marks et al, 2001). They include shared situational awareness, team norms, team cohesion, and team trust. Finally, teams facilitate higher performance by defining clear performance criteria, providing feedback to individual members and to the team as a whole about these criteria, and incorporating a team-based reward structure. These social dimensions of team performance have been highlighted in a number of team taxonomies (e.g., Fleishman & Zaccaro, 1992; Marks et al., 2001).

Similar social performance processes also occur at the MTS level. However, the focus shifts to establishing (a) what kinds of teams need to work closely together (as opposed to merely coexisting or working minimally together in the same organizational space), (b) what responsibilities each team will have, and (c) what specific proximal goals will be shared by particular teams (e.g., see Figure 2.2). Also of central importance to MTS-level performance are the states of shared understanding, cohesion, trust, collective confidence, and behavioral norms that emerge *between* teams. No matter how strong each component team is in an incident response MTS, overall performance will suffer if they do not trust one another or have different understandings of and expectations about how they are supposed to work together. Thus, establishing these conditions becomes a crucial performance process at the MTS level (DeChurch et al., 2011; Zaccaro et al., 2012).

Preliminary Validation

Table 2.1 displays an abbreviated version of the cyber security incident response performance process taxonomy. The elaborated version of this taxonomy consists of three dimensions: (a) proactive versus reactive performance, (b) planning versus execution activities, and (c) individual versus team versus MTS levels of action. The resulting 12 taxonomic cells contain between four and six taxa, for a total of 65 taxa. Included under each taxon are sets of representative activities (see column two in Table 2.1).[2]

The validity of a taxonomic structure depends upon on how well it captures the domain being classified (Fleishman & Quaintance, 1984). Our research team conducted a preliminary validation of the proposed taxonomy using interviews with cyber security personnel. We conducted 47 focus groups and interviews with 118 members, 19 team leaders, and 10 MTS leaders. These interviews were then transcribed and deconstructed into codeable segments of incident response activities. Two raters then coded each activity segment (i.e., unit) into one of the taxonomy cells. Any units that could not be coded were set aside for further discussion and recoding or used to propose new taxa.

The results of the focus group and interview coding indicated that each of the 65 taxa in the proposed taxonomy was mentioned as characteristic of incident response performance in at least two interviews. The average number of focus groups and interviews that mentioned a particular taxonomic activity was 17.6. Thus, all of the taxa in the proposed taxonomy were represented in the data gathered from cyber security personnel. Accordingly, the results of this first validation indicated substantial support for the tripartite structure of the proposed taxonomy. Incident responders differentiated among individual, team, and multiteam performance activities. They also affirmed a clear delineation between proactive and reactive activities proposed by this and other incident response taxonomies (e.g., Alberts et al., 2004; Cichonski et al., 2012; Killcrece et al., 2003; Maj et al., 2010). Finally, the proposed taxonomy contains a greater elaboration of cognitive performance activities than is found in prior classifications, reflecting models of complex problem-solving (Mumford et al., 1991) and situational awareness (Endsley, 1995). This taxonomy also reflects models of externalized cognition, or collective information processing (i.e., *thinking together*; Fiore, Rosen, et al., 2010; Hinsz et al., 1998). The focus group interviews provided support for the distinction between cognitive and behavioral activities and for collective cognition at both the team and the multiteam level. Indeed, the average number of focus groups that mentioned activities coded into one of the team-level taxa was 15.9, and the average number for the multilevel taxa was 19.3.

This preliminary validation provides encouraging support for the proposed taxonomy. However, additional work and refinement is necessary. Comparisons should be made with other taxonomies of incident response performance. Likewise, further analysis is necessary to determine whether the taxa display appropriate levels of discriminant validity—do they actually reflect conceptually distinct cognitive and behavioral performance processes, or should particular taxa be combined into a more parsimonious classification? Such research will help to refine the taxonomy and increase its utility for cyber security incident response personnel.

Cyber Security Incident Response Performance Outcomes

Our generic model of incident response performance posits cognitive and behavioral performance processes leading to categories of incident response performance outcomes (see Figure 2.1). Our focus in this chapter has been on describing a framework for classifying incident response performance processes. Full description of a performance outcomes taxonomy would require another chapter. However, our proposed process framework does suggest particular categories of performance outcomes that should be included in a taxonomy of outcomes. In Table 2.2, we provide a preliminary classification of incident response outcomes that would be the product of one or more of the processes defined in the proposed performance process taxonomy.

TABLE 2.2 Incident Response Performance Outcomes

Outcome category	Outcome examples

Objective outcomes	• Quantity of incidents handled (individual, team, MTS)
	• Quality of incident solutions (individual, team, MTS)
	  • Comprehensiveness
	  • Innovation
	• Efficiency of incident handling (individual, team, MTS)
	• Speed of incident handling
	• Reduction in system vulnerability

Subjective outcomes	• Managerial performance ratings and assessments (individual, team, MTS) • Reputation (individual, team, MTS) • Customer satisfaction (individual, team, MTS) • Customer commitment to the incident responder (individual, team, MTS)
Individual withdrawal outcomes	• Absenteeism • Lateness • Turnover
Individual disruption outcomes	• Accidents • Disciplinary actions
Motivational and affective individual outcomes	• Task efficacy • Job satisfaction • Organizational commitment
Knowledge/cognitive individual outcomes	• Knowledge and skill acquisition • More complex expertise models
Motivational and affective collective outcomes	• Collective efficacy (team and MTS) • Trust (team and MTS) • Cohesion (team and MTS)
Knowledge/cognitive collective outcomes	• Shared mental models (team and MTS) • Transactive memory systems (team and MTS)
Individual well-being	• Physical • Psychological

Note: MTS = multiteam system.

Organizational psychologists have identified several categories of performance measures, including objective, subjective, withdrawal, disruption, motivational and affective, knowledge, and well-being outcomes (Campbell et al., 1993; Guion & Highhouse, 2006; Quiñones, Ford, & Teachout, 1995; Van Katwyk, Fox, Spector, & Kelloway, 2000). A few of these outcomes mainly reflect individual-level products (e.g., absenteeism, lateness, turnover, well-being), whereas most can be seen as a result of individual, team, and/or MTS performance processes. Objective outcomes for incident responders can include number of incidents handled, quality of incident response, speed and efficiency of response handling, and overall reduction of system vulnerability or enhancement of system security. Additional outcomes that are not direct performance products, but indicative of other personnel activities include absenteeism, lateness, turnover, accidents, and disciplinary actions. A comprehensive assessment of incident response performance outcomes should not be limited to only one or two of these measures; instead a more integrated approach should be adopted that is consistent with the team or organization's overall mission and goals (Kaplan & Norton, 2007).

Subjective outcomes for incident responders include a variety of judgment- or evaluation-based measures (Chew et al., 2008; Cichonski et al., 2012). These may be managerial performance ratings both for individual responders and for teams and/or MTSs as a whole. Likewise, customers' satisfaction with the incident response team, and their commitment to continue using the team, represents another key outcome of incident response handling. Finally, the reputation of a particular individual, team, or MTS within the professional and cyber security community is a critical outcome. Given the severity of potential consequences resulting from cyber security attacks, the reputation of a particular team in terms of its knowledge, responsiveness, and competence may be its most valuable outcome.

Incident response performance outcomes can also include an array of psychological end states, such as motivation and affective and knowledge-based indices. Motivational and affective states include increased task confidence, job satisfaction, and organizational commitment. At the team level, these outcomes would include emergent states (Marks et al., 2001), such as cohesion, trust, and collective efficacy. At the MTS level, these states would emerge between particular teams (e.g., trust between network monitoring and threat intelligence teams) that must work closely together on a particular task or across all component teams in an MTS. Finally, individual well-being, in terms of both physical and psychological health, can also be considered a relevant outcome.

Knowledge gains represent another important outcome derived from completing incident response processes. As individual responders work through novel or unusual events, they accrue a better understanding of incident response that they will apply in future response handling and problem-solving (Mumford et al., 2001). At the team and MTS levels, engaging in collective knowledge work and externalized cognitive processes increases several critical shared knowledge states. One is *transactive memory* (Pearsall, Ellis, & Bell, 2010; Wegner, 1987; Yuan, Fulk, Monge, & Contractor, 2010), which refers to a shared understanding of which members in a team have which kinds of unique expertise. Such knowledge is important when members need to call on others to resolve a particular incident that may be outside of their particular understanding. A second form of collective knowledge is a *shared mental model* (Cannon-Bowers, Converse, & Salas, 1993), which includes team members' collective understanding of the cyber security operating environment and how they should work together to complete particular tasks and the overall mission. Such shared mental models are critical drivers of team performance and adaptation (Marks, Zaccaro, & Mathieu, 2000; Mathieu, Heffner, Goodwin, Salas, & Cannon-Bowers, 2000).

Finally, individual well-being, in terms of both physical and psychological health, can also be considered a relevant outcome. Given the stressful context of cyber security work and the high cognitive demands of such work, felt stress and burnout, along with their physical concomitants, can result in lower performance (Sonnentag & Frese, 2003; Van der Doef & Maes, 1999). Achieving team goals but burning out in the process likely means lower levels of the other outcomes shown in Table 2.2.

Taxonomy Applications

This taxonomy was constructed not only to provide a better and more comprehensive depiction of cyber security incident response processes but also to offer a basis for a number of applications and strategies for facilitating better performance in this domain. One important and direct application of this classification is its capacity to inform the contents of performance-appraisal tools that CSIRT managers may wish to develop and utilize in their teams. Such instruments are most useful when they specifically describe the key individual and collective behaviors critical for effective performance (Banks & Murphy, 1985; Schrader & Steiner, 1996). Also, greater item specificity in performance appraisals can facilitate more informative feedback to subordinates (DeShon, Kozlowski, Schmidt, Milner, & Wiechmann, 2004; Larson, 1984). The taxa and their representative behaviors listed in Table 2.1 can provide a strong basis for such specificity.

A second application of the taxonomy lies in its capacity to contribute to the derivation of KSAs that drive effective performance (Fleishman & Quaintance, 1984). This can be accomplished by having subject-matter experts define KSAs that will lead to successful enactment of the activities noted within each taxon (Baranowski & Anderson, 2005; Vinchur, Prien, & Schippmann, 1993). A second approach would be to have experts link a predetermined set of KSAs to the accomplishment of each of the taxa in the taxonomy (Baranowski & Anderson, 2005; Hughes & Prien, 1989). Although such a set could come from different sources, it could be validated though this linkage analysis.

The specification of both effective incident response performance activities and KSAs contributes, in turn, to the development of higher quality CSIRT training and selection systems (e.g., Brannick, Levine, & Morgeson, 2007; Stevens & Campion, 1994). KSAs that are validated against the taxonomy can inform learning objectives in a variety of different types of individual- and team-level training programs. The more specific performance activities listed within each taxon can also be used to guide the development of targeted programs of instruction for use in training and the content of evaluation tools used to gauge skill acquisition from training. Rank ordering of KSAs in terms of their importance for incident response performance can provide the basis for more effective selection of cyber security personnel. Thus, the taxonomy can offer a number of applications that can improve the overall effectiveness of cyber security incident response.

Summary and Conclusions

Our purpose in this chapter has been to contribute a more comprehensive performance taxonomy to the literature on cyber security incident response. Prior classifications have included several of the elements and activities listed in our proposed framework. However, we have sought to expand this work in three ways. First, we have elaborated on the proactive activities that can set the stage for effective reactive performance and responses to detected cyber threats. We have also defined in greater detail the types of cognitive processes that contribute to successful incident response. In particular, we have highlighted a cognitive process—forecasting—that emphasizes planning activities and has not been mentioned in prior classifications. Finally, we have described incident response activities in fairly specific terms ways and not only as performed not only by individual incident responders but also as performed by teams and MTSs. Several prior taxonomies have listed collaboration as a key performance activity, and a few have indicated that such collaboration happens between multiple teams. However, the present taxonomy goes further by using models of team and MTS performance to define more specific interdependent activities that drive effective cognitive and behavioral performance processes at both of these levels.

In our opening paragraphs, we noted the high and escalating costs of cyber threats and attacks. These costs increase the need to select and develop effective incident responders, incident response teams, and MTSs. Strategies to improve incident responders' performance need to be rooted in an understanding of the performance requirements and performance processes of effective cyber incident response. Also, the examination of the dynamics and drivers of such response by computer and organizational scientists should rest on models of incident response performance. We hope that the proposed taxonomy in this chapter contributes to such an examination and to derived strategies that increase the effectiveness of cyber security incident response.

NOTES

1 This chapter is based in part on research sponsored by the U.S. Department of Homeland Security Science and Technology Directorate, Homeland Security Advanced Research Projects Agency, Cyber Security Division (BAA 11-02), and by the Air Force Research Laboratory Information Directorate under agreement FA8750-12-2-0258. The U.S. government is authorized to reproduce and distribute reprints for governmental purposes notwithstanding any copyright notation thereon. We acknowledge the contribution of team members on this research effort who are not authors of this chapter.

2 For the expanded and latest form of the taxonomy, please e-mail Stephen J. Zaccaro at szaccaro@gmu.edu.

REFERENCES

Alberts, C., Dorofee, A., Killcrece, G., Ruefle, R., & Zajicek, M. (2004, October). *Defining incident management processes for CSIRTs: A work in progress* (CMU/SEI-2004-TR-015). Retrieved from http://www.dtic.mil/dtic/tr/fulltext/u2/a453378.pdf

Alexander, K. B. (2012). An introduction by General Alexander. *The Next Wave, 19*(4). Retrieved from http://www.nsa.gov/research/tnw/tnw194/article2.shtml

Amason, A. C., & Sapienza, H. J. (1997). The effects of top management team size and interaction norms on cognitive and affective conflict. *Journal of Management, 23*, 495–516.

Bailey, K. D. (1994). *Typologies and taxonomies: An introduction to classification techniques.* Thousand Oaks, CA: Sage Publications.

Baranowski, L. E., & Anderson, L. E. (2005). Examining rating source variation in work behavior to KSA linkages. *Personnel Psychology, 58*, 1041–1054.

Brannick, M. T., Levine, E. L., & Morgeson, F. P. (2007). *Job and work analysis: Methods, research, and applications for human resource management* (2nd ed.). Thousand Oaks, CA: Sage Publications.

Baard, S. K., Rench, T. A., & Kozlowski, S. W. J. (2013). Performance adaptation: A theoretical integration and review. *Journal of Management, 40*, 48–99.

Banks, C. G., & Murphy, K. R. (1985). Toward narrowing the research–practice gap in performance appraisal. *Personnel Psychology, 38*, 335–345.

Bantel, K. A., & Jackson, S. E. (1989). Top management and innovations in banking: Does the composition of the top team make a difference? *Strategic Management Journal, 10*(S1), 107–124.

Bolstad, C., Endlsey, M. R., Costello, A. M., & Howell, C. D. (2010). Evaluation of computer-based situation awareness training for general aviation pilots. *International Journal of Aviation Psychology, 20*, 269–294.

Borman, W. C., & Brush, D. H. (1993). More progress toward a taxonomy of managerial performance requirements. *Human Performance, 6*, 1–21.

Borman, W. C., Bryant, R. H., & Dorio, J. (2010). The measurement of task performance as criteria in selection research. In J. L. Farr & N. T. Tippins (Eds.), *Handbook of employee selection* (pp. 439–461). New York: Routledge.

Bronk, H., Hakkaja, M., & Thorbruegge, M. (2007, December 22). *A basic collection of good practices for running a CSIRT*. Retrieved from https://www.enisa.europa.eu/activities/cert/support/guide2/files/a-collection-of-good-practice-for-cert-quality-assurance

Burke, C. S., Stagl, K. C., Salas, E., Pierce, L., & Kendall, D. (2006). Understanding team adaptation: A conceptual analysis and model. *Journal of Applied Psychology, 91*, 1189–1207.

Byrne, C. D., Shipman, A. S., & Mumford, M. D. (2010). The effects of forecasting on creative problem-solving: An experimental study. *Creativity Research Journal, 22*, 119–138.

Campbell, J. P., McCloy, R. A., Oppler, S. H., & Sager, C. E. (1993). A theory of performance. In N. Schmitt & W. C. Borman (Eds.), *Personnel selection in organizations* (pp. 35–70). San Francisco: Jossey-Bass.

Cannon-Bowers, J. A., Salas, E., & Converse, S. A. (1993). Shared mental models in expert team decision making. In N. J. Castellan Jr. (Ed.), *Individual and group decision making: Current issues* (pp. 221–246). Hillsdale, NJ: Erlbaum.

Chen, T. R., Shore, D. B., Zaccaro, S. J., Dalal, R. S., Tetrick, L. E., & Gorab, A. K. (2014, September/October). An organizational psychology perspective to examining computer security incident response teams. *IEEE Security & Privacy, 12*(5), 61–67.

Chew, E., Swanson, M., Stine, K., Bartol, N., Brown, A., Robinson, W., & Gutierrez, C. M. (2008, July). *Performance measurement guide for information security* (Special Publication No. 800-55, Rev. 1). Gaithersburg, MD: National Institute of Standards and Technology, U.S. Department of Commerce.

Cichonski, P., Millar, T., Grance, T., & Scarfone, K. (2012). *Computer security incident handling guide: Recommendations of the National Institute of Standards and Technology* (Special Publication no. 800-61, Rev. 2). Gaithersburg, MD: National Institute of Standards and Technology, U.S. Department of Commerce.

DeChurch, L.A., Burke, C. S., Shuffler, M., Lyons, R., Doty, D., & Salas, E. (2011). A historiometric analysis of leadership in mission critical multiteam environments. *The Leadership Quarterly, 22*, 152–169.

DeShon, R. P., Kozlowski, S. W. J., Schmidt, A. M., Milner, K. R., & Wiechmann, D. (2004). A multiple-goal, multilevel model of feedback effects on the regulation of individual and team performance. *Journal of Applied Psychology, 89*, 1035–1056.

Ely, K., Zaccaro, S. J., & Conjar, E. A. (2009). Leadership development: Training design strategies for growing adaptability in leaders. In R. J. Burke & C. L. Cooper (Eds.), *The peak performing organization* (pp. 175–196). London: Routledge.

Endsley, M. R. (1995). Toward a theory of situation awareness in dynamic systems. *Human Factors, 37*, 32–64.

Fiore, S. M., Rosen, M. A., Smith-Jentsch, K., Salas, E., Letsky, M., & Warner, N. (2010). Toward an understanding of macrocognition in teams: Predicting processes in complex collaboration. *Human Factors, 52*, 203–224.

Fiore, S. M., Smith-Jentsch, K. A., Salas, E., Warner, N., & Letsky, M. (2010). Towards an understanding of macrocognition in teams: Developing and defining complex collaborative processes and products. *Theoretical Issues in Ergonomics Science, 11*, 250–271.

Fleishman, E. A., Mumford, M. D., Zaccaro, S. J., Levin, K. Y., & Hein, M. B. (1991). Theoretical efforts in the description of leader behavior: A synthesis and functional integration. *The Leadership Quarterly, 2*, 245–287.

Fleishman, E. A., & Quaintance, M. K. (1984) *Taxonomies of human performance: The description of human tasks*. San Francisco: Academic Press.

Fleishman, E. A., & Zaccaro, S. J. (1992). Taxonomic classifications of team tasks. In R. W. Swezey & E. Salas (Eds.), *Teams: Their training and performance* (pp. 31–56). Norwood, NJ: Ablex.

Forum of Incident Response and Security Teams. (n.d.). *FIRST history*. Retrieved from https://www.first.org/about/history

Grance, T., Kent, K., & Kim, B. (2004). *Computer security incident handling guide: Recommendations of the National Institute of Standards and Technology* (Special Publication No. 800-61). Washington, DC: U.S. Government Printing Office.

Guion, R. M., & Highhouse, S. (2006). *Essentials of personnel selection: Personnel assessment and selection*. Mahwah, NJ: Erlbaum.

Hargrove, A. K., Winslow, C., & Kaplan, S. (2013). Self-guided activities for improving employee emotions and emotion regulation. In P. L. Perrewé, C. C. Rosen, & J. R. B. Halbesleben (Eds.), *The role of emotion and emotion regulation in job stress and well eing* (pp. 75–102). Bingley, England: Emerald.

Hinsz, V. B., Tindale, R. S., & Vollrath, D. A. (1997). The emerging conceptualization of groups as information processors. *Psychological Bulletin, 121*, 43–64.

Hughes, G. L., & Prien, E. P. (1989). Evaluation of task and job skill linkage judgments used to develop test specifications. *Personnel Psychology, 42*, 283–292.

Hunter, S. T., & Cushenbery, L. 2011. Leading for innovation: Direct and indirect influences. *Advances in Developing Human Resources, 13*, 248–265.

Ilgen, D. R., Hollenbeck, J. R., Johnson, M., & Jundt, D. (2005). Teams in organizations: From input-process-output models to IMOI models. *Annual Review of Psychology, 56*, 517–543.

Jervis, S. (2014, June 4). *Cyber attack! 60% of small companies out of business in six months.* Retrieved from http://www.huffingtonpost.co.uk/shivvy-jervis/cyber-attacks-business_b_5083906.html

Joshi, A., & Roh, H. (2009). The role of context in work team diversity research: A meta-analytic review. *Academy of Management Journal, 52*, 599–627.

Kaplan, R., & Norton, D. (2007, July/August). Using the balanced scorecard as a strategic management system. *Harvard Business Review, 85*(6), 150–161.

Kennedy, D. M., & McComb, S. A. (2010) Merging internal and external processes: Examining the mental model convergence process through team communication. *Theoretical Issues in Ergonomics Science, 11*, 340–358.

Killcrece, G., Kossakowski, K.-P., Ruefle, R., & Zajicek, M. (2003, December). *Organizational models for computer security incident response teams (CSIRTs)* (CMU/SEI-2003-HB-001). Pittsburgh, PA: Software Engineering Institute, Carnegie Mellon University.

Kossakowski, K.-P., Allen, J., Alberts, C., Cohen, C., Ford, G., Fraser, B., … Wilson, W. (1999, February). *Responding to intrusions* (CMU/SEI-SIM-006). Pittsburgh, PA: Software Engineering Institute, Carnegie Mellon University.

Kozlowski, S.W.J., & Ilgen, D. R. (2006). Enhancing the effectiveness of work groups and teams. *Psychological Science in the Public Interest, 7*, 77–124.

Larson, J. R. (1984). The performance feedback process: A preliminary model. *Organizational Behavior and Human Performance, 33*, 42–76.

Lemos, R. (2013, November 8). From event gatherers to network hunters. *BusinessWeek Dark Reading*. Retrieved from http://www.darkreading.com/analytics/threat-intelligence/from-event-gatherers-to-network-hunters/d/d-id/1140848?

McFeely, R. A. (2013, June 12). *Cyber security: Preparing for and responding to the enduring threat: Testimony before the Senate Appropriations Committee.* Retrieved from http://www.fbi.gov/news/testimony/cyber-security-preparing-for-and-responding-to-the-enduring-threat

Maj, M., Reijers, R., & Stikvoort, D. (2010). *European Network and Information Security Agency (ENISA) good practice guide for incident management.* Retrieved from https://www.enisa.europa.eu/activities/cert/support/incident-management

Marks, M. A., Mathieu, J. E., & Zaccaro, S. J. (2001). A temporally based framework and taxonomy of team processes. *Academy of Management Review, 26*, 356–376.

Marks, M. A., Zaccaro, S. J., & Mathieu, J. E. (2000). Performance implications of leader briefings and team interaction training for team adaptation to novel environments. *Journal of Applied Psychology, 85*, 971–986.

Mathieu, J. E., Heffner, T. S., Goodwin, G. F., Salas, E., & Cannon-Bowers, J. A. (2000). The influence of shared mental models on team process and performance. *Journal of Applied Psychology, 85*, 273–283.

Mathieu, J. E., Marks, M. A., & Zaccaro, S. J. (2001). Multiteam systems. In N. Anderson, D. S. Ones, & C. Viswesvaran (Eds.), *Handbook of industrial, work, and organizational psychology: Vol. 2* (pp. 289–312). London: Sage.

Mathieu, J. E., Maynard, M. T., Rapp, T., & Gilson, L. (2008). Team effectiveness 1997–2007: A review of recent advancements and a glimpse into the future. *Journal of Management, 34*, 410–476.

Morgeson, F. P., DeRue, D. S., & Karam, E. P. (2010). Leadership in teams: A functional approach to understanding leadership structures and processes. *Journal of Management, 36*, 5–39.

Mumford, M. D., Medeiros, K. E., & Partlow, P. J. (2012). Creative thinking: Processes, strategies, and knowledge. *Journal of Creative Behavior, 36*, 30–47.

Mumford, M. D., Mobley, M. I., Uhlman, C. E., Reiter-Palmon, R., & Doares, L. (1991). Process analytic models of creative capacities. *Creativity Research Journal, 4*, 91–122.

Mumford, M. D., Schultz, R. A., & Van Doorn, J. R. (2001). Performance in planning: Processes, requirements, and errors. *Review of General Psychology, 5*, 213–240.

National Institute of Standards and Technology, National Initiative for Cybersecurity Education. (2013). *National cybersecurity workforce framework*. Retrieved from http://csrc.nist.gov/nice/framework/

Obama, B. (2015, January 13). The president speaks about cybersecurity [Video file]. Video posted to http://www.whitehouse.gov/photos-and-video/video/2015/01/13/president-speaks-about-cybersecurity

Osorno, M., Millar, T., & Rager, D. (2011, June). Coordinated cybersecurity incident handling: Roles, processes, and coordination networks for crosscutting incidents. In *Proceedings of the 16th International Command and Control Technology Symposium*. Retrieved from http://www.dtic.mil/dtic/tr/fulltext/u2/a547075.pdf

Pearsall, M. J., Ellis, A. P., & Bell, B. S. (2010). Building the infrastructure: The effects of role identification behaviors on team cognition development and performance. *Journal of Applied Psychology, 95*, 192–200.

Peterson, N. G., Mumford, M. D., Borman, W. C., Jeanneret, P. R., & Fleishman, E. A. (1999). *An occupational information system for the 21st century: The development of O*NET*. Washington, DC: American Psychological Association.

Pfleeger, S. L. & Caputo, D. D. (2012). Leveraging behavioral science to mitigate cybersecurity risk. *Computers and Security, 31*, 597–611.

Piaget, J. (1952). *The origins of intelligence in children*. New York: International Universities Press.

Ponemon Institute. (2010, July). *First annual cost of cyber crime study: Benchmark study of U.S. companies*. Retrieved from http://www.greycastlesecurity.com/resources/documents/Ponemon_Cost_of_CyberCrime_Study_07-10.pdf

Ponemon Institute. (2014, October). *2014 global report on the cost of cyber crime*. Retrieved from http://h20195.www2.hp.com/v2/getpdf.aspx/4AA5-5207ENW.pdf?ver=1.0

Pulakos, E. D., Arad, S., Donovan, M. A., & Plamondon, K. E. (2000). Adaptability in the workplace: Development of a taxonomy of adaptive performance. *Journal of Applied Psychology, 85*, 612–624.

Quiñones, M. A., Ford, J. K., & Teachout, M. S. (1995). The relationship between work experience and job performance: A conceptual and meta-analytic review. *Personnel Psychology, 48*, 887–910.

Reinhardt, W., Schmidt, B., Sloep, P., & Drachsler, H. (2011). Knowledge worker roles and actions—Results of two empirical studies. *Knowledge and Process Management, 18*, 150–174.

Sackett, P. R. (2002). The structure of counterproductive work behaviors: Dimensionality and relationships with facets of job performance. *International Journal of Selection and Assessment, 10*, 5–11.

Salazar, M., Lant, T., Fiore, S., & Salas, E. (2012). Facilitating innovation in diverse science teams through integrative capacity. *Small Group Research, 43*, 527–558.

Schrader, B. W., & Steiner, D. D. (1996). Common comparison standards: An approach to improving agreement between self and supervisory performance ratings. *Journal of Applied Psychology, 81*, 813–820.

Sessa, V. I. (1996). Using perspective taking to manage conflict and affect in teams. *Journal of Applied Behavioral Science, 32*, 101–115.

Smith, E., Ford, J. K., & Kozlowski, S. W. J. (1997). Building adaptive expertise: Implications for training design. In M. A. Quiñones & A. Ehrenstein (Eds.), *Training for a rapidly changing workplace: Applications of psychological research*. Washington, DC: American Psychological Association.

Sonnentag, S., & Frese, M. (2003). Stress in organizations. In W. C. Borman, D. R. Ilgen, & R. J. Klimoski (Eds.), *Handbook of psychology: Vol. 12. Industrial and organizational psychology* (pp. 453–491). Hoboken, NJ: Wiley.

Sony Corporation. (2015). *Consolidated financial results forecast for the third quarter ended December 31, 2014, and revision of consolidated forecast for the fiscal year ending March 31, 2015*. Retrieved from http://www.sony.net/SonyInfo/IR/financial/fr/150204_sony.pdf

Steiner, I. (1972). *Group process and productivity*. New York: Academic Press.

Steinke, J., Bolunmez, B., Fletcher, L., Wang, V., Tomassetti, A. J., Repchick, K. M., Zaccaro, S. J., Dalal, R. S., & Tetrick, L. E. (2015). Improving cyber security incident response team effectiveness using teams-based research. *Security and Privacy, IEEE, 13*, 20–29.

Stevens, M. J., & Campion, M. A. (1994). The knowledge, skill, and ability requirements for teamwork: Implications for human resource management. *Journal of Management, 20*, 503–530.

Thomas, K. W. (1992). Conflict and conflict management: Reflections and update. *Journal of Organizational Behavior, 13*, 265–274.

Van der Doef, M., & Maes, S. (1999). The job demand-control(-support) model and psychological well-being: A review of 20 years of empirical research. *Work & Stress, 13*, 87–114.

Van Katwyk, P. T., Fox, S., Spector, P. E., & Kelloway, E. K. (2000). Using the Job-Related Affective Well-Being Scale (JAWS) to investigate affective responses to work stressors. *Journal of Occupational Health Psychology, 5*, 219–230.

Vinchur, A. J., Prien, E. P., & Schippmann, J. S. (1993). An alternative procedure for analyzing job analysis results for content-oriented test development. *Journal of Business and Psychology, 8*, 215–226.

Viswesvaran, C. (1993). *Modeling job performance: Is there a general factor?* (Unpublished doctoral dissertation). University of Iowa, Iowa City.

Wegner, D. M. (1987). Transactive memory: A contemporary analysis of the group mind. In B. Mullen & G. R. Goethals (Eds.), *Theories of group behavior* (pp. 185–208). New York: Springer.

Werlinger, R., Muldner, K., Hawkey K., & Beznosov, K. (2010). Preparation, detection, and analysis: The diagnostic work of IT security incident response. *Information Management & Computer Security, 18*, 26–42.

West-Brown, M., Stikvoort, D., & Kossakowski, K.-P. (1998). *Handbook for computer security incident response teams (CSIRTS)* (CMU/SEI-98-HB-001). Pittsburgh, PA: Software Engineering Institute, Carnegie Mellon University.

West-Brown, M. J., Stikvoort, D., Kossakowski, K.-P., Killcrece, G., Ruefle, R., & Zaijicek, M. (2003, April). *Handbook for computer security incident response teams (CSIRTs)* (CMU/SEI-2003-HB-002). Retrieved from http://resources.sei.cmu.edu/library/asset-view.cfm?assetid=6305

Wildman, J. L., Bedwell, W. L., Salas, E., & Smith-Jentsch, K. A. (2011). Performance measurement at work: A multilevel perspective. In S. Zedeck (Ed.), *APA handbook of industrial and organizational psychology: Vol 1. Building and developing the organization* (pp. 301–341). Washington, DC: American Psychological Association.

Yuan, Y. C., Fulk, J., Monge, P. R., & Contractor, N. (2010). Expertise directory development, shared task interdependence, and strength of communication network ties as multilevel predictors of expertise exchange in transactive memory work groups. *Communication Research, 37*, 20–47.

Zaccaro, S. J., & DeChurch, L. A. (2012). Leadership forms and functions in multiteam systems. In S. J. Zaccaro, M. A. Marks, & L. A. DeChurch (Eds.), *Multiteam systems: An organization form for dynamic and complex environments* (pp. 253–288). London: Routledge.

Zaccaro, S. J., Heinen, B., & Shuffler, M (2009). Team leadership and team effectiveness. In E. Salas., J. Goodwin, & C. S. Burke (Eds.), *Team effectiveness in complex organizations: Cross disciplinary perspective and approaches* (pp. 83–111). San Francisco: Jossey-Bass.

Zaccaro, S. J., Marks, M. A., & DeChurch, L. A. (2012). Multiteam systems: An introduction. In S. J. Zaccaro, M. A. Marks, & L. A. DeChurch (Eds.), *Multiteam systems: An organization form for dynamic and complex environments* (pp. 3–32). London: Routledge.

Zaccaro, S. J., Rittman, A. & Marks, M. A. (2001). Team leadership. *The Leadership Quarterly, 12*, 451–484.

Zaccaro, S. J., Weis, E., Hilton, R., & Jeffries, J. (2011). Building resilient teams. In. P. Sweeney, M. Matthews, & P. Lester (Eds.), *Leading in dangerous contexts* (pp. 182–201). Annapolis. MD: Naval Institute Press.

3

THE ROLE OF PROCESSES IN SECURITY OPERATIONS CENTERS

Sandeep Bhatt, William Horne, Sathya Sundaramurthy, and Loai Zomlot

Cyber security incident response teams (CSIRTs) are the front lines of defense for many organizations against cyber security attacks. CSIRTs are complex organizations that work around the clock to analyze a huge volume of potential attacks and respond appropriately.

The importance of security notwithstanding, there is tremendous pressure on businesses to be as efficiently manage the tradeoff between operations costs versus the risks of being attacked. Thus, it is imperative that the work of a CSIRT be consistent, efficient, predictable, and accurate. Having well-defined processes is critical to meeting these business objectives.

Several process models of CSIRTs appear in the literature. These models generally describe CSIRTs at a very high level. These models can serve many useful purposes, such as training and educating people who have had little exposure to what these organizations do and serving as a guide when establishing a new organization. However, these models are not very useful for improving the operational efficiency of organizations.

One might hope that a more detailed model would remedy these limitations. Although detailed processes can describe some of the work that happens in a CSIRT, other aspects are fundamentally difficult to model. As a result, using process models to improve the operational efficiency of a CSIRT seems to be an elusive goal. It is possible that adaptive case management, which is an alternative to process modeling, will provide some help.

In this chapter, we briefly review what CSIRTs are, how they work, and some history of how they have evolved into the types of organizations they are today. We review the existing literature on process models of CSIRTs and describe their benefits and shortcomings. We end with a short discussion of how an adaptive case management (ACM) approach, guided by appropriate cognitive task analyses (CTAs) of CSIRTs, may help with some of these problems.

Background

Just as the demonstration of Marconi's wireless telegraph was about to begin at the Royal Institution in London in June 1903, the device, seemingly of its own accord, started tapping out rude messages in Morse code (Hong, 2001). Marconi's system had been hacked! The century that has since passed saw the growth of phreaking, hacks to exploit telephone networks for fun and profit, which later morphed into hacking computers and computer networks.

In 1988, Robert Morris, then a first-year graduate student at Cornell University, launched the first worm, a piece of code that exploited a vulnerability in a target and spread from computer to computer, consuming resources at every step (Orman, 2003). The Morris worm spread to thousands of computers, which became unresponsive. It took several days for teams of experts to identify the worm and to return computers to a normal state. In hindsight, it is clear that Morris did not act with malice; quite likely, he never realized the extent to which the worm would spread.

Anticipating similar widespread and perhaps even malicious security incidents in the future, the U.S. government funded the CERT Coordination Center, the first CSIRT, at Carnegie Mellon University in November 1988. The threat landscape that unfolded over the next few years primarily included curious hackers who wanted to prove that something could be done without any clear nefarious objective. As the Internet outgrew its academic and military origins and became a platform for commercial activity, criminal activity thrived with the abundance of insecure software, naïve users, and economic incentives. Reports of stolen credit card information from commercial enterprises, theft of intellectual property from industries, and denial-of-service attacks on corporations and on government and military agencies routinely appear in the newspapers. Prominent too are revelations of espionage and attacks on control systems conducted by nation states.

As businesses and governments have grown increasingly dependent on their IT infrastructures, the role, responsibilities, and organization of CSIRTs have evolved accordingly. Today, CSIRTs are widespread—major corporations and government agencies have CSIRTs either in house or partially outsourced. These CSIRTs perform a wide variety of functions, from detecting security breaches and analyzing their scope to coordinating responses with technical teams as well as with legal, corporate communications, executive, and external entities (including law enforcement and CSIRTs of other organizations and nations).

The Security Operations Center

In the early days of wide-area computer networking, informal groups of IT experts in different parts of an organization, perhaps spread across a few sites, responded to a security breach by meeting periodically to appraise the situation and figure out the next steps. Given that these experts were taking time off from their regular tasks, this ad hoc process was ineffective and unsustainable.

In contrast, today a corporate CSIRT is a formal entity with full-time staff, including the following:

- a team of security analysts who track security events and alerts and analyze these to determine the extent of a security breach;
- an incident response team that determines how to respond to breaches;
- forensics investigators who try to uncover how the breach occurred and collect evidence for potential legal action;
- an engineering team to develop and maintain specialized tools that support the CSIRT; and
- a coordination team to communicate and coordinate responses with other technical, legal, marketing, and executive teams.

In this chapter, we focus on the first line of defense of a CSIRT: the security operations center (SOC) that receives alerts from different sources, triages them to identify actual breaches, analyzes the extent of the breach, and coordinates responses. To facilitate understanding of the scope and complexity of an SOC, we next describe the workings of an SOC for a large organization.

What the SOC Sees

A goal of an SOC is to look for evidence of active attacks against the organization. This includes monitoring traditional security detection mechanisms, such as intrusion detection and prevention systems, and monitoring devices within the organization for evidence of infection. An organization may also deploy automated agents that scour the web and social media feeds and report signs of illicit activity (such as postings of proprietary company software on a public site) to the SOC. In addition, an SOC will receive notifications or advisories via e-mail or on the web from government agencies and security companies and e-mails from employees or external organizations who may notice suspicious activity. The task of the SOC is to receive events from all of these sources, then identify and prioritize security incidents that indicate likely malicious behavior that requires a response.

For a large multinational corporation with, say, hundreds of thousands of employees and devices, the total number of events sent to the SOC can be in the billions every day; this number could conceivably rise higher as more devices come on the network and sensors are deployed. There is simply no way that a team of humans can consume this much data.

Fortunately, most events sent to an SOC are not the result of a security breach. A sensor only responds to a local observation—it cannot tell whether harmless or malicious activity resulted in the observation. In fact, the vast majority of events result from harmless activity, so the problem facing the SOC is like looking for a needle in a haystack.

To deal with this problem, the primary workhorse in modern SOCs is a security incident and event management (SIEM) system (Bhatt, Manadhata, & Zomlot, 2014). SIEM systems collect and manage events from diverse sources and filter out as many events as possible that are harmless while retaining the events corresponding to malicious activity. The main strength of SIEM systems is their ability to cross-correlate logs from diverse sources using common attributes to define meaningful attack patterns and scenarios, which, when they occur, can alert a security analyst. This feature makes the SIEM like radar that detects objects in a timely manner. Ultimately, from billions of events per day, the SIEM system identifies a few hundred alerts that the SOC analyst sees.

What the SOC Does

An analyst manually processes incoming alerts from the SIEM system. The first task of the analyst is to triage the alert by quickly assessing the likelihood that the event is truly indicative of a compromise or is a false positive and, if the former, evaluating the likely impact of the incident before prioritizing it and creating a case for further analysis. Because events arrive at a rapid pace even under normal circumstances, it is imperative to triage them as quickly and accurately as possible—typically within a few minutes. The large volume of alerts flowing into an enterprise SOC leads to overwhelming amounts of work. SOC teams usually work around the clock in 10–12-hour shifts.

Many SOCs use an escalation model in which the SOC consists of several levels of security analysts (SAs); the higher the level, the more experienced and specialized the function of the SA. Level 1 SAs mainly monitor the incoming alerts. If the SA can definitively classify the alert as corresponding to an attack, he or she is able to initiate some actions to remediate the problem. If the SA can definitively classify the alert as a false positive, it can be dismissed. If the same rule triggers many false positives, the Level 1 SA can request that the engineering team tune the rule to reduce the false-positive rate. When a Level 1 SA is unable to classify an alert as either an attack or a false positive, he or she escalates the alert to a Level 2 SA for further investigation.

Level 2 SAs have more experience and, thus, can handle more complex alerts. As with Level 1 SAs, they perform an investigation and can either remediate the problem directly, dismiss the event as a false positive, request a change by the engineering team, or escalate the event further. Typically, the further up the chain, the more time can be spent on the alert and the deeper the skill set that is required to deal with the alert. The escalation process is illustrated in Figure 3.1.

Not all SOCs use this kind of escalation model. In some cases, the SOC may only have a single tier of analysts. At Hewlett-Packard, we use a Level 2 assist model, in which Level 2 analysts are brought in to assist Level 1 analysts for

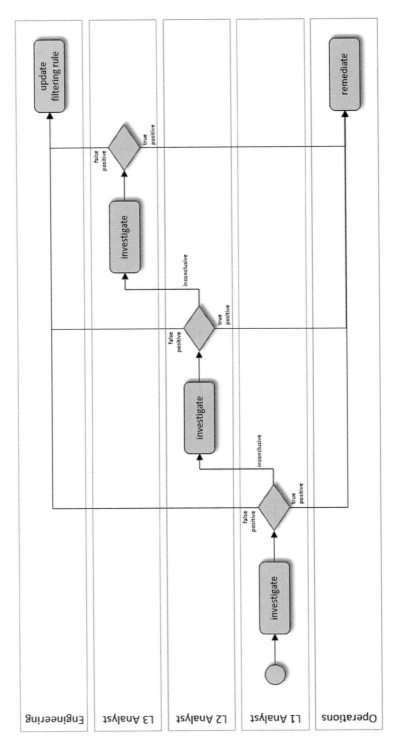

FIGURE 3.1 Escalation Swim Lane Diagram [L = level]

complex cases, but the Level 1 analysts are still primarily responsible for the events. In other organizations, totally separate groups, such as incident management or forensic teams, may handle events that cannot be handled within the SOC.

If the alert cannot be dismissed immediately, a case is typically opened and tracked using another invaluable tool in the SOC—the case management system. Case management systems, which evolved from ticketing systems, are used to create and manage the life cycle of an incident that is identified by a security analyst for further inspection. Originally designed for help desks, these systems manage processes with a prespecified workflow. It is easy to see that when multiple people, each of whom is simultaneously handling multiple cases, work together on a case, some aspect of the case is likely to fall through the cracks. This is especially important across escalation boundaries and shift changes or when a case stalls while information is being gathered from parties outside the SOC. Such communications often take hours or days to complete, so cases can be kept open while this information is collected.

Upon analysis of an attack and its impact, the next step it to respond by taking remedial actions. This may include reimaging infected machines, developing and applying new patches to vulnerable software applications, and reconfiguring defense devices to block the attack that was the root cause of the breach. Responding to an attack requires technical coordination with other teams—for example, network and application software configuration. Given the breadth of the activities that need to be carried out to ensure that the attack cannot recur, full response may take several weeks. Although the SOC focuses on the technical details, it may have to coordinate with wider CSIRT teams—such as corporate legal and communications, for example—depending on the severity of the attack to the business.

What the SOC Investigates

Analyzing an alert is by no means a straightforward task. Alerts themselves have very little information content. Yet the task of the analyst is to try to answer questions such as these:

- Who conducted the attack?
- What did they do (or try to do)?
- Why did they do it?
- When did they do it?
- Where did they attack?
- How did they go about it?

Analysts have to recreate as much of the context surrounding the alert as possible, formulate various hypotheses about what may have caused the alert, and then find evidence to back up one of the hypotheses. Indeed, at some level, the entire purpose of the SOC is to create context around events.

The problem is that in large, diverse information technology (IT) environments, all sorts of things happen that are unpredictable. There is often a legitimate explanation for seemingly malicious or anomalous behavior. The analyst, thus, typically collects information to try to understand why systems are behaving as they are. He or she might use a diverse set of tools to gather that information. Often, the information is simply not available, which makes the job even harder. For example, most organizations have asset management systems for tracking all of the machines and devices on their network, who those devices belong to, what applications they are running, and so on. However, maintaining a complete and accurate asset management system is a huge challenge. With the increasing popularity of BYOD (bring your own device) models, open wireless access points for mobile devices, and the inevitability of "shadow IT," there are many devices that are not tracked. Often, these are the devices involved in an incident.

Eventually, a deeper analysis of the incident might be needed to figure out whether a security breach actually occurred and, if so, identify the infected network component or computer. This would include a forensic analysis of the machine, attempting to identify any resident malware, reverse engineering the malware to figure out other potentially compromised resources, and identify the root cause and method of attack. Forensic analysts and reverse engineers have their own set of specialized tools for doing their jobs. Depending on the complexity of the attack and its spread within the organization, a deep analysis can require days or weeks to complete.

One of the challenges is that all of the tools—including the SIEM system, ticketing systems, asset management systems, and various investigation tools—are only weakly integrated. As a result, analysts can spend a great deal of time going back and forth between the different tools, cutting and pasting text. Although case management systems enable analysts to enter information from each step of their analysis in case logs, these must be entered manually; as a result, much of the activity is not logged and tracked, and it is difficult to document all of the steps that an analyst might have taken to resolve a problem.

Challenges Facing SOC Investigations

SOC investigations are challenging primarily because of the scale and complexity of the enterprise being monitored, the variety in types and meanings of events sent to the SOC, and the rate at which events arrive at the SIEM system from security devices and sensors. These pose technical as well as operational challenges for an SOC. Although the SIEM system reduces the amount of data so that the number of alerts is orders of magnitude smaller than the number of events, the SOC analyst is still confronted with looking for a needle in a haystack, albeit a somewhat less enormous one.

A fundamental issue that makes analysis difficult is the high rate of false-positive alerts that the SIEM rules trigger. The source of this problem is deeply rooted in the base-rate fallacy phenomenon that any detector suffers (Axelsson, 2000; Zomlot, 2014). Suppose there is a detector that, given an event, looks for some security problem and fires an alert. Suppose, further, that given an event, the detector only fires an alert falsely 1 percent of the time, which would be considered a very low false-positive rate. Finally, suppose that the security problem only occurs very rarely, say in one out of every 10,000 events. Of the 9,999 events on which it does not occur, the detector fires falsely on 1 percent of them (i.e., on about 100 events), whereas on the one event that should be turned into an alert, the detector correctly identifies it 99 percent of time. Therefore, in such a situation, for every correctly identified alert, about 100 false positives are generated.

The only way to resolve this problem is to write better alerts that have vanishingly small probabilities of false positives. This is why constant feedback from SOC analysts to the engineering team is important. However, such rules tend to be specific to one kind of attack, and unless one writes an exhaustive set of rules, the false-negative rate will be high, which is even worse because the SOC then misses potential attacks completely. In short, there is no easy solution to this problem. The SOC must make a tradeoff between false positives and false negatives.

A different challenge facing the SOC is the isolation from the operations of the enterprise network. SOC personnel are not involved in the details of configuring, testing, and maintaining enterprise assets. Routine activities such as patching, backup, and testing may trigger alerts in the SIEM system that are designed to detect security breaches; tracking down the cause of such alerts creates unnecessary overhead in the SOC. Therefore, it is important that the SOC coordinate with the operations teams to have advanced notice of when such activities might take place. Whereas SOC analysts can make requests of the SOC engineering teams to fine-tune rules, they often do not have similar interactions with operations teams that might configure and maintain intrusion-prevention systems, for example. Finally, when SOC analysts request data from other IT organizations, there is typically some delay in getting the information. This creates delays in investigations and adds to the backlog of open cases (Mathieu, Marks, & Zaccaro, 2001).

Formulating SOC Processes

SOCs handle huge numbers of events around the clock. It is important that the work carried out by an SOC be performed consistently, efficiently, predictably, and accurately. For that to happen, the organization needs to have well-defined processes and procedures that their employees should follow.

There are several advantages to having well-defined processes for an SOC. To begin with, when members of a team working in an environment with an overwhelming workload that requires coordination with external organizations follow well-defined procedures, the team becomes more productive. Moreover, well-defined processes are especially useful in establishing communication protocols during incident handling. For example, when the SOC has to collaborate with the vulnerability management and forensics teams to handle certain incidents, well-defined processes clearly specify what types of information must be shared with each of the teams.

Another benefit of defining a set of processes is consistency. Following processes assures that incidents are handled in a consistent manner from detection through remediation. It is less likely that an incident will fall through the cracks. Also, even though there may be frequent turnover in personnel, the output of the SOC remains consistent, because the results depend on the processes, not on the particular analysts.

Processes are also critical in training a new incoming analyst. Each SOC is unique in the way it operates because of the differences in the context, which include business and technical aspects like network infrastructure. The new analyst will take quite some time to internalize this contextual knowledge, which happens only through on-the-job experience. The new analyst relies on the documented processes during this time to perform his or her job.

Finally, processes can improve the efficiency of an SOC. They can be continuously monitored and modified to improve SOC performance (Curtis, Kellner, & Over, 1992; Ko, Lee, & Lee, 2009; van der Aalst, 2013). They can also help to identify where automation can reduce the amount of routine work, allowing SOC analysts more time for critical tasks requiring their technical skills.

At Hewlett-Packard, SOC processes are divided into the following four categories (Hewlett-Packard, n.d.), depending on the main function of the process. Depending on each person's role, SOC workers are aware of the processes for which they are responsible. At the same time, this categorization helps every SOC worker understand his or her role in the larger workings of the SOC:

- **business processes** that describe all the administrative and management components that are required to effectively operate a CSIRT;
- **technology processes** that describe all the information relating to system administration, configuration management and conceptual design;
- **operational processes** that describe the mechanics of the daily operations, like shift schedules and handover procedures; and
- **analytical processes** that describe all activities designed to detect and better understand malicious events.

How Should SOC Processes Be Defined?

There are several ways one can describe the functions and interactions of an SOC. One method is to break down the work of the SOC into different functions and write down in sufficient detail how to carry out each function, including protocols for how to communicate information across functional boundaries.

At a minimum, processes should be documented and communicated to all of the employees of the SOC and other stakeholders. This may be accomplished with something as simple as a web page with the appropriate information or a Microsoft Word or Adobe PDF document.

A more disciplined approach would be to create a formal model of the process—for example, using languages like Business Process Modeling Language or Unified Modeling Language—or to use visual representations of processes, such as flowcharts or business process diagrams. The intent of using a more disciplined approach is that an accurate model can be used to measure and optimize the productivity of the organization, enabling prediction of the impact of changes to the organization or the environment.

There is a rich literature on *business process management* (BPM), which can be described as "a discipline involving any combination of modeling, automation, execution, control, measurement and optimization of business activity flows, in support of enterprise goals, spanning systems, employees, customers and partners within and beyond the enterprise boundaries" (Workflow Management Coalition, n.d.). BPM has been successfully adopted to describe processes in industrial engineering, organizational psychology, business process management communities, and software engineering (van der Aalst, 2013). One of the major applications of BPM to IT governance is the Information Technology Infrastructure Library (ITIL), specifically its information technology service management component (Cartlidge, et al., 2012).

There are two approaches to BPM that can be used to define SOC process models. The first method is *prescriptive*; steps in the model are high-level prescriptions for the functions that an SOC should carry out. An alternative approach is *descriptive*; these models aim to gather all the current activities of a SOC and document them to develop process diagrams.

Related Work

There have been several attempts to define SOC and CSIRT processes in the literature. Typically, these have been prescriptive models describing analytical processes. They often consist of a cycle describing high-level workflows that occur in an organization. For example, in Alberts, Dorofee, Killcrece, Ruefle, and Zajicek (2004), at the highest level, the process can be summarized as shown in Figure 3.2. The cycle begins with planning and implementation of an initial CSIRT capability. The next step is to define how the organization's infrastructure can be protected against attack. There is then a process to detect events and triage them into high-priority incidents. Finally, the SOC must respond by mitigating the event and communicating to the appropriate parties. On the basis of lessons learned, the processes may be improved. Each of the five steps is refined in one additional level of detail. For example, triage events step is further refined into three additional steps: categorize and correlate events, prioritize events, and assign events.

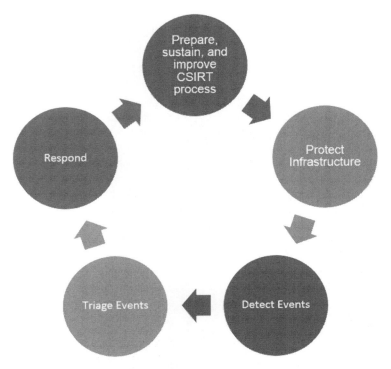

FIGURE 3.2 High-Level Process Diagram as Described in Figure 3.1 [CSIRT = cyber security incident response team]

Several other accounts have appeared in the literature with similar cycles. Some of the earliest work can be traced back to the observe–orient–decide–act loop suggested by military strategist John Boyd (1987) or the plan–do–check–act cycle, which has its origins in Japanese quality control (Moen & Norman, 2010). Other similar cycles can be found in Calder and Watkins (2010); Chairman of the Joint Chiefs of Staff (2009); Cichonski, Millar, Grance, and Scarfone (2012); Daley, Millar, and Osorno (2011); European Union Agency for Network and Information Security (2010); and Osorno, Millar, and Rager (2011).

These kinds of process models can serve several purposes. They can be used by organizations to guide the development of their SOC or CSIRT. They can serve as a baseline from which to evaluate and measure the maturity of an existing incident management capability. And they can be used for training and educational purposes to give new employees or outsiders a high level view of what happens in the SOC.

However, they are not particularly helpful from an operational perspective, because they are not detailed enough to reflect the work that employees within the SOC do on a daily basis. As a result, it is difficult to obtain some of the benefits of process modeling with these approaches, such as process improvement and predictive analysis. This situation is similar to the following observation about ITIL:

> Though standards such as the ... ITIL ... offer the potential for cost savings through the use of formal processes and best practices, such top-down approaches tend to be either high-level—often far removed from the actual work—or low-level—often inflexible given the rapid pace of technology and market change. (Bailey, Kandogan, Haber, & Maglio, 2007)

One might wonder if more detailed process models could be developed that would provide such capabilities. However, we are not aware of any such models in the literature. In fact, it may be difficult to create a usable process model with enough details to enable some of the advantages of process modeling.

By its very nature, investigation and analysis is unstructured work, sometimes requiring novel, unorthodox methods to arrive at a conclusion. The IT environment and attack methods are frequently changing in ways that the analyst cannot see. When an event arrives, the analyst must create a mental model of the context, or environment, when the event triggered. Creating this mental model may require running known scripts that have proven useful in the past, asking around to see if anyone is aware of a recent change in the IT infrastructure, or perhaps searching the Internet to see if a new type of attack has recently been detected. Sometimes a series of benign events can conspire to trigger a security alert. For example, one SOC analyst relayed a story about how an alert caused a great deal of concern and took up many analyst resources, only for them to later find out from a network administrator that the anomalous traffic that triggered the alert was from an internal server applying security patches to specific application software. This example illustrates the complex, unpredictable paths that analysts have to figure out their way through. Such cases cannot be represented in any detail on a process diagram.

However, wherever possible, SOC analysts are encouraged to document their investigative findings and turn them into procedures that other analysts can follow when they encounter a similar set of circumstances. Although this may not comprehensively cover all of the investigative work that happens in an SOC, it can help to improve the efficiency of handling events that occur repeatedly.

Another complicating fact stems from the large and ever-increasing variety of events that can confront an analyst. Because different types of alerts may require different steps to analyze, the number of scenarios to consider can be enormous, well beyond any number that makes sense to insert into a process model diagram.

The types of process models described here only cover a narrow aspect of the types of processes that occur in an SOC. In particular, these process models are mostly focused on analytical processes and have very little to say about the business, technical, and operational processes described at the beginning of this section. This may be due in large part to the fact that these types of processes are highly dependent on the particular organizational structure and IT infrastructure in which the SOC operates.

The Downside of Processes

Processes do have certain limitations in SOCs, in fact influencing operations negatively. Requiring analysts to repeat rigid processes and procedures all day every day leads, inevitably, to job fatigue. This has been noted in other contexts as well, including locomotive engineering (Roth & Multer, 2009). This rigid nature of processes has some causal effect on the high employee turnover in SOCs. This is exacerbated by the fact that the effectiveness of SOCs is measured in terms of process maturity. Processes also hinder creativity. For example, an analyst, when realizing that there is a better way to perform a certain task than following the process, is encouraged still to follow the process. Although there are continuous process-improvement programs in SOCs, the iteration frequency of the processes does not keep up with the dynamic nature of incidents. There is also a tendency in SOCs to define processes without clearly documenting why they exists in the first place. Because most analysts do not understand the purpose of the processes, the realization that a certain process does not work comes only after its failure in some situations.

There are definite advantages to being a more adaptive organization that can be flexible in how it handles events. In one of our own interviews with a CSIRT manager, when asked about the models in Alberts et al. (2004), the manager responded, "It is a very academic view of [practiced processes]. I mean, obviously working these events is a little more organic than that." It appears, too, that during emergency situations, carefully crafted processes are sometimes ignored. According to one focus group interviewed in Shedden, Ahmad, and Ruighaver (2011),

> It's absolutely astounding to see people that have spent 3 months planning for a security incident previously with beautifully constructed documentation, throw it all out the window and go "OK, yes, that's to keep the auditors happy. Now, what are we really going to do?" (p. 6)

Adaptive Case Management

Background

As mentioned in the previous section, the lack of contextual information associated with an event complicates investigative tasks. Security analysts recreate as much of the context as they need using multiple tools, cutting and pasting information obtained from one tool into another, or perhaps e-mailing colleagues for missing information they may have. Perhaps they may have seen the event frequently in the past and have a mental store of useful auxiliary information built from experience. This mental store is often referred to as tacit knowledge (Polanyi, 1967), and it is what separates experienced analysts from new employees.

From a high level, an analyst receives an alert, tries a variety of methods (such as those mentioned earlier) to create as much context around the alert as necessary, forms a hypothesis, looks for evidence to validate the hypothesis, and iterates as needed. These small steps govern the investigation process. However, there are a considerable number of possible variations at each step (e.g., different sources of information, different experts to consult, different tools to use). Which path an analyst chooses depends on the tacit knowledge specific to the analyst.

Unfortunately, much of the knowledge of how the SOC handles incidents is tacit knowledge. Consequently, when analysts leave the organization, all of their tacit knowledge leaves with them. This can also cause problems when different analysts have different tacit knowledge, which can lead to communication failure, especially when cases are passed down across shift boundaries.

To better capture the variability in low-level work, and to address the issue of tacit knowledge, we need an approach that is better suited to the situation. A viable alternative to BPM is ACM (Swenson, 2010). ACM aims to increase the efficiency of the knowledge workers, "who have high degree[s] of expertise, education or experience, and the primary purpose of their jobs involves the creation, distribution, or application of knowledge" (Davenport, 1993, p. 10).

ACM represents a shift from a static process-modeling approach to a data-centric—or, in our context, an incident-based—paradigm. Therefore, ACM is an approach to manage work by gathering and organizing information necessary for knowledge workers to accomplish their goals, with less focus on enforcing a particular process (Swenson, 2010).

An ACM method centers on each incident; the first step is to gather all available data that are relevant to the incoming incident. These data can be acquired using tools, as before, but also by querying a database of previous incidents. As more incidents are analyzed, the database is updated so that the results and techniques of analyzing each incident can benefit responses to future incidents. By recording the choices made at each step of analyzing each incident—for example, the tools used, experts consulted, and event correlations checked—the ACM solution attempts to explicitly create and store some of the tacit knowledge that analysts have today.

In summary, we envision a solution that follows these principles:

- Automate and customize repetitive parts of incident investigation by automatically creating the context around the SIEM alert as opposed to the current practice of having the analyst figure and ferret out relevant information from multiple sources.
- Free analysts to adapt to each incident by allowing them to take ownership of an incident and to decide and design their investigation processes. This

will give analysts the freedom to assign tasks or collaborate within the system seamlessly.
- Manage the content of each incident by collecting all of the related information and communications and storing it in the system. The system uses the stored incidents to learn and propose recommendations and guidance for similar future incidents. This may also help in cutting the number of unnecessary investigations.
- Integrate the system with all SOC tools (e.g., the SIEM system) to enable and facilitate all of the foregoing characteristics.

Finally, we do not envision an ACM solution replacing process models entirely. Static process models are adequate to describe the functions and communications structure of an SOC at a high level. However, we need tools adhering to the principles just outlined to ease the pressure on analysts who carry out tasks that are dynamic and unpredictable but nonetheless have a repetitive structure at a high level.

Having a system that provides contextual information and guides, but does not fully automate, the security analyst in his or her investigations is an ambitious next step in the evolution of SOC systems. The current trend of integrating rigid, predesigned investigative process models into the case management system is ridden with insurmountable obstacles. The hybrid approach we propose is better suited to the SOC environment. It integrates high-level SOC process models from the literature with an ACM-style system for facilitating and guiding the low-level, detail-oriented analysis process. Ultimately, our focus is on improving SOC performance, using appropriate methods where they apply.

The Importance of CTA to ACM System Design

In principle, an ACM system can ease the task of an analyst by automatically creating much of the context surrounding a security event. However, this presumes that we have a working definition of the context associated with each type of event. Moreover, it is critical to present this context to the analyst in a way that reduces the cognitive load on the analyst; without such a guarantee, the system would be useless!

The definition of context, as well as its presentation, must be guided by an understanding of the cognitive processes of an analyst—both to identify tacit knowledge and to identify opportunities for better automation support. CTA of CSIRTs can guide the design of the functional requirements of an ACM system. CTA methods can play an important role in identifying tacit knowledge as well (Clark, Feldon, van Merriënboer, Yates, & Early, 2008; Militello & Hutton, 1998). There has been prior work on using CTA to aid in designing incident response visualization tools for CSIRTs (D'Amico, Goodall, Tesone, & Kopylec, 2007; D'Amico & Whitley, 2008; D'Amico, Whitley, Tesone, O'Brien, & Roth, 2005). These works report on CTA of CSIRT workers, discussing how information assurance analysts progress through different stages of situational awareness and how visual representations are likely to facilitate cyber defense situational awareness. Similar studies will be needed to define requirements for the kind of ACM system that we envision.

Another important consideration in the design and deployment of new technologies is that they often introduce new modes of failure. This may happen, for example, because the new technologies create a cognitive overload (Roth & Multer, 2009). Here too, we expect that a detailed CTA will be needed to anticipate potential problems before deployment. By providing automation in an intelligent manner so that the tools fit into the cognitive workflow of an analyst, we aim to design tools that are more useful and avoid the problem of cognitive overload introduced by new technology.

REFERENCES

Alberts, C., Dorofee, A., Killcrece, G., Ruefle, R., & Zajicek, M. (2004, October). *Defining incident management processes for CSIRTs: A work in progress* (CMU/SEI Report No. CMU/SEI-2004-TR-015). Retrieved from http://www.dtic.mil/dtic/tr/fulltext/u2/a453378.pdf

Axelsson, S. (2000). The base-rate fallacy and the difficulty of intrusion detection. *ACM Transaction on Information System Security, 3*, 186–205.

Bailey, J., Kandogan, E., Haber, E., & Maglio, P. P. (2007, March). *Activity-based management of IT service delivery*. Paper presented at the First Symposium on Computer Human Interaction for Management of Information Technology, Cambridge, MA.

Bhatt, S., Manadhata, P. K., & Zomlot, L. (2014, September/October). The operational role of security information and event management systems. *IEEE Security and Privacy Magazine, 12*(5), 35–41.

Boyd, J. R. (1976, September 3). *Destruction and creation*. Leavenworth, KS: U.S. Army Command and General Staff College.

Calder, A., & Watkins, S. G. (2010). *Information Security Risk Management for ISO27001/ISO27002*. Cambridgeshire, England: IT Governance.

Cartlidge, A., Rudd, C., Smith, M., Wigzel, P., Rance, S., Shaw, S., & Wright, T. (2012). *An introductory overview of ITIL 2011*. Retrieved from http://www.itsm.info/ITSM.htm

Chairman of the Joint Chiefs of Staff. (2012, July 10). *Cyber incident handling program*. Retrieved from http://www.dtic.mil/cjcs_directives/cdata/unlimit/m651001.pdf

Cichonski, P., Millar, T., Grance, T., & Scarfone, K. (2012, August). *Computer security incident handling guide: Recommendations of the National Institute of Standards and Technology* (Special Publication No. 800-61, Rev. 2). Gaithersburg, MD: National Institute of Standards and Technology, U.S. Department of Commerce.

Clark, R. E., Feldon, D. F., van Merriënboer, J.J.G., Yates, K. A., & Early, S. (2008). Cognitive task analysis. In J. M. Spector, M. D. Merrill, J. van Merriënboer, & M. P. Driscoll (Eds.), *Handbook of research on educational communications and technology* (3rd ed., pp. 577–593). New York: Erlbaum.

Curtis, B., Kellner, M. I., & Over, J. (1992, September). Process modeling. *Communications of the ACM, 35*(9), 75–90.

Daley, R., Millar, T., & Osorno, M. (2011, November). *Operationalizing the coordinated incident handling model*. Paper presented at 2011 IEEE International Conference on Technologies for Homeland Security (HST), Waltham, MA.

D'Amico, A., Goodall, J., Tesone, D., & Kopylec., J. (2007, September/October). Visual discovery in computer network defense. *IEEE Computer Graphics and Applications*, *27*(5), 20–27.

D'Amico, A., & Whitley, K. (2008). The real work of computer network defense analysts. In J. R. Goodall, G. Conti, & K.-L. Ma (Eds.), *VizSEC 2007: Proceedings of the Workshop on Visualization for Computer Security* (pp. 19–37). New York: Springer.

D'Amico, A., Whitley, K., Tesone, D., O'Brien, B., & Roth, E. (2005). Achieving cyber defense situational awareness: A cognitive task analysis of information assurance analysts. *Proceedings of the Human Factors and Ergonomics Society Annual Meeting*, *49*, 229–233.

Davenport, T. H. (1993). *Process innovation: Reengineering work through information technology*. Boston: Harvard Business School Press.

European Union Agency for Network and Information Security. (2010). *Good practice guide for incident management*. Retrieved from https://www.enisa.europa.eu/activities/cert/support/incident-management

Hewlett-Packard. (n.d.). *Building a successful security operations center*. Retrieved from http://www.hp.com/go/sioc

Hong, S. (2001). *Wireless: From Marconi's Black-box to the Audion*. Cambridge, MA: MIT Press.

Ko, R. K., Lee, S. S., & Lee, E. W. (2009). Business process management (BPM) standards: A survey. *Business Process Management Journal*, *15*, 744–791.

Mathieu, J. E., Marks, M. A., & Zaccaro, S. J. (2001). Multiteam systems. In N. Anderson, D. S. Ones, & C. Viswesvaran (Eds.), *Handbook of industrial, work, and organizational psychology* (pp. 289–312). London: Sage.

Militello, L. G., & Hutton, R. J. B. (1998). Applied cognitive task analysis (ACTA): A practitioner's toolkit for understanding cognitive task demands. *Ergonomics*, *41*, 1618–1641.

Moen, R. D., & Norman, C. L. (2010). Circling back. *Quality Progress*, *43*(11), 22–28.

Orman, H. (2003, September/October). The Morris worm: A fifteen-year perspective. *IEEE Security & Privacy*, *1*(5), 35–43.

Osorno, M., Millar, T., & Rager, D. (2011). Coordinated cybersecurity incident handling: Roles, processes, and coordination networks for crosscutting incidents. In *Proceedings of the 16th International Command and Control Technology Symposium*. Retrieved from http://www.dtic.mil/dtic/tr/fulltext/u2/a547075.pdf

Polanyi, M. (1967). *The tacit dimension*. New York: Anchor Books.

Roth, E., & Multer, J. (2009, January). *Technology implications of a cognitive task analysis for locomotive engineers* (DOT/FRA/ORD-09/03). Washington, DC: Office of Research and Development, Federal Railroad Administration, U.S. Department of Transportation.

Shedden, P., Ahmad, A., & Ruighaver, A. B. (2011). Informal learning in security incident response teams. In P. Seltsikas, D. Bunker, L. Dawson, & M. Indulska (Eds.), *Proceedings of the 22nd Australasian Conference on Information Systems* (Paper 37). Retrieved from http://aisel.aisnet.org/acis2011/37/

Swenson, K. D. (2010). *Mastering the unpredictable: How adaptive case management will revolutionize the way that knowledge workers get things done*. Tampa, FL: Meghan-Kiffer Press.

van der Aalst, W.M.P. (2013). Business process management: A comprehensive survey. *ISRN Software Engineering, 2013* (Article No. 507984). http://dx.doi.org/10.1155/2013/507984

Workflow Management Coalition. (n.d.). *What is BPM?* Retrieved from http://www.wfmc.org/what-is-bpm

Zomlot, L.M.M. (2014). Base-rate fallacy in intrusion analysis. In *Handling uncertainty in intrusion analysis* (pp. 121–125; doctoral dissertation). Retrieved from K-State Research Exchange website: http://krex.k-state.edu/dspace/handle/2097/17603

4

ESCALATION

An Understudied Team Decision-Making Structure

Reeshad S. Dalal, Balca Bolunmez, Alan J. Tomassetti, and Zitong Sheng

> An email bombing incident is being handled by a novice staff member. During correspondence with the sites involved, new information is identified that indicates that the account being used to launch the attacks is itself compromised. The account contains password files from over 1,000 different systems. Given both the number of hosts involved in the incident and the staff member's lack of experience, the incident will require escalation.
>
> (West-Brown et al., 2003, p. 129)

> Yeah, I mean the key … is … when to get leadership involved. That's a big decision about when to start escalating things. It's part of the process that we have in place of: I pass it to Tier 2, Tier 2 will look at it. If this is going to go something bigger, then he'll get his management involved, and it'll go up the chain. But you have to understand when that needs to happen.
>
> (Personal communication with cyber security incident response analyst)

This chapter examines the concept of escalation decision making. Decision making of this kind is prevalent in cyber security incident response teams (CSIRTs) but is also relevant in a variety of other organizational settings. Curiously, however, the academic literature has not paid particular attention to this decision-making structure. This chapter therefore aims to explain escalation decision making and to suggest an agenda for future basic research in the area.

West-Brown et al. (2003) define *escalation* as follows: "[E]scalation is concerned with raising the importance of an activity regardless of its priority. Escalation invariably requires at least one level of management to become involved for decision-making purposes" (p. 128). As suggested by this definition, escalation is primarily concerned with raising the responsibility for a decision to a higher level in the organizational hierarchy. In other words, we do not focus, in the present chapter, on "handoffs" or "notifications," which involve passing responsibility for a decision to others at the same level of a hierarchy, albeit perhaps to those individuals or teams with higher expertise relevant to the incident at hand (Alberts, Dorofee, Killcrece, Ruefle, & Zajicek, 2004; Daley, Millar, & Osorno, 2011; Killcrece, Kossakowski, Ruefle, & Zajicek, 2003; West-Brown et al., 2003). We also limit our focus to escalation initiated by an analyst within a CSIRT rather than escalation from, say, a help desk to a CSIRT.

A similar escalation phenomenon can be observed in other professions that require incident response. For example, models of nuclear power plant decision making (e.g., Carvalho, Dos Santos, & Vidal, 2005) suggest that, when something goes wrong with automation systems, a control room operator (who is responsible for monitoring the automation systems) can escalate the decision to the shift supervisor with or without a suggested solution. After receiving this information, the shift supervisor makes the final decision regarding what action to take. As another example, a nurse in a hospital may escalate a situation involving a patient to a rapid response team when (among other things) the patient exhibits unexpected symptoms and the nurse believes that something is wrong but cannot identify it using objective data (Mitchell, Schatz, & Francis 2014). Yet another example involves the triage of urgent care patients during prehospital emergency medical response. Dispatchers, who receive the medical assistance request either directly from a patient or from a third party, assess the severity of the case and make the decision whether to transfer the patient to a nurse advice telephone line or alternative emergency medical services (e.g., escalate to a hospital-based specialized nurse or an emergency physician; Gijsenbergh, Nieuwenhof, & Machiels, 2003; Neely, Eldurkar, & Drake, 2000).

However, escalation may also be relevant in many domains other than incident response. For example, Doraiswamy and Shiv (2012) suggest that the handling of escalation is one of the top 50 information technology project management challenges. In fact, we suggest that escalation may be especially common in hierarchical organizations in which a subordinate is given initial authority over certain decisions but is permitted (or required) to relinquish control over the decision to his or her supervisor under certain circumstances (e.g., when the subordinate has never encountered such a decision situation previously and/or when the decision is likely to have severe consequences for the organization or external constituencies). Given the ubiquity of hierarchical organizations, we suggest that escalation is itself ubiquitous.

Yet the academic research on decision making has not considered escalation as one of the standard decision-making structures. As a result, sufficient basic research attention has not been focused on escalation. Accordingly, this chapter has two primary objectives.

Objectives of This Chapter

The first objective of this chapter is to introduce cyber security professionals to research conducted by organizational psychologists and judgment and decision-making researchers. Although the decision-making structures studied by these researchers differ somewhat from the escalation decision-making structure prevalent in CSIRTs, they can nonetheless inform an understanding of escalation. To that end, in the next section, we discuss the decision-making structures more commonly studied in academic research.

The second objective of this chapter is to introduce researchers in the fields of organizational psychology and judgment and decision making to the escalation decision-making structure present in CSIRTs and several other applied decision-making teams.[1] Although this decision-making structure has not yet received much scrutiny from academic researchers, it may, as discussed previously, be a fairly common structure in the "real world." Escalation decisions may therefore be an area where practice should inform basic scientific research such that the latter should begin to study the escalation decision-making structure both in field settings, such as functioning CSIRTs, and in more controlled settings, such as the laboratory. We therefore echo Pfleeger and Caputo (2012) in the belief that studying the intersection between cyber security, on the one hand, and research on human decision making and behavior, on the other, will lead to "innovative experimental designs … that can form the basis of experimental replication and tailoring of applications to particular situations" (p. 609).

Decision-Making Structures, Old and New

The judgment and decision-making—and, to a lesser extent, organizational psychology—academic literature discusses three primary decision-making structures (Dalal, et al., 2010): (1) the individual decision maker (who does not involve other people in the decision-making process), (2) the decision-making team (which uses a collective decision-making process characterized by information sharing and, ultimately, a decision rule such as unanimity, two-thirds majority, simple majority, or plurality), and (3) the *judge–advisor system* (in which one person—the decision maker or "judge"—makes decisions after receiving advice from one or more other people). These decision-making structures are depicted in Figure 4.1.

In contrast, an escalation decision-making structure involves a first-order decision maker who relinquishes responsibility over the decision to a second-order decision maker. The second-order decision maker is at least one level higher in the organizational hierarchy than the first-order decision maker (e.g., the second-order decision-maker may be a Level 2 analyst, whereas the first-order decision maker may be a Level 1 analyst). The second-order decision maker then makes a decision either unilaterally or in consultation with the first-order decision maker. After making the decision, the second-order decision maker may or may not delegate the implementation of the decision back to the first-order decision maker. This decision-making structure is depicted in Figure 4.2.

We acknowledge at the very outset that escalation can take several forms in practice and that our aforementioned description and depiction of escalation are

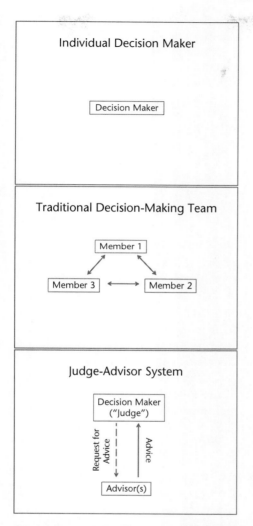

FIGURE 4.1 Individual, Team, and Judge–Advisor System Decision-Making Structures [The dashed arrow indicates communication that may or may not occur.]

somewhat stylized or simplified. Yet a somewhat simplified definition of escalation (albeit one that captures the core features of the phenomenon) is necessary so that the phenomenon is not so diffuse as to be useless to contemplate. A somewhat simplified definition also permits future basic research to capture this phenomenon in controlled laboratory settings—and to compare escalation with the more traditional decision-making structures studied in basic research. With regard to this latter aspect, as can be seen from a juxtaposition of Figures 4.1 and 4.2, none of the three commonly studied decision-making structures closely approximates

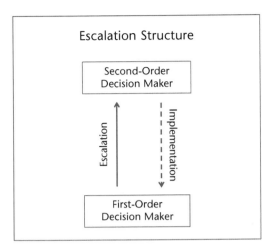

FIGURE 4.2 Escalation Decision-Making Structure [The dashed arrow indicates communication that may or may not occur.]

the escalation structure. This indicates the need for considerable future research on escalation. Yet findings pertaining to the more commonly studied structures can serve as starting points for research on escalation. We therefore briefly touch upon the relevance of each of the three more commonly studied structures.

The individual decision-making structure can be viewed as a special case of the escalation decision-making structure. In cases in which a first-order decision maker decides not to escalate, the two structures are identical except that the escalation structure includes not just a decision regarding how to handle the incident but also a decision not to escalate. In cases in which a first-order decision maker does decide to escalate, the first stage of the escalation structure (i.e., initial consideration by the first-order decision maker prior to the decision to escalate) is nonetheless closely related to the individual decision-making structure. In terms of substantive findings that are likely to be relevant, research on the individual decision maker suggests that, contrary to some economic models, decision makers often make decisions with incomplete information and that they are often unable to accurately weigh the pieces of information they do possess (Dawes, 1979). Instead, decision makers tend to use heuristics—that is, mental shortcuts—to make decisions (Bazerman & Moore, 2012; Tversky & Kahneman, 1974). For instance, individual decision makers may frame information in a way that colors their future thinking (e.g., they may view a firewall either as admitting good traffic or as blocking bad traffic; Pfleeger & Caputo, 2012). Similarly, they may search only for new information that confirms their preconceptions rather than a balance of confirming and disconfirming information (e.g., they may believe that abnormally high outbound traffic to a server with a ".ru" domain reflects data exfiltration, and they might only seek out information confirming this hypothesis rather than information suggesting that the traffic simply reflects normal international business transactions). Although heuristics such as these frequently work well, they sometimes lead to spectacularly biased decisions (Bazerman & Moore, 2012; Tversky & Kahneman, 1974). It is therefore not entirely surprising that the failure rate for major decisions by top managers has been estimated at approximately 50 percent (Nutt, 2002). Yet decision makers—including experts—are often greatly overconfident about the quality of the decisions they make (Russo & Schoemaker, 1992).

Research on decision-making team and judge–advisor system structures is relevant to the escalation structure because it reminds researchers that individuals frequently do not make decisions on their own. In other words, "no decision maker is an island" (cf. Donne, 1624 & 1630/1999, p. 103). At a more specific level, however, research on the team decision-making structure suggests that information sharing and joint decision making are not always a panacea: For instance, teams may suffer from "groupthink" (such that a desire for harmony and conformity overrides dissent and the examination of alternative solutions), team members may share and then reiterate common information (whereas sharing and reiterating unique information would be more beneficial), teams may reach decisions that are more extreme than the prediscussion preferences of *any* of their members, and teams—like individuals—may suffer from overconfidence (Gigone & Hastie, 1997; Stasser, 1999; Sunstein, 2009).

Perhaps the extant decision-making structure most similar to the escalation structure is the judge–advisor system (or hierarchical decision-making team) structure (see Bonaccio & Dalal, 2006, for a review). As in the case of escalation, research in this area explicitly emphasizes the hierarchical nature of much organizational decision making. Moreover, this research focuses on what advice is, how advice taking should be measured, what motivates decision makers to seek and accept advice, and what motivates advisors to provide advice. For instance, research indicates that decision makers rarely seek sufficient advice because they fear appearing incompetent to advisors—even though being asked for advice frequently *increases* advisors' perceptions of decision-makers' competence (Brooks, Gino, & Schweitzer, 2015; see also Bonaccio & Dalal, 2006). The following section uses insights from these existing decision-making structures to inform research on escalation decision making.

Understanding Escalation Decision Making

To understand escalation decision making, we use Lasswell's (1948) classic formulation regarding human communication *per se*: "who says what to whom with what effect" (p. 37). This is similar to Dorofee, Killcrece, Ruefle and Zajicek's (2007) guidance to cyber security professionals: "Criteria or procedures for escalation should define how and when to escalate, [and] to whom" (p. 96). In the current context, "who" refers to the first-order decision maker: namely, the initiator of the escalation. "To whom" refers to the second-order decision maker:

namely, the recipient of the escalation. "What" and "how" refer to the content of communication from the first-order decision maker to the second-order decision maker.[2] "When" refers to how soon during the decision-making process and/or under what conditions the first-order decision maker escalates. Finally, "with what effect" refers to the upshot of the escalation. We discuss each of these in turn.

Who Escalates?

Both person-level factors (individual differences) and person-in-situation factors might cause a person—a first-order decision maker—to escalate. Although several factors are likely to be implicated, here we extrapolate from the literature on the judge–advisor system (Bonaccio & Dalal, 2006) and discuss three factors likely to influence whether the first-order decision maker escalates.

The first major factor is the first-order decision maker's expertise (or competence) level. CSIRT analysts differ in the number and nature of certifications they possess, their level of experience, and so forth. Members will be more likely to escalate in general if they have lower expertise in incident handling (a person-level factor), and they will be more likely to escalate *on a particular incident* if they have lower expertise with regard to that particular incident (a person-in-situation factor). For example, when recounting how a particularly memorable incident was handled, an analyst we interviewed stated, "I was like, 'No, this is too odd, it's entirely too odd.' So the final decision that [I] made was [to] escalate it."

A second factor likely to influence whether the first-order decision maker escalates is his or her confidence level. The organizational psychology literature has focused on person-level differences in confidence across domains (e.g., Judge & Bono, 2001) or in specific domains such as incident handling. This literature suggests that CSIRT analysts whose confidence—either as a domain-general dispositional trait or as a self-evaluation specific to the domain of incident handling—is low will be more likely to escalate on average. In contrast, the judgment and decision-making research literature (e.g., Harvey, 1997) has usually focused on decision-specific confidence. This literature suggests that CSIRT analysts whose confidence about handling a particular incident is low will be more likely to escalate that particular incident.

Whereas confidence in this context may be thought of as the first-order decision maker's (fallible) perceptions of his or her own expertise, the first-order decision maker also needs to manage the impressions held about him or her by others—for example, the second-order decision maker's perceptions about the first-order decision maker's expertise. Therefore, impression-management motives (Ashford, Blatt, & VandeWalle, 2003) may be implicated in escalation: CSIRT analysts who score low on impression-management motives will be more likely to escalate in general. The role of impression-management motives is implicitly addressed in the European Network and Information Security Agency incident management guide (European Union Agency for Network and Information Security [ENISA], 2010, p. 21), which refers to the "'cry wolf' risk," in which analysts "annoy [their] management with too many false alarms," thereby "[losing] credibility" (p. 21). Impression management was also discussed implicitly by a senior analyst we interviewed:

> I know one of the big things that people always worry about when they're escalating is that somebody's going to look at them and say, "Well, why didn't you know this?" [But] there's a reason why you're called a *novice*. It's because you don't know everything.... So it's up to the professionals to mentor those novices through things like this.

As mentioned previously, the three factors under discussion were chosen by extrapolation from the literature on the judge–advisor system. Future research in the field and the laboratory will be necessary to examine whether these and other factors (e.g., the dependent decision-making style; Scott & Bruce, 1995) are indeed relevant in the case of escalation. Assuming, however, that they are, several practical implications present themselves. Obviously, CSIRTs must either hire people who already possess sufficient expertise or must train them quickly so that they acquire sufficient expertise. However, CSIRTs must also ensure that their employees are well calibrated: that is, neither overconfident nor underconfident. Given that overconfidence tends to be more prevalent and, therefore, a greater concern than underconfidence, CSIRTs could employ decision-making protocols involving simple (and quick) evidence-based strategies to combat overconfidence during decision making: for instance, strategies that require them to "consider the opposite" or to conduct a "pre-mortem" (Klein, 2007; Lord, Lepper, & Preston, 1984). Finally, CSIRTs should not be composed of analysts who are overly motivated to manage impressions. This issue, too, can be addressed at the hiring stage.

To Whom Are Decisions Escalated?

As discussed previously, the second-order decision maker is usually one level higher in the hierarchy than the first-order decision maker. Often, as illustrated by one of the quotations with which we opened this chapter (see also Flinders Ports, 2008), escalation will proceed from one level to the level immediately above it—and then, if needed, to the level immediately above that second level. "Chain" communication networks (Shaw, 1978) such as this one tend to work well for routine problems involving adjacent levels of a hierarchy, but they tend not to work as well with repeated escalation that eventually covers multiple levels of the hierarchy, because such communication takes longer and may suffer from inaccuracies due to filtering and exaggeration (Gaines, 1980). For example, as noted in the European Network and Information Security Agency incident management guide (ENISA, 2010),

> An escalation model that follows the chain of command—step-by-step from low to high—will lead to unacceptable delays or misinterpretations when a grave incident occurs and is therefore not recommended in such cases. Of course, for incidents that are not grave and do not need urgent escalation, informing the next higher level of management is acceptable if this can help improve the issue.... [S]everity and urgency can and should be used to decide what to escalate and to where. (p. 21)

A practical implication is that CSIRTs should have protocols requiring that, in high-severity and/or urgent cases, escalation occurs not just to the next level above the first-order decision maker but also, simultaneously, to the higher level at which the incident can most efficiently be resolved. However, because CSIRT analysts may not be very familiar with employees several rungs above them in the organizational hierarchy, the escalation protocols should be quite specific as to which higher level employees (e.g., data protection officer vs. director of IT risk management; Universities and Colleges Information Systems Association [UCISA], n.d.) would constitute good second-order decision makers in which situations.

It is also the case that specific threats are usually not escalated (or not escalated *effectively*) all the way to the level of upper management. This could be because IT management does not like sharing bad news with the organization's upper management and/or does not know how to communicate threats in metrics most relevant to upper management (e.g., financial cost) as well as because upper management finds cyber threat information to be too technical (Ponemon Institute, 2014).

Before moving on, we note that we have been assuming that escalation is initiated by a person lower in the hierarchy ("who") and that the recipient is a person higher in the hierarchy ("to whom"). An examination of our interviews with CSIRT analysts and team leaders does suggest this to generally be the case: In our interviews, the initiator was the person lower in the hierarchy in 51 of the 64 cases that involved escalation and in which it was possible for us to clearly discern both the initiator and recipient. Still, just as the leadership literature (DeRue & Ashford, 2010) has noted a distinction between being granted leadership by others and claiming leadership for oneself, it is possible that, in some cases, the initiator of the escalation is actually the person higher in the hierarchy. Future research should examine why this occurs (a lack of trust on the part of the higher level person, knowledge on the part of the higher level person regarding the high severity or unusual nature of the incident in question, etc.). It would also be desirable to compare this top-down strategy with the more common bottom-up strategy in terms of effects: for instance, success in handling the incident in question, success in handling future incidents involving the same two people, future trust between the same two people, and so forth.

Another important and understudied issue is how the escalation process ends. After second-order decision makers receive incidents, they may finish handling the incidents themselves. However, there are several other possibilities.

Second-order decision makers may instead further escalate the incidents (to third-order decision makers). Alternately, they may instruct first-order decision makers on how to handle the incidents and may then delegate the implementation back to the first-order decision makers. Yet another possibility is that they may handle the incidents jointly with the first-order decision makers.

Our aforementioned interviews with cyber security analysts and team leaders do provide preliminary data on this issue, but, because we had not specifically asked interviewees to tell us how the escalation process ended, it was only possible for us to retrospectively discern this information in 37 of the 64 cases of escalation. Out of these 37 cases, the second-order decision maker (1) handled the incident alone in 28 cases, (2) further escalated the incident in zero cases, (3) delegated the implementation back to the first-order decision maker in one case, and (4) handled the incident jointly with the first-order decision maker in eight cases. These preliminary data suggest that second-order decision makers generally handle escalated decisions on their own. However, additional research is needed to replicate these preliminary findings and to investigate the conditions under which each of the variants is more likely to occur.

What Is Communicated During Escalation?

Formal escalation protocols in CSIRTs often provide a predetermined format for escalation reports. For instance, escalation reports may include the following:

- Suspected date/time of incident
- Detection date/time
- Method of detection
- Incident category
- Current incident classification
- Basis for current classification
- Current status of investigation
- Current mitigating actions
- Potential incident classification
- Basis for potential incident classification (i.e.[,] impact category)
- Estimate of actions/events that may lead to potential classification/impact
- Estimate of likelihood of potential classification/impact
- Notes and/or specific actions required of the [individuals to whom the incident is being escalated]

(UCISA, n.d., p. 205)

Essentially, escalation reports such as these serve to identify the substantive features of the problem using an "ordered list" format (von Winterfeldt, 1980, p. 73). Future research in this area could systematically examine the utility (versus lack thereof) of requiring escalation reports to contain each of the forms of advice discussed by previous researchers (Dalal & Bonaccio, 2010): For instance, information about options that is primarily descriptive rather than evaluative (i.e., information that does not explicitly prescribe or proscribe options), recommendations in favor of one or more options, recommendations against one or more options, and recommendations about decision process (i.e., recommendations about how the decision maker should go about making the decision). Preliminary evidence from judge–advisor systems using hypothetical decision scenarios in the laboratory (Dalal & Bonaccio, 2010) suggests that decision makers appreciate all forms of advice[3] but that they prefer nonevaluative information to evaluative recommendations[4] and that there is a slight tendency for diminishing returns when multiple types of advice are provided simultaneously. However, additional research is needed to determine whether this preference for information over recommendations will extend to second-order decision makers in highly time-constrained field settings.

Because escalation reports often include subjective probability judgments—for example, "Estimate of likelihood of potential classification/impact" (UCISA, n.d., p. 205)—and because research suggests that even expert decision makers and advisors are often highly overconfident in such judgments (e.g., Russo & Schoemaker, 1992), the escalation report itself may provide a good vehicle for implementing ways of reducing overconfidence, such as the aforementioned pre-mortem (Klein, 2007). This would involve the first-order decision maker briefly indicating ways in which he or she thinks the incident could be handled *badly*. Previous research using individual decision makers suggests that pre-mortems are successful in reducing overconfidence (Klein, 2007). An escalation context, due to the multiple decision makers involved, has the potential to provide an even greater effect by reducing overconfidence in both the first-order and second-order decision makers.

When Does Escalation Occur?

The severity of an incident may determine when escalation occurs. For instance, very serious incidents may be escalated immediately, whereas less serious incidents may be escalated after more investigation (e.g., after determining whether a breach involves personal data), and very minor incidents may not be escalated at all but, rather, may be the subject of periodic reporting (UCISA, n.d.). Thus, the timing of escalation may follow psychological ideas regarding "strong situations" (Meyer, Dalal, & Hermida, 2010): There may be less personal discretion—and therefore less room for personality factors to play a role—when the stakes are high. Future research should test this idea by examining whether the impact of personality factors (such as dependent decision-making style; Scott & Bruce, 1995) on the timing of escalation differs as a function of the severity of the incident in the manner suggested earlier.

It is important to note that the previous discussion of the content of the escalation report may also have implications for the timing of escalation. For instance, if first-order decision makers are expected only to provide nonevaluative information, they are likely to be able to escalate more rapidly than they will be if they are additionally expected to provide recommendations in favor of and against various options as well as recommendations regarding how to proceed. CSIRTs will need to consider whether quicker escalations focusing primarily on description are more or less useful than slower escalations focusing on both description and evaluation. This is a complex issue, because the answer probably depends on a variety of other factors, including the expertise levels of the first-order and second-order decision makers. For instance, a recommendation from an inexperienced first-order decision maker may not be particularly useful to a veteran second-order decision maker—and, therefore, such a situation may call for quicker escalations focusing primarily on description.

The issue of the timing of escalation is further complicated by the fact that escalation may not be a one-time event. The first-order decision maker may provide an update when the status of the incident changes (UCISA, n.d.). The second-order decision maker may request clarification or additional information. The second-order decision maker may also instruct the first-order decision maker on how to handle the incident, and he or she may then delegate the implementation back to the first-order decision maker. Therefore, although initial laboratory studies of escalation may begin by studying the simpler case of one-time escalation, escalation research will eventually need to account for the seemingly iterative nature of escalation.

What Are the Results of Escalation?

Ultimately, escalation should facilitate the functioning of the CSIRT. This means that future research on escalation should use CSIRT performance as criteria (i.e., dependent variables) of interest. An in-depth treatment of CSIRT performance is beyond the scope of this chapter. But, in brief, CSIRT performance can (1) be thought of as having both reactive and proactive components;[5] (2) be studied at the individual, team (i.e., within-team), and multiteam system (i.e., between-team) levels of analysis; and (3) consist of outcomes (assessing effectiveness), behavior (assessing execution), and processes (assessing planning).

Of primary (though not sole) interest in the study of escalation is reactive performance at the team and multiteam system levels of analysis, as operationalized by effectiveness outcomes. It is more important for research on escalation to study reactive performance than proactive performance, because escalation by definition occurs in the context of incident *response*. It is likewise more important to study the team and multiteam system levels of analysis than the individual analyst level of analysis, because escalation, as we have defined it, involves more than one analyst within an incident response team or multiteam system. Finally, it is more important to study effectiveness outcomes than execution behavior or planning processes, because effectiveness outcomes reflect the end products of CSIRT activities and because many of these outcomes can be measured objectively.

Within the category of reactive effectiveness outcomes at the team and multi-team system levels, several specific outcomes can be studied in research on escalation. A complete listing of these is beyond the scope of this chapter, but we provide a few examples. One subcategory of outcomes, of course, represents outcomes related to the effectiveness with which the team completes its core tasks. This subcategory includes outcomes such as solution quantity (e.g., the speed with which the team handled an incident, perhaps as a function of the severity of the incident) and solution quality (e.g., client/customer ratings of the extent to which the team's handling of an incident was comprehensive and innovative).

However, escalation researchers should also consider other types of outcomes: for instance, cognitive, affective (emotional), and reputational outcomes. An example of a *cognitive* outcome is knowledge and skill acquisition by team members (which can be measured objectively via knowledge tests). In the context of escalation, this outcome may reflect the extent to which second-order decision makers use escalation as a vehicle not only for incident handling but also for providing developmental feedback to first-order decision makers. An example of an *affective* outcome is client/customer satisfaction with the CSIRT. An example of a *reputational* outcome is media reports of security breaches involving the CSIRT client/customer. In our interviews, members of various types of CSIRTs often noted that they considered bad publicity in the media to be the ultimate indicator of their CSIRT's (in)effectiveness.

The Road Ahead

Because escalation has thus far rarely been studied as a decision-making structure, research opportunities abound—and future research has the potential to simultaneously make large contributions to scientific understanding and to practical application. The following is a preliminary list of research questions that arise from previous sections of this chapter:

- Which organizational settings are characterized by escalation decision making? For instance, how common is escalation in settings other than incident response?
- Overall, what proportion of incident response decisions can be characterized by the escalation decision-making structure? And how does this proportion compare with the proportion of decisions that are better characterized by other decision-making structures (e.g., the judge–advisor system)?
    o Under conditions in which multiple decision-making structures are possible for a given employee in a particular case, what factors determine which decision-making structure will be used?
- Our examination of escalation protocols and our interviews with CSIRT members both suggest that escalation is typically initiated by the employee

lower in the hierarchy. But might other research methods (e.g., observations during regular CSIRT functioning) indicate that escalation is initiated more often than popularly believed by the employee higher in the hierarchy (e.g., a higher-level employee "yanking" an incident from a lower level employee)?
  - All else being equal, does the effectiveness of escalation depend on whether it is initiated by the lower level versus the higher level employee?
- Do first-order decision makers' expertise/competence, confidence, impression-management motives, and dependent decision-making style predict how often these first-order decision makers escalate?
- How does the escalation process typically end (and why)? Do second-order decision makers typically handle the incidents themselves, escalate the incidents still further up the chain of command, delegate implementation back down to the first-order decision makers, or handle the incidents jointly with the first-order decision makers?
  - All else being equal, which of these strategies is most effective (and in which conditions)?
- What is the most effective format for escalation reports? For instance, should such reports consist primarily of descriptive information, or should they additionally include evaluative recommendations of various kinds? Are strategies like pre-mortems useful when built into escalation reports, or do their costs (e.g., in terms of time) exceed their benefits (e.g., in terms of reducing overconfidence)?
- Does the timing of escalation—that is, how soon escalation occurs—depend on the first-order decision maker's personality (e.g., dependent decision-making style)? And, if so, is this more true for less severe incidents than for more severe ones?
- Is escalation typically a one-time occurrence, or is it more accurately described as an episode of multiple but discontinuous instances of communication between first- and second-order decision makers?
  - All else being equal, which of these two strategies is most effective (and in which conditions)?

Several of these research questions pertain to the effectiveness of escalation. However, as discussed previously, the success of escalation can be evaluated in terms of several outcomes—and there is no requirement that these outcomes will move in concert. For instance, decision speed and decision quality may be higher when a second-order decision maker "yanks" an incident from a first-order decision maker, but future intrateam trust and future first-order decision-maker knowledge may suffer as a result. Therefore, to generate best practices (that can, for instance, be used to design escalation protocols) while steering clear of unintended consequences, researchers and practitioners should always consider a relatively complete (or at least representative) set of outcomes simultaneously.

Caveats aside, however, the study of escalation opens up a new direction for decision-making researchers: a road less traveled, if you will. Of course, as we have discussed in this chapter, research on escalation can be informed by research on other, more studied decision-making structures. However, research on escalation can also *inform* research on the other decision-making structures. For instance, research on the judge–advisor system has typically focused on a narrow range of effectiveness outcomes (primarily those related to decision quality)—and could therefore benefit from the broader perspective advocated here.

We end this chapter by stating that, in our opinion (1) few important real-world decisions are made by individuals acting completely alone, and (2) few real-world decisions *per se* are made by teams acting consensually (or according to some other decision rule). Instead, we assert that many real-world decisions are made by individuals who frequently request and receive advice from others in the organization: in other words, by a judge–advisor system. We are not the first to make such assertions: Previous research on the judge–advisor system has done so as well (see, e.g., Bonaccio & Dalal, 2006). However, we further assert that many other real-world decisions are not well characterized even by a judge–advisor system. Rather, it is frequently the case that individuals have initial responsibility for a decision but, for various reasons, end up "passing the buck" to other individuals at higher levels in the organizational hierarchy. Such escalation decisions have not yet been studied with any regularity in the academic literature. We believe that future research will vindicate our belief that the escalation decision-making structure, together with the judge–advisor system, characterizes the majority of important real-world decisions. This chapter has therefore aimed to catalyze research in this important but understudied area.

NOTES

1 The judgment and decision-making literature (e.g., Sleesman, Conlon, McNamara, & Miles, 2012; Staw, 1981) does study a phenomenon—often adjudged to be irrational by researchers—whereby decision makers continue to "escalate" commitment to a course of action well beyond the point at which objective evidence indicates that this course of action is suboptimal relative to cutting one's losses and moving on. The escalation of commitment to a failing course of action is a very different phenomenon from the focus of the current chapter: namely, the escalation of responsibility for a decision. Although we acknowledge the possibility of confusion among judgment and decision-making researchers, we nonetheless use the *escalation* terminology because of its widespread use in cyber security and other applied settings.
2 "How" could also refer to the specific communication media used (e.g., e-mail, instant message, telephone). For instance, the University of Scranton CSIRT operational standards manual (University of Scranton, Information Security Office, 2009) indicates that escalation should happen via e-mail for incidents adjudged to be moderate in severity but via telephone or in person (through an ad hoc meeting) for incidents

adjudged to be high in severity. In the interest of space, we do not address the issue of communication media any further.

3 An exception involves cases in which the advice is unsolicited, which is not characteristic of escalation decisions.

4 An exception involves cases in which advisors greatly exceed decision makers in expertise, which is not characteristic of escalation decisions.

5 In other words, a CSIRT can perform well not only in response to incoming incidents (reactive performance) but also in its attempts to decrease the number of incoming incidents by, for example, flagging network vulnerabilities (proactive performance).

REFERENCES

Alberts, C., Dorofee, A., Killcrece, G., Ruefle, R., & Zajicek, M. (2004). *Defining incident management processes for CSIRTs: A work in progress* (CMU/SEI Report No. CMU/SEI-2004-TR-015). Retrieved from http://www.dtic.mil/dtic/tr/fulltext/u2/a453378.pdf

Ashford, S. J., Blatt, R., & VandeWalle, D. (2003). Reflections on the looking glass: A review of research on feedback-seeking behavior in organizations. *Journal of Management, 29*, 773–799.

Bazerman, M. H., & Moore, D. A. (2012). *Judgment in managerial decision making* (8th ed.). Hoboken, NJ: Wiley.

Bonaccio, S., & Dalal, R. S. (2006). Advice taking and decision-making: An integrative literature review, and implications for the organizational sciences. *Organizational Behavior and Human Decision Processes, 101*, 127–151.

Brooks, A. W., Gino, F., & Schweitzer, M. (in press). Smart people ask for (my) advice: Seeking advice boosts perceptions of competence. *Management Science*.

Carvalho, P. V., Dos Santos, I. L., & Vidal, M. C. (2005). Nuclear power plant shift supervisor's decision making during microincidents. *International Journal of Industrial Ergonomics, 35*, 619–644.

Dalal, R. S., & Bonaccio, S. (2010). What types of advice do decision-makers prefer? *Organizational Behavior and Human Decision Processes, 112*, 11–23.

Dalal, R. S., Bonaccio, S., Highhouse, S., Ilgen, D. R., Mohammed, S., & Slaughter, J. E. (2010). What if industrial–organizational psychology decided to take workplace decisions seriously? *Industrial and Organizational Psychology, 3*, 386–405.

Daley, R., Millar, T., & Osorno, M. (2011, November). *Operationalizing the coordinated incident handling model*. Paper presented at 2011 IEEE International Conference on Technologies for Homeland Security (HST), Waltham, MA.

Dawes, R. M. (1979). The robust beauty of improper linear models in decision making. *American Psychologist, 34*, 571–582.

DeRue, D. S., & Ashford, S. J. (2010). Who will lead and who will follow? A social process of leadership identity construction in organizations. *Academy of Management Review, 35*, 627–647.

Donne, J. (1999). *Devotions upon emergent occasions* and *Death's duel*. New York: Vintage Books. (Original works published 1624 and 1630)

Doraiswamy, P., & Shiv, P. (2012). *50 top IT project management challenges*. Cambridgeshire, England: IT Governance.

Dorofee, A., Killcrece, G., Ruefle, R., & Zajicek, M. (2007, April). *Incident management capability metrics Version 0.1* (CMU/SEI No. CMU/SEI-2007-TR-008). Retrieved from http://resources.sei.cmu.edu/library/asset-view.cfm?assetid=8379

European Union Agency for Network and Information Security. (2010). *Good practice guide for incident management*. Retrieved from https://www.enisa.europa.eu/activities/cert/support/incident-management

Flinders Ports. (2008). *Emergency management plan*. Retrieved from http://www.flindersports.com.au/pdf/EmergencyManagementPlan.pdf

Gaines, J. H. (1980). Upward communication in industry: An experiment. *Human Relations, 33*, 929–942.

Gigone, D., & Hastie, R. (1997). The impact of information on small group choice. *Journal of Personality and Social Psychology, 72*, 132–140.

Gijsenbergh, F., Nieuwenhof, A., & Machiels, K. (2003). Improving the first link in the chain of survival: The Antwerp experience. *European Journal of Emergency Medicine, 10*, 189–194.

Harvey, N. (1997). Confidence in judgment. *Trends in Cognitive Sciences, 1*, 78–82.

Judge, T. A., & Bono, J. E. (2001). Relationship of core self-evaluations traits—self-esteem, generalized self-efficacy, locus of control, and emotional stability—with job satisfaction and job performance: A meta-analysis. *Journal of Applied Psychology, 86*, 80–92.

Killcrece, G., Kossakowski, K.-P., Ruefle, R., & Zajicek, M. (2003, October). *State of the practice of computer security incident response teams (CSIRTs)* (CMU/SEI Report No. CMU/SEI-2003-TR-001). Retrieved from http://resources.sei.cmu.edu/library/asset-view.cfm?assetid=6571

Klein, G. (2007, September). Performing a project premortem. *Harvard Business Review, 85*(7), 18–19.

Lasswell, H. D. (1948). The structure and function of communication in society. In L. Bryson (Ed.), *The communication of ideas: Religion and civilization series* (pp. 37–51). New York: Harper & Row.

Lord, C. G., Lepper, M. R., & Preston, E. (1984). Considering the opposite: A corrective strategy for social judgment. *Journal of Personality and Social Psychology, 47*, 1231–1243.

Meyer, R. D., Dalal, R. S., & Hermida, R. (2010). A review and synthesis of situational strength in the organizational sciences. *Journal of Management, 36*, 121–140.

Mitchell, A., Schatz, M., & Francis, H. (2014). Designing a critical care nurse–led rapid response team using only available resources: 6 years later. *Critical Care Nurse, 34*, 41–56.

Neely, K. W., Eldurkar, J. A., & Drake, M. E. (2000). Do emergency medical services dispatch nature and severity codes agree with paramedic field findings? *Academic Emergency Medicine, 7*, 174–180.

Nutt, P. C. (2002). *Why decisions fail: Avoiding the blunders and traps that lead to debacles*. San Francisco: Berrett-Koehler.

Pfleeger, S. L., & Caputo, D. D. (2012). Leveraging behavioral science to mitigate cyber security risk. *Computers & Security, 31*, 597–611.

Ponemon Institute. (2014, January). *Cyber security incident response: Are we as prepared as we think?* Retrieved from http://www.lancope.com/system/files/Lancope-Ponemon-Report-Cyber-Security-Incident-Response.pdf

Russo, J. E., & Schoemaker, P. J. (1992, Fall). Managing overconfidence. *MIT Sloan Management Review, 33*(2), 7–17.

Scott, S. G., & Bruce, R. A. (1995). Decision-making style: The development and assessment of a new measure. *Educational and Psychological Measurement, 55*, 818–831.

Shaw, M. E. (1978). Communication networks fourteen years later. In L. Berkowitz (Ed.), *Group process* (pp. 351–362). New York: Academic Press.

Sleesman, D. J., Conlon, D. E., McNamara, G., & Miles, J. E. (2012). Cleaning up the big muddy: A meta-analytic review of the determinants of escalation of commitment. *Academy of Management Journal, 55,* 541–562.

Stasser, G. (1999). A primer of social decision scheme theory: Models of group influence, competitive model-testing, and prospective modeling. *Organizational Behavior and Human Decision Processes, 80,* 3–20.

Staw, B. M. (1981). The escalation of commitment to a course of action. *Academy of Management Review, 6,* 577–587.

Sunstein, C. R. (2009). *Going to extremes: How like minds unite and divide.* Oxford, England: Oxford University Press.

Tversky, A., & Kahneman, D. (1974). Judgment under uncertainty: Heuristics and biases. *Science, 185,* 1124–1131.

Universities and Colleges Information Systems Association. (n.d.) *Resources for Chapter 11—When things go wrong: Non-conformities and incidents.* Retrieved from http://www.ucisa.ac.uk/~/media/Files/members/activities/ismt/Resources%20for%20Chapter%2011.ashx

University of Scranton, Information Security Office. (2009). *Computer security incident response team: Operational standards.* Retrieved from http://www.scranton.edu/pir/documents/CSIRT%20Operational%20Standards%20Manual.pdf

von Winterfeldt, D. (1980). Structuring decision problems for decision analysis. *Acta Psychologica, 45,* 71–93.

West-Brown, M. J., Stikvoort, D., Kossakowski, K.-P., Killcrece, G., & Ruefle, R., & Zajicek, M. (2003). *Handbook for computer security incident response teams (CSIRTs)* (CMU/SEI Report No. CMU/SEI-2003-HB-002). Retrieved from http://resources.sei.cmu.edu/library/asset-view.cfm?assetid=6305

5

INSIDER THREAT IN CYBER SECURITY

What the Organizational Psychology Literature on Counterproductive Work Behavior Can and Cannot (Yet) Tell Us

Reeshad S. Dalal and Aiva K. Gorab

The insider was employed as a systems and network administrator by the victim organization, an internet service provider (ISP). The insider oversaw the operation of, and had complete control of, the organization's entire computer network. The insider left the company abruptly and without explanation. Subsequently, the organization declined the insider's request for back pay. The insider sued his former employer to collect approximately $2,000. Four months after his termination, the insider remotely attacked the victim organization's network on two occasions. The first attack wiped out all data, including all data and configuration settings on 12 machines in the organization's network, temporarily crippling the system for 15 hours. The organization's customers continued to experience sporadic service for several days, causing the organization's business to suffer. The organization took steps to secure its system against similar attacks. Ten days after the first attack, the organization was hit with another electronic intrusion. The second attack erased various operating systems and configuration settings on unprotected machines not previously targeted. Computer forensics analyses revealed that the insider attempted to erase all electronic traces of his identity, but the attacks on the organization's system could be linked to other computers outside the organization that were in use or otherwise controlled by the insider. Among those outside computers was a computer that the insider was surreptitiously controlling as a slave intermediary computer from a remote location. The slave computer was sitting in the insider's former cubicle at a company where the insider had worked prior to joining the victim organization. The insider was arrested, convicted, ordered to pay $118,000 restitution, and sentenced to five months of imprisonment followed by five months of home confinement. (Silowash, 2013, pp. 3–4)

Data from surveys and case studies of cyber security attacks—such as the one in the foregoing example—demonstrate that insider attacks pose a major risk in both government and private industry (Greitzer & Hohimer, 2011). According to a U.S. Department of Defense, Office of the Inspector General (1997) report, 87 percent of all identified intruders into Department of Defense information systems were internal to the organization (i.e., employees or other individuals with access to the organization, such as contractors). In a similar vein, in his 2014 Worldwide Threat Assessment report to the Senate Select Committee on Intelligence, the Director of National Intelligence, James Clapper (2014), stated that "[t]rusted insiders with the intent to do harm. ...will continue to pose a critical threat" (p. 3). Based on yearly Cybersecurity Watch Survey responses from government and private sector firms, *CSO Magazine* (2011–14) reported that although insider attacks made up a minority (22 percent to 49 percent) of all cyber attacks overall, the insider attacks were often more damaging than attacks from external sources. In general, the deleterious impact of insider threat is grave and includes (but is not limited to) the following: damage to organizational or national reputation, financial loss, disruption of operations, decrease in competitive edge, and harm to individuals. Better understanding of the insider threat phenomenon is hindered by the failure to detect (let alone solve) many insider attacks as well as targeted firms' attempts to underreport insider attacks and handle them internally in an attempt to reduce negative reputational impact to the organization (Sarkar, 2010, p. 115; Shaw, Ruby & Post, 1998).

It is perhaps at this stage that we should confess that this chapter was originally intended to be a discussion of what cyber (and physical) security professionals interested in insider threat behavior could learn from the academic organizational psychology literature on counterproductive work behavior: in other words, how basic scientific knowledge could be put into application. After all, as noted by Shaw (2006),

> Lack of empirical data and accepted typologies of insider activity have slowed the development of theoretical and other research efforts designed to advance our understanding of insider behavior, despite the availability of a great deal of anecdotal information. (p. 22)

It seemed, in other words, as though the comparatively large literature on counterproductive work behavior could fruitfully be brought to bear on the problem of insider threat. However, the more we read up on insider threat (e.g., Nurse et al., 2014; Ophoff, Jensen, Sanderson-Smith, Porter, & Johnston, 2014; Posey, Bennett, & Roberts, 2011; Shaw, 2006), the more we became convinced that the extant literature on counterproductive work behavior was already approaching the limits of its potential contribution to the literature on insider threat. In fact, the insider threat literature suggests several "holes" in the extant counterproductive work behavior literature. Filling these holes would serve an important applied purpose by making the counterproductive work behavior literature more useful to the insider threat literature in the future. However, filling these holes would also serve an important basic research purpose by advancing the research literature on counterproductive work behavior and thereby facilitating a better scientific understanding of the phenomenon. Such research, in other words, would be located in *Pasteur's quadrant*, meaning that it would simultaneously enhance use and understanding (the traditional goals of applied and basic research, respectively; Stokes, 1997).

To that end, we begin by formally defining insider threat and counterproductive work behavior and by discussing typologies that have been proposed in each case. We then briefly discuss what the extant literature on counterproductive work behavior has already contributed to the literature on insider threat. Here, we add some nuance that may provide incremental value. After that, we turn to several important holes in the counterproductive work behavior literature that are uncovered through an examination of the insider threat literature—and we suggest ways in which future research on counterproductive work behavior could be designed to fill these holes and, therefore, to be more useful to the insider threat literature.

Formal Definitions and Typologies

Insider Threat

Insider threat refers to any "action of an insider that puts an organization's data, processes, or resources at risk in a disruptive or unwelcome way" (Pfleeger, Predd, Hunker, & Bulford, 2010, p. 170). *Insider* simply refers to an individual with legitimate access to the resources or networks of the organization (Pfleeger et al., 2010).

Multiple approaches have been used to define and study insider threat. The first approach simply outlines the insider actions that pose a threat to the organization without specifying or examining the motivation behind these actions. Consistent with this approach, Theoharidou, Kokolakis, Karyda and Kiountouzis (2005) define insider threat as the misuse of privileges and/or the violation of an organization's information system security policy, which includes both accidental and intentional misuse without differentiating between the two categories.

In contrast, the second approach differentiates between malicious (e.g. information technology sabotage) and accidental insider threat actions, such as naïve or careless use of information technology (Carroll, 2006; Pfleeger et al., 2010; Sarkar, 2010). In addition, based on the motive behind the insider threat, Pfleeger et al. further describe two types of unintentional and four types of intentional insider threat. Specifically, these authors suggest that unintentional insider threat can occur as mistakes (e.g., when individuals fail to pay attention) or lack of knowledge. Intentional insider threat, conversely, can be (1) malicious and externally motivated, (2) malicious and internally motivated (e.g., individual financial needs or wants, retribution for perceived organizational injustice by a disgruntled employee), (3) designed to demonstrate a proof of concept (such as a vulnerability), or (4) based on deception (Pfleeger et al., 2010).

However, according to a third approach, only insider actions that are both intentional and malicious should be considered insider threat (Schultz, 2002). This last conceptualization of insider threat most closely represents counterproductive work behavior—in particular, the more severe forms of counterproductive work behavior.

Counterproductive Work Behavior

Counterproductive work behavior is considered to be an important component of overall employee performance (Dalal, Lam, Weiss, Welch, & Hulin, 2009; Rotundo & Sackett, 2002). *Counterproductive work behavior* is defined as "any intentional behavior on the part of an organization member viewed by the organization as contrary to its legitimate interests" (Gruys & Sackett, 2003, p. 30). Behavior contrary to the legitimate interests of the organization is typically interpreted as behavior that could harm the organization itself or its stakeholders—for instance, employees, customers/clients, and suppliers—and that the organization is legitimately entitled to view as being harmful. Although this definition takes the organization's perspective, it does so within limits: As Sackett and DeVore (2001) note, an organization cannot legitimately expect employees to routinely work 14-hour days or to refrain from leaving the organization for better job opportunities. Counterproductive work behavior is often motivated by intent to harm the organization, but intent to harm is viewed as neither necessary nor sufficient: Behavior intended to harm may not actually result in harm (e.g., if an employee is inept in his or her attempt to harm the organization), and behavior enacted without an intent to harm may nonetheless result in harm (e.g., if an employee has motives other than harming the organization, but harm nonetheless results; Gruys & Sackett, 2003; Spector & Fox, 2005). Instead of intent to harm, a weaker standard is used: namely, that the behavior must be intentional. In other words, accidental behavior—despite its potential to harm the organization—is typically excluded from the domain of counterproductive work behavior.

Several typologies of counterproductive work behavior have been proposed. Here, we focus on the three that have probably been most influential. Bennett and Robinson (2000) make a distinction between behavior directed at the organization itself (e.g., "Discussed confidential company information with an unauthorized person," p. 360) and behavior directed at individual employees within the organization (e.g., "Publicly embarrassed someone at work," p. 360). Gruys and Sackett (2003) discuss several forms of counterproductive work behavior, including theft and related behavior (e.g., "Help another person or advise them how to take company property or merchandise," p. 34), destruction of property (e.g., "Deface, damage, or destroy property, equipment, or product belonging to the company," p. 34), misuse of information (e.g., "Destroy or falsify company records or documents," p. 34), misuse of time and resources (e.g., "Use company resources you aren't allowed to use," p. 34), unsafe behavior (e.g., "Endanger coworkers by not following safety procedures," p. 34), poor attendance (e.g., "Intentionally come to work late," p. 35), poor quality work (e.g., "Intentionally do work badly or incorrectly," p. 35), alcohol use (e.g., "Have your performance affected due to a hangover from alcohol," p. 35), drug use (e.g., "Come to work under the influence of drugs," p. 35), inappropriate verbal actions (e.g., "Verbally abuse a coworker," p. 35), and inappropriate physical actions (e.g., "Make unwanted sexual advances toward a subordinate," p. 35). Spector et al. (2006) also discuss several forms of counterproductive work behavior, including sabotage (e.g., "Purposely damaged a piece of equipment or property," p. 456), withdrawal (e.g., "Left work earlier than you were allowed to," p. 456), production deviance (e.g., "Purposely did your work incorrectly," p. 456), theft (e.g., "Took money from your employer without permission"), and abuse (e.g., "Threatened someone at work with violence," p. 456).

As can be seen from these examples, the typologies include several forms of behavior relevant to insider threat. In one sense, however, these typologies are as noteworthy for what they omit as for what they include: None of the typologies includes an explicit focus on the severity of the behavior. Interestingly, some early work (Robinson & Bennett, 1995) did suggest that counterproductive work behavior varies along a dimension ranging from minor to serious behavior. However, the same authors subsequently (see Bennett & Robinson, 2000) decided to deemphasize severity and to instead include both minor and serious behavior within each category of counterproductive work behavior.

Other researchers have largely adhered to this idea. Consider, for example, Spector and Fox's (2005) list of factors that may (or may not) be considered when describing counterproductive work behavior: whether a person can be the target, whether the organization itself can be a target, whether physical acts are included, whether an intent to harm is necessary, whether the behavior necessarily violates norms or standards, and whether a pattern of behavior is required.[1] The severity of the behavior is notably absent as a consideration: At best, one can infer that serious acts are included in some fashion because not just verbal but also physical acts—for instance, getting into fistfights at work—are included.

We agree that typologies should have psychological meaning and should reflect the extent to which behavior within each category is essentially interchangeable both conceptually and empirically. On the basis of the existing typologies of counterproductive work behavior, it would appear that organizational psychologists have concluded that the severity of behavior does not have psychological meaning and/or that minor and severe behavior are essentially interchangeable within each category of counterproductive work behavior. It may turn out to be true that differences in severity are best thought of as differences of degree, not kind. Still, the lack of attention to severity limits the extent to which counterproductive work behavior research is relevant to the insider threat phenomenon. Moreover, in a subsequent section of this chapter, we suggest why it may be premature—even from a purely basic research perspective—to conclude that severity is not an important aspect of typologies of counterproductive work behavior. These caveats notwithstanding, research on counterproductive work behavior has already contributed insights to the insider threat literature.

What Counterproductive Work Behavior Research Can Tell Us about Insider Threat

The insider threat literature has already recognized, and gleaned certain insights from, the counterproductive work behavior literature. This section describes these insights and provides additional nuance that may not have transferred cleanly across disciplinary boundaries.

Antecedents to Counterproductive Work Behavior[2]

Certain types of employees are predisposed toward engaging in counterproductive work behavior. Research suggests that the dispositional characteristic of integrity predicts counterproductive work behavior (Berry, Sackett, & Wiemann, 2007; Van Iddekinge et al., 2012). This would appear to support the use of criminal background checks and credit scores during the hiring process for positions of trust (e.g., those involving the handling of money or confidential information, those involving work with vulnerable populations, those involving public safety responsibilities). However, other organizational psychology research (e.g., Connerley, Arvey, & Bernardy, 2001; Volpone, Tonidandel, Avery, & Castel, in press) suggests that background checks and credit scores are likely to demonstrate a disproportionately greater negative impact on ethnic minorities, leading to both fairness concerns and legal (e.g., Civil Rights Act) concerns. Firms may therefore wish to instead assess job applicants' personality traits (e.g., conscientiousness, agreeableness, emotional stability), which provide the psychological underpinnings for the dispositional characteristic of integrity (Berry et al., 2007)[3] and also predict counterproductive work behavior well (Berry, Ones, & Sackett, 2007). Importantly, these personality traits do not exhibit adverse impact on ethnic minorities (Hogan, Hogan, & Roberts, 1996), thereby precluding the need to choose between predictive power and fairness. Research on the predictive power of the personality traits of conscientiousness, agreeableness, and emotional stability (though perhaps not research on the added benefit of their lack of adverse impact) has specifically been cited in the insider threat literature (e.g., Greitzer, Kangas, Noonan, Brown, & Ferryman, 2013).

Of course, employees' appraisals of situational factors at work also predict counterproductive work behavior. For instance, employees who are dissatisfied with their jobs and uncommitted to their firms are more likely to engage in counterproductive work behavior (Dalal, 2005). Interventions that, for instance, target stressors are therefore likely to improve job satisfaction and consequently reduce counterproductive work behavior. For example, Greenberg (1990) has found that, compared with an inadequate explanation, a thorough and sensitive explanation for temporary pay cuts will meaningfully reduce employee theft. The insider threat literature has also cited the importance of job satisfaction (often by referring to the *disgruntled* employee; e.g., Greitzer et al., 2013; Shaw, 2006).

At a more molecular level, specific instances of counterproductive work behavior are often triggered by discrete negative events that are a function of stable negative situational factors at work and that are interpreted in light of one's personality (Douglas et al., 2008; Weiss & Cropanzano, 1996). These negative events lead to negative emotional reactions that, in turn, lead to enactments of counterproductive work behavior as a way of "repairing" negative mood (Dalal et al., 2009). The insider threat literature also often discusses the impact of triggering events (e.g., Leach, 2009), though it seemingly has not yet drawn connections to the theories discussed in the analogous organizational psychology literature.

Before moving on, we must note a caveat. Due to the aforementioned lack of research attention devoted to the severity of behavior, little research has been brought to bear on whether severe forms of counterproductive work behavior—for instance, sabotage and physical assault—share the same set of antecedents and the same theoretical mechanisms as counterproductive work behavior *per se*. The prevailing assumption is that they do, but we believe that this is an assumption that deserves further scrutiny, because insider threat is most akin to severe forms of counterproductive work behavior.

Methods of Elicitation

The primary tool for the elicitation of counterproductive work behavior (and its antecedents) is the employee survey. Although some work on insider threat does use employee surveys to detect insider threat (e.g., Computer Security Institute, 2011), cyber security practitioners may be skeptical of the practice of determining the prevalence of counterproductive work behavior by asking employees to rate their own behavior (Shaw & Stock, 2011) and may instead rely on technologically based or indirect detection methods of insider threat, such as linguistic changes in employee electronic communications (Brown, Watkins, & Greitzer, 2013; Taylor et al., 2011). Many organizational psychology researchers have been similarly skeptical of such self-reports of behavior and have preferred to rely instead on "other reports" (typically, ratings by supervisors or coworkers). However, a recent quantitative review of the literature (Berry et al., 2012) suggests that such concerns are overstated. Specifically, the review found that (1) counterproductive work behavior scores are actually higher when assessed via self-ratings than when assessed via other ratings (in other words, people own up to more of such behavior than can be detected by others); (2) self- and other ratings of counterproductive work behavior are moderately to strongly interrelated (in other words, people who rate themselves as performing a lot of counterproductive work behavior are also rated as doing so by others, and vice versa); and (3) for the most part, self- and other ratings of counterproductive work behavior exhibit similar relationships with other variables—and, where they do not, it is self-ratings that provide more added value.

Why might this be the case? Although researchers have rightly been concerned about the fact that employees may be unwilling to respond accurately to questions about socially undesirable behavior, their unwillingness may be tempered by promises that their responses will be treated as confidential and will not be traced back to them by organizational authorities. Moreover, it is important to note that other reports of behavior are hardly a panacea: Counterproductive work behavior is often performed covertly, and therefore coworkers—and especially supervisors—may not have much opportunity to observe such behavior. Other ratings may therefore be based less on specific information and more on general beliefs about the job performance and/or personality of the focal employee: in other words, a *halo effect* (Dalal et al., 2009).

Looking beyond surveys, objective data on counterproductive work behavior can be obtained through electronic performance monitoring data—for example, through analysis of an employee's Internet browsing history, recording of the employee's network activity, use of insider threat–focused (as opposed to externally focused) "honeypots" in internal networks, and even in-depth text mining of the employee's e mail and social media communication (D'Arcy, Hovav, & Galletta, 2009; Greitzer et al., 2013; Spitzner, 2003).[4] However, the organizational psychology literature (e.g., Stanton, 2000) suggests several cautions regarding the manner in which such electronic performance systems are designed and used. First of all, this research suggests that the effects of electronic performance monitoring should be examined not only in terms of performance (including counterproductive work behavior) but also in terms of several other outcomes, such as stress reactions and job satisfaction. Second, the devil is in the detail: Outcomes depend on a large number of characteristics of the monitoring system. These characteristics include (but are not limited to) the extent to which the employee can control the onset or timing of monitoring, how often monitoring occurs, whether all aspects or only some aspects of performance are monitored, whether monitoring is conducted at the level of the individual employee or groups of employees, the nature of the person or group reviewing and acting upon the data gathered, and the extent to which that person or group acts in a considerate manner toward the employee being monitored. Inattention to these characteristics may well result in unintended negative consequences that defeat the stated purposes of electronic performance monitoring. For instance, although the focus of electronic monitoring is often on deterring counterproductive work behavior, research suggests that monitoring is perceived more negatively when it is viewed as a deterrent rather than when it is viewed as developmental (Wells,

Moorman, & Warner, 2007). Greitzer et al. (2013) state that the insider threat literature appears to have been slow to acknowledge such issues, noting, for example, that "two of the most comprehensive books devoted exclusively to insider threat research … lacked any discussion of privacy/ethics/legal considerations" (p. 131).

In our view, this is a mistake. Firms should realize that employees are likely to find certain forms of monitoring (e.g., the use of insider threat-focused honeypots) more acceptable than others (e.g., in-depth text mining of e-mail and social media communication). Firms could focus their performance-monitoring efforts primarily on employees occupying positions of trust. Moreover, firms could consider monitoring only serious forms of counterproductive work behavior (those analogous to insider threat) and could consider communicating that they will do this, as well as the rationale for the monitoring, very clearly to employees. Attempts to deter even very minor and occasional forms of counterproductive work behavior, such as sporadic browsing of news headlines or sporadic social media activity, are probably inadvisable, because in most cases they are likely to yield more negative than positive effects. Specifically, such policies are not only likely to decrease job satisfaction but are also unlikely to boost performance, because they fail to recognize that taking short breaks can restore employees' regulatory resources and thereby increase future performance (Dalal, Bhave, & Fiset, 2014). Just because firms *can* (in terms of technical ability and absence of legal restraints) electronically monitor vast quantities of employee behavior does not mean that they *should* do so without careful forethought.

What Counterproductive Work Behavior Research Cannot (Yet) Tell Us about Insider Threat

Perhaps more interesting than what research on counterproductive work behavior can tell us about insider threat is what it cannot. This is because a focus on these questions would not only facilitate a better understanding of insider threat in cyber (and physical) security but would also facilitate a better understanding of counterproductive work behavior itself. Before we address these holes in the counterproductive work behavior literature, however, we discuss a terminological barrier to entry.

Caveat Venditor: The Large Cost of Small Differences

The organizational psychology literature on negative workplace behavior has had the unfortunate tendency to refer to the same concept using a bewildering array of names—an example of the *jangle fallacy* (Kelley, 1927). Several forms of behavior have been mooted: counterproductive work behavior, workplace deviance behavior, workplace aggression, organizational retaliation behavior, antisocial workplace behavior, and so on and so forth. Small differences have been noted in the definitions of these forms of behavior: For instance, norm violation is a prerequisite for deviant behavior but not for counterproductive work behavior (Spector & Fox, 2005). However, one does not have to be a "lumper" (as opposed to a "splitter"; Darwin, 1919) to note that these are distinctions without differences: After all, the items used to measure these forms of behavior are essentially identical in all cases. The proliferation of labels presents an unnecessary barrier to entry by outsiders, such as cyber security professionals interested in counterproductive work behavior from an insider threat perspective. In fact, insider threat researchers have explicitly criticized the organizational psychology literature for "not [having] a consistent terminology" (Pfleeger et al., 2010, p. 174). Organizational psychology researchers should settle on one label post haste—probably a popular one that has the benefit of being definitionally nonrestrictive (e.g., counterproductive work behavior)—and should then stick to it.

The Role of Severity

As mentioned previously, extant taxonomies of counterproductive work behavior mix mild and severe behavior within each type of counterproductive work behavior.[5] However, there is no guarantee that the structure of counterproductive work behavior at the person level of analysis (in which the focus is on comparing people with each other) will generalize to its structure at the within-person level (in which the focus is on comparing a given person with him- or herself on a different occasion). At the within-person level, it is important to study not only the temporal co-occurrence of various forms of behavior (e.g., Behavior A generally occurs at the same time as Behavior B but not at the same time as Behavior C) but also temporal sequences of behavior (e.g., Behavior A generally transitions into Behavior B, but the converse does not hold; see Dalal et al., 2014).

Of particular interest in this regard is the within-person relationship between minor and severe forms of counterproductive work behavior. Several possibilities arise (Andersson & Pearson, 1999; Rosse & Miller, 1984). One possibility is that minor and severe forms of behavior are relatively independent of each other. A second possibility is that each form of counterproductive work behavior "spills over" into others because of the similarity of their antecedents. A third possibility is that the expression of any form of counterproductive work behavior serves as a sort of relief valve, reducing the need for other forms of counterproductive work behavior. A fourth possibility is that mild counterproductive work behavior "progresses" or "spirals" into more severe behavior. If the first possibility is found to be true, the insider threat literature may be better served by focusing on the research literatures on the more severe forms of counterproductive work behavior, such as sabotage and theft. However, if any of these last three possibilities is found to be true, the counterproductive work behavior literature *per se* is likely to be quite relevant to the insider threat literature.

Future research could therefore test these models (and others) against each other using actual data on the within-person relationships between various forms of counterproductive work behavior, thereby more cleanly examining the role of severity. We would, however, note that, due to the low base rate of high-severity counterproductive work behavior, such research would necessarily be massive in scope, entailing both a large number of research participants and a large number of time points at which the behavior of each participant would be assessed.[6]

Relationship with Unintentional Behavior

As mentioned previously, counterproductive work behavior researchers typically agree that unintentional behavior, though potentially harmful to the organization, falls outside the ambit of counterproductive work behavior. For instance, intentional negligence is considered to be counterproductive work behavior, whereas unintentional negligence is not. In contrast, those interested in insider threat differ on the point of whether unintentional behavior should be included within the ambit of insider threat.

Unfortunately, extant research on counterproductive work behavior cannot help to answer this question. To our knowledge, there is little extant research examining whether traditionally conceptualized counterproductive work behavior can be differentiated empirically (e.g., via measurement techniques such as factor analysis) from errors/accidents. Worse yet, it appears that organizational psychologists have rarely even attempted to develop taxonomies of performance-related (i.e., behavioral as opposed to, say, cognitive) errors/accidents. Indeed, it may be difficult to formulate error/accident taxonomies that generalize across jobs, because the nature of errors/accidents may be highly job specific. We therefore suggest that researchers (1) use task analysis to construct taxonomies of performance-related errors/accidents for jobs sampled from several job "families" and that, for each of these jobs, they then (2) use factor analysis to examine the extent to which these errors/accidents can be distinguished empirically from counterproductive work behavior (and, in particular, from the high-severity forms of counterproductive work behavior that most resemble insider threat behavior). Researchers should, moreover, examine the extent to which various forms of counterproductive work behavior and various forms of performance-related errors/accidents are predicted by the same antecedents (and to the same extent). Such research would finally provide an empirical answer to the question of whether unintentional behavior should be included within the ambit of insider threat.

The Role of Motives

The cyber and physical security literatures on insider threat have devoted considerable emphasis to articulating motives for insider threat—for instance, revenge, the exploitation of opportunity (whether the employee works alone on the night shift, whether the employee oversees money or weaponry, etc.), addiction (Maasberg & Beebe, 2014), and the possibility of financial gain (Casey, 2011; Shaw, 2006; Silowash et al., 2012). In contrast, the organizational psychology literature has focused little attention on motives (Thau, 2006).

A preliminary list, obtained from the insider threat literature (e.g., Casey, 2011; Shaw, 2006) as well as organizational psychology theories of the antecedents of counterproductive work behavior, might include the following motives: harming the organization, violating norms, restoring self-worth, retaliating for real or imagined wrongs, repairing one's mood, gaining control, exploiting opportunity, profiting financially or otherwise, and serving a (perceived) greater good. We call for future organizational research to adopt a more systematic approach. Such an approach would begin by using a clear definition of the term *motive* (see, e.g., Kagan, 1972) and by using this definition to distinguish between motives, on the one hand, and both dispositional antecedents (e.g., the personality trait of conscientiousness) and situational appraisals (e.g., job satisfaction), on the other hand. Next, a comprehensive and definitionally consistent list of motives could be derived by examining existing case studies, organizational theories of counterproductive work behavior, surveys of organizational psychology researchers, and surveys of practitioners in the areas of cyber (and physical) security and organizational psychology. Finally, researchers could determine the manner in which motives in this list cluster together empirically via an assessment of the "proximity" of the motives to each other (Borg, Groenen, & Mair, 2013): for example, by asking people to rate the similarity of the motives or by empirically assessing the co-occurrence of motives in insider threat case studies. If, for instance, a desire to violate workplace norms clusters empirically with a desire to harm the firm, then these should not really be regarded as two distinct motives. Such an approach would yield an empirical taxonomy of motives, which could then be used to predict counterproductive work behavior. It should be noted that severe forms of counterproductive work behavior (those most akin to insider threat) may well exhibit motives that differ somewhat from mild forms of counterproductive work behavior.

The Use of Case Studies

The insider threat literature in both the cyber security and the physical security domains is awash in case studies (e.g., Silowash, 2013). Similarly, case studies—often in the form of legal cases—exist for several other serious forms of counterproductive work behavior (e.g., sexual harassment). Yet the research literature on counterproductive work behavior has not used these case studies except as illustrative anecdotes.[7] We believe that because many of these case studies were the result of investigations into the causes and consequences of specific acts of insider threat and other forms of counterproductive work behavior, an analysis of them can be particularly useful in testing existing models of the antecedents and consequences of counterproductive work behavior. Moreover, because (as we discuss subsequently) there is as yet little understanding of the design and effectiveness of interventions to reduce counterproductive work behavior, an analysis of case studies of interventions targeting counterproductive work behavior either directly or through its antecedents (see, e.g., Greenberg, 2009) would be helpful.

However, we do not advocate the use of single case studies for such purposes. Instead, we advocate the use of a cross-case synthesis via a pattern-mapping procedure in which expected patterns of antecedents are tested against empirical patterns in the body of cases analyzed (Yin, 2013; for an example from the insider threat literature, see Moore et al., 2011). In the organizational psychology literature, such work has been done in the area of voluntary turnover (Lee, Mitchell, Wise, & Fireman, 1996) but not yet in the area of counterproductive work behavior. Yet such work is sorely needed—and it would be fairly easy to do. For instance, empirical patterns obtained from a body of case studies could be used to validate *a priori* models such as (1) the event–emotion–behavior process, as well as the role of dispositional and chronic situational factors proposed in this process, expected for specific instances of counterproductive work behavior on the basis of theories of triggering events (Weiss & Cropanzano, 1996), and (2) the *critical pathway* to insider violations, which describes the expected role of dispositional characteristics, work and life stressors, and attention from management (Shaw, 2006).

The Development of Evidence-Based Interventions

Ultimately, from a practical standpoint, research on counterproductive work behavior would be most useful to the insider threat literature if it resulted in a series of evidence-based interventions: procedures aimed at reducing the prevalence of counterproductive work behavior in firms. Yet methodologically sound research on such interventions—which, in this case, would consist of experiments (i.e., randomized control trials) or quasi-experiments (i.e., nonrandomized control trials) in the field—is almost completely absent. This is more an indictment of the field of organizational psychology as a whole than of research solely on counterproductive work behavior, because most interventions aimed at deterring counterproductive work behavior focus on its antecedents and consequences. Yet there exist very few organizational psychology field experiments or quasi-experiments on improving organizational justice perceptions (Greenberg, 2009), increasing job satisfaction, effecting change in an organization's ethical climate, modifying employee selection procedures to screen out unconscientious job applicants, and so forth. There even exist very few organizational psychology field experiments or quasi-experiments on the implementation and modification of electronic performance monitoring. Perhaps the only area of interventions in which field experiments and quasi-experiments are (somewhat) common is that of stress interventions (see, e.g., Sonnentag & Frese, 2012).

On the basis of the foregoing, it would perhaps come as a surprise to few readers that we endorse field experiments and quasi-experiments on interventions aimed at reducing counterproductive work behavior in firms. However, we would go further to say that such research also needs to examine the common phenomenon of *fade out*: namely, that the effect of many interventions is greatest in the short term but decreases over time (Billings et al., in press; Kühnel & Sonnentag, 2011). Thus, research is needed that compares a variety of interventions in terms of their short-term and long-term benefits vis-à-vis the reduction of counterproductive work behavior.

These benefits would ideally then be juxtaposed with the costs of developing and administering these interventions such that, ultimately, the literature was able to propose a list of interventions with high benefit-to-cost ratios. It is, however, important to note that both benefits and costs may be contingent on a variety of factors (e.g., performance monitoring may be easier to implement for some jobs than for others, some jobs may be easier to redesign than others, the costs of sabotage may be higher in some industries or organizations than in others). Ultimately, therefore, the literature should produce quantitative reviews (meta-analyses) of the benefits and costs of interventions, along with estimates of how these benefits and costs are affected by various factors. Cost–benefit calculations (Cascio & Boudreau, 2010) could then be presented to managers under a range of conditions found to influence these calculations.

Conclusion

We began work on this chapter by thinking that the organizational psychology literature on counterproductive work behavior would be very useful to cyber (and physical) security practitioners concerned about insider threat. To that end, it is in fact true that some of the academic work on the antecedents of counterproductive work behavior has been cited in insider threat publications. However, as we delved deeper into the insider threat literature, we became convinced that the counterproductive work behavior literature, as it stands today, is approaching the limits of its contributions. Therefore, in this chapter, we have discussed several areas in which future counterproductive work behavior research could be made more useful to the insider threat literature. One way of interpreting the current paucity of insights is that it reveals a stark disconnect between current academic research on counterproductive work behavior, on the one hand, and the concerns of practitioners dealing with severe forms of counterproductive work behavior such as insider threat, on the other hand. Although there is some truth to this perspective, we prefer to emphasize a more optimistic alternative perspective: namely, that there exist important opportunities for collaboration and cross-fertilization between these two communities of interest. Moreover, as we mentioned near the beginning of this chapter, filling the gaps in the counterproductive work behavior research revealed by the insider threat literature would also serve the basic research goal of improving researchers' understanding of counterproductive work behavior itself. That sounds to us like a "win–win" situation.

NOTES

1 On the basis of typical definitions of counterproductive work behavior, the answers are yes, yes, yes, no, no, and no, respectively.
2 Two forms of research on the relationships between various antecedents and counterproductive work behavior are particularly informative. Quantitative reviews (meta-analyses) of the literature are provided by Berry, Carpenter, and Barratt (2012); Berry, Ones, and Sackett (2007); Dalal (2005); Grijalva and Newman (2015); Herschcovis et al. (2007); and Van Iddekinge, Roth, Raymark, and Odle-Dusseau (2012). Conceptual models are provided by Douglas et al. (2008); Martinko, Gundlach, and Douglas (2002); Spector and Fox (2002); and—despite not explicitly being billed as a model of counterproductive work behavior—Weiss and Cropanzano (1996).
3 Survey measures that purport to assess integrity directly, as opposed to via personality, are also common. One concern with these "integrity tests," however, is that they are typically copyrighted by for-profit test publishers that may have an incentive for not releasing unfavorable results or, more generally, details regarding the development and validation of these tests (see, e.g., Van Iddekinge et al., 2012).
4 In cyber security terminology, *honeypots* are traps intended to attract attackers and to alert defenders that an attack has occurred (Spitzner, 2003). They could include anything from computers to network sites to Excel spreadsheets to credit card numbers (Spitzner, 2003). Honeypots are typically designed to have no regular or authorized use, meaning that any use is by definition unauthorized and triggers an alert.
5 In this regard, it should be noted that existing research on taxonomies of counterproductive work behavior has run into measurement-related difficulties, possibly as a result of the low base rates and highly skewed distributions of counterproductive work behavior items. We request the indulgence of our cyber security readers, because a discussion of this issue necessarily involves psychometric jargon. Bennett and Robinson (2000) first used exploratory factor analysis to remove items that either had low loadings on focal factors or high loadings on other factors (i.e., high cross-loadings). They subsequently used confirmatory factor analysis on the same sample. Because fit was suboptimal, they then examined the modification indices and re-estimated the confirmatory factor analysis model. Gruys and Sackett (2003) first used confirmatory factor analysis on item parcels. These authors found that the model did not exhibit good fit. They then created composite scores for counterproductive work behavior facets and conducted a principal components analysis on the composite facet scores, concluding—despite somewhat ambiguous results—that there existed a single underlying principal component. Spector et al. (2006) contended that counterproductive work behavior is a formative rather than a reflective construct and so did not conduct factor analyses. We discuss this history of measurement-related difficulties by way of noting that the nondifferentiation of severe from mild behavior in extant taxonomies may not reflect "settled science."
6 We would, moreover, note that because of the importance of time and the within-person nature of relationships between minor and severe behavior, recent research examining these relationships at the level of the person (e.g., Berry, Lelchook, & Clark, 2012) is not directly relevant here.
7 We are ourselves guilty of this, as exemplified by the brief case study with which we opened this chapter.

REFERENCES

Andersson, L. M., & Pearson, C. M. (1999). Tit for tat? The spiraling effect of incivility in the workplace. *Academy of Management Review, 24*, 452–471.

Bennett, R. J., & Robinson, S. L. (2000). Development of a measure of workplace deviance. *Journal of Applied Psychology, 85*, 349–360.

Berry, C. M., Carpenter, N. C., & Barratt, C. L. (2012). Do other-reports of counterproductive work behavior provide an incremental contribution over self-reports? A meta-analytic comparison. *Journal of Applied Psychology, 97*, 613–636.

Berry, C. M., Lelchook, A. M., & Clark, M. A. (2012). A meta analysis of the interrelationships between employee lateness, absenteeism, and turnover: Implications for models of withdrawal behavior. *Journal of Organizational Behavior, 33*, 678–699.

Berry, C. M., Ones, D. S., & Sackett, P. R. (2007). Interpersonal deviance, organizational deviance, and their common correlates: A review and meta-analysis. *Journal of Applied Psychology, 92*, 410–424.

Berry, C. M., Sackett, P. R., & Wiemann, S. (2007). A review of recent developments in integrity test research. *Personnel Psychology, 60*, 271–301.

Billings, D. W., Leaf, S. L., Spencer, J., Crenshaw, T., Brockington, S., & Dalal, R. S. (in press). A randomized trial to evaluate the efficacy of a web-based HIV behavioral intervention for high-risk African American women. *AIDS and Behavior*.

Borg, I., Groenen, P.J.F., & Mair, P. (2013). *Applied multidimensional scaling.* Heidelberg, Germany: Springer.

Brown, C. R., Watkins, A., & Greitzer, F. L. (2013). Predicting insider threat risks through linguistic analysis of electronic communication. In *Proceedings of 46th Hawaii International Conference on System Sciences* (pp. 1849–1858). Washington, DC: IEEE Computer Society.

Carroll, M. D. (2006). Information security: Examining and managing the insider threat. In *Proceedings of the 3rd Annual Conference on Information Security Curriculum Development* (pp. 156–158). New York: Association for Computing Machinery.

Cascio, W., & Boudreau, J. (2010). *Investing in people: Financial impact of human resource initiatives* (2nd ed.). Upper Saddle River, NJ: Pearson Education.

Casey, E. (2011). *Digital evidence and computer crime: Forensic science, computers and the Internet* (3rd ed.). Waltham, MA: Academic Press.

Clapper, J. R. (2014, January 29). *Statement for the record: Worldwide threat assessment of the U.S. intelligence committee.* Retrieved from http://www.dni.gov/files/documents/Intelligence%20Reports/2014%20WWTA%20%20SFR_SSCI_29_Jan.pdf

Computer Security Institute. (2011). *2010/2011 computer crime and security survey.* Retrieved from http://gatton.uky.edu/FACULTY/PAYNE/ACC324/CSISurvey2010.pdf

Connerley, M. L., Arvey, R. D., & Bernardy, C. J. (2001). Criminal background checks for prospective and current employees: Current practices among municipal agencies. *Public Personnel Management, 30*, 173–183.

Dalal, R. S. (2005). A meta-analysis of the relationship between organizational citizenship behavior and counterproductive work behavior. *Journal of Applied Psychology, 90*, 1241–1255.

Dalal, R. S., Bhave, D. P., & Fiset, J. (2014). Within-person variability in job performance: A theoretical review and research agenda. *Journal of Management, 40*, 1396–1436.

Dalal, R. S., Lam, H., Weiss, H. M., Welch, E. R., & Hulin, C. L. (2009). A within-person approach to work behavior and performance: Concurrent and lagged citizenship–counterproductivity associations, and dynamic relationships with affect and overall job performance. *Academy of Management Journal, 52*, 1051–1066.

D'Arcy, J., Hovav, A., & Galletta, D. (2009). User awareness of security countermeasures and its impact on information systems misuse: A deterrence approach. *Information Systems Research, 20*, 79–98.

Darwin, C. (1919). *The life and letters of Charles Darwin* (Vol. 1). New York: D. Appleton and Company.

Douglas, S. C., Kiewitz, C., Martinko, M. J., Harvey, P., Kim, Y., & Chun, J. U. (2008). Cognitions, emotions, and evaluations: An elaboration likelihood model for workplace aggression. *Academy of Management Review, 33*, 425–451.

Greenberg, J. (1990). Employee theft as a reaction to underpayment inequity: The hidden cost of pay cuts. *Journal of Applied Psychology, 75*, 561–568.

Greenberg, J. (2009). Everybody talks about organizational justice, but nobody does anything about it. *Industrial and Organizational Psychology, 2*, 181–195.

Greitzer, F. L., & Hohimer, R. E. (2011). Modeling human behavior to anticipate insider attacks. *Journal of Strategic Security, 4*, 25–28.

Greitzer, F. L., Kangas, L. J., Noonan, C. F., Brown, C. R., & Ferryman, T. (2013). Psychosocial modeling of insider threat risk based on behavioral and word use analysis. *e-Service Journal, 9*, 106–138.

Grijalva, E., & Newman, D. A. (2015). Narcissism and counterproductive work behavior (CWB): Meta analysis and consideration of collectivist culture, Big Five personality, and narcissism's facet structure. *Applied Psychology, 64*, 93–126.

Gruys, M. L., & Sackett, P. R. (2003). Investigating the dimensionality of counterproductive work behavior. *International Journal of Selection and Assessment, 11*, 30–41.

Hershcovis, M. S., Turner, N., Barling, J., Arnold, K. A., Dupré, K. E., Inness, M., … Sivanathan, N. (2007). Predicting workplace aggression: A meta-analysis. *Journal of Applied Psychology, 92*, 228–238.

Hogan, R., Hogan, J., & Roberts, B. W. (1996). Personality measurement and employment decisions: Questions and answers. *American Psychologist, 51*, 469–477.

Kagan, J. (1972). Motives and development. *Journal of Personality and Social Psychology, 22*, 51–66.

Kelley, T. L. (1927). *Interpretation of educational measurements*. Yonkers, NY: World Book.

Kühnel, J., & Sonnentag, S. (2011). How long do you benefit from vacation? A closer look at the fade out of vacation effects. *Journal of Organizational Behavior, 32*, 125–143.

Leach, E. C. (2009). *Mitigating insider sabotage and espionage: A review of the United States Air Force's current posture* (Unpublished master's thesis). Air Force Institute of Technology, Wright-Patterson Air Force Base, OH.

Lee, T. W., Mitchell, T. R., Wise, L., & Fireman, S. (1996). An unfolding model of voluntary employee turnover. *Academy of Management Journal, 39*, 5–36.

Maasberg, M., & Beebe, N. L. (2014). The enemy within the insider: Detecting the insider threat through addiction theory. *Journal of Information Privacy and Security, 10*, 59–70.

Martinko, M. J., Gundlach, M. J., & Douglas, S. C. (2002). Toward an integrative theory of counterproductive workplace behavior: A causal reasoning perspective. *International Journal of Selection and Assessment, 10*, 36–50.

Moore, A. P., Cappelli, D., Caron, T. C., Shaw, E. D., Spooner, D., & Trzeciak, R. F. (2011). *A preliminary model of insider theft of intellectual property* (CMU/SEI Technical Report No. CMU/SEI-2011-TN-013). Retrieved from http://repository.cmu.edu/sei/726

Nurse, J. R. C., Buckley, O., Legg, P. A., Goldsmith, M., Creese, S., Wright, G. R., & Whitty, M. (2014). Understanding insider threat: A framework for characterizing attacks. In *2014 IEEE Privacy and Security Workshops* (pp. 214–228). Washington, DC: IEEE Computer Society.

Ophoff, J., Jensen, A., Sanderson-Smith, J., Porter, M., & Johnston, K. (2014). A descriptive literature review and classification of insider threat research. In *Proceedings of Informing Science & IT Education Conference (InSITE) 2014* (pp. 211–223). Retrieved from http://Proceedings.InformingScience.org/InSITE2014/InSITE14p211-223Ophoff0543.pdf

Pfleeger, S. L., Predd, J. B., Hunker, J., & Bulford, C. (2010). Insiders behaving badly: Addressing bad actors and their actions. *IEEE Transactions on Information Forensics and Security, 5*, 169–179.

Posey, C., Bennett, R. J., & Roberts, T. L. (2011). Understanding the mindset of the abusive insider: An examination of insiders' causal reasoning following internal security changes. *Computers & Security, 30*, 486–497.

Robinson, S. L., & Bennett, R. J. (1995). A typology of deviant workplace behaviors: A multidimensional scaling study. *Academy of Management Journal, 38*, 555–572.

Rosse, J. G., & Miller, H. E. (1984). Relationship between absenteeism and other employee behaviors. In P. S. Goodman & R. S. Atkin (Eds.), *Absenteeism: New approaches to understanding, measuring, and managing employee absence* (pp. 194–228). San Francisco: Jossey-Bass.

Rotundo, M., & Sackett, P. R. (2002). The relative importance of task, citizenship, and counterproductive performance to global ratings of job performance: A policy-capturing approach. *Journal of Applied Psychology, 87*, 66–80.

Sackett, P. R., & DeVore, C. J. (2001). Counterproductive behaviors at work. In N. Anderson, D. S. Ones, H. Kepir Sinangil, & C. Viswesvaran (Eds.), *Handbook of industrial, work, and organizational psychology: Vol. 1. Personnel psychology* (pp. 145–164). London: Sage.

Sarkar, R. K. (2010). Assessing insider threats to information security using technical, behavioral and organizational measures. *Information Security Technical Report, 15*, 112–133.

Schultz, E. E. (2002). A framework for understanding and predicting insider attacks. *Computers & Security, 21*, 526–531.

Shaw, E. D. (2006). The role of behavioral research and profiling in malicious cyber insider investigations. *Digital Investigation, 3*, 20–31.

Shaw, E. D., Ruby, K. G. & Post, J. M. (1998). *The insider threat to information systems: The psychology of the dangerous insider.* Retrieved from http://www.pol-psych.com/sab.pdf

Shaw, E. D., & Stock, H. V. (2011). *Behavioral risk indicators of malicious insider theft of intellectual property: Misreading the writing on the wall.* Retrieved from http://zadereyko.info/downloads/Malicious_Insider.pdf

Silowash, G. J. (2013, June). *Insider threat attributes and mitigation strategies* (CMU/SEI Technical Report No. CMU/SEI-2013-TN-018). Retrieved from http://repository.cmu.edu/sei/741

Silowash, G. J., Cappelli, D. M., Moore, A. P., Trzeciak, R. F., Shimeall, T., & Flynn, L. (2012, December). *Common sense guide to mitigating insider threats* (4th ed.; CMU/SEI Technical Report No. CMU/SEI-2012-TR-012). Retrieved from http://repository.cmu.edu/sei/677

Sonnentag, S. & Frese, M. (2012). Stress in organizations. In N. Schmitt & S. Highhouse (Eds.), *Handbook of psychology: Vol. 12. Industrial and organizational psychology* (2nd ed., pp. 560–592). Hoboken, NJ: Wiley.

Spector, P. E., & Fox, S. (2002). An emotion-centered model of voluntary work behavior: Some parallels between counterproductive work behavior and organizational citizenship behavior. *Human Resource Management Review, 12*, 269–292.

Spector, P. E. & Fox, S. (2005). Concluding thoughts: Where do we go from here? In S. Fox & P. E. Spector (Eds.), *Counterproductive work behavior: Investigations of actors and targets* (pp. 297–305). Washington, DC: American Psychological Association.

Spector, P. E., Fox, S., Penney, L. M., Bruursema, K., Goh, A., & Kessler, S. (2006). The dimensionality of counterproductivity: Are all counterproductive behaviors created equal? *Journal of Vocational Behavior, 68*, 446–460.

Spitzner, L. (2003). Honeypots: Catching the insider threat. In *Proceedings of the 19th Annual Computer Security Applications Conference, 2003* (pp. 170–179). New York: Institute of Electrical and Electronics Engineers.

Stanton, J. M. (2000). Reactions to employee performance monitoring: Framework, review, and research directions. *Human Performance, 13*, 85–113.

Stokes, D. E. (1997). *Pasteur's quadrant: Basic science and technological innovation*. Washington, DC: Brookings Institution Press.

Taylor, P. J., Dando, C. J., Ormerod, T. C., Ball, L. J., Jenkins, M. C., Sandham, A., & Menacere, T. (2013). Detecting insider threats through language change. *Law and Human Behavior, 37*, 267–275.

Thau, S. T. (2006). *Workplace deviance: Four studies on employee motives and self-regulation* (Doctoral dissertation). Retrieved from University of Gronigen, Research Database website: http://irs.ub.rug.nl/ppn/296072389

Theoharidou, M., Kokolakis, S., Karyda, M., & Kiountouzis, E. (2005). The insider threat to information systems and the effectiveness of ISO17799. *Computers & Security, 24*, 472–484.

U.S. Department of Defense, Office of the Inspector General. (1997). *DoD management of information assurance efforts to protect automated information systems* (Technical Report No. PO 97-049). Retrieved from http://www.dodig.mil/sar/972semi.pdf

Van Iddekinge, C. H., Roth, P. L., Raymark, P. H., & Odle-Dusseau, H. N. (2012). The criterion-related validity of integrity tests: An updated meta-analysis. *Journal of Applied Psychology, 97*, 499–530.

Volpone, S. D., Tonidandel, S., Avery, D. R., & Castel, S. (in press). Exploring the use of credit scores in selection processes: Beware of adverse impact. *Journal of Business and Psychology*.

Weiss, H. M., & Cropanzano, R. (1996). Affective events theory: A theoretical discussion of the causes and consequences of affective experiences at work. In B. M. Staw & L. L. Cummings (Eds.), *Research in Organizational Behavior* (Vol. 18, pp. 1–74). Greenwich, CT: JAI Press.

Wells, D. L., Moorman, R. H., & Werner, J. M. (2007). The impact of the perceived purpose of electronic performance monitoring on an array of attitudinal variables. *Human Resource Development Quarterly, 18*, 121–138.

Yin, R. K. (2013). *Case study research: Design and methods* (5th ed.). Thousand Oaks, CA: Sage.

6

CREATIVITY AND INNOVATION IN CYBER SECURITY WORK[1]

Julie A. Steinke, Laura Fletcher, Qikun Niu, and Lois E. Tetrick

Cyber security is a relatively new field that involves the protection of organizations' assets from harm or loss through digital technologies. Organizational assets can include connected computing devices, personnel, infrastructure, technology applications, services, telecommunication systems, and all of the transmitted and stored information in the cyber environment. Therefore, cyber security includes organizational policies and practices relative to the cyber environment aimed at protecting the assets of the system's users and the organization, including various security concepts, security safeguards, and risk-management approaches. Despite these technologies and tools, a major challenge facing cyber security is the potential for attacks from a variety of sources. These potential attacks create an ever-changing work environment that challenges cyber security analysts to stay one step ahead of those trying to infiltrate their systems (e.g., hackers).

In order to keep hackers at bay, cyber security workers not only must successfully react and respond to a range of problems posed by hackers but also must proactively design innovative systems or tools that prohibit hackers from breaking through in the first place. Thus, effective cyber security work can be dependent upon workers' abilities to be creative and innovative problem-solvers in an attempt to remain adaptable to their ever-changing work demands. In fact, a report published by the National Academies Press (Blumenthal, Inouye, & Mitchell, 2003) on information technology (IT), creativity, and innovation stated that many in the IT field might think "that the keys ... are simply equipment and software—developing and providing access to standard, commercial IT tools" and that "this perspective ... is an insufficiently rich or flexible one" (p. 3) that would benefit from the merging of technical and creative considerations. In addition, behavioral science perspectives, such as those from the viewpoint of organizational psychology, provide insights into how individual characteristics and various processes (e.g., cognitions, behaviors) impact creativity and innovation in the workplace. Throughout this chapter, we aim to provide a framework for conceptualizing creativity and innovation from an organizational psychology perspective within the domain of cyber security work. Our framework has two primary goals: (1) to enhance the development of cyber security incident response team (CSIRT) analysts' creative problem-solving skills and (2) to elaborate ways that the incident-handling process can benefit from creative problem-solving.

We begin with a review of the nature of cyber security work and research on creativity and innovation. We then provide insights into how the cyber security domain can foster creativity and innovation among cyber security workers, with a particular focus on the role of CSIRT analysts as creative problem-solvers. The chapter concludes with considerations for future research on creativity, innovation, and creative problem-solving within the cyber security domain.

The Cyber Security Domain

Due to the increasing demand for effective cyber security, the National Institute of Standards and Technology (NIST) began the National Initiative for Cybersecurity Education (NICE) to cultivate an effective cyber security workforce in the United States. The subsequently developed NICE framework defined cyber security work and workers using a common lexicon that placed specialty areas of cyber security work into seven categories that describe a wide variety of incident response–related tasks: securely provision, analyze, operate and maintain, protect and defend, investigate, collect information, and oversight and development (U.S. Department of Homeland Security, 2013a). This framework identified unique workload and workforce requirements that were specifically important to cyber security, including being able to expand resources and capabilities in response to prolonged demands (i.e., manage surge capacity); sustain multiple work streams that rapidly occur (i.e., be fast paced); adapt to fundamental changes to technology, processes, and threats (i.e., be transformative); and employ a large number of intricate technologies and concepts (i.e., work in highly complex settings).

In addition, individuals working within the cyber security domain must demonstrate particular characteristics. Our focus in this chapter is on the ability of cyber security workers to be creative problem-solvers, although more in-depth reviews of other characteristics can be found in the NICE framework as well as other chapters in this book (e.g., Jose, LaPort, & Trippe, Chapter 7; Zaccaro, Hargrove, Chen, Repchick, & McCausland, Chapter 2). When cyber threats occur, cyber security workers must be able to shift between a variety of roles (e.g., be agile) and be able to maintain and execute a variety of activities at any given point in time (e.g., be multifunctional). Cyber security workers also must be dynamic in that they need to constantly learn in order to effectively approach new endeavors and problems, often while remaining flexible enough to move into new roles or environments throughout sometimes unconventional work hours or shifts (U.S. Department of Homeland Security, 2013b).

Further, many cyber security workers are members of CSIRTs, which comprise two or more individuals who interact with each other as well as IT infrastructure, other IT personnel, end users, management, and other CSIRTs to provide proactive and reactive cyber security services to support the mission of a defined constituency (Chen et al., 2014; Ruefle, 2007). In addition to their responsibilities of coordinating and supporting cyber events or incident responses (Ruefle, 2007), CSIRTs must effectively manage vast amounts of information that is required to solve unfamiliar, complex problems (Steinke et al., 2015). The environment in which cyber security workers operate is one of constant change that adds complexity to the interactions between CSIRT members (Steinke et al., 2015). The complex nature of these environments have many implications for the ways in which cyber security workers interact and collaborate, which can influence problem-solving by altering who analysts and other CSIRT members might collaborate with and under what circumstances such collaborations occur.

The Case for Creativity and Innovation in Cyber Security

Effective cyber security work is dependent upon workers' abilities to demonstrate creativity and innovation when responding to constantly changing work demands. Many of these changing work demands are the result of hacking attempts, requiring analysts to not only react to hackers' actions but also to take a proactive approach that enables them to remain one step ahead of hackers. In order to remain "ahead of the game," analysts must anticipate new ways in which they might be attacked and attempt to secure those pathways. Thus, analysts must not only take time to know their work but also be able to view that work creatively and see new ways that their work could be attacked by hackers. A CSIRT analyst reiterated this viewpoint while participating in a focus group conducted by a research team involving the authors of this chapter:

> There are specific pitfalls to being an analyst that hackers count on. If I flood you with all the same type of events and then I try to execute an attack in the middle of that, that [attack] looks very, very similar to all the false positives that I'm triggering for your environment. That's what we call cognitive bias, when they look at that. So we teach them to recognize when that type of attack is happening, right, when somebody's counting on their cognitive bias failing them. They recognize this and are able to deal with that mentally. The last thing we want is an analyst watching events scroll by on screen. It's extremely boring, it's a grind. I mean we literally call it "the grind" when you're on console, because that's all you're doing is grinding through events. And so we teach them to approach it differently, to think about it differently than just sitting there grinding through event

after event. If they're seeing events that are closing out, that they're just closing without doing nothing, why? There's no such thing as a false positive on channel. If it's a true false positive, it needs to be presented to the engineers so they can fix it so that false positives are not presented anymore.

Lately, there has been an increased focus on the alignment between creativity and technology (Blumenthal et al., 2003), suggesting that the IT field could benefit from nontechnical approaches to technical work. Further, many cyber analysts are often told to "think like a hacker" in an effort to help them consider other ways to view their work. The focus group conversation mention above continued with the same individual saying the following:

Analyst: One [thing to look at is] the thought processes that need to happen with the analysts when they look at the event. We do not "run book." *Run book* is when, [in] a network operations center, something breaks. They have very specific processes they follow to fix it. We cannot do that. Run books are not flexible. And if our analysts are not as flexible as the attacker, then we're dead in the water. So our analysts have a considerably deep skill set. And this is why we say we train them to hack. We train them to think like [a] hacker, to investigate events the way a hacker would look at an event.

Interviewer: *If I can push that a little bit. So when you say to train them to think like a hacker, what does that mean?*

Analyst: So one of the things that they do during their training process ... one of the very first things they have to do is read a book. It's called the *Psychology of an Intelligence Analyst*. It's a book that all analysts that join [organization] have to read.... It's incredibly valuable and it teaches [them] ... to approach an event as if it's new each time they see [it]. Because it is new each time they see [it].

Hackers must be creative and innovative when trying to find new ways to infiltrate a system. Thus, it is also important for cyber security workers to be creative and innovative in order to combat hackers, because both entities are competing against each other in a continuous cycle. To be effective, cyber security workers must not only screen, select, and evaluate alternative solutions but also generate ideas and transform those ideas into new solutions, a process known as *creative problem-solving* (e.g., Basadur & Basadur, 2011; Buijs, Smulders, & Van Der Meer, 2009). As the competitive cycle between cyber security workers and hackers continues, these two sides are continually embedded in a cycle of creativity and innovation surrounding digital technologies, and in the end, the side that creatively solves the problems posed by the other wins, at least until their opponent develops new innovations that pose further challenges that must be dealt with in new ways, thus starting the cycle again.

Figure 6.1 demonstrates this potential cycle, illustrating how cybersecurity workers (e.g., analysts) and hackers continually interact responsively and proactively with each other. For example, hackers demonstrate creativity when they find new ways to infiltrate networks. In response to these actions, analysts must then use creative problem-solving to evaluate the attacks and develop new, innovative tools and technologies that detect or defend against similar hacking attempts. These actions in turn create new challenges for hackers to analyze, which then inspire hackers to seek new, innovative ways of breaking into similar or new technical systems. The cycle then continues when analysts must again view their work from new, creative perspectives. Creative problem-solving can potentially aid analysts in this approach.

Overall, one thing is clear: Cyber security workers must constantly attempt to deal with novel events that sometimes require novel solutions. Therefore, many workers could benefit from developing their skills as creative problem-solvers, although this viewpoint is not necessarily new to some cyber security workers. Another CSIRT analyst who participated in a different focus group conducted during the same research project supported this viewpoint:

> You can have education aimed towards security. However, we're looking for true security people, and that's more of a mindset than it is something you can teach. You have a lot of certified ethical hackers in this world, and they get security jobs, managing firewalls and stuff. But for our team, we want to find the really creative people, the ones that can actually think outside of the box.

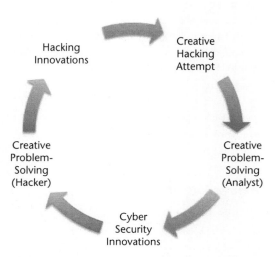

FIGURE 6.1 Model Depicting the Interactive Cycle between Cyber Security Workers and Hackers

The question remains: How can cyber security workers enhance their creative and innovative abilities as well as their creative problem-solving skills to improve their own cyber security effectiveness and, ultimately, that of the CSIRT in which they work? Fortunately, creativity and innovation have garnered a substantial amount of research attention, addressing topics such as conditions that contribute to employee creativity and how digital technologies can enhance individual creativity and influence innovation (Oldham & Da Silva, 2015). Increased attention to these topics might be attributable to the nature of cyber security work, which benefits from the identification of new problems and the development of novel solutions. The influence of creativity has permeated the organizational mindset such that many researchers and organizational leaders have focused on how to promote creativity and innovation among individuals (e.g., Anderson, Potočnick, & Zhou, 2014). For instance, focused attention is often placed on how to design innovative products (e.g., Griffin, 1997) or ways to promote the creative process by establishing policies that enhance the development of environments that are supportive of creativity (Blumenthal et al., 2003; Oldham & Da Silva, 2015). Cyber security defense could benefit from other aspects of this research, such as how to hire and train creative individuals who have the potential to more effectively solve problems in creative and innovative ways. In fact, as the following focus group quote from a cyber security analyst suggests, some individuals actually seek out cyber security work because of the opportunity to be creative and innovative in response to threats, be these new viruses, malware, newly recognized software vulnerabilities, or so forth:

> The reason I joined security, for example, is I used to work in the administrative–engineering department, and they knew very well how to configure a router. But if I asked, "What does this actually do?" they couldn't tell me. And in security, you need to know what you're actually doing, because you can't defend against it if you don't know what it actually does. And that's a very rare breed of people that can teach themselves, that are creative, that are curious, and that's a small market [we] are trying to search.

In the next section, we review research on creativity, innovation, and the process of creative problem-solving. We then provide insights into how cyber security analysts can become effective and creative problem-solvers.

An Overview of Creativity, Innovation, and Creative Problem-Solving

The terms *creativity* and *innovation* are often used interchangeably, though they actually differ. Guilford (1950) referred to creativity as a set of abilities found among most creative individuals that determined whether people could exhibit a significant amount of creative behaviors. In the cyber security domain, these behaviors might be reflected in one individual's ability to develop more unique coding techniques than another. Other researchers (e.g., Mumford, 2003; Torrance, 1966) have viewed creativity as an adaptive process in which individuals notice problems and attempt to seek novel solutions to those problems. An analyst might notice that a specific type of attack occurs repeatedly and might design a new automated system that identifies characteristics of such attacks, ultimately allowing the analyst to focus on other potential threats. In addition, creativity is not characterized at only the individual level but can also involve interactions between individuals, as defined by Csikszentmihalyi (1999), who considered creativity to be "a phenomenon that is constructed through an interaction between producers and audience. Creativity is not the product of single individuals, but of social systems making judgments about individuals' products" (p. 314). In fact, the influence of contextual aspects, such as characteristics of the situation (Mumford & Gustafson, 1988) or environment (Plucker, Beghetto, & Dow, 2004) that are reflected in differences in organizational resources or climate are also considered by some researchers to impact creativity. Thus, creativity and innovation can be demonstrated in individual cyber security work, within a CSIRT team, or within the larger organizational structure.

Whereas creativity involves the generation of ideas that are unique and novel, innovation primarily involves putting those creative ideas into action. West and Farr (1990) defined innovation as "the intentional introduction and application within a role, group or organization of ideas, processes, products or procedures, new to the relevant unit of adoption, designed to significantly benefit the individual, the group, the organization or wider society" (p. 9), and Amabile, Conti, Coon, Laenby, and Herron (1996) defined innovation as "the successful implementation of creative ideas within an organization" (p. 1155). Although innovation requires creative ideas to be generated, it is important to note that those ideas do not necessarily need to be generated among those involved in the implementation. Within the cyber security domain, for example, a hacker might find a creative way to infiltrate a computer network. In response, the analyst who notices the hacker's attempt to access the network could discuss the issue with other analysts, who then could provide a creative solution (e.g., how to develop a new tool to catch similar hacking attempts) that is later implemented by the first analyst. In this example, the first analyst uses the creative ideas of another analyst to develop an innovative strategy that makes the CSIRT more effective and blocks similar future attempts. In any case, the interactive nature of creativity and innovation suggests that an integrated approach to both might work best. In other words, creativity and innovation can work together as a process that results in outcomes and new products that ultimately lead to "new and improved ways of doing things" (Anderson et al., 2014, p. 1299).

In an effort to identify strategies that enhance creativity, several models of the creative process have been developed over the past several decades. Osborn's (1953) seven-stage process was among the first and was later revised into a three-stage model of fact finding, idea finding, and solution finding (Osborn, 1963). Subsequently, the Osborn–Parnes (1967) model of creative problem-solving (reviewed in more detail later) has formed one of the foundational methods used to understand the creative process and help individuals identify novel and creative solutions to existing problems. Puccio, Firestien, Coyle, and Masucci (2006) further elaborated on creative problem-solving as a balance between convergent (i.e., screening, selecting, and evaluating alternatives) and divergent (i.e., generating diverse alternatives) types of thinking and considered this "dynamic balance … the hallmark of [creative problem-solving]" (p. 20). According to these authors, individuals strong in creative problem-solving feel "the need to define problems, generate ideas, transform ideas into solutions, and construct action plans" using both convergent and divergent thinking strategies (Puccio et al., 2006, p. 20). Cyber security workers who use creative problem-solving would demonstrate this process by screening network systems to detect potential security threats and then develop a variety of alternative solutions to those threats, some of which might be novel (e.g., a new software program), in addition to standardized responses (e.g., implementing an existing tool, such as a firewall). In general, creative problem-solving involves the ability of individuals or groups to develop novel and useful ideas (e.g., be creative) that can be applied throughout various processes to ultimately result in innovative developments that are implemented as solutions.

Creative Problem-Solving Models

In this section we review several specific models that focus on creativity and innovation as part of creative problem-solving approaches. It is important to note that many of these models fail to distinguish between creativity and innovation, often using the terms interchangeably, although we attempt to maintain these distinctions.

Because "there is something creative about all genuine problem-solving" (Guilford, 1967, p. 312), many attempts at conceptualizing creativity and innovation center on the creative process, attempting to identify individual differences (e.g., personality traits) that make one creative, or on creative products themselves, which include objects and ideas that are both novel and appropriate for fulfilling necessary requirements (Lan & Kaufamn, 2012). Rhodes (1961) identified four aspects of creativity: people, processes, products, and press. The *people* aspect of creativity refers to characteristics that make someone creative. These characteristics can include personality traits or motivational attributes. *Processes* are the ways people become creative, such as by engaging in collaborative behaviors and communicating with others or attempting to reconceptualize information. Often creativity results in a product, the third aspect. *Products* are usually considered proxies of creativity because they are the end results of individual and group efforts, or what Rhodes (1961) called "an idea [that] becomes embodied into tangible form" (p. 309). However, Hennessey and Amabile (2010) suggested that focusing on creative products is a fleeting attempt that is largely situation dependent. Thus, the fourth aspect of creativity—*press*—reflects how environmental influences might interact with an individual to either help or hinder the development of creativity. Possible contextual factors include aspects of organizations, such as culture (e.g., risk taking, available resources) or even team composition. Many perspectives on creativity, innovation, and creative problem-solving specifically address only one of these aspects, and we summarize them in the following sections.

The People Aspect

Theories on creativity and innovation that examine individual characteristics attempt to identify attributes of the creative person (e.g., personality traits) or influences that promote creative expression (e.g., inspiration). For instance, Guilford (1950) identified the notion of a "creative personality" and believed that creative abilities influenced individuals' behavior and the extent to which those behaviors were noteworthy in new ways. As a result, several personality tests were developed to evaluate individuals' tendency to be creative, such as the Creativity Personality Scale (Gough, 1979), the Torrance Tests of Creative Thinking (Torrance, 1966), and the Wallach–Kogan Creativity Tests (Wallach & Kogan, 1965). In addition to personality, numerous studies have identified factors that can impact the expression of creativity in individuals, including motivations, values, thinking styles, self-concepts and identify, and knowledge and abilities (see Anderson et al., 2014, for a review). Similarly, in a review of organizational innovation literature, Mumford and Hunter (2005) identified four key influences on a person or group's willingness to engage in, and capability for, innovation. Three of these influential factors are individual characteristics—knowledge, dispositional characteristics, and motivation—whereas the fourth factor addresses processes, which are reviewed next.

Creative Processes

Creativity and innovation can involve processes, or progressions of actions that occur when developing and implementing novel ideas (Schroeder, Van de Ven, Scudder, & Polley, 1986). Early process models identified linear progressions (stages) that individuals and groups might move through in attempts to be creative and innovative. A four-stage model of the creative process developed by Wallas (1926) formed the foundation for many of these approaches (e.g., Guilford, 1967). In these models, individuals first begin by conducting preliminary analyses of the problem at hand in order to effectively define the problem (preparation). Individuals then rely on their knowledge and analytical skills to prepare for engagement in effective problem-solving. Once a problem has been identified, individuals unconsciously work on the problem, identifying patterns of associations that prepare them for idea generation (incubation). Eventually, a promising idea might rise to the conscious level and appear as a flash of enlightenment (illumination). At this point, individuals work on evaluating and refining ideas (verification). This process of refinement could involve returning to earlier stages to rethink problems in the initial idea. Guilford (1967) refined this process by suggesting that individuals direct attention once it has been aroused by a problem (filtering) and then cycle through thoughts in which they sense and structure the problem (cognition) before finally generating ideas through convergent and divergent thinking (production). Further, individuals are expected to conduct an evaluation process between each of these stages in which they develop new hypotheses on the basis of available information. Other stage/process models exist, including Amabile's (1983) five-stage creative process model, which also identifies domain-relevant and creative-relevant skills as well as task motivations that might contribute to initial problem identification.

Osborn and Parnes (Parnes, 1967) developed a five-step process model of creative problem-solving that identified mental processes used to develop novel solutions to problems. These five steps are fact finding (discovering relevant facts), problem finding (identifying the problem), idea finding (generating new ideas), solution finding (evaluating ideas), and acceptance finding (putting the idea into action). Many researchers (e.g., Isaksen & Treffinger, 1985) have applied or adapted this process model in order to address potentially malleable aspects of creativity and innovation, such as motivational and contextual influences on the process. Rather than using a strictly linear approach to creativity, many current models now view creative problem-solving as cyclical or continuous processes, with the possibility that some stages occur simultaneously or in differing orders depending on the context or task (Lubart, 2001). As for how this process is reflected in the integration of creativity–innovation, Paulus (2002) suggested that creativity occurs not only in the beginning stages of innovation but also throughout the stages of idea generation and implementation through recursive cycles of generation and implementation. A primary reason supporting this recent approach is that problems discovered in the beginning implementation stage can serve as stimuli that generate new or improved solutions.

Current approaches to creative problem-solving (e.g., Basadur, Runco, & Vega, 2000; Mumford, Bedell-Avers, & Hunter, 2008) model ways in which individuals and groups can be adaptive throughout various stages of the creative process. According to Basadur et al., people possess innate cognitive-processing styles that influence stages of creative problem-solving. Mumford et al. (2008) considered planning vital to the creative and innovative process and described various elements at the individual, group, and organizational levels that assist in the development of successful innovations. Earlier stages of the process are exploratory in nature and tend to occur at the organizational level. These processes involve scanning the external environment and monitoring the internal organization for patterns or trends that could spark creative ideas. Identification of ideas allows for the development of themes or projects to pursue and establishes criteria with which to evaluate ideas as they develop among project teams. At the team level, project teams use planning to identify their required resources (e.g., partnerships) and facilitate a creative and innovative climate. The project team's work process is heavily influenced by the individual level, which includes the impact of leadership, group abilities, and the overall engagement of group members involved with the project. The key to successful innovation is that elements across all three levels of the organization interact accordingly.

Bledow, Frese, Anderson, Erez, and Farr (2009) provided a similar idea of how individuals and groups might engage in what they termed *innovative ambidexterity*, or "the ability of a complex and adaptive system to manage and meet conflicting demands by engaging in fundamentally different activities" (p. 320). This ability represents successfully managing both the exploration (e.g., creating new ideas and products) and exploitation (e.g., production and implementation of those ideas and products) stages. Overall, effective navigation through the creative problem-solving process depends upon the availability of appropriate knowledge and the proper application of strategies during process execution (Mumford, Medeiros, & Partlow, 2012).

Analysts continually face attacks from various hackers who are always looking for new ways to infiltrate technical systems. Once these attacks are identified, analysts sometimes must respond to them by finding new and useful solutions to problems as they occur (a reactive approach). Other times, analysts attempt to anticipate attacks before they occur (a proactive approach). In either case, the understanding and application of creative problem-solving models could prove potentially valuable for cyber security workers. Although many of these attacks might target similar aspects of the system (e.g., the same software program), these attacks are often distinctly different from each other, as one focus group conversation indicated:

Interviewee 1: Most of the team members are very creative, and that's, in my opinion, a very strong aspect you need in any security related team.

Interviewee 2: "Yeah, well, you need a lot of improvisation, because we have like standard workflows for incidents, but they are only on a high level, so it's more like a reminder.... But it's not like, oh, if you have a problem with this system, go and do this, or—because it's too unpredictable....You need to improvise quite a lot. And that's actually what I like most about it. You get to do a lot of stuff you haven't done before.

Interviewer: How repetitive is your work?

Interviewee 2: Not at all.

Creative problem-solving could benefit cyber security analysts because one of their main duties is to solve unexpected problems. If such problems are not anticipated, then cyber security is potentially less effective than it could be for no other reason than it must wait for hacking attempts to occur before they can be responded to. Thus, the ability to identify new solutions to new, unexpected problems could greatly enhance the work of cyber security analysts. In the next section, we attempt to outline how cyber security analysts can benefit from the use of a creative problem-solving approach.

Cyber Security Analysts as Creative Problem-Solvers

The U.S. Department of Homeland Security (2013a) has released guidelines for effective incident response that describe four main phases of incident response: preparation, detection and analysis, containment/eradication/recovery, and postincident activity. The preparation phase reiterates the point that organizations should ensure that their cyber security workers are skilled and have the necessary tools (e.g., hardware, software) and resources for effective incident response. In addition, well-established processes should be in place surrounding coordination and communication throughout the organization. Detection and analysis refers to identifying characteristics of the incident and its underlying root cause. Incidents should be "triaged," which often involves categorizing the type of incident according to type and/or severity and prioritizing it to mitigate the chances that large-scale incidents will develop. Additional information, such as which aspects of the system are infected or at risk for damage, should be clarified as well so that the attack can be properly contained and eradicated and recovery actions put in place.

The third phase of incident response involves actual containment, eradication, and recovery. In this phase, analysts respond to incidents by developing and implementing action plans with the aim to return systems to preincident status. Effective communication is paramount in this phase, because all involved parties should be aware of procedures and their implications.

Many incidents have the potential to be extremely costly for the organization, either in terms of time (e.g., system downtime) or financial costs (e.g., time spent on salaries during incident response; financial repercussions to the organization, such as when orders cannot be taken or products produced due to an attack). Thus, it is beneficial for organizations to conduct some sort of postincident activity survey to review how each incident was handled and ensure that similar incidents do not occur in the future. These activities can be very beneficial in terms of capturing lessons learned during incidents and identifying possible improvements in the CSIRT's incident response process (e.g., software improvements, policy changes). Other types of postincident activities include compiling logs of actions taken throughout the incident response process; conducting evaluations and assessments of technical systems and personnel; and further development and implementation of new or improved procedures, tools, or applications. Throughout all of these phases, creative problem-solving can help cyber security workers address the complicated problems they often face.

Creative Problem-Solving Applied to Incident Response

Although the U.S. Department of Homeland Security (2013a) guidelines help to inform effective incident response, they only focus on technical aspects of incidents and do not expand upon nontechnical aspects of incident response, such as how to improve communication skills or solve unknown problems. In this respect, models of incident response can be expanded to address these missing perspectives. Figure 6.2 presents a model of creative problem-solving applied to cyber security incident response. Consideration of both the technical aspects of incident response (U.S. Department of Homeland Security, 2013a) and the non-technical aspects of creative problem-solving (i.e., people, processes, products, and press/context) provides a solid framework for how cyber security analysts can attempt to solve the problems of unexpected and unknown threats.

The overarching goal of creative problem-solving is to provide individuals with procedures or techniques that will help them use their skills to develop new and useful solutions to encountered or potential problems. These processes are supported by cognitive skills, such as divergent and convergent thinking, that help one generate possible solutions to a problem and then select the most appropriate course of action. Across several models of creative problem-solving, individuals flow through various phases involving problem identification and idea generation, as well as idea implementation, often resulting in innovations.

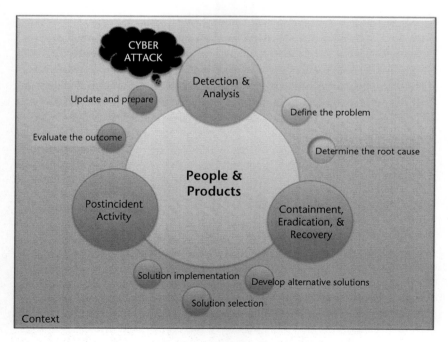

FIGURE 6.2 Creative Problem-Solving Applied to Incident Response

However, sometimes cyber security analysts need to identify problems (e.g., attacks) before they actually appear. To effectively deal with those attacks, analysts must try to generate ideas about what those problems might be and then transform their predictions into solutions and innovations that protect technical systems. Although attacks can be overt (i.e., known or recognized) or concealed (i.e., unrecognized at first), potential problems can arise at any point in this process. For illustrative purposes, in Figure 6.2, we show a problem (a cyber attack) occurring between the preparation and detection phases, based on the assumption that most CSIRTs are proactively attempting to keep hackers from infiltrating their systems by updating hardware, software, and individuals skills (e.g., certifications, trainings). At some point, the attack, real or anticipated, is detected and further analyzed (represented by the medium-sized circle labelled *Detection & Analysis* in Figure 6.2; U.S. Department of Homeland Security, 2013a, guidelines). This phase coincides with the problem-identification phase of creative problem-solving. Aspects of the problem-identification phase are depicted as smaller circles related to detection and analysis. At this point, analysts must define the parameters of the attack as clearly as possible, including determining the root cause of the problem (i.e., source or entry point of the attack). Determining the root cause of the attack is essential to effective cyber security, because often cyber attacks appear to be one type of problem when in fact they are masking other aspects of an attack.

CSIRT analysts can employ specific creative problem-solving techniques when viewing or anticipating problems. For instance, many analysts might try attempting to hack into their own systems through a practice called *red teaming* (Peake, 2003), enabling them to identify potential weak spots in the network or system security and design. Considering how an attack might relate to or affect other parts of the system might also enable analysts to discover unknown relationships between system parameters that could identify unknown sources of entry or undiscovered relationships between systems that hackers could use to their advantage.

In addition, analysts could implement penetration strategies at the beginning of the creative problem-solving process to improve their abilities to plan around problems, which are associated with improved creative performance (Osburn & Mumford, 2006). Penetration strategies like red teaming involve identifying root causes of a problem as well as identifying possible restrictions, resources, and contingencies associated with the problem (Bishop, 2007). Analysts can ask themselves (or colleagues) simple questions like these: "What is the problem?" "Why is it important?" "How do I identify causes that can be changed?" Once these contextual questions have been answered, analysts can identify main causes for the situation, eliminating any causes that are not under the analyst's control or that cannot be acted on due to time or resource constraints, resulting in the identification of target areas that will have the biggest impact for the amount of investment needed to be solved. However, it should be noted that these strategies have not been empirically tested in the domain of cyber security. Thus, how various creative problem-solving strategies influence analysts' abilities to determine incident root causes could be an interesting avenue for future research.

In addition, analysts should be aware that although novel contributions have been found to be beneficial early in a project's lifespan (e.g., when the main goals are to explore the problem and understand it better), researchers (e.g., Ford & Sullivan, 2004) have suggested that once the transition towards executing the idea or proposal begins, any additional attempts to introduce new ideas might interfere with performance and induce frustration. CSIRT managers and researchers would therefore benefit from research that explores the impact of the development of new ideas or alternative root causes at various stages of the incident response process.

Once all aspects of an attack have been identified, categorized, and prioritized, analysts must begin to address the attack in order to stop it and limit any potential negative side effects. These actions occur during the containment, eradication, and recovery phase outlined in the U.S. Department of Homeland Security (2013a) guidelines (again, represented by the medium-sized circle labeled *Containment, Eradication, & Recovery* in Figure 6.2). To effectively perform these actions, analysts must perform two main functions: stop the spread of the attack and prevent further damage by the attack. Many CSIRTs, as shown in Chapter 3—by Bhatt, Horne, Sandaramurthy, and Zomlot (this volume)—and the following quote from a CSIRT focus group, have well-developed strategies in place for handling known, familiar attacks:

> We have a ticketing system....Within our ticketing system and within the infrastructure, there are certain types of incidents that are fairly well defined. A server goes down, a site loses power, somebody loses their laptop, their laptop gets stolen, or there's a virus attack or something like that. These are things that are easily quantifiable and can raise an alert pretty easily, and that's something that gets flagged and doesn't take much in terms of analysis.... There's a fairly standard response for that. We need to work better on what our response is, but those are fairly well defined within the company and within the team. There are other types of threats that require a little bit more analysis, that are not as standard, at least within our company at this point, and also globally.

Regardless of whether an attack is known or unknown, important decisions must be made about who to coordinate with and when.

In the case of novel attacks, processes for incident handling are much less clear, potentially affecting the quality of many of those decisions. At this point, analysts must use the information gained earlier during detection and problem identification to develop solutions. Analysts can use creative problem-solving strategies to develop alternative solutions about ways to contain or eradicate attacks before selecting one or more for implementation, as represented by the smaller circles related to the containment, eradication, and recovery phase in Figure 6.2. In addition, novel solutions might aid in system recovery, potentially involving new insights that lead to system enhancements.

One way to generate possible solutions to identified problems is through brainstorming activities. Although typical brainstorming focuses on producing a large quantity of ideas while individuals react to each others' ideas, Girotra, Terwiesch, and Ulrich (2010) examined processes that improve brainstorming outcomes and found that teams in which individuals first worked independently before coming together as a team to discuss ideas produced the highest quality creative ideas. Thus, after analysts identify a problem (given that it is not a high-urgency problem), they could spend a short amount of time separately developing their own ideas before coming together to share and discuss those ideas with their team. Hunter and Cushenbery (2011) provided additional support for this strategy by claiming that although creative ideas develop from individuals, the actual implementation of those ideas is often a collective and collaborative effort. Thus, individual brainstorming activities followed by team discussions could result in the development and selection of the strongest solution.

In addition, when developing possible solutions, analysts could benefit from the implementation of forecasting techniques. These techniques involve attempts to predict possible outcomes (both good and bad), problems that could occur during solution implementation, and possible contingency plans (Osburn & Mumford, 2006).

Types of creative resourcing—the manipulation and recombination of objects in novel and useful ways to solve problems—might also prove useful to cyber security workers. In autonomous resourcing, a method useful when resources are limited, managers motivate employees to be creative and think of themselves as "creative owners," so they feel responsible for their own solutions (Sonenshein, 2014). Through direction of resourcing, managers demonstrate more direct control over creative resourcing and use their ability to withhold or provide resources as a source of motivation for employees (Sonenshein, 2014). Directed resourcing is useful when more resources are available and can be used to motivate workers to engage in creative behaviors such as play or friendly competition. Although time constraints can provide strong boundary conditions for potential solutions, the more cyber security analysts are able to use brainstorming, penetration strategies, creative resourcing, or other creative idea-generation methods, the more effective they may be in thwarting hacker attacks.

Naturally, effective incident response does not end once solutions have been implemented. In order to truly be effective, some sort of postincident activity must occur. These activities are the final step suggested in the U.S. Department of Homeland Security (2013a) guidelines (again represented by the medium-sized circle in Figure 6.2 labeled *Postincident Activity*) and could take the form of after-action reviews or other methods that involve members of a CSIRT evaluating incident outcomes and identifying other useful pieces of information, such as lessons learned or gaps in existing services, procedures, or policies. By reviewing information gained at the end of incident response, CSIRTs can learn from experience to better prepare for future potential problems (e.g., new types of incidents). For example, once an incident has been contained and eradicated and all systems have recovered from any detrimental effects, the involved team could employ creative problem-solving techniques (e.g., evaluate the outcome, as depicted in Figure 6.2) during an after-action review, in which several questions should be asked about the incident-handling process. These questions could be as simple as these: "What happened?" "What was done well?" "What went wrong (and why did it go wrong)?" "What could be done better in the future?" "How should it be done next time?" Creative problem-solving strategies could be used when developing and responding to these questions. CSIRT members could continue to use techniques such as brainstorming and alternative solution generation to help guide after-action reviews in an effort to produce potential new insights and innovations enabling CSIRTS to be better prepared for future incidents. Thus, the creative problem-solving process could help the incident-handling cycle to continue by providing ways for CSIRTs to update their systems, policies, and so forth in order to be better prepared for detecting future attacks. This notion is evident in Figure 6.2, in which the initial stage of preparation identified in the U.S. Department of Homeland Security (2013) guidelines also serves as the end stage of the creative problem-solving process component of postincident activities, thus continuing the cycle of effective, creative, and innovative incident response.

Research on creative problem-solving training indicates that people who were taught how ideas could be used and how to prepare for implementation of those ideas were able to contribute higher quality, more original, and more elegant ideas (Barrett et al., 2013). Thus, major incidents or problems could be framed as learning opportunities, in which experts within an organization help individuals and teams to understand any mistakes that occurred during the idea-generation and implementation processes. This information sharing would also lead to improved mental models, which have been found to positively impact creativity (Mumford et al., 2012).

Rhodes (1961) and Mumford et al. (2008) suggested that other factors are at play in addition to problem-solving processes. Rhodes suggested that in addition to processes, people (e.g., individual differences), products (e.g., developed outcomes, innovations), and press (i.e., contextual influences) are important to creativity. Mumford et al. (2008) claimed that planning is vital for creativity and innovation because it helps to facilitate new idea generation throughout various processes. These notions are depicted in our model (see Figure 6.2) as we believe that the characteristics of each individual (e.g., personality traits, intellect, technical skills) and the products they use (e.g., software systems, collaboration tools) facilitate various team and incident-response processes (e.g., help analysts with idea generation and planning throughout the creative problem-solving process as applied to incident response). In addition, incident response circumstances can differ from one context to another, and these contextual influences should be considered. Analysts can invoke creative problem-solving not only during various processes of incident response but also when considering characteristics of the people involved, the products used, and the context in which the problem exists. For instance, CSIRT managers can consider team composition when establishing incident response teams so that specific incidents are addressed by teams that comprise individuals with specific characteristics that might enhance incident response (e.g., a member high in curiosity might work well on a team addressing novel incidents, because he or she might be more likely to explore alternative solutions). In addition, products might be used in new or nontraditional methods to solve problems that they were not originally designed to address. Further, once an incident is properly handled, after-action reviews may identify new products that could be helpful if similar incidents were to occur, leading to innovations that expand cyber security technologies.

Future Considerations for Creativity and Innovation in Cyber Security

Creative problem-solving is a potentially valuable tool that could enhance cyber security and CSIRT effectiveness. However, the applications of creative problem-solving in the cyber security domain are relatively new, leaving many avenues of its usefulness unexplored.

Individual Differences

Future research on individual differences in the creative process could be beneficial not only to cyber security but to the field of creative problem-solving in general. Some researchers have examined individual differences, such as the Big Five personality traits (e.g., Raja & Johns, 2010), cognitive style (e.g., Arieli, Goldenberg, & Goldschmidt, 2010), motivation (e.g., Amabile, 1996), and personal values (e.g., Zhou, Shin, Brass, Choi, & Zhang, 2009). However, few such studies have specifically examined the cyber domain. Further, the role of individual differences in creativity has been addressed with mixed success, indicating the potential moderating effects of context. How individual differences might influence creativity within the specific context of cyber security could provide additional insight into creative problem-solving itself.

The Downside of Creativity

Another topic for future research is the assumption that increased levels of creativity always result in more productive and/or innovative work. Although creativity is likely to result in innovations that enhance productivity, there is evidence to suggest that high levels of creativity could lead to negative results. The meaning and impact of creative ideas can differ depending on the stage of problem-solving in which they occur. As previously mentioned, novel contributions could prove beneficial to early stages of a project's life span but might interfere in later stages. Future research that attempts to identify *when* creativity results in increased productivity or new innovations during the life span of various projects might prove useful by helping to identify when individuals can benefit most from creative behaviors.

In addition, Gino and Ariely (2012) have suggested that people who are more dispositionally creative are more likely to engage in unethical behavior, and those who were less dispositionally creative, when primed to be creative, also demonstrated unethical behaviors. These findings suggest that high levels of creativity in cyber security workers, or attempts to increase creativity in workers, might not be in the best interests of organizations. Thus, future research should examine the potential relationship between creativity and other potential negative organizational outcomes such as insider threat. In addition, insights gleaned from this stream of research might provide insights into the psychological differences between cyber security workers ("the good guys" who protect systems) and hackers ("the bad guys" who attempt to infiltrate systems without permission). For example, Gino and Ariely also found that individuals high in creativity who demonstrated unethical behaviors justified unethical behaviors that resulted in their own profit, although they were able to maintain positive self-concepts while doing so (e.g., their behaviors served a better purpose). The "justified"-behavior perspective is sometimes apparent among some hackers, who believe they are exposing protected information for a better cause.

Flow

Future research examining the idea of flow could also benefit the application of creative problem-solving to cyber security. *Flow* refers to a mental state of being in which one is fully immersed in an activity (Csikszentmihályi, 1990). How one obtains flow, as well as outcomes produced during flow, could differ between analysts and hackers. For one thing, analysts are often constrained in their work by shift hours, although they might work longer shifts with less breaks during times when they have to handle large-scale incidents. Hackers, conversely, are free to work at their own pace and, often, on their own schedules. Thus, it might be easier for hackers to attain a state of flow in their work, because they are not constrained by a shift coming to an end. In addition, cyber security workers can also be constrained by policies and procedures, unlike hackers, who may not be bound by or care about such regulations.

In a study of hacker motivations, Lakhani and Wolf (2005) confirmed that the intrinsic motivation to reach a creative flow when working on projects was the strongest motivator and driver of hackers' behaviors. However, flow might not be that beneficial to cyber analysts due to various contextual constraints impacting their work (e.g., fixed work hours requiring handoff of an incident to analysts on incoming shifts). Thus, an analyst might achieve flow but not be able to work long enough to complete the handling of an incident while fully benefiting from that psychological state. In addition, it might be that analysts, compared with hackers, function within a work environment that makes extrinsic motivation more salient.

However, when attempts to handle incidents require longer shift durations, analysts may be more likely to reach a state of flow and could potentially benefit from doing so. Differences in the amount of time to reach a state of flow could have implications for creative problem-solving if individuals who reach that state demonstrate greater tendencies to solve problems creatively. Thus, an analyst's inability to attain a state of flow during a limited work shift could have broader implications for the nature of his or her creative work.

Multilevel Considerations

Finally, the majority of this chapter has focused on creativity, innovation, and creative problem-solving at the individual level. Several researchers (e.g., Anderson et al., 2014; Csikszentmihalyi, 1999; Hunter & Cushenbery, 2011) have defined creativity, innovation, and creative problem-solving as interactive processes that cross levels through the interactions of individuals and teams. Anderson et al. (2014) also pointed out that greater collaboration across these levels could result in recognizable benefits at multiple levels. Such benefits are likely to develop because "innovation—the successful *instantiation* of creative thinking" (Hunter & Cushenbery, 2011, p. 250) is the result of teams that function within broader structures than individuals (e.g., departments, organizations), therefore enabling teams to incorporate information across various levels of analysis (i.e., individual, team, and organizational; Hunter & Cushenbery, 2011; Mumford & Hunter, 2005). Future research should continue to explore creativity and innovation at these levels to determine differences in processes that can be accounted for by level and potential outcomes of creativity and innovation at various levels.

Conclusion

Overall, creative problem-solving provides a suitable framework to help cyber security analysts develop new methods for dealing with novel problems. Enhancing individuals' abilities to see problems in new ways and explore alternative and novel solutions to those problems could increase those individuals' tendency to "think like hackers." Hacking itself is based upon the very notion of creativity, because it involves people trying to gain unauthorized access to technical systems. Therefore, hackers need to seek out novel, and sometimes unconventional, ways to achieve entry into those systems. Our model of creative problem-solving applied to incident response (see Figure 6.2) could potential aid cyber security analysts throughout the process of interacting with hackers demonstrated in Figure 6.1. Although cyber security workers are often problem-solvers who are trained in formal ways, they could benefit from learning how to view traditional methods with new insights and, subsequently, discover potential problems/attacks or solutions to unexpected problems/attacks before these have the ability to cause harm. Ultimately, enhancing cyber security analysts' creative problem-solving skills could allow cyber security workers and the CSIRTs in which they work to be more effective and to achieve the goal of remaining one step ahead of hackers.

NOTE

1 This material is based in part on research sponsored by the Department of Homeland Security (DHS) Science and Technology Directorate, Homeland Security Advanced Research Projects Agency, Cyber Security Division (DHS S&T/HSARPA/CSD), BAA 11-02 and the Air Force Research Laboratory, Information Directorate under agreement number FA8750-12-2-0258. The U.S. Government is authorized to reproduce and distribute reprints for Governmental purposes notwithstanding any copyright notation thereon.

REFERENCES

Amabile, T. M. (1983). The social psychology of creativity: A componential conceptualization. *Journal of Personality and Social Psychology, 45,* 357–376.
Amabile, T. M. (1996). *Creativity in context.* Boulder, CO: Westview Press.
Amabile, T M., Conti, R., Coon, H., Lazenby, J., & Herron, M. (1996). Assessing the work environment for creativity. *Academy of Management Journal, 39,* 1154–1184.
Anderson, N., Poto nik, K., & Zhou, J. (2014). Innovation and creativity in organizations: A state-of-the-science review, prospective commentary, and guiding framework. *Journal of Management, 40,* 1297–1333.
Barrett, J. D., Peterson, D. R., Hester, K. S., Robledo, I. C., Day, E. A., Hougen, D. P., & Mumford, M. D. (2013). Thinking about applications: Effects on mental models and creative problem-solving. *Creativity Research Journal, 25,* 199–212.
Basadur, M., & Basadur, T. (2011). Where are the generators? *Psychology of Aesthetics, Creativity, and the Arts, 5,* 29–42.
Basadur, M., Runco, M. A., & Vega, L. (2000). Understanding how creative thinking skills, attitudes and behaviors work together: A causal process model. *Journal of Creative Behavior, 34,* 77–100.
Bishop, M. (2007, November/December). About penetration testing. *IEEE Security & Privacy, 5*(6), 84–87.
Bledow, R., Frese, M., Anderson, N., Erez, M., & Farr, J. (2009). A dialectic perspective on innovation: Conflicting demands, multiple pathways, and ambidexterity. *Industrial and Organizational Psychology, 2,* 305–337.

Buijs, J., Smulders, F., & Van Der Meer, H. (2009). Towards a more realistic creative problem solving approach. *Creativity and Innovation Management, 18,* 286–298.

Blumenthal, M. S., Inouye, A. S., & Mitchell, W. J. (Eds.). (2003). *Beyond productivity: Information, technology, innovation, and creativity.* Washington, DC: National Academies Press.

Chen, T. R., Shore, D. B. Zaccaro, S. J., Dalal, R. S., Tetrick, L. E. & Gorab, A. K. (2014, September/October). An organizational psychology perspective to examining computer security incident response teams. *IEEE Security & Privacy, 12*(5), 61–67.

Csikszentmihályi, M. (1990). The domain of creativity. In M. A. Runco & R. S. Albert (Eds.), *Theories of creativity* (pp. 190–212). Newbury Park, CA: Sage.

Csikszentmihalyi, M. (1999). Implications of a systems perspective for the study of creativity. In R. J. Sternberg (Ed.), *Handbook of creativity* (pp. 313–328). Cambridge, England: Cambridge University Press.

Ford, C., & Sullivan, D. M. (2004). A time for everything: How the timing of novel contributions influences project team outcomes. *Journal of Organizational Behavior, 25,* 279–292.

Gino, F., & Ariely, D. (2012). The dark side of creativity: Original thinkers can be more dishonest. *Journal of Personality and Social Psychology, 102,* 445–459.

Girotra, K., Terwiesch, C., & Ulrich, K. T. (2010). Idea generation and the quality of the best idea. *Management Science, 56,* 591–605.

Gough, H. G. (1979). A creative personality scale for the Adjective Check List. *Journal of Personality and Social Psychology, 37,* 1398–1405.

Griffin, A. (1997). The effect of project and process characteristics on product development cycle time. *Journal of Marketing Research, 34,* 24–35.

Guilford, J. P. (1950). Creativity. *American Psychologist, 5,* 444–454.

Guilford, J. P. (1967). *The nature of human intelligence.* New York: McGraw-Hill.

Hennessey, B. A., & Amabile, T. M. (2010). Creativity. In S. Fiske (Ed.), *Annual review of psychology* (pp. 569–598). Palo Alto, CA: Annual Reviews.

Hunter, S. T., & Cushenbery, L. (2011). Leading for innovation: Direct and indirect influences. *Advances in Developing Human Resources, 13,* 248–265.

Isaksen, S. G., & Treffinger, D. J. (1985). *Creative problem solving: The basic course.* New York: Bearly Limited.

Lakhani, K. R., & Wolf, R. G. (2005). Why hackers do what they do: Understanding motivation and effort in free/open source software projects. In J. Feller, B. Fitzgerald, S. A. Hissam, & K. R. Lakhani (Eds.), *Perspectives on free and open source software* (pp. 3–21). Cambridge, MA: MIT Press.

Lan, L., & Kaufman, J. C. (2012). American and Chinese similarities and differences in defining and valuing creative products. *Journal of Creative Behavior, 46,* 285–306.

Lubart, T. I. (2001). Models of the creative process: Past, present and future. *Creativity Research Journal, 13,* 295–308.

Mumford, M. D. (2003). Where have we been, where are we going? Taking stock in creativity research. *Creativity Research Journal, 15,* 107–120.

Mumford, M. D., Bedell-Avers, K. E., & Hunter, S. T. (2008). Planning for innovation: A multi-level perspective. In M. D. Mumford, S. T. Hunter, & K. E. Bedell-Avers (Eds.), *Research in multi-level issues: Vol. 7. Multi-level issues in creativity and innovation* (pp. 107–154). Bingley, England: Emerald.

Mumford, M. D., & Gustafson, S. B. (1988). Creativity syndrome: Integration, application, and innovation. *Psychological Bulletin, 103,* 27–43.

Mumford, M. D., & Hunter, S. T. (2005). Innovation in organizations: A multi-level perspective on creativity. In F. Dansereau & F. J. Yammarino (Eds.), *Research in multi-level issues: Vol. 4. Multi-level issues in strategy and methods* (pp. 9–73). London: Elsevier.

Mumford, M. D., Medeiros, K. E., & Partlow, P. J. (2012). Creative thinking: Processes, strategies, and knowledge. *Journal of Creative Behavior, 46,* 30–47.

Oldham, G. R., & Da Silva, N. (2015). The impact of digital technology on the generation and implementation of creative ideas in the workplace. *Computers in Human Behavior, 42,* 5–11.

Osborn, A. F. (1953). *Applied imagination: Principles and procedures of creative problem-solving.* New York: Scribner's.

Osborn, A. F. (1963). *Applied imagination: Principles and procedures of creative problem-solving* (3rd ed.). New York: Scribner's.

Osburn, H. K., & Mumford, M. D. (2006). Creativity and planning: Training interventions to develop creative problem-solving skills. *Creativity Research Journal, 18,* 173–190.

Parnes, S. J. (1967). *Creative behavior guidebook.* New York: Scribner's

Paulus, P. B. (2002). Different ponds for different fish: A contrasting perspective on team innovation. *Applied Psychology, 51,* 394–399.

Peake, C. (2003). *Red teaming: The art of ethical hacking.* Bethesda, MD: SANS Institute.

Plucker, J. A., Beghetto, R. A., & Dow, G. T. (2004). Why isn't creativity more important to educational psychologists? Potentials, pitfalls, and future directions in creativity research. *Educational Psychologist, 39,* 83–96.

Puccio, G. J., Firestien, R. L., Coyle, C., & Masucci, C. (2006). A review of the effectiveness of CPS training: A focus on workplace issues. *Creativity and Innovation Management, 15,* 19–33.

Raja, U., & Johns, G. (2010). The joint effects of personality and job scope on in-role performance, citizenship behaviors, and creativity. *Human Relations, 63,* 981–1005.

Rhodes, M. (1961). An analysis of creativity. *Phi Delta Kappan, 42,* 305–310.

Ruefle, R. (2007, January). *Defining computer security incident response teams.* Retrieved from https://buildsecurityin.us-cert.gov/articles/best-practices/incident-management/defining-computer-security-incident-response-teams

Sagiv, L., Arieli, S., Goldenberg, J., & Goldschmidt, A. (2010). Structure and freedom in creativity: The interplay between externally imposed structure and personal cognitive style. *Journal of Organizational Behavior, 31,* 1086–1110.

Schroeder, R., Van de Ven, A., Scudder, G., & Polley, D. (1986). Managing innovation and change processes: Findings from the Minnesota Innovation Research Program. *Agribusiness, 2,* 501–523.

Sonenshein, S. (2014). How organizations foster the creative use of resources. *Academy of Management Journal, 57,* 814–848.

Steinke, J., Bolunmez, B., Fletcher, L., Wang, V., Tomassetti, A. J., Repchick, K. M., … Tetrick, L. E. (2015). *Improving cyber security incident response team effectiveness using teams-based research.* Manuscript submitted for publication.

Torrance, E. P. (1966). *The Torrance Tests of Creative Thinking—Norms, Technical Manual Research Edition—Verbal Tests, Forms A and B—Figural Tests, Forms A and B.* Princeton, NJ: Personnel Press.

U.S. Department of Homeland Security. (2013a). *Interactive national cybersecurity workforce framework.* Retrieved from http://niccs.us-cert.gov/training/tc/framework

U.S. Department of Homeland Security (2013b). *National Initiative for Cybersecurity Education (NICE).* Retrieved from http://csrc.nist.gov/nice/

Wallach, M. A., & Kogan, N. (1965). *Modes of thinking in young children: A study of the creativity–intelligence distinction.* New York: Holt, Rinehart and Winston.

Wallas, G. (1926). *The art of thought.* New York: Franklin Watt.

West, M. A., & Farr, J. L. (Eds.). (1990). *Innovation and creativity at work: Psychological and organizational strategies.* Chichester, England: Wiley.

Zhou, J., Shin, S. J., Brass, D. J., Choi, J., & Zhang, Z.-X. (2009). Social networks, personal values, and creativity: Evidence for curvilinear and interaction effects. *Journal of Applied Psychology, 94,* 1544–1552.

7
CYBER SECURITY EXECUTIVE LEADERSHIP

Richard Klimoski and James Murray

Introduction

This chapter is written with the goal of describing how effective organizational leadership plays a critical role when comes to promoting cyber security in work organizations. It begins it with the notion that the essence of leadership is influence. Accordingly, when it comes to creating the conditions thought to be instrumental to securing data or key organizational assets, organizational leaders must make use of their capacity for influence to ensure that the right people, policies, programs, and processes are in place.

The focus is on those organizational leaders who are felt to have the greatest responsibility for organizational success and who would have the greatest control over company resources. Inevitably, this leads us to describe the nature, responsibilities, and functions of those individuals who are operating in the *C-suite*. This includes the chief executive officer (CEO), chief operating officer (COO), chief financial officer (CFO), chief information officer (CIO), and chief technology officer (CTO). But here we pay special attention to the title or position of chief information security officer (CISO). Whereas all senior leaders are responsible for creating the conditions that support cyber security, we point out how the CISO can add value to how a firm addresses this initiative. Moreover, as senior organizational leaders, each of the people in these positions must find ways to propagate their vision across levels of responsibility (Fitzgerald & Krause, 2008).

We start with the premise that, to be effective, senior organizational leaders must understand and address the complexity of doing business in today's global markets and be capable of dealing with the uncertainty that this implies. We then show how managing risk is part of this obligation. With this as background, we emphasize the operational and functional requirements for organizational leaders when it comes to promoting cyber security. We note that these requirements must be effectively addressed in some fashion by senior leaders. Moreover, because fulfilling these requirements is often challenging, doing so will call for collective, integrated, aligned, and sustained effort on the part of all of the members of the C-suite. In this regard, we propose that it is the CISO who is in the best position to become first among equals—in effect, leading leaders to do the right thing. If, as they say, it takes a village to raise a child, it will take collective leadership at the most senior levels of the firm to ensure that it has the greatest capacity to protect against cyber threats and/or to deal with the threats that are realized. We see it is likely that it is the CISO who has the right perspective and the set of capabilities to accomplish this.

But we also recognize that the nature of cyber threats will be constantly changing. This implies that those in the CISO position must have the skill mix to be prepared not only to lead in the present but also to address future challenges in this arena. Along these lines, we review what we know about the qualities and qualifications required of today's CISO to be effective as well as those felt to be needed for an incumbent to be able to continue to learn, adjust, and adapt to emerging business and cyber risks. Similarly, we cover the ways that companies or individuals can develop these competencies. In doing this, we highlight the potential value of using both formal and experiential learning opportunities and programs. In particular, we show how an individual who aspires to be the CISO can come to be seen as both competent and credible.

This chapter also recognizes that when it comes to effective cyber leadership, context matters. This implies that such things as enterprise type and scale often present novel threats to or unique opportunities for addressing cyber risks. So too will forces within the firm. As an example, when it comes to cyber security leadership, an executive's location within the company hierarchy and his or her functional position will shape what must be done or how it gets done. Although we cannot be definitive in laying out all such contingencies, we address those that we feel have the greatest implication for how to promulgate or implement cyber security policy, practices, or processes.

Our final section recognizes the dynamic, or even volatile, nature of cyber threats and when leadership initiatives might be called for at the macro level. Thus, it is not enough for senior organizational leaders to be able to react to developments in the larger society that imply cyber threats (e.g., new technology). They must take every opportunity to be proactive, individually and collectively, to shape such things as new legislation, new (technical) standards, and public policy. In all of this, we see the CISO as having a particular role to play. By virtue of his or her technical background, work experience, and leadership capabilities, this individual would be in the best position to identify emerging potential cyber risks and to know where to exert external influence to advantage his or her firm and industry sector, and even society generally.

Organizations and Uncertainty

Most of us would agree that modern work organizations have been designed to accomplish certain goals, whether it be to produce things (e.g., manufacturing), to invent things (e.g., research and development [R&D] labs), or to provide services (e.g., law firms). But many writers have pointed out that for these goals to be achieved, the work arrangements created and the management responsibilities adopted must deal with uncertainty (Katz & Kahn, 1978). Simply stated, there are a lot of things that are unknown. Organization theory has highlighted three sources for this uncertainty (Thompson, 1967). One source stems from the fact that work organizations exist in a larger society. Thus, such things as the dynamism of the economy, shifting political pressures, the volatile nature of the competition, and the need to acquire scarce resources (e.g., capital, raw materials, good workers) will produce challenges, threats, or opportunities for a company. A second source of uncertainty derives from what theorists call the *transformation process*. This refers to uncertainty about how a company takes raw materials (e.g., iron, wood, oil) and converts them into products or services. Some fields understand this well. In other cases, there is more art than science involved. For example, we know a lot about how to produce high-quality steel. We know a lot less about how to ensure that uneducated children (the raw materials for school systems) learn and can come to perform intellectually. The people employed by a firm are seen as a third source of uncertainty. Human nature being what it is, current or potential employees will vary considerably in such things as skills, interests, motivation, loyalty, and commitment to the firm. Some will require a great deal of training or supervision; others will be well prepared and intrinsically motivated to perform. In fact, it is often the variability across such worker attributes that creates the most uncertainty for the company.

To deal with these sources of uncertainty, most companies set up structures, policies, practices, or business processes. But, ultimately, it falls to a class of employees and managers to ensure that goal striving and goal accomplishment can occur with minimal disruption. In light of this, Marion (2014) and his colleagues (e.g., Uhl-Bien, Marion, & McKelvey, 2007) refer to the need for what they call *complexity leadership*. This form of leadership involves seeking out leaders who have a profound understanding of the sources and nature of complexity facing modern work organizations. Marion makes a case that although administrative leadership (e.g., using traditional systems and structures) can sometimes drive business results, in light of an increasingly uncertain world business environment, a substantially new approach to leadership is called for.

These authors' recommendation is to seek out or prepare individuals who can effectively demonstrate "enabling leadership." Enabling leaders will adopt best business practices but can temper such things as the specificity of rules to encourage long-term creative solutions to business challenges. They promote adaptability and resilience. In this view, enabling leaders act "in the interface between adaptive and administrative leadership" (Marion, 2014, p. 194) to foster effective operations. In doing this, enabling leaders find ways to mediate the demands of a volatile business environment and the kinds of company policies and practices that promote both efficiencies and effectiveness.

How might this be done? Along these lines, the writers in this arena offer several ideas. One tool that can be adopted by leaders is to promote appropriate contact and interpersonal trust. This simply means that the enabling leader finds ways to encourage open, formal or informal, interaction among personnel. It also involves removing physical or administrative barriers to the interactions among individuals and groups who must learn from one another to share information. As another example, enabling leaders support process-related conflicts in which "agents differ over how tasks or preferences are to be performed" (Marion, 2014, p. 195). In a similar way, enabling leaders are capable of managing "the diversity of skills, preferences, ethnicities, world views, visions and goals, knowledge and ideas among network participants" (Marion, 2014, p. 195). By behaving in such ways, enabling leaders foster work environments of psychological comfort, trust, and appropriate risk taking. To be sure, these practices are not unique to this framework. Advice on how to enable others can be found in several streams of writing, including work on servant leadership (e.g., Graham, 1991), employee engagement or empowerment (e.g., Spreitzer, 2008), moral leadership (e.g., Travino & Brown, 2004), psychological safety (e.g., Edmondson, 1999), building a culture of trust (e.g., Ciancutti & Steding, 2001), workplace justice (e.g., Colquitt, 2012), promoting creativity and innovation (e.g., Amabile, 1997), and high-involvement organization designs (e.g., Lawler, 1992).

Such an approach to leadership promotes an adaptable and resilient work force, one that can deal with the uncertainty that most modern organizations face with increasing frequency. To put it differently, effective leaders do not shy away from complexity; they embrace it and then go on to create new capabilities for employees such that they too contribute to the building of an adaptive and resilient company (Argote, 2012; Hitt, Keats, & DeMarie, 1998).

Assessment of Business-Level Risk

This section considers the various aspects of the CISO as the enabler of an organization. The management of complexity and trading off of organization and business objectives is central to the risk process. The CISO's characteristics of expert leader, communicator, influencer, business partner, and collaborator are identified, and implementation examples are provided. We begin our discussion with a focus on business savvy and relationship building—key skills for any C-suite professional.

The CISO or cyber executive manager's role in the cyber security arena is truly to be a risk manager and to focus on business-level risks. This executive will align organizational policies and procedures to comply with federal laws and statutes and also to accomplish the corporation's strategic goals. His or her focus will be to enable the organization to achieve its business goals and to enable new ways of doing business to facilitate efficient interactions. The classic management characteristics of communication and collaboration are the executive's greatest tools when focused by an understanding of business strategy and culture.

The CISO, or the executive with a related management title, will inform and translate business-level goals and their related risks. The CISO works within the corporation's C-suite and lines of business to identify enabling technologies and characteristics of an enabling leader (described earlier). Always working in a positive manner, the CISO conveys a supportive and enabling perspective on the business issues being addressed. A lesson learned from past failed practices is the need to ensure that the overall organization views the CISO and the security team as helping to find ways to accomplish business goals rather than being negative or impediments to the achievement of organizational objectives. For example, a policy desired by the cyber leader (e.g., no personal thumb drives can be used for business purposes) often is perceived as an obstacle to getting work done. Finding ways to promote the cyber security goals of the CISO while enabling the achievement of organizational goals is a must.

The CISO and his or her direct reports are uniquely required to be able to understand broad and specific business objectives and to translate the constraints or risks and opportunities of the business level into the cyber security realm. This process requires an embrace of the complexity of federal, state, local, and industry security standards and practices. These requirements are then translated into the corporation's organizational implementations by application of the legacy architectural approaches adopted by the organization. In this translation and interpretation, the CISO and the management team must be experts at providing clear business-level feedback to technology, process, or policy questions and at aiding or partnering with the organization's lines of business in their strategic and tactical implementations. To achieve this synergy within the business, it is essential to establish the foundation of an organizational risk or governance board or integrated product team. This governance body would be chaired by the CISO or the chief risk officer (CRO) and include representation from all key stakeholder groups addressing overall policies and processes and providing templates or guidelines for procedures. Although a governance body is intended to facilitate organizational inclusion and comprehensive decision making, it must enable agile methods and responsiveness at all organizational levels, establishing and empowering a decision-making structure for organizational protection and services.

Within the governance and management structure of the corporation, risk management is defined in three basic levels by a risk management framework, as portrayed in Figure 7.1. The Deloitte Risk Intelligence Enterprise framework is represented as a triangle with the oversight layer at the top, the common risk infrastructure in the center, and the risk processes and risk classes at the base

FIGURE 7.1 Deloitte Risk Intelligence Enterprise Framework

(Deloitte & Touche LLP, 2012). The oversight layer provides the "tone at the top" and is owned by the board of directors, ensuring concurrence across the organization for enterprise risk governance. The common risk infrastructure layer represents the people, processes, and technology elements owned by executive management, the CISO and team, providing risk infrastructure and management. The base layer of the framework identifies the risk process and risk classes owned by the business units and supporting functions that demonstrate risk ownership of the various stakeholders. The overall integrated risk management framework is intended to develop and deploy risk strategies of the enterprise while sustaining and continuously improving the risk environment.

The global reach of cyber threats must be considered not only in multinational organizations but with the growing focus on international cyber espionage. New and more tenacious actors have emerged, with nation and state proxies being well-funded and part of an advanced persistent threat. These emerging risk elements require the CISO to understand international issues, including access to international information technology and cyber law resources, and to leverage industry or governmental collaboration to understand threats and to marshal resources for planning and coordination for advanced preparation, informing the C-suite of revised procedures beyond the scope of the corporation and coordinating with local and federal authorities (i.e., the Federal Bureau of Investigation, the U.S. Computer Emergency Readiness Team, U.S. Cyber Command, and the Financial Services Information Sharing and Analysis center).

Corporations of all types have an increased focus on international law and regulation due to the diversity of suppliers, complex supply chains, and the distribution of sensitive specification. These elements of the supply chain increasingly contain proprietary or confidential data relating to intellectual property for competitive advantage. Even if a CISO has a managed risk environment at his or her enterprise, consideration of an interconnected supply chain with appropriate policies and procedures must be given to the extended enterprise of suppliers, and the protection of data critical to the enterprise but outside of its direct control is of special interest.

In larger corporations, or those doing business with international suppliers, the international laws and requirements for cyber security and privacy may be considerable; these laws need to be considered at the outset of an initiative. Although it is challenging to consider all of the legal and international standards, a key resource for the CISO is his or her chief council and legal staff. Periodic rotation of risk meetings to various locations of a corporation and specific reviews on targeted issues in a country or line of business have proven to be best practices within the industry to ensure a well-rounded perspective.

Privacy Management

Privacy management is often seen as an element of risk management for contemporary work organizations. It typically involves giving special attention to personally identifiable information (PII) and any related privacy data. Privacy management also includes the rights to privacy of employees (or customers) in relation to the organization's rights to monitor communications and employee behavior. As such, the senior leader may use such things as policies, practices, or protocols to ensure that there is a balance. But often issues of privacy protection revolve around the capabilities of information systems and technology to analyze or store information and communications (e.g., e-mail) as authorized or sanctioned by senior leaders. Although this is also within the purview of the CISO for privacy management, it requires special considerations and potentially compartmentalized information. The organization's response can be to create a structure to deal with the complexities and competing tensions within it. For some larger organizations, the competing tensions between cyber security and privacy are dealt with by creating a chief privacy officer role separate from the CISO. In small- to medium-size organizations, an individual or a team will focus on PII and ensure that proper national and international laws are followed, depending on the scope and type of data. Social and cultural norms also need to be considered in risk management so as to align with corporate ethics, standards, and trends. Industry interviews identify a healthy tension between PII data stewards and marketing/sales departments, for example, that want to know everything about a customer so as to identify the most focused subgroup. This tension decomposes to a legal and ethical assessment by the corporations so as to protect and aid their customers while respecting their privacy.

The CISO as Cyber Educator

As a C-suite member, the CISO has a fundamental responsibility to educate and inform the board, other executive leadership, business units, and the corporation as a whole about system risks. The CISO must characterize the dynamic environments across the world, nation, industry, and business sectors. It is the CISO's responsibility to lead cyber risk awareness discussions and education, including efforts directed toward those in the executive suite. A key issue in communications is appropriately informing and not scaring or overstating a case for action to the business leadership. In a 2010 study by the IT Policy Compliance group, only 6 percent of survey respondents correctly understood the cyber threat to their organization, and 90 percent of the respondents underestimated the threat (IT Policy Compliance Group, 2010). The CISO, through industry and technology sources, must be in tune with the measures and metrics for cyber threat assessment at a number of levels. The CISO must promote a solid understanding of the base rate of event occurrence and the forces that might reduce the accuracy of industry threat awareness. As identified by Tversky and Kahneman (1974), there are too many reasons to expect bias in executive decision making. One way to appropriately calibrate the enterprise risk to management is frequently updating and reviewing factual and consistent metrics and measures in a structured manner and correlating them within the corporation and environment.

The risk management process is fundamental to leading an organization in uncertain times. With the dynamic evolution of the cyber security field, risk must be assessed across the whole enterprise in a coordinated fashion. In this regard, one of the initial areas that must to be considered is the current operational requirements for cyber security. Such a focus ensures that there can be a managed migration of security enhancement relative to the current operational baseline.

Operational Leadership for Cyber Security

Different models are available to the CISO of cyber risk management. Most models emphasize the operational aspects of cyber security and give attention to the details of governance, policy, procedures, and methods. This includes a requirement that security audits are routinely performed to assess compliance and verification of those standards agreed upon by stakeholders. In a comparison of risk models and an assessment of governance methodologies, industry practitioners recognize that an organization may select from a variety of candidates. It is recommended that the CISO select the model closest to company culture and processes for integration and adoption.

The supporting staff of the CISO can be thought of as operating in a multi-team environment that spans the organization's hierarchy and supports the technical disciplines required (DeChurch & Marks, 2006). Simply stated, people are arranged in work units that may be team based but depend on the interflow of information and the coordination of efforts across team boundaries in order for both the unit and the larger organization to succeed. Some of the work may be outsourced to consultants for specialized expertise or for periodic and part time participation. The leadership needs to consider points of impact within, between, and across component teams at the strategy and coordinating levels. The CISO needs to carefully select a leadership style that takes into account organizational needs, budgets for resources, personnel and their skills, the maturity of teams, and the ability to leverage capabilities on an interim basis. All other things being equal, it is highly likely that a style that communicates respect for and trust of employees will be more effective than one that appears controlling (Ciancutti & Steding, 2001).

PricewaterhouseCoopers, a major consulting organization, defines cyber security risk management as consisting of the six elements identified in Figure 7.2 (PricewaterhouseCoopers, 2011). Moving clockwise through their model, *security strategy* will set the direction for the organization and needs to be integrated

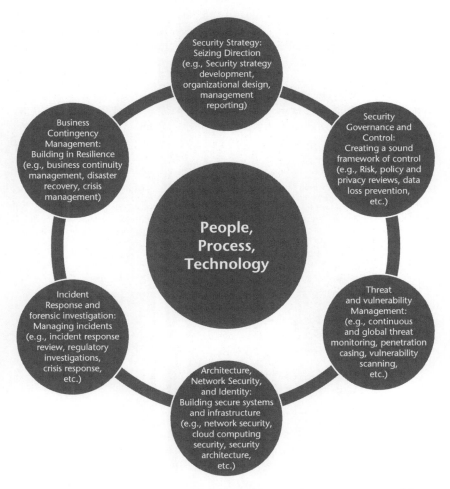

FIGURE 7.2 PricewaterhouseCoopers Cyber Security Risk Management Model

with the overall business as a "plank" in the business strategic platform. *Security governance and control* creates a framework for control and communications in the dynamic and time-critical business function. *Threat and vulnerability management* begins the operational implementation functions managing organizational exposure. The *architecture, network security, and identity* portion of the model describes the details of building secure systems and the infrastructure. *Incident response and forensic investigation* describes managing security incidents, and the final portion of the model, *business contingency management*, is designed to build in operational resilience. Note that operational leadership (i.e., keeping business processes going) is implied throughout the model.

At the time of this writing, the U.S. National Institute of Standards and Technology (NIST) has been very active in producing, revising, and evolving their own set of cyber security standards and guides to aid industry, corporations, and government agencies. The NIST risk management framework is depicted in Figure 7.3; this model emphasizes the process view of cyber security operations and contains both architectural descriptions and organizational inputs for each step in the six-step process (Ross, 2010).

The type of model just briefly described makes it clear that it is the cyber leader's responsibility to put in place a structure that is adapted to the needs of the overall organization and to select the appropriately skilled personnel to follow through and implement these operational governance processes. The form of

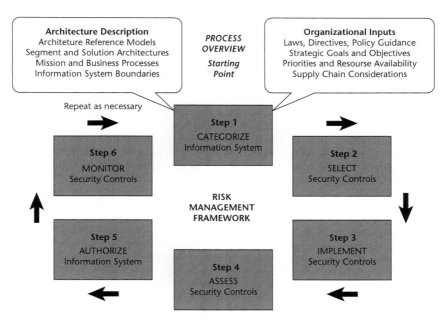

FIGURE 7.3 National Institute of Standards and Technology Risk Management Framework

organization involves components from many departments within corporate internal audit, the CIO's operational organization, or other line of business or business units. Management of the diversity in organizational reporting and functional alignment will test the CISO's abilities as an "enabling" leader managing complexity.

Yet operational leadership is only one functional obligation of cyber leaders. In the next section, we explore additional requirements to be addressed by the cyber leader.

The Challenge of "Defining Victory"

For a cyber leader and member of the executive team, it is important to understand what a successful cyber security leader needs in order to contribute across the organization. In previous, very narrow interpretations, the expectation from the C-suite was for the CISO to fully protect the organization and, thus, *have no security breaches or losses of information* while complying with all federal, state, local, international, and industry regulations. Although this may be a laudable goal, it is not realistic in today's dynamic corporate cyber environment.

Current thinking is for the CISO to participate as a member of the executive management team and to help form and shape a managed risk environment in which the corporation can operate. Usually, this involves a "defense in depth" approach and an agile response plan for incidents (Holmes, 2015). In this regard, today's companies must assess their annualized data-loss exposure, their business downtime, and regulatory audit spending relative to security (these items are addressed as best practices in the chapter summary).

In order to accomplish the goal of having a managed risk environment, the CISO may be held accountable for carrying out the following functions:

- Advise the CEO or equivalent management (COO/CRO) and, ultimately, the board of directors in setting priorities and controlling expectations.
- Collaborate and influence members of the executive team along with the CIO, chief marketing officer, lines of business, CTO, and CFO.
- Lead the security team, which may be composed of components from other parts of the organization.
- Lead cyber education and awareness within the organization and promote continuous learning and improvement.
- Establish a governance, policy, and management approach to enable effective use of corporate resources.
- Engage the industry group and peer companies to understand, characterize, benchmark, and defend against attacks.
- Define meaningful measures and metrics to help quantify and categorize the threats to the organization and assess whether volumes and types are increasing or decreasing.

- Understand and implement cyber security requirements, compliance, implementation, and validation from all sources applicable to the industry.
- Maintain awareness of technological advances and threats/opportunities that the technology may present for the enterprise.

With these in mind, how should a corporation recognize cyber security effectiveness at a managerial level? A concise response might be the following:

- manages programs that affect the corporation's business and reputation in a politically sensitive manner;
- understands the corporation's business objectives and the environment in which it operates;
- acts as a high-level consultant to the executives and upper-level managers on security, legal, and threat issues affecting their programs;
- oversees the corporation's cyber defenses and has programs, procedures, and quality controls (measures and metrics) in place to ensure their effectiveness; and
- efficiently manages the organization and leverages professional knowledge and experience in crisis and is able to respond under pressure.

There are many other criteria and perspectives, which will depend on what is unique about an organization's corporate culture or the particular industry sector it is involved in. For example, a company in a regulated industry (e.g., a financial institution) will have to meet certain compliance requirements or lose the franchise. The cyber security status of publically traded companies is often revealed by the close scrutiny given by market analysts. Those companies that contract with the U.S. federal government will face many specific obligations regarding their cyber security posture. But it could also be said (perhaps somewhat cynically) that victory is often best defined as engendering "no bad press" whereby the CEO must face public scrutiny or even scorn for major breaches of security or loss of personal information.

The next section leverages organizational and industry considerations. These are applied for the cyber security leader in relation to title, organizational position, potential business/industry, and industry factors that affect or influence the characteristics of the position.

Cyber Leadership Demands and Context

Reporting Relationships

Within any organization, a person's title carries with it a number of characteristics that relate to the power and influence of the position in the organization. At what level is the person within the organization? To whom does he or she report: the CEO or the board of directors? What resources does the person control?

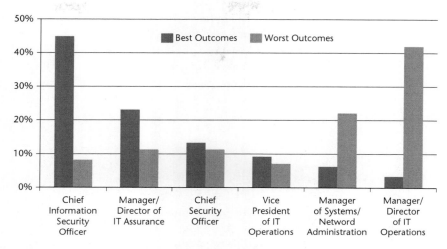

FIGURE 7.4 Information Security Title Related to Outcomes

These carry over to all leadership positions and influence power from political, leadership, social, and technical perspectives (Boulton, 2015; Shumard, 2013).

Reporting relationships appear to make a considerable difference. Figure 7.4 identifies six different titles of individuals occupying a cyber leadership role. As the bar chart indicates by ranking the outcomes of the titles from best to worst (left to right), the information technology (IT) operations positions are at the underperforming or low-performing end of the spectrum. The conclusion that can be drawn from this, and backed up by other industry studies, is that cyber operations should not be placed in an operational organization where the focus is on keeping costs down and economizing on resources (IT Policy Compliance Group, 2010). Also, as shown by IT Policy Institute data, functional obligation matters (IT Policy Compliance Group, 2010). Cyber leadership in IT will differ from its manifestations in marketing, finance, technology leadership, human resources, supply chain, operations management, and so forth.

As shown in Figure 7.4 the best outcomes were realized by firms with the cyber leader identified as CISO. These data are reinforced by results from Fitzgerald and Krause (2008, p. 9), which indicate that reporting relations matter and that the level of chief or C-suite member is of great importance to enable access and the ability to provide coaching to the leadership of the organization. This level in the organization enables insights into critical business issues, allowing the cyber security leader to be informed and responsive to organizational issues.

Scale of Operations

Another factor that affects cyber leadership is the scale of the enterprise. Enterprise scale significantly affects the strategies, methods, and policies that are deployed to achieve a risk-managed enterprise. The business scale factors include the phases of the organization life cycle: startup scale, mature firm, or declining market. Other considerations are the scale and scope of the enterprise, with a focus on the diversity of the organization's locations and processing. Firms of multinational and global scale will face increased complexity from legal requirements and regulations as well as factors such as differing cultural approaches and possible language challenges.

Company Life Cycle

Companies have a range of risk profiles over their life cycle and at various economic phases. Startup firms tend to take more risks as they grow and expand their product lines and customer base. MacCrimmon, Wehrung, and Standbury (1986) demonstrate that measures of risk taking gathered from the same individual or organization change over time. Mature organizations usually have more assets to protect but also have more resources to devote to risk/threat management. For example, a large organization is more likely to be able to afford having a CISO and a CIO.

Products/Services

An organization's types of work products or services will affect cyber capabilities and cyber risks. The issues to consider are IT services supplier management from outsourcing, supply chain management, degree of participant integration, and scale of the product suppliers. Gartner, Inc. obtained 200 security program assessments across industries (Casper, Stegman, & McMillan, 2014). The analysts used IT spending per employee, an indicator of total security investment, and quantified industry characteristics such as risk, applications, and infrastructures. Using IT security spending per employee (see Figure 7.5) provides a more stable baseline because number of employees tends to vary less year to year than does IT spending. Visibly, average spending varies very much by industry, with insurance companies spending four times as much as the average retail or wholesale company.

With this industry characterization as a background, Gartner, Inc. examined the elements of cyber security across industries. As indicated in Figures 7.5 and 7.6, different industry sectors are identified on a multidimensional scale, with comparison of ten maturity and performance criteria. These assessments provide compelling results and identify the highest level of IT security maturity in insurance (3.0) and the lowest in retail (2.2). This study correlates and emphasizes IT security program maturity and IT security spending. By way of illustrating comparative benchmarking, the center point of the chart in Figure 7.6 indicates a maturity of 1.7, and the ring designating the retail industry sector indicates a maturity level of 2.7.

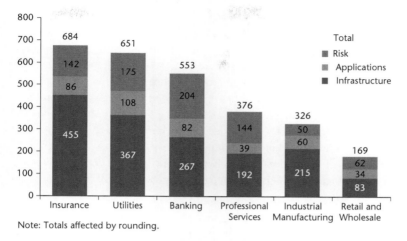

FIGURE 7.5 IT Spending per Employee by Industry (Gartner IT Key Metrics 2013), with permission

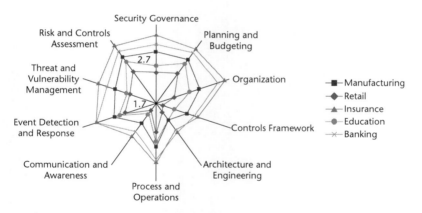

FIGURE 7.6 Cyber Security Maturity by Industry

So far, we have explored leadership challenges, elements of risk, and organizational requirements in relation to operational and functional components. We next consider the leadership competencies needed for the cyber leaders throughout the organization.

Functional Requirements of Cyber Leaders

Most cyber leaders know it is not the case of *if* their company will be broken into but rather a matter of *when* their company will be broken into. This sober reality leads to a natural uneasiness and vigilance in the field. This perspective can be driven to an extreme and result in paranoia, or it can be used positively to promote continuous improvement, verification, and validation and a team mentality. Teamwork, cooperation, and building a community within a corporation and across industry and IT environments are key to risk awareness, even while building a team to protect from and respond to incidents when they happen. The cyber leaders in today's organizations must continuously scan and assess their corporate and technological environments, aligning current and future needs with technology, qualifying the risks of the technology, and implementing processes with appropriately skilled personnel.

As we discussed in the section on risk management, strategic competencies are called for in cyber security leadership. Strategic competencies enable performance of a variety of roles:

- business and organizational leadership;
- excellent communications and relationship building;
- change management and teamwork; and
- policy, governance, and risk management.

From these roles, functional requirements can be derived. A brief list of the top requirements for cyber leaders is presented in the following paragraphs:

Aligning cyber security within the business: The cyber leader must be an enabler of mission goals and objectives. Although the tendency will always be to look for potential threats implied by business arrangements being proposed by others, it will be important to find ways that facilitate the accomplishment of mission goals. The cyber leader must avoid being thought of as a negative force or a roadblock. Ideally, he or she will be able to develop a reputation as an enabler for the managers of the company's lines of business or business units.

Making a business case for cyber security: The cyber leader must be able to articulate the needs of the business and the risks and opportunities associated with the deployment of technology or information-handling systems. This skill requires having business and industry metrics so as to assess risks and opportunities by qualitative and quantitative measures. Such measures would describe the impact of business decisions in terms of cost, schedule, quality, and impact to the reputation of the corporation. The business case to be shaped involves deciding how much risk of what type is worth the cost of mitigation.

Aligning stakeholders and coalitions: The cyber leader should use communication and collaboration skills to inform, educate, and persuade other business leaders in the organization as well as in the industry at large or environment.

Shaping organizational design (authority, reporting communication structures): The cyber leader often selects a cyber security approach that is initially in alignment with organizational structures and processes. His or her goal is to facilitate protection of the corporate "crown jewels" and enable a rapid and empowered response to threats/incidents. In a mature cyber security organization, there may be key reasons for organizational redesign to better align resources, authority, and responsibility with overall needs. Of course, this will also be affected by such things as the organization's tendency to grow organizational assets (e.g., acquiring a company may change risk exposure) or to invest in intellectual property.

Managing change: The work of the cyber leader takes place in the presence of emerging technology and threats. As such, there will be a constant need to develop and continuously upgrade a security strategy, security architecture, governance plan, implementation policies, and procedures. Capabilities must always be (re)aligned and be sensitive to assessment of enterprise systems (e.g., supply chain arrangements). The cyber leader should continually improve upon structured acceptance and verification processes with solid configuration management, penetration testing, and systems audits.

Promoting the right culture: The cyber leader must strike the right balance between open and closed business processes. He or she must routinely contribute to discussions regarding recruiting and socializing the right people and motivating appropriate behaviors in these individuals once on the job. The cyber leader must contribute to the design and management of programs to instill a sense of constant vigilance while encouraging continuous improvement and learning. This will be particularly challenging for high-reliability organizations (e.g., ones controlling critical infrastructure, like power plants), which are often the targets of cyber threats.

Guiding policy and practice through governance: The cyber leader must help lead the organization to create and manage data governance. He or she must contribute to high-level discussions that will determine the appropriate policies, procedures, and practices associated with data governance and participate in any decisions that are likely to change or upgrade these. This may depend on organizational design—whether the CISO executes his or her own projects or manages the project governance from which the projects are executed and then implemented through the business council or other areas.

Coordination execution of security projects: The progressive organization is constantly investing in new business processes. These usually open the company to new cyber risks. Such initiatives may come out of the cyber leader's own projects (e.g., system upgrades designed to detect penetration threats). But often they will come out of changes being made by virtually every function of the business operation (finance, purchasing, manufacturing, R&D, etc.). In any event, as these are designed and brought online, great attention must be given to the information-processing requirements involved and implications for potential new threats. For example, human resources policies may change to allow employees to work remotely. This would strongly affect (and compromise) any existing security perimeter.

The foregoing requirements must be met by a cyber leader to manage his or her organization while responding to an asymmetric threat. The CISO must be broadly prepared and able to learn quickly and adapt to changing conditions.

In the next section, we explore how these functional requirements contribute to the success of an organization and how a cyber leader will leverage these capabilities to achieve the organization's goals as well as his or her goals.

Cyber Leadership Competencies

As implied, cyber leadership requires personal characteristics suitable for functioning well in "high-velocity environments." In fact, the role is still in flux and evolving. Senior executives of many organizations are still uncertain about the scope of work responsibilities to be assigned to the CISO. One study of 200 U.S.-based C-level executives (e.g., CEOs, presidents, chief legal officers) reveals a great deal of skepticism among respondents that traditionally technically trained individuals are ready to function effectively as part of an organization's senior leadership team (ThreatTrack Security, n.d.). This is particularly true of respondents from the retail and health-care industry sectors, whose companies are often the targets of cyber attacks. The prevailing sense is that many incumbents in or candidates for the CISO role possess only a narrow (technical) skill set. Although technical acumen is felt to be a needed foundation for the role, the respondents believe that a fully qualified CISO must "possess a broad awareness of organizational objectives and business needs outside of information security" (ThreatTrack Security, n.d., p. 2).

Stewart (2013) provides advice to those seeking a career in cyber security and reinforces the stereotype that technical competencies are needed or expected as his paper relies on the International Organization for Standardization (ISO) standards pertaining to staffing requirements (27001 and 27002). Reports like this tend to support those who would subordinate the senior cyber security officer to executives holding the titles of CIO or even COO (Boulton, 2015).

When competencies are explored for senior cyber security positions, surveys of industry leaders are often used. As a recent example, one study first examined the job descriptions and functional roles for the CISO found in a variety of reports (Fitzgerald, 2008). This initial information was supplemented by interviews of incumbents in the position. The data provided for a summarized set of capabilities. These were then incorporated into a survey, along with open-ended questions, and administered to a sample of 200 respondents occupying a variety of positions in the CISO category. The respondents identified a range of items, shown in Figure 7.7. Of these themes, the areas of oral and written communications, influence, teamwork, collaboration, and self-confidence were ranked as very important.

In a similar manner, a recent report by IBM highlighted what was offered as "a new standard for security leaders" (van Zadelhoff, Lovejoy, & Jarvis, 2013). The report emphasized the need to deal with such risk as loss of brand reputation, operational downtime, and compliance violations. But it then went on to argue

Cyber Security Executive Leadership   **153**

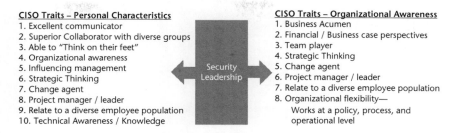

FIGURE 7.7 Personal Characteristics and Organizational Awareness Traits of Security Leadership

that this can be best accomplished by having leaders who have the skill to set up and manage core business practices. These include having

- a strong strategy and policy framework,
- comprehensive risk management practices,
- effective business relations,
- communications protocols, and
- effective business-relevant measures and metrics.

It can be noted that the portfolio of competencies needed to perform as a CISO does not seem too dissimilar from what might be expected of any senior level leader in today's global business environment (e.g., Zaccaro, 2007). But it does appear that unlike many others who aspire to the C-suite, those aspiring to be the CISO may find negotiating their career path somewhat daunting. One reason for this may stem from fact that early promotions for the aspiring CISO often come as a result of being effective in a technical (IT) role. This implies that there is something of a disconnect between the skill set required to perform well at a lower level and the skill set needed or expected at the most senior level. Although such disconnects occur for other specialists (e.g., for those coming out of an accounting background who want to become CFOs), this seems to be more of a liability for technologists.

Although we must speculate, one reason for the disconnect is that other specialists, even at lower levels, are usually positioned to be exposed to at least one aspect of business operations. Thus, they are often able to see the need for—and, therefore, make a "business case" for—their decisions or requests. In a related way, lower level specialists can, over time, build up some of the competencies required to function well at the highest levels of leadership. When given the opportunity to perform at that level, they are then able to "speak the language of the boardroom" (Citrix, 2014). In related way, over time, they are also able to build up their credibility as potential candidates for senior positions. And credibility is often easier to earn as a result of a documented record of meeting what are

Yesterday's CISO	New CISO
Subject Matter Expert	Trusted Adviser
Analyst	Facilitator and Leader
Technical Risk Expert	Risk Manager
Individual Contributor	Integrative Business Thinker
Chief Security Officer	Chief Risk Officer
Administrator	Strategist
Manager	Visionary

FIGURE 7.8 Evolution of Chief Information Security Officer Capabilities

nominally seen as business (not technology) challenges. Recent studies have documented or implied the evolution of the CISO position and, therefore, the required competencies. As pointed out over the past few years in particular, the business world has expectations that the CISO must to go beyond being a technical specialist and become a business leader, as shown in Figure 7.8.

Under the ideal scenario, the CISO will be a strategist and visionary and an integrative business thinker. Incumbents, therefore, need to understand the business needs of their firm and to develop the security strategies being shaped by such forces as new technologies, new political realities in society, and new threats emerging nationally and internationally and to assess in a risk-based manner the new solutions proposed by the lines of business or marketing/sales departments. Although the CISO will of course be sought out for security and cyber security expertise, he or she must constantly assess aspects of technology security to reassess the interests of the organization and the technology investment required, as is described in the following section.

There is one another capability that seems important to the role of the CISO at this time in history. This is to be able to adapt and to grow as a professional. It seems apparent that the CISO must be a person able to learn quickly and adapt to a changing technology base. His or her portfolio of competencies will require continual honing and development within the business but also in the broader industry and corporate environment. The dynamic nature of the forces that must be dealt with also implies that the CISO must be adaptable. In this regard, one report called for the CISO to be a more *versatile* security leader:

> [S]ecurity leaders must combine strong security strategy with a holistic risk management that considers the economic impact of IT security, while developing effective business relations and engendering trust with senior leaders. They have to maintain foundational security technologies, but not at the expense of implementing more advanced and strategic capabilities. ... They must create the right feedback loops as well. ... Both security

technology and business metrics must be fed into the risk management process.... Those metrics must translate into the language of the organization.

(van Zadelhoff et al., 2013, p. 9)

Cyber Technology/Investment Strategy

One of the key areas requiring attention from a CISO is the constant reassessment of technology and policy portfolios related to cyber and technology investments. Management of a cyber security portfolio or technologies and processes is essential to the long-term stability and security of the organization. Cyber investments need to be carefully managed and nurtured with the C-suite and the CTO and lines of businesses executives to stay ahead of the evolving threats and to have credible alternatives to offer that can enhance cyber security but also be implemented in functional organizations (Christiansen, 2008; Sanovic, 2008). The CISO and his or her team would have to develop and reassess a list of candidate responses to the evolving threats. In a constant threat and response assessment, the CISO would leverage his or her technological and process awareness to determine alternatives to threats and appropriate times to pilot or deploy solutions. This activity requires an important set of skills, involves cross-organizational tasks, and has a wide organizational impact.

The breadth of this area can be extensive as technology, processes, and organizations' needs are constantly being reassessed and tradeoffs determined. Figure 7.9 identifies a few significant explanations from the Gartner (2014) report as to why organizations invest in some areas and not in others. This is a risk assessment process coordinated by the CISO with the corporate risk management board, corporate audit, and the CFO. Three trends can be derived from the data:

1. There is a need to continuously improve/optimize security, risk processes, and functions. Even though organizations have foundational IT security elements in place, they know they can still do better in terms of network, endpoint, and application security.
2. The people factor is critical. There will be a need to invest in people and develop their expertise, with the goal of improving customer confidence. Senior leaders of organizations need to be made to understand that security technologies work best in combination with well-trained staff.
3. It is surprising that the item "we will protect our know-how" was ranked so low. This suggests that many organizational leaders do not understand that information is a strategic competitive asset. Cyber security leaders must seek out ways in which they can become strategic partners with business leaders rather than artisans whose work can easily be commoditized or outsourced. It could also be that many respondents marked this area so low out of a sense of frustration:

They have no expectations that they can prevent their data from leaking—and this is key when dealing with emerging markets that do not protect

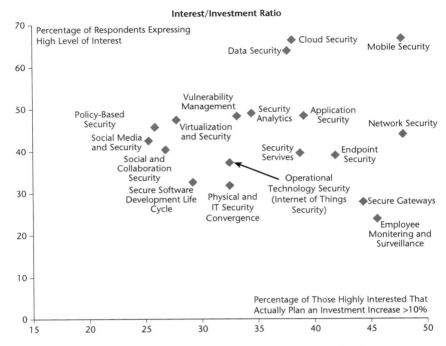

FIGURE 7.9 Cyber Security Transformational Interest versus Technology Investment Ratio

intellectual property rights as hoped. Companies exploit and utilize their know-how as quickly as possible, recognizing that you can't keep it a secret for long. (Casper et al., 2014, p. 5)

The Challenges of Maintaining Competency and Credibility

The senior cyber security leader and other members of the C-suite need to maintain vigilance from the organizational perspective regarding a corporation's threats and weaknesses as well as the weaknesses that result from the pace of technology introducing new threats and opportunities for breaches. As implied, they will also face new political realities from emerging laws and regulations. Fortunately, there are a number of resources available to support continuous learning.

Continuous Learning as the CISO

There are a number of organizations and societies with which a CISO can engage, such as International Information System Security Certification Consortium, the Information Systems Security Organization (ISSA), and the Information Audit and Control Association. Any Google Internet search will provide a list of local chapters of such organizations. If the CISO is seeking a more comprehensive or broad experience, a number of excellent university and government programs are available to broaden his or her background and scope. The CISO will need to investigate his or her industry or trade associations to identify already-formed group or subcommittees. The U.S. Department of Homeland Security has also identified a number of critical infrastructure sectors; these can be reviewed at http://www.dhs.gov/critical-infrastructure-sectors.

Building and Maintaining Cyber Security as a Core Competency of the Firm

One way to promote continuous learning is to allow staff time for creativity and innovation. Cyber security staff should not be located in an operational department where time is allocated to the maximum and procedures are already well defined. There will always be new and emerging threats, and, thus, the cyber leader needs to find ways to inspire creativity to protect the organization and manage risk.

Growing and maintaining competency and credibility might be accomplished by attending to the design of the organizational unit lead by the CISO. When building out the cyber security business unit and supporting its capabilities, the CISO might consider such parameters as these:

- careful vetting (insider threats),
- levels of education and skill mix required,
- continuous education policies,
- staff rotation practices,
- degrees of internal client contact,
- support for professional engagement,
- involvement in decision making,
- overlap in staff or capability (business, technical, management, political), and
- management of staff strengths and desires (many cyber specialists want to stay technical, so be careful not to promote beyond skills or desired level).

Team building and effective cyber team utilization are key factors underlying success in the CISO role. To promote this goal, a diverse team of technical, policy, business, and risk personnel is needed. The cyber leader will also have to leverage his or her team in order to continuously communicate up and down the chain of command, to educate company personnel on critical issues, and reinforce relationships.

Cyber Security Thought Leadership

At a high level of aspiration, the CISO may want to become known as a thought leader and position his or her company as the benchmark for certain cyber security practices. Here, cyber leadership takes on a different meaning. It will involve taking on key roles at national or international levels in professional organizations, participating on task forces and working groups, or partnering with universities in order to stay well informed regarding research discoveries in those areas of IT security most related to the firm's suppliers, markets, or competition.

Developing Cyber Leadership

Becoming a cyber leader typically involves going through stages development and awareness to experience and leadership. Clearly, there is the need to build a skill base rooted in an understanding of the components of IT (down to the chip level) and their applications. Although this capability is important to performance and credibility at the lower levels of an organization, the CISO or C-suite member would not be expected to know every bit or byte in security protocols or systems. A basic understanding of the implications of security issues and the ability to relate these to the company's weaknesses so as to derive threats and be able to articulate risks is the essential quality for CISO success. Global Knowledge, a security technology trainer/educator, has identified areas of competency formally defined in ISO standards 27001 and 27002 to include the following (Stewart, 2013):

- security policy;
- organization of information security;
- assessment management;
- human resource security;
- physical and environmental security;
- communications and operations management;
- access control;
- information systems acquisition, development, and maintenance;
- information security incident management;
- business continuity management; and
- regulatory compliance.

The protocols further state,

> As you can see, there is an astounding breath of concern for the cyber professional. For smaller firms with fewer staff, cybersecurity job positions will require competence across all of these areas of concern. For larger organizations with very large staffing abilities, a team of cyber professionals may be assembled, with each member being a skilled practitioner in one primary topic.
> (Stewart, 2013, p. 3)

The next phase of the cyber leader's education is in the areas of management and process awareness. This phase addresses the cyber leader's understanding of management theory and application of it to form strategies and address strategic issues as well as having the "street smarts" to implement strategies for the company at multiple levels. This awareness may come from years of experience in the industry or company, a college MBA program, or military training in organizations and personnel awareness.

The final phase is a leadership phase and may be the most important. Although this is not a sequential process, leadership is something developed from experience and performance of a wide variety of tasks. Leadership is shaped through self-awareness and awareness of one's environment. Leadership can be developed and nurtured through industry experience, higher education, coaching, or military service. It requires an individual to exhibit "authoritativeness, influence, command, effectiveness; sway, clout" ("Leadership," n.d.).

At the time of this writing, there is no single path to developing the attributes that are needed to be a seen as a leader in the cyber security arena at the level of the firm, in professional organizations, or at standards-setting debates or in policy discussions. The ISSA has identified a career framework, but it is very general and aimed at helping individuals grow professionally for success in the cyber field at different points in the career life cycle. It does not offer a map or path to a job as the CISO (Drolet, 2015).

However, Klimoski and Amos (2014) have offered a rubric that might be used to outline some feasible approaches for those who aspire to senior cyber leadership positions at the firm level. They referred to it as the "three C" rubric. The first C refers to *competence*, the second C refers to *confidence*, and the third C refers to *credibility*.

Competence

There is no doubt that that competencies for the effective performance of cyber security leadership roles are what most people think about when trying to answer the question of how to develop future cyber leaders. However, in the cyber leadership arena, there are several areas of domain knowledge and skill that a leader needs in order to be effective; several sets of these were outlined earlier in this section. Simply stated, when it comes to personal or professional development, the current thinking is that someone who aspires to cyber leadership must be both technically well prepared and able to make a "business case."

Formal university education is usually part of the prescription. In this regard, there are many technical schools and universities that now offer undergraduate and graduate degrees in various aspects of cyber security. Many are offered in a traditional format (e.g., George Mason University), and some are online (e.g., Bay Path College). There are many opportunities for development of the necessary technical knowledge and skills through certificate programs (e.g., the Certified Information Systems Security Professional exam). When it comes to business-related acumen, it would be helpful to be exposed to formal education covering such topics as finance, accounting, and marketing as well as the people side of managing a business.

Consistent with what we know about adult learning (McCall, 2004), in order to translate knowledge into skills and performance, those seeking to develop their competencies need to do so by working in the area. As Allen Paller, Director of Research at the SANS Institute, has stated, "the more technically adept security technicians are more cultivated than taught" (as quoted in Lemos, 2013, p. 2). Along these lines, many cyber security companies (e.g., Dell Secure Works) are partnering with universities (e.g., Georgia Tech, Purdue) to recruit promising candidates and to develop their own "farm league." Other companies make use of hacking or cyber defense competitions to identify young people with potential. Individuals with this raw talent or aptitude are then offered scholarships to technical schools, community colleges, or universities along with co-op or summer internship arrangements to help them grow professionally (Lemos, 2013).

At the more senior level, advanced levels of competence develop over the course of a sequence of jobs or positions in the field. Some industries require industry-sector cyber security experts as there are special regulatory obligations on the firm (e.g., a health-care organization) or threats to company assets (e.g., a financial institution). But a case has been made that to become fully capable as a future cyber leader, it is desirable to move across companies and sectors. In fact, it is not unusual for companies to "poach" talent from other organizations, making it easier for someone to develop the needed breadth of experience (Lemos, 2013).

There is some evidence that both the U.S. government and the U.S. military have become "suppliers" of midcareer cyber leadership talent. Much as the U.S. military trains pilots capable of high levels of performance who then go on to private sector careers, some have observed this happening in the cyber security sector. Thus, individuals gain years of experience dealing with advanced IT and special protocols for dealing with cyber threats in the public sector and then are well prepared to handle the needs of the private sector when they transfer to a private company.

When it comes to developing competence among midcareer professionals, some universities employ a supply chain-like arrangement. For example, George Mason University, located only a few miles from federal agencies and the Pentagon in northern Virginia, recruits technically trained individuals into their master of science program in secure information systems. In the course of studies, students raise their competence relative to many areas covered in a typical MBA program (e.g., financial models, new product development, leadership). However, it is a unique academic degree program—jointly produced by the School of

Business, the School of Engineering, and the School of Public Policy—and additionally provides the advanced management training that program graduates would need in order to perform well at the senior levels of cyber leadership.

Self-Confidence

Self-confidence is the second C in the Klimoski and Amos (2014) rubric. Most of us have observed instances in which competent people are not recognized as such because they lack confidence. This often manifests in the form of "self-handicapping." When taking on important and career-relevant assignments (often involving professional risk) or promoting him- or herself for career moves that might produce professional development, the less confident individual is slow to act. This closes off opportunities to perform well or to grow personally or professionally.

Achieving high levels of competence will usually engender high levels of self-confidence. But this is not always the case. Thus, several writers have offered guidance to those who seek to boost self-confidence as individuals or as mentors. For example, Hollenbeck and Hall (2004) suggested that in order to increase their self-confidence, individuals should watch and learn from confident others and talk to these people so as to understand how they developed their self-confidence. In a more prescriptive vein, they recommended that one should develop the capacity to more accurately assess one's capabilities relative to the perceived task requirements involved in a particular situation (i.e., do not underestimate the former or overestimate the latter). Lester, Hannah, Harms, Vogelgesang, and Avolio (2011) described the impact of a formal program in the military in which mentors provided honest and constructive feedback to protégés, which increased the protégé's leadership self-efficacy (or self-confidence as a leader).

Credibility

The third C stresses credibility, the capacity for eliciting confidence in one from others (Klimoski & Amos, 2014). There are several ways that one might develop credibility. Certainly it helps to be competent, and, as implied, credibility is also enhanced when competence in reflected in self-confidence. For example, as Yukl (2010) has pointed out, one of the quickest ways to lose respect as a leader is to misuse the power that you already have.

Credibility is enhanced through several mechanisms. A record of accomplishments is one of these. Being able to point to a list of successfully completed projects, a set of goals accomplished, or a history of awards or accolades usually enhances credibility. As such, an individual seeking to develop credibility as a future cyber security leader must be selective regarding the kind of jobs to apply for, assignments to take on, and awards to aspire to obtain. Of course, once goals are aimed for, the aspirant must perform well in order for his or her records of accomplishments to contribute to credibility. Along these lines, it would be wise to have a clear idea of the kind of senior leadership position being sought and to build up the set of accomplishments in one's professional portfolio accordingly.

Credibility is often linked to social capital, or the network of social relationships that are developed over time, which reflect not just who you know but who can speak to your talents (Klimoski & Amos, 2014). There has been a great deal of research on how best to develop social capital (e.g., Anand & Conger, 2007; Ibarra & Hunter, 2007; Uzzi & Dunlap, 2005). Usually, it involves engaging with a wide range of people in order to find similar interests and leveraging these interests in activities that build the relationships over time. Thus, credibility is often linked to one's reputation regarding how one deals with a range of people or one's inclination to help others to achieve their goals.

Along these lines, a reputation for integrity plays a special role in promoting credibility. This is where one's character comes into play. How confident one is in one's abilities, how well one lives up to one's values, and one's willingness to make ethical decisions are at the heart of one's charter and often form the foundation for one's reputation.

In order to be suitable for a senior cyber leadership position, one's competence and confidence will certainly come into play. But to truly be successful as a CISO, one must win the backing of other executives in the firm and be effective at "selling information security" (Christiansen, 2008; Granneman, 2013). Therefore, establishing credibility is the key. Thus, in order to develop as a professional, one's work strengthening the third C would represent time and effort well spent.

The Organizational Value of Cyber Leadership

The value of cyber security leadership is ultimately realized in a more effective and efficient organizational operating environment and the ability to achieve organizational strategies within a market. As a measure of "success," the IT Policy Compliance Group (2010) surveyed a variety of organizations in relation to their cyber security and, as a result, issued a *Best Practices for Managing Information Security* report. Of the organizations considered in the survey, the companies with the best outcomes attributed their success to the following factors:

- Information security is reported to a CRO, CISO, or assurance manager.
- The manager of information security is a CISO or senior manager of IT assurance.
- IT provides and manages information integrity, availability, and confidentiality standards.
- Productivity and security are managed by policies and targets for minimum acceptable downtime and maximal acceptable risks.
- Standardized procedures and controls are implemented.
- Information security is managed by the CISO.

- Day-to-day operations are managed by the CISO and IT security operations specialists.
- Policies, procedures, and controls are nearly fully automated.
- Measures and reporting occur daily, weekly, and monthly.
- A quality-improvement program is implemented.

Over the course of a year, the organizations with these best practices experienced the following:

- data loss exposure: 0.4% of revenue;
- business downtime: less than 4 hours;
- regulatory audit spending: $1.30 relative to security;
- revenue: 8.5 percent higher than industry average; and
- profit: 6.4 percent higher than industry average.

Summary

In this chapter, we have presented the cyber leadership challenges facing the modern work organization in terms of enterprise risk management, focusing on the role of the CISO. The responsibility for cyber security must be widely shared, involving commitments and energy from the board of directors, the members of the C-suite, the managers of the business units or lines of business, and even the typical employee, with the CISO best equipped to orchestrate all of these people and efforts. We have described some of the operational leadership requirements for the CISO, including the need to inspire teamwork, to integrate cyber security preparations and execution within the business strategy, and to provide the common services needed to protect the organization as a whole. In an attempt to help the organization "know what success looks like," we have defined cyber

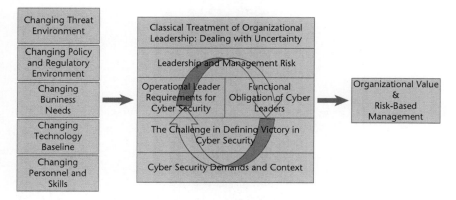

FIGURE 7.10 Recapping the Themes of the Chapter

security leadership to guide and inform our readers. Finally, we have described the cyber security demands and evolving context of the CISO role, identifying the skills needed by the individual and his or her team from industry surveys.

The chapter can be summarized in the form of an input–process–outcome diagram, as shown in Figure 7.10. Most organizations want to see that the CISO adds value to enterprise risk management. Inputs absorbed by the system are numerous, but we have highlighted a set of these in this chapter, with special emphasis on the dynamic threat environment that must be confronted.

The core of the chapter is the exploration of the key processes to be managed by the CISO and his or her business unit in order to be seen as credible. As such, we have emphasized that the qualities needed by someone who aspires to be the senior cyber leader go beyond demonstrated technical expertise. In fact, as we have portrayed, it is the same qualities required for effective senior leaders coming from all backgrounds that make a cyber security leader successful.

REFERENCES

Amabile, T. M. (1997). Motivating creativity in organizations: On doing what you love and loving what you do. *California Management Review, 40*, 39–58.

Anand, N. & Conger, J. A. (2007). Capabilities of the consummate networker. *Organizational Dynamics, 36*, 13–27.

Argote, L. (2012). Organizational learning and knowledge management. In S. W. J. Kozlowski (Ed.), *The Oxford handbook of organizational psychology* (Vol. 1, pp. 933–955). New York: Oxford University Press.

Baker, W., Hutton, A., Hylender, C. D., Pamula, J., Porter, C., & Spitler, M. (2011). *2011 data breach investigations report: A study conducted by the Verizon RISK Team in cooperation with the U.S. Secret Service and the Dutch High Tech Crime Unit.* Retrieved from http://www.secretservice.gov/Verizon_Data_Breach_2011.pdf

Boulton, C. (2015, February 6). Data breaches spark debates on CISO, CIO dynamic. *CIO Journal.* Retrieved from http://blogs.wsj.com/cio/2015/02/06/data-breaches-spark-debates-on-ciso-cio-dynamic/

Casper, C., Stegman, E., & McMillan, R. (2014, April 8). *Don't be the next target—IT security spending priorities 2014.* Retrieved from https://www.gartner.com/doc/2703221/dont-target--it-security

Ciancutti, A., & Steding, T.L. (2001) *Built on trust: Gaining competitive advantage in any organization.* Chicago: Contemporary Books.

Citrix. (2014). *Security strategies for success.* Retrieved from https://www.citrix.com/content/dam/citrix/en_us/documents/products-solutions/security-leadership-series-security-strategies-for-success-en.pdf

Christiansen, J. S. (2008). Selling information security. In T. Fitzgerald and M. Kraus (Eds.), *CISO leadership: Essential principles for success* (pp. 151–162). Boca Raton, FL: Auberbach.

Colquitt, J. A. (2012) Organizational justice. In S. W. J. Kozlowski (Ed.), *The Oxford handbook of organizational psychology* (Vol. 1, pp. 526–547). New York: Oxford University Press.

DeChurch, L. & Marks, M. (2006). Leadership in multi-team systems. *Journal of Applied Psychology, 91*, 311–329.

Deloitte & Touche LLP. (2013). *Risk intelligent governance in the age of cyber threats: What you don't know could hurt you*. Retrieved from http://www2.deloitte.com/content/dam/Deloitte/us/Documents/risk/us-aers-risk-intelligent-governance-in-the-age-of-cyber-threats.pdf

Drolet, M. (2015, February 9). Bridging the cybersecurity skills gap: 3 big steps. *InformationWeek Dark Reading*. Retrieved from http://www.darkreading.com/operations/bridging-the-cybersecurity-skills-gap-3-big-steps---/a/d-id/1318766

Edmondson, A. C. (1999). Psychological safety and learning behavior in work teams. *Administrative Science Quarterly, 44*, 350–383.

Fitzgerald, T. (2008). What you told us: A CISO survey. In T. Fitzgerald & M. Krause (Eds.), *CISO leadership: Essential principles for success* (pp. 3–27). Boca Raton, FL: Auerbach.

Fitzgerald, T., & Krause, M. (Eds.) (2008). *CISO leadership: Essential principles for success*. Boca Raton, FL: Auerbach.

Graham, J. W. (1991). Servant-leadership in organizations: Inspirational and moral. *Leadership Quarterly, 2*, 105–119.

Granneman, J. (2013, December 5). *What attributes are necessary to have success in the CISO role?* Retrieved from http://searchsecurity.techtarget.com/tip/What-attributes-are-necessary-to-have-success-in-the-CISO-role

Hitt, M. A., Keats, B. W., & DeMarie, S. M. (1998). Navigating the new competitive landscape: Building strategic flexibility and competitive advantage. *Academy of Management Executive, 12*(4), 22–42.

Hollenbeck, G. P., & Hall, D. T. (2004). Self-confidence and leader performance. *Organizational Dynamics, 33*, 254–269.

Holmes, D. (2015, January 30). How the skills shortage is killing defense in depth. *InformationWeek Dark Reading*. Retrieved from http://www.darkreading.com/operations/how-the-skills-shortage-is-killing-defense-in-depth/a/d-id/1318885

Ibarra, H., & Hunter, M. (2007, January). How leaders create and use networks. *Harvard Business Review, 85*(1), 40–57.

IT Policy Compliance Group. (2010, February). *Best practices for managing information security*. Retrieved from http://eval.symantec.com/mktginfo/enterprise/other_resources/b-best_practices_for_managing_information_security-february_2010_OR_2876547.en-us.pdf

Joint Task Force Transformation Initiative. (2010, February). *Guide for applying the risk management framework to federal information systems: A security life cycle approach* (NIST Special Publication No. 800-37). Retrieved from http://nvlpubs.nist.gov/nistpubs/SpecialPublications/NIST.SP.800-37r1.pdf

Katz, D., & Kahn, R. (1978). *The social psychology of organizations* (2nd ed.). New York: Wiley.

Klimoski, R. J., & Amos, B. (2014). To act as a leader. In J. K. Ford, J. B. Hollenbeck, & A. M. Ryan (Eds.), *The nature of work: Advances in psychological theory, methods, and practice* (pp. 94–135). Washington, DC: American Psychological Association.

Lawler, E. E., III (1992). *The ultimate advantage: Creating high involvement organizations*. San Francisco: Jossey-Bass.

Leadership [Definition 2]. (n.d.). In *Dictionary.com*. Retrieved from http://dictionary.reference.com/browse/leadership?s=t

Lemos, R. (2013, September 3). *Bridging the IT security gap*. Retrieved from http://searchsecurity.techtarget.com/feature/Bridging-the-IT-security-skills-gap

Lester, P. B., Hannah, S. T., Harms, P. D., Vogelgesang, G. R., & Avolio, B. J. (2011). Mentoring impact on leader efficacy development: A field experiment. *Academy of Management Learning & Education, 10*, 409–429.

McCall, M. W. (2004). Leadership development through experience. *Academy of Management Executive, 18,* 127–130.

MacCrimmon, K., Wehrung, D., & Standbury, W. (1986). *Taking risks: The management of uncertainty* (Vol. 1). New York: Free Press.

Marion, R. (2014). Organizational leadership and complexity mechanisms. In M. G. Rumset (Ed.), *The many sides of leadership* (pp. 184–202). New York: Oxford University Press.

PricewaterhouseCoopers. (2011). *Delusions of safety? The cyber savvy CEO: Getting to grips with today's growing cyber-threats.* Retrieved from https://www.pwc.nl/nl/assets/documents/pwc-delusions-of-safety.pdf

Sanovic, R. (2008). The importance of IT security strategy. In T. Fitzgerald & M. Krause (Eds.), *CISO leadership: Essential principles for success* (pp. 163–170). Boca Raton. FL: Auerbach.

Shumard, C. (2013, July 16). *Opinion: Definition of the role of the CISO still a work in progress.* Retrieved from http://searchsecurity.techtarget.com/opinion/Opinion-Definition-of-the-role-of-CISO-still-a-work-in-progress

Spreitzer, G. (2008). Taking stock: A review of more than twenty years of research on empowerment at work. In J. Barling & C. L. Cooper (Eds.), *The SAGE handbook of organizational behavior: Vol. 1. Micro perspectives* (pp. 54–72). Thousand Oaks, CA: Sage.

Stewart, J. (2013). *Planning a career path in cybersecurity.* Retrieved from http://www.ocio.gov.nl.ca/ocio/im/im_as_career/cybersecurity_jobs.pdf

Thompson, J. D. (1967) *Organizations in action: Social science bases of administration.* New York: McGraw-Hill.

ThreatTrack Security. (n.d.). *No respect. Chief information security officers misunderstood and underappreciated by their C-level peers.* Retrieved from http://www.threattracksecurity.com/getmedia/b970d014-d47e-43f4-8a35-65e782bd1285/the-role-of-the-ciso.aspx

Travino, L. K., & Brown, M. E. (2004). Managing to be ethical: Debunking five business ethics myths. *Academy of Management Executive, 18,* 69–81.

Tversky, A., & Kahneman, D. (1974). Judgment under uncertainty: Heuristics and biases. *Science, 185,* 1124–1131.

Uhi-Ben, M., Marion, R., & McKelvey, B. (2007). Complexity leadership theory: Shifting leadership from the industrial age to the knowledge era. *The Leadership Quarterly, 18,* 296–296.

U.S. Department of Homeland Security. (2014, June 12). *Critical infrastructure sectors.* Retrieved from http://www.dhs.gov/critical-infrastructure-sectors

Uzzi, B., & Dunlap, S. (2005, December). How to build your network. *Harvard Business Review, 83*(12), 53–60.

van Zadelhoff, M., Lovejoy, K., & Jarvis, D. (2013). *A new standard for security leaders: Insights from the 2013 IBM Chief Information Security Officer Assessment.* Armonk, NY: IBM Corporation.

Yukl, G. (2010). *Leadership in organizations* (7th Eed.). Upper Saddle River, NJ: Prentice Hall.

Zaccaro, S. J. (2007). Trait-based perspectives of leadership. *American Psychologist, 62,* 6–16.

8

REQUISITE ATTRIBUTES FOR CYBER SECURITY PERSONNEL AND TEAMS

Cyber Risk Mitigation through Talent Management

Irwin Jose, Kate LaPort, and D. Matthew Trippe

The potential of a cyber attack is an operating reality for today's organizations, large and small. Private and public sectors alike cannot ignore the security concerns that have emerged due to threats originating from cyberspace—where hackers are constantly seeking network vulnerabilities and developing new malware for methods of attack, espionage, and sabotage (National Research Council, 2002). If the high profile cyber attacks of the early 21st century can teach organizations anything, it would be that there is an extreme shortage of the talent required to effectively monitor, maintain, and secure organizational networks that house sensitive information and intellectual capital (Libicki, Senty, & Pollak, 2014).

The recent hacking of the Sony Corporation, in which sensitive employee information and e-mails were illegally obtained and utilized as political leverage, has reinvigorated the global debate on state-sponsored cyber attacks. As a result of this breach, Sony has estimated an approximate loss of $44 million. Weeks later, another cyber attack was launched against Sony in which the PlayStation network was hacked and rendered inoperable to its users. This attack on the PlayStation network was preceded by a cyber attack in April 2011 in which the personal information, including credit card numbers, of its 70 million users was leaked, and a loss of $171 million was estimated (Richwine, 2014). In addition to the immediate costs of such attacks, corporations with a history of data breaches may experience losses in customer/client loyalty, which will affect bottom lines in the long term. A recent poll of corporations found that loss of reputation was the greatest perceived cyber risk leading to economic loss, followed by business interruption and loss of customer data (Allianz Global & Corporate Specialty, 2015).

In the public sector, hackers have accessed designs for more than 24 major U.S. weapons systems, ranging from the F-35 and F-22 stealth fighters to numerous air-defense missiles, advanced communications technologies, lasers, RC-135 River Joint spy planes, and even the Navy's Aegis antimissile system (Ingersoll, 2013). Recognizing the increasing threats, the federal government has approved a major expansion of its cyber security force. To strengthen the nation's ability to protect critical computer systems and defend its network from adversaries, the U.S. Department of Defense has set out to improve its entire cyber security workforce plan (U.S. Department of Defense Cyber Workforce Strategy, 2013).

It is important to note that a secure network is the result of a larger system including technological *as well as* human capital aspects. The following pages focus solely on human capital and do not address required technological advances and best practices in securing networks. The human capital aspect, however, is as critical as the technological. In evaluating of the Sony attacks, industry experts have highlighted that a major vulnerability was the fact that there were merely *three* full-time employees dedicated to monitoring a company network with 7,000 employees (Tribbey, 2014). Tribbey's article went on to conclude that sufficient job training for employees and subsequent surprise testing of these trainees is needed before these types of attacks will end. Unfortunately, a recent poll revealed that among the top cyber risk mitigation strategies organizations use, not a single strategy is focused on strengthening talent management systems for the personnel supporting the security networks these organizations are building (Allianz Global & Corporate Specialty, 2015).

This current chapter argues that an organization's ability to effectively manage its cyber security talent is vital to its security and success. In short, cyber security networks and risk mitigation strategies are only as strong as the human operators behind the screens. This reality should drive researchers and human resources (HR) practitioners to action. To gain advantage in the cyber fight, employers need cyber security personnel who possess the knowledge, skills, abilities, and other characteristics (KSAOs) required to effectively carry out cyber security operations. As the demands for effective cyber personnel increase, the labor pool is struggling to meet them (Beidel & Magnuson, 2011; Libicki et al., 2014). Workforce planning on the part of the employer will be critical in sustaining an effective cyber security workforce. However, to respond to the current needs and plan for future requirements, it is first important to identify job requirements that are critical to the cyber security workforce. The purpose of this chapter is to review and explore the requisite attributes of cyber security personnel at the individual level as well as multilevel conceptualizations (e.g., cyber security teams).

Toward these ends, the following sections (1) review a common framework in which to define and describe the work conducted by cyber security personnel, (2) map cyber jobs to unique workload and workforce requirements, (3) provide and discuss a multistage model of critical cyber security personnel attributes that has implications for the selection and training of cyber security personnel, and (4) discuss a multilevel approach to understanding cyber security personnel attributes within the context of cyber security teams and multiteam systems (Mathieu, Marks, & Zaccaro, 2001). The chapter concludes with a summary and implications for future research.

Defining Cyber Jobs

To date, the cyber security industry has not adopted a common lexicon through which to describe cyber security jobs. The absence of a common language restricts an organization's ability to implement effective talent management solutions. For example, organizations will be challenged to implement effective selection, training, and workforce planning initiatives without a full understanding of the KSAOs needed for these positions.

In 2012, the National Initiative for Cybersecurity Education (NICE) released a cyber security framework, developed in an attempt to describe cyber security work agnostic of organizational structures, job titles, or other potentially idiosyncratic attributes. This approach assumes that any given individual may perform tasks in more than one skill-based specialty area (e.g., information assurance compliance *and* system administration), or an individual may work within a single specialty area (e.g., information assurance *or* system administration). One potential determinant of how these positions may be defined and structured is the organization's size and resources allocated toward cyber security (NICE, 2012b). Thus, as the NICE framework notes, due to a host of organizational variables, there may not be one-to-one crosswalks of jobs to individual specialty areas.

Within the NICE framework, types of cyber work are grouped into the larger organizing constructs of *categories* and *specialty Areas*. The categories group related specialty areas together and create an overarching structure for the framework. The requisite KSAOs within each specialty area are provided. As a result, specialty areas in a given category are more similar *within* a specialty area than *between* specialty areas. A summary of the seven categories and descriptions of the types of positions included in each can be found in Table 8.1.

Workload requirements help define the unique characteristics that differentiate one professional field from another. A critical component to identifying requisite attributes for cyber security personnel is understanding the unique workload requirements of such jobs and, effectively, the KSAO requirements for effective personnel. The NICE framework synthesizes and documents a set of unique workload and workforce requirements for cyber security personnel. A summary of these requirements can be found in Table 8.2.

We have inferred from these descriptions of cyber security personnel performance requirements that successful cyber personnel would likely possess

TABLE 8.1 Categories from the Workforce Framework

Category	Description	Sample job areas
Securely provision	Conceptualizing, designing, and building secure information technology (IT) systems (i.e., responsible for some aspect of systems development)	• Information assurance compliance • Technology research and development • Systems development
Operate and maintain	Providing support, administration, and maintenance necessary to ensure effective and efficient IT system performance and security	• Data administration • Knowledge management • Systems security analysis
Protect and defend	Identification, analysis, and mitigation of threats to internal IT systems or networks	• Computer network defense analysis • Vulnerability assessment and management • Incident response
Investigate	Investigation of cyber events and/or crimes of IT systems, networks, and digital evidence	• Digital forensics • Investigation
Collect and operate	Specialized denial and deception operations and collection of cyber security information that may be used to develop intelligence	• Collection operations • Cyber operations • Cyber operations planning
Analyze	Highly specialized review and evaluation of incoming cyber security information to determine its usefulness for intelligence	• Threat analysis • All source intelligence • Exploitation analysis
Oversight and development	Providing leadership, management, direction, and/or development and advocacy so that individuals and organizations may effectively conduct cyber security work	• Legal advice and advocacy • Education and training • Strategic planning and policy development

combinations of important attributes. The existing body of literature on predictors of cyber personnel success lends initial evidence to this assertion. The following section draws from this nascent literature and from the cyber security personnel performance requirements delineated earlier to outline individual characteristics likely to be needed by cyber security personnel for effective performance. Moreover, we propose a multistage model that provides guidance regarding the attributes on which organizations should focus their selection and/ or training efforts (see Figure 8.1).

TABLE 8.2 National Initiative for Cybersecurity Education Framework for Cyber Security Workload and Workforce Requirements

Requirement	Description
Workload requirements	
Surge capacity	The need to expand resources and capabilities in response to prolonged demand
Fast paced	The need to sustain multiple work streams occurring rapidly
Transformative	The need to adapt to fundamental changes to technology, processes, and threats
High complexity	The need to employ a large number of intricate technologies and concepts
Workforce requirements	
Agile	The ability to shift between roles or needs should a threat warrant different support
Multifunctional	The ability to maintain and execute a variety of activities at any given time
Dynamic	The ability to provide for constant learning to effectively approach new endeavors and problems
Flexible	The ability to move into new roles or environments quickly to increase knowledge and skills
Informal	The ability to work in a nontraditional environment

Multistage Model for Understanding Cyber Security Personnel Attributes

Individual characteristics can be conceptualized as trait-like individual differences (e.g., cognitive ability), whereas others are more malleable attributes, such as technical knowledge (Ackerman & Humphreys, 1990; Chen, Gully, Whiteman, & Kilcullen, 2000; Hough & Schneider, 1996; Kanfer, 1990, 1992). Used in other areas of industrial and organizational psychology for years (e.g., motivation [see Barrick, Stewart, & Piotrowski, 2002], selection [Schmitt, Cortina, Ingerick, & Weichmann, 2003]), multistage models are an increasingly popular way of portraying the relationships between a broad range of individual characteristics. These models consider both types of individual differences and place them along a distal–proximal continuum, with distal traits representing stable individual differences that influence the development of proximal, malleable characteristics, which in turn have a more direct influence on employee performance at work. For example, in Zaccaro, Kemp, and Bader's (2004) multistage model of leader effectiveness, distal, stable personality attributes are expected to influence the

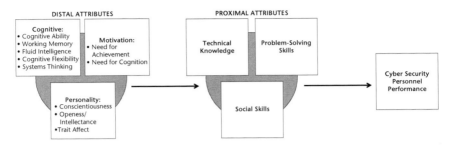

FIGURE 8.1 A Multistage Model of Cyber Security Personnel Performance

development of more proximal social skills, which in turn influence leader effectiveness.

Capturing individual attributes within multistage models is particularly important for organizational talent management personnel. It draws the critical distinctions between distal, trait-like attributes, appropriate for targeting selections systems, and proximal, malleable attributes, appropriate for targeting both selection and training programs. We propose a multistage model (see Figure 8.1) to highlight the distal and proximal attributes important for predicting cyber personnel effectiveness. The attributes included in this model are driven by the performance requirements and tasks necessary for successful performance in these positions. The complexity and diversity of cyber security personnel performance requirements suggests that cyber personnel would need multiple traits from the following categories of attributes: (1) cognitive abilities, (2) personality, (3) motivational drivers of behavior, (4) social appraisal and interpersonal skills, and (5) technical knowledge/cyber expertise. We focus first on the distal attributes likely to contribute to effective cyber personnel performance.

Distal Attributes: Cognitive

Cognitive Ability

Cognitive ability involves the collection of mental abilities that involve the capacity to reason, plan, and solve problems (Landy & Conte, 2004). It has been repeatedly related to job performance in a number of different contexts (Schmidt & Hunter, 1998). Although little empirical work exists linking cognitive ability to cyber personnel success, it has clear links to complex identification and analysis performance requirements. For example, computer network defense analysis personnel are responsible for conducting research, analysis, and correlations across a wide variety of source data sets (e.g., indications, warnings). Other cyber personnel working in legal advice and advocacy areas need to maintain knowledge of emerging relevant laws and regulations in order to resolve conflicts in standards and procedures. Employees lacking the cognitive ability to reason and plan would be ill-equipped to successfully perform these activities.

Working Memory

Related to general cognitive ability, *working memory* is the system that holds multiple pieces of transitory information in the mind, where they can be manipulated (Baddeley & Hitch, 1974). Those with enhanced working memory can store and manipulate increased visual and verbal information to reach their goals. Given the amount of information that cyber security personnel must digest and manipulate in order to, for example, monitor risk on a daily basis, it is expected that individuals with better working memory will be more effective cyber security personnel. Employees lacking working memory would find themselves unable to track the large quantities of information necessary for providing effective systems monitoring and data administration, among other requirements.

Fluid Intelligence

Also related to general cognitive ability, *fluid intelligence* includes such abilities as pattern recognition and abstract reasoning (Cattell, 1963). It has been shown to be critical in positions involving problem-solving when individuals encounter novel situations. The performance requirements of cyber personnel point to a need to problem-solve in a dynamic environment characterized by emerging and novel information. For example, cyber personnel involved in computer network defense analysis must recognize and quickly adapt to vulnerabilities in security systems on the basis of information gathered while conducting vulnerability scans. Given these performance requirements, it is expected that individuals with higher fluid intelligence will be better equipped to succeed in the cyber workforce.

Cognitive Flexibility

Cognitive flexibility refers to a person's ability to restructure his or her knowledge as an adaptive response to changing situational demands. According to Spiro and Jehng (1990), this flexibility is a function of both the way the knowledge is represented (e.g., along multiple, rather than single, conceptual dimensions) and the processes that operate on those mental representations. Cognitive flexibility is expected to assist cyber personnel while they are performing dynamic analyses in digital forensics, reacting to emerging computer-based technology that has potential for exploitation by adversaries, and developing algorithms to analyze data structures, among other demanding activities. Without cognitive flexibility, cyber personnel could not adapt their knowledge to successfully fulfill these cyber performance requirements.

Systems Thinking

Systems thinking can be defined as an approach to problem-solving in which an individual possesses an understanding of how multiple parts of a system interact and influence each other (Aronson, 1996). Systems thinking, related to the cognitive attributes already discussed, has been posited to be a key characteristic for cyber personnel (Boardman & Sauser, 2008; Richmond, 1993; Squires, Wade, Dominick, & Gelosh, 2011). Cyber personnel who demonstrate the ability to understand interactions among various system parts would be able to understand how elements within systems change over time, identify nonlinear relationships between system parts, and consider both short- and long-term consequences of actions (Sterman, 2002). As cyber personnel need to, for example, monitor and evaluate a system's compliance with information technology security, resilience, and dependability requirements and develop security-compliance processes, systems thinking has been pointed to as a key attribute of effective cyber security personnel.

Given the lack of research specific to examining the role of cognitive attributes in cyber security personnel, it is hard to make definitive statements about the relative importance of the cognitive attributes that have been presented here. However, given the inherent complexity and abstract nature of the knowledge and skills required to achieve expertise in cyber security and network defense, cognitive ability is likely to be a prominent predictor of knowledge and skill acquisition in this field (Ackerman, 1988; Gottfredson, 2002). In addition to general cognitive ability, systems thinking is also likely to play a relatively strong role in predicting cyber security job performance. The complex and intricate structures of networks require a full understanding of any particular network as a system of interrelated parts. This is particularly critical for cyber security responsibilities regarding network defense and digital forensics. Future research should examine the predictive validity of these constructs in cyber security personnel as well as their relationships with each other.

Distal Attributes: Personality

Although a number of the cyber personnel job requirements shown in Table 8.3 are largely cognitive in nature, personality attributes are also expected to play a role in cyber personnel success. *Personality* refers to individual differences in characteristic patterns of thinking, feeling, and behaving (McCrae & Costa, 1987). As these patterns affect the ways individuals behave, they have been shown to be important predictors of performance in a variety of employment contexts. Those personality attributes expected to be most relevant to performance in the cyber security context are conscientiousness, openness/intellectance, and dispositional affect.

Conscientiousness

Individuals high in *conscientiousness* are efficient and organized, with excellent attention to details. They exhibit a tendency to show self-discipline, act dutifully,

TABLE 8.3 Sample Cyber Security Job Tasks and Knowledge, Skills, and Abilities (KSAs)

Job	Sample tasks	Sample KSAs
Information assurance compliance	• Develop methods to monitor and measure risk, compliance, and assurance efforts • Monitor and evaluate a system's compliance with information technology security, resilience, and dependability requirements • Recommend new or revised security, resilience, and dependability measures on the basis of results of reviews • Develop security compliance processes and/or audits for external services (e.g., cloud service providers, data centers)	• Knowledge of computer network defense and vulnerability assessment tools and their capabilities • Knowledge of data administration and standardization policies and standards • Knowledge of system diagnostic tools and fault-identification techniques • Skill in identifying measures or indicators of system performance and the actions needed to improve or correct performance relative to the goals of the system
Data administration	• Analyze and define requirements and specifications • Monitor and maintain databases to ensure optimal performance • Provide recommendations on new database technologies and architectures • Develop data standards, policies, and procedures	• Knowledge of data administration and standardization policies and standards • Knowledge of sources, characteristics, and use of the organization's data assets • Skill in designing databases
Computer network defense analysis	• Develop content for computer network defense tools • Perform computer network defense trend analysis and reporting • Conduct tests of information assurance safeguards in accordance with established test plans and procedures • Conduct research, analysis, and correlation across a wide variety of source data sets (e.g., indications, warnings)	• Knowledge of intrusion-detection system tools and applications • Knowledge of information assurance principles and organizational requirements that are relevant to confidentiality, integrity, availability, authentication, and nonrepudiation • Skill in conducting vulnerability scans and recognizing vulnerabilities in security systems

(*Continued*)

TABLE 8.3 Sample Cyber Security Job Tasks and Knowledge, Skills, and Abilities (KSAs) (Continued)

Job	Sample tasks	Sample KSAs
Digital forensics	• Collect and analyze intrusion artifacts and use discovered data to enable mitigation of potential computer network defense incidents within the enterprise • Identify digital evidence for examination and analysis in such a way as to avoid unintentional alteration • Perform dynamic analysis to boot an image of a drive to see the intrusion as the user may have seen it in a native environment • Recognize and accurately report forensic artifacts indicative of a particular operating system	• Knowledge of basic concepts and practices of processing digital forensic data • Knowledge of server diagnostic tools and fault-identification techniques • Skills in developing, testing, and implementing network infrastructure contingency and recovery plans
Legal advice and advocacy	• Acquire and maintain a working knowledge of relevant laws, regulations, policies, standards, and procedures • Evaluate, monitor, and ensure compliance with information communication technology security policies and relevant legal and regulatory requirements • Interpret and apply laws, regulations, policies, standards, and procedures to specific issues • Resolve conflicts in laws regulations, policies, standards, and procedures	• Knowledge of emerging computer-based technology that has potential for exploitation by adversaries • Skill in tracking and analyzing technical and legal trends that will affect cyber activities • Knowledge of international traffic in arms regulations and relevance to cyber security

and aim for achievement (Thompson, 2008). Conscientiousness has been linked to job performance across contexts (Barrick & Mount, 1991; Dudley, Orvis, Lebiecki, & Cortina, 2006), but certain facets of it may have important implications for cyber security personnel. Although the self-discipline and achievement-striving nature of highly conscientious individuals may assist in cyber performance, findings in the adaptability literature (LePine, Colquitt, & Erez, 2006) have demonstrated that those facets reflecting deliberation and order may hinder cyber personnel's ability to adapt to new situations For example, whereas conscientiousness may greatly facilitate cyber personnel in data administration's ability to maintain databases to ensure optimal performance and other activities requiring great attention to detail, too much of a focus on structure and order may hinder cyber personnel who need to respond quickly to improve or correct system performance in response to a vulnerability.

Openness/Intellectance

Openness/intellectance (Costa & McCrae, 1992) involves active imagination; aesthetic sensitivity; attentiveness to inner feelings; preference for variety; and, most relevant to cyber personnel, intellectual curiosity. People high in openness/intellectance are more motivated to engage in intellectual pursuits that increase their knowledge in areas of interest (Furnham, Swami, Arteche, & Chamorro-Premuzic, 2008). These individuals, particularly those who also are highly achievement driven by virtue of their conscientiousness, are likely to continue acquiring knowledge to facilitate their job performance. Cyber personnel may also benefit from higher levels of openness as it has been linked to creativity and "thinking outside the box." Given that the cyber world requires the seeking out and development of knowledge of a rapidly evolving technical nature (e.g., cryptology, available diagnostic tools, fault-identification techniques) and skill in developing solutions to emerging threats (NICE, 2012b), it is likely that our future superior cyber personnel will have high openness and intellectance driving them to learn more about their field and develop creative solutions to promote network defense.

Trait Affect

In addition to the major personality components already described, it is likely that affect also plays a role in cyber security personnel success. *Trait affect* is the overall tendency to perceive things through a positive or negative lens. Whereas individuals higher in trait positive affect have a propensity to experience positively activated emotional states, individuals higher in trait negative affect have a propensity to attend to negative stimuli (Moriya & Tanno, 2008). This is critical to the ability to detect threats quickly (Augustine, Larsen, & Elliot, 2013), which is critical for successful cyber personnel performance, particularly for those in computer network defense analysis and digital forensics positions. Effectively, individuals who are higher in trait negative affect are likely to demonstrate higher levels of job performance than are individuals low in trait negative affect.

Given the lack of research specifically examining the role of personality attributes in cyber security personnel, it is hard to make definitive statements about the relative importance of the personality attributes described here. However, it can be argued that openness/intellectance may be relatively more critical given the complex nature of cyber security threats. That is, openness/intellectance predisposes an individual to think creatively about solutions, which may be required to effectively manage ever changing cyber threats demanding novel solutions. In addition, constant changes in technology necessitate continuous learning, which may lead an individual high in openness/intellectance to be more successful over time than an individual low in openness/intellectance.

Distal Attributes: Motivation

In addition to the cognitive and personality attributes just described, individual motivations, notably need for achievement and need for cognition, are also likely important for cyber security personnel success. Individual differences in motivation have been considered to influence learning and performance for a considerable time (Heggestad & Kanfer, 2000).

Need for Achievement

Need for achievement refers to an individual's desire to succeed and achieve goals. Individuals high in need for achievement believe that they are the drivers of their own success (McClelland, 1987). Need for achievement has been noted as an important motivator across positions, in information technology positions more specifically (Eyob, 1994), and is likely to predict performance in cyber positions as well. Notably, individuals with high cognitive ability or systems thinking skills are unlikely to be successful in cyber security without the associated drive to direct these abilities toward effective performance. In effect, cognitive attributes are likely to interact with motivational attributes in understanding effective cyber security performance.

Need for Cognition

Need for cognition is a second motivational variable likely to contribute to success in cyber roles; it reflects the extent to which individuals are inclined toward effortful cognitive activities (Cacioppo & Petty, 1982). Not surprisingly, need for cognition has been shown to be moderately related to fluid intelligence (Fleischhauer et al., 2009). Given the cognitive nature of many of the performance requirements of cyber personnel, the best candidates are likely to be those who are motivated toward cognitive activities. Along with high cognitive abilities, these individuals have both the drive and intellectual ability to continually develop and absorb the technical knowledge necessary to fulfill their positions' performance requirements. Similar to need for achievement, cognitive attributes are likely to interact with need for cognition in understanding effective cyber security performance.

Proximal Attributes

The attributes already described are those that are stable, trait-like individual differences. In other words, it is unlikely that they will change drastically throughout an individual's adulthood. It is those distal attributes that an organization cannot readily train, and they are, therefore, more appropriate for targeting in selection procedures as opposed to training interventions. Proximal attributes are the more malleable knowledges and skills that provide the critical link between distal attributes and on-the-job behaviors and, ultimately, performance. It is important to note that as these attributes are malleable, they are appropriate for not only selection initiatives but also for training interventions. Those proximal attributes particularly important for linking the aforementioned distal attributes to cyber security personnel performance are technical knowledge, problem-solving skills, and social skills.

Technical Knowledge

In order to effectively perform the cyber security job tasks outlined in Table 8.3, individuals must have expertise in a number of technical knowledge areas. The specific technical knowledge areas vary by position. For example, information assurance compliance personnel require knowledge of computer network defense and vulnerability assessment tools, whereas individuals in legal advice and advocacy positions need thorough knowledge of relevant laws, regulations, policies, standards, and procedures. Without knowledge of intrusion-detection system tools, a computer network defense analyst could not successfully perform computer network defense trend analyses.

The acquisition of such technical knowledge is likely driven by a combination of the distal attributes described earlier and other contextual/situational factors. For example, individuals high in cognitive ability, need for cognition, and conscientiousness are likely to have both the underlying ability to digest technical information and the drive to seek it out on their own. In this way, technical knowledge serves as the critical link mentioned earlier between some of the distal attributes and subsequent cyber security personnel performance.

Problem-Solving Skills

Problem-solving skills refers to a complex higher order cognitive process that requires the use of multiple fundamental skills to reach a desired goal (Goldstein & Lewin, 1987). Problem-solving skills are a second individual attribute important for fulfilling cyber performance requirements. For example, problem-solving skills are needed to effectively identify indicators of system performance and the actions needed to improve or correct performance relative to the goals of the system. This is essentially a problem-solving task, in which the employee must gather information on the current state of the system (problem identification), compare the current state to the desired state (problem representation), develop a strategy to move the system from the current to the desired state (solution generation), execute that strategy, and monitor its effectiveness. Without ample problem-solving skills, an individual could not successfully navigate this process.

Note that the development of problem-solving skills has been shown to be related to fluid intelligence, working memory, and cognitive ability (Hambrick & Engle, 2003), three of the distal attributes described earlier. Problem-solving skills are also facilitated by extensive technical knowledge in an area (Pretz, Naples, & Sternberg, 2003). In this way, problem-solving skills, in combination with other proximal attributes, serve as an additional link between distal attributes and cyber performance. For example, systems thinking may serve as an antecedent to effective problem-solving skills, which in turn are positively related to cyber security performance.

Social Skills

Although the majority of cyber security personnel job requirements are cognitive in nature, there is a notable amount of social interaction underlying these requirements (NICE, 2012b). For example, some investigative positions explicitly require interaction with witnesses, and legal positions require interaction with policy makers. Therefore, the social skills of individuals should not be ignored when considering those attributes likely to contribute to successful cyber security personnel performance. Of the broad spectrum of social-appraisal skills, it is likely that communication skills and situational awareness are particularly important for cyber security personnel. *Situational awareness* refers to a person's ability to perceive and integrate the elements within his or her environment as they interact and change over time (Sarter & Woods, 1991).

As for many of the attributes previously, there is no existing research specifically examining the theoretical links between the proximal attributes noted here and cyber security personnel performance. However, the proximal attribute that may prove to be relatively more critical is technical knowledge. This is an intuitive assumption to make—possessing the requisite technical knowledge to do a job would be a minimum standard for selection into any position. However, the implication of emphasizing the importance of technical knowledge in predicting cyber security personnel success is that extensive efforts would need to be taken to develop the technical expertise within the existing workforce given that the current demand for such expertise far exceeds the supply.

In recognition of this reality, the U.S. Department of Defense has focused most of its resources on selecting enlisted personnel with the aptitude for success in technical training rather than attempting to enlist personnel with extant cyber-related certifications (Gould, 2012; Trippe, Moriarty, Russell, Carretta, & Beatty, 2014). Federal agencies like the National Security Agency and the Central Intelligence Agency and large government contractors also develop talent from within, but they often begin with degreed personnel in science, technology, engineering, and math disciplines (Libicki et al., 2014).

Cyber Security Personnel Attributes: A Multilevel Approach

Up to this point, we have discussed cyber security personnel at the individual level. This does not fully capture the nature of cyber security jobs/positions as these functions are often completed in the context of *cyber security teams* (CSTs). In its current iteration, the NICE framework does not include teamwork KSAO requirements as part of the workload and subsequent workforce requirements of cyber security jobs/positions. However, in recent reports, the Pentagon has unveiled plans to deploy more than 100 CSTs by the end of 2015 (Sternstein, 2013), highlighting the reality of cyber security as existing within a team context and necessitating a consideration of attribute requirements beyond the individual level.

Researchers have argued that team performance is a function of both collective levels of task-specific competencies and teamwork skills (Cannon-Bowers, Tannenbaum, Salas, & Volpe, 1995). As such, teamwork among cyber security personnel presents a unique set of considerations for requisite attributes. One framework through which one can identify these unique requisite attributes was proposed by Orvis and Zaccaro (2008), in which the authors noted that in team staffing, one should give consideration to both transportable and contextual personnel attributes. *Transportable attributes* refer to the KSAOs that team members must have regardless of their assigned team and/or the tasks they are assigned to. *Contextual attributes*, conversely, refer to KSAOs that are directly aligned with the specific task being completed by the team and are not applicable outside of the task context.

Transportable Attributes

Collectivism

Authors have identified collectivism as a critical transportable attribute when considering team staffing (Orvis & Zaccaro, 2008). *Collectivism* refers to one's generic desire for group solidarity and preference toward teamwork (Zaccaro & DiRosa, 2012). Conceptualizing the attribute as a context-free construct, earlier investigations have provided support for the importance of team collectivistic composition as a driver of team performance (Eby & Dobbins, 1997). In 2007, Bell meta-analytically examined the importance of collectivistic orientation in team performance across team types. She separated this construct into (1) preference for group harmony and (2) preference for teamwork (vs. preference for autonomous teamwork). Analyses revealed that, although preference for harmony predicted team performance, team context was a critical factor to consider. However, although preference for working in teams predicted team performance, team context was not shown to be a critical factor to consider.

Personality

The Big Five personality dimensions (Barrick, Stewart, Neubert, & Mount, 1998) have also been examined as transportable team attributes. Through a meta-analysis, Barrick et al. (1998) found that team personality composition was related to team performance, with emotional stability (mean score) and agreeableness (mean and minimum scores) showing the strongest relationships. "The true-score correlation for agreeableness was quite high (.35) and indicates that it is a particularly important predictor in jobs involving cooperative and interdependent work" (Barrick et al., 1998, p. 181). Along the same lines, Peeters, van Tuijl, Rutte, and Reymen (2006) found that agreeableness was positively associated with team performance and that variability in this construct predicted team performance negatively. Various composition scores (e.g., mean, minimum) of team personality have also been found to have significant relationships with team performance, with the strongest relationships observed for agreeableness and conscientiousness (both mean and minimum), suggesting that the social harmony and subsequent performance of a team can be influenced by a single disagreeable member. Subsequent analyses suggested that the ability of these attributes to predict team performance was not dependent on job context.

Cannon-Bowers et al. (1995) provided a delineation of the teamwork knowledge and skills that they considered to be transportable: (1) morale building, (2) conflict resolution, (3) information exchange, (4) task motivation, (5) cooperation, (6) consultation with others, and (7) assertiveness. In one study specifically examining teamwork within cyber security jobs, Rajivan et al. (2010) found that simply encouraging analysts to work as a team (e.g., cooperation, consultation with others, information exchange) and providing team-level rewards (i.e., task motivation) led to better team performance. Meta-analytic results and primary studies have suggested that transportable KSAOs are important for team effectiveness.

In contrast, as mentioned earlier, contextual attributes are KSAOs that are directly aligned to the specific tasks being completed by a team and are less applicable outside of the task context. One important characteristic of workload requirements that may affect contextual attributes for CSTs is *cognitive load*. As outlined in the NICE framework, cyber security jobs present unique workload requirements, including surge capacity, a fast-paced work context, transformative demands, and a high degree of complexity. Collectively, these workload requirements—along with the workforce requirements that incumbents be multifunctional, dynamic, and flexible—establish the case for cyber security jobs as jobs operating in a complex, dynamic, high-stakes environment. The existing literature on adaptive and crisis-oriented teams highlights a number of potential requirements to consider for effective performance in CSTs (Pulakos, Arad, Donovan, & Plamondon, 2000). These requirements are discussed in the following sections.

Contextual Attributes

The cyber security workforce environment presents an occupational context in which there is a high degree of pressure and dynamism. Technological advances and software changes require personnel to constantly learn and adapt to new systems (NICE, 2012b). In addition, with the continuous and growing threat of cyber attacks, constant vigilance is required to avoid/defend against potential network breaches. These realities are reflected in the NICE framework's identified workload and workforce requirements. Given these environmental characteristics, there may be some contextual team attributes that are more relevant for CSTs than others. Some of these may be (1) team cohesion, (2) transactive memory, and (3) shared mental models. It is important to recognize that these constructs are sometimes referred to as *team processes/emergent states* rather than attributes (i.e., inputs) of the team. However, given the episodic nature of team effectiveness (Marks, Mathieu, & Zaccaro, 2001), a focus on these constructs attempts to highlight how team emergent states, in and of themselves, become inputs (i.e., attributes) of teams as they undergo the developmental process (Mathieu, Maynard, Rapp, & Gilson, 2008).

Cohesion

Cohesion refers to a team's collective commitment to an overall task and to each other (Goodman, Ravlin, & Schminke, 1987). Meta-analytic results have identified three distinct dimensions of cohesion: interpersonal attraction, task commitment, and pride (Beal, Cohen, Burke, & McLendon, 2003). Beal et al. (2003) also provided evidence of each construct's unique contribution to team performance and noted that "as team workflow increased, the cohesion–performance relationship became stronger" (p. 998). Given the nature of the workload requirements for CSTs, cohesion represents a potentially critical factor in ensuring team success. Specifically, with the need for cyber security personnel to expand their resources and capabilities in response to prolonged demand (surge capacity) and to sustain multiple work streams occurring rapidly (fast pace), this context is likely to require a high degree of motivation and commitment (among team members) to perform in such a cognitively and physically taxing work environment.

Transactive Memory Systems

Transactive memory systems refers, in this context, to a set of individual memory systems in combination with the communication among the individuals composing a team (Wegner, 1987). In other words, transactive memory systems capture the collective knowledge of who knows what. Transactive memory systems benefit team performance through enhanced communication and coordination as a function of the group's awareness of its collective knowledge. On the basis of this notion, empirical evidence has linked transactive memory systems and team performance (Lewis, 2004; Rulke & Rau, 2000). In addition, researchers have linked transactive memory systems within a team to learning transfer (Lewis, Lange, & Gillis, 2005). These authors provided evidence that transactive memory systems affect a team's ability to apply prior learning to new tasks. As such, transactive memory systems represent a critical team attribute to consider as an antecedent of effective CST performance. Specifically, given that workforce requirements necessitate CST members to possess the ability to shift between roles and needs (i.e., be agile) as well as the ability to be constantly learning to effectively approach new problems (i.e., be dynamic), high transactive memory systems increase the likelihood of being able to identify and tap into the requisite knowledge, skills, and abilities distributed among team members and enhance team learning to address existing threats in a fast-paced environment.

Shared Mental Models

Shared mental models represent an organized understanding or mental representation of knowledge that is shared by team members (Mathieu, Heffner, Goodwin, Cannon-Bowers, & Salas, 2005). *Task* shared mental models suggest that team members share a common mental schema regarding their tasks and their operating environment. Conversely, *team* shared mental models reflect collective understanding among team members regarding how they interact with one another. Evidence has implicated both task and team shared mental models as predictors of team performance. However, whereas team shared mental models show a direct effect on team performance, task shared mental models show an indirect effect on performance through team processes (Mathieu et al., 2005). Given the workload and workforce requirements found in cyber security, shared mental models represent a potentially critical predictive attribute of team success. Specifically, given that workforce requirements necessitate that team members to possess the ability to shift between roles and needs in response to changing threats and to employ a large number of intricate technologies and concepts, having a clear shared mental model within a team with respect to *what* needs to be done as well as *how* it is going to be done would prove beneficial to cyber team performance.

Given the lack of existing empirical research focused on the team attributes noted here and CST performance, the relative importance of the discussed attributes is difficult determine. However, among the contextual attributes, transactive memory systems may have a relatively stronger role in predicting CST performance. This supposition is based on the notion that transactive memory systems may support CSTs in meeting the fast-paced, dynamic, knowledge-based workload requirements that characterize cyber security threats. Future research is needed to support this assertion.

Cyber Security Multiteam Systems

Whereas the previous sections described important attributes for individuals' performance in cyber security positions and attributes important for the success of cyber security teams, the following consider a third, higher level of attributes—those of cyber security multiteam systems (MTSs). Former Homeland Security secretary Michael Chertoff recently noted that single teams are not sufficient to ensure cyber security; rather, "everyone has to be part of the battlefield," and multiple groups working toward minimizing risk are necessary (Armerding, 2014). Mathieu et al. (2001), described such teams as *MTSs*, or "two or more teams that interface directly and interdependently in response to environmental contingencies toward the accomplishment of collective goals" (p. 290). MTSs often appear in environments where goals are too large for a single team to accomplish (e.g., incident command systems [Moynihan, 2007], space missions [Caldwell, 2005]).

The complexity and the time-sensitive nature of cyber security issues has given rise to the creation of at least one such MTS in cyber security: the cyber security incident response teams (CSIRT; Zaccaro, Chen, Winslow, & Hargrove, 2014). Although there are a number of CSIRT structures, a sample structure consists of teams of platform specialists, artifact analyst staff, vulnerability handlers, incident handlers, hotline/help desk/triage staff, their respective team leaders, and an overall CSIRT manager. Other variations may include law enforcement and public relations teams. Each of these teams has its own responsibilities and proximal goals to achieve in reaction to a cyber security incident. Notably, as part of an MTS, the teams share at least one common distal goal (e.g., eradicating a threat, communicating subsequent learned intelligence).

In pursuit of their common goal, individual component teams in CSIRTs, as in other MTSs, exhibit input, process, and outcome interdependence with at least one other team in the CSIRT (Mathieu et al., 2001). *Input interdependence* refers to the sharing of human, informational, technological, or financial resources, whereas *process interdependence* refers to the degree of interteam interaction required during completion of the overall CSIRT mission. For example, forensics team processes may be interdependent with those of threat intelligence teams as they require information from threat intelligence in order to determine the nature of an incident. *Outcome interdependence* refers to the degree to which the outcomes for each of the CSIRT component teams depend upon the goal accomplishments of other teams in the CSIRT.

Just as CSIRTs' component teams share a common overall goal and exhibit input, process, and outcome interdependencies, they also share common requirements for success. Among others, information sharing, knowledge management, collective problem-solving, and adaptation and innovation have been pointed to as critical factors in MTS effectiveness (Zaccaro et al., 2014). In other words, processes occurring between component teams are critical drivers of MTS success

(Davison, Hollenbeck, Barnes, Sleesman, & Ilgen, 2012; DeChurch & Marks, 2006; Marks, DeChurch, Mathieu, Panzer, & Alonso, 2005). In the context of CSIRTs, component teams must effectively and efficiently share information. They must share this information among teams that are often geographically dispersed and composed of individuals with different technical backgrounds. They must also participate in problem-solving processes, not only within single teams but at the interteam level, with different teams providing portions of critical input in the problem-definition and problem-resolution phases (Zaccaro et al., 2014). In order to successfully fulfill these requirements for performance, successful CSIRTs are likely to be characterized by shared mental models and leadership coordination, among other attributes.

Shared Mental Models

Described earlier at the team level, shared mental models represent understandings or mental representations that are shared among team members (Mathieu et al., 2005). Within an MTS, the concept of shared mental models can be extended to represent an organized understanding of task and team knowledge that is shared by component teams within the MTS. Hinsz and Betts (2011) noted that these shared understandings among component teams are likely to facilitate MTS performance. For example, a shared multiteam-interaction mental model describes a shared understanding of the appropriate between-teams activities (Murase, Carter, DeChurch, & Marks, 2014). Likewise, the shared understanding of the MTS's distal goal ensures that the component teams are each working toward the same ultimate outcome. In CSIRTs, shared mental models can ensure that critical activities (e.g., determining the nature of an event) are being investigated by the appropriate component teams and only the appropriate component teams. This allows for timely investigations without sacrificing resources of other component teams that may be needed to focus on eradicating the threat.

Leadership Coordination

Leadership has long been pointed to as a key driver of followers' understanding of their tasks and strategies for achieving proximal and distal goals (e.g., Fiedler, 1967; House, 1971; Murase, Resick, Jiménez, Sanz, & DeChurch, 2011). In an MTS context, research by Murase et al. (2014) has provided initial evidence of the critical role that boundary-spanning leadership plays in facilitating critical between-teams processes in MTSs (e.g., multiteam-interaction mental models). Notably, leaders, through their strategic communications, can enable the between-teams coordination critical for MTS success (Murase et al., 2014). In a CSIRT, these leaders must create strategic communications that drive teams toward their shared distal goal of threat eradication in addition to outlining and monitoring the achievement of the proximal goals each team is responsible for.

Compositional Attributes

Although CSIRTs' component teams are driven to success with effective shared mental models and leadership coordination, we recognize that they can vary among a number of different MTS features that may affect how these are fostered. These features have been categorized as compositional attributes, linkage attributes, and developmental attributes. *Compositional attributes*, to name a few, include the number of component teams, total number of individual members across teams, number of organizations represented, and degree of heterogeneity in the core purposes and missions of component teams. *Linkage attributes* include the ordering of teams according to levels of responsibility, degree of integrated coordination among members of different component teams, and communication structure. Finally, *developmental attributes* include the source of initial CSIRT formation (e.g., appointed, emergent), anticipated duration, membership constancy, and constancy of linkages among component teams.

These compositional attributes likely affect the importance of factors that foster CSIRT effectiveness and the actions that CSIRT team members and leaders should take to facilitate this effectiveness. For example, although shared mental models are important drivers of success across CSIRTs, leaders may not need to spend as much time facilitating these models among component teams from the same organization that have constant members, similar existing communication structures, and limited integrated coordination among members of different component teams. Future research and practice could benefit from further exploration of CSIRT dynamics to outline best practices in this area that take into account the different compositional attributes of CSIRTs.

Summary

The proposed multistage model includes a comprehensive set of individual difference characteristics that have been demonstrated to be reliable and valid predictors of human performance (Ackerman, 1992; Barrick & Mount, 1991; Schmidt & Hunter, 1998). The desirability of these characteristics from both theoretical and empirical perspectives represents the accumulation of many contributions of personnel psychology to the fundamental design of selection and classification systems. In recognizing the wide selection of potential attributes that may affect cyber security personnel performance, it is important to note that an emphasis on any one attribute (above another) should (1) be supported by empirical research and (2) be informed by and aligned with the talent-management strategy adopted by the organization.

To the former point, there is a lack of existing research focused primarily on cyber security personnel. In the absence of this research, determining the relative importance among the proposed constructs is difficult. However, this chapter has highlighted the relative theoretical importance of cognitive ability, systems thinking, openness/intellectance, technical knowledge, and transactive memory systems as potential avenues for future research. The selection of these attributes was based on the assumptions that they are more strongly tied than others to the workload/workforce requirements of cyber security personnel. Future research should examine the criterion-related validity of these attributes and explore the relationships among them to strengthen our understanding of cyber security personnel performance.

To the latter point, the current labor market, in which the demand for cyber security talent far exceeds the supply (Beidel & Magnuson, 2011; Libicki et al., 2014), necessitates an emphasis on the development of talent within the existing workforce, thus suggesting the relative importance of proximal attributes over distal attributes as the former are considered to be more trainable. This does not negate the use of selection, because as selection may be applied to the existing workforce to identify individuals who are more likely to be successful in training. However, to meet workforce demands, selection ratios are likely to be high, thus decreasing the utility (Taylor & Russell, 1939) of a purely selection-based approach and an emphasis on distal attributes. Until the workforce market for cyber security personnel changes, in regard to application, the relative importance and emphasis on any of the attributes noted in this chapter will have to be driven by the existing labor force. As a whole, this chapter presents a foundation on which organizations may base their talent-management systems. The management of cyber security talent is a cyber risk–mitigation strategy that should be adopted by all organizations seeking to secure their computer networks. However, as noted in the opening of the chapter, organizations do not place an emphasis on talent management in their risk-mitigation strategies. This presents an opportunity for organizational researchers, HR practitioners, and security risk managers to work collaboratively in addressing this challenge.

REFERENCES

Ackerman, P. L. (1988). Determinants of individual differences during skill acquisition: Cognitive abilities and information processing. *Journal of Experimental Psychology: General, 117*, 288–318.

Ackerman, P. L. (1992). Predicting individual difference in complex skill acquisition: Dynamics of ability determinants. *Journal of Applied Psychology, 77*, 598–614.

Ackerman, P. L., & Humphreys, L. G. (1990). Individual differences theory in industrial and organizational psychology. In M. D. Dunnette & L. Hough (Eds.), *Handbook of industrial and organizational psychology* (2nd ed., Vol. 1, pp. 223–282). Palo Alto, CA: Consulting Psychologists Press.

Allianz Global & Corporate Specialty. (2015). *Allianz risk barometer 2015*. Retrieved from http://www.agcs.allianz.com/insights/white-papers-and-case-studies/risk-barometer-2015/

Armerding, T. (2014, November 5). *Chertoff: Cybersecurity takes teamwork*. Retrieved from http://www.csoonline.com/article/2844133/data-protection/chertoff-cybersecurity-takes-teamwork.htm

Aronson, D. (1996). *Overview of systems thinking.* Retrieved from http://www.thinking.net/Systems_Thinking/OverviewSTarticle.pdf

Augustine, A. A., Larsen, R. J., Elliot, A. J. (2013). Affect is greater than, not equal to, condition: Condition and person effects in affective priming paradigms. *Journal of Personality, 81,* 355–364.

Baddeley, A. D., & Hitch, G. (1974). Working memory. In G. A. Bower (Ed.), *Psychology of learning and motivation* (Vol. 8, pp. 47–89). New York: Academic Press.

Barrick, M. R., & Mount, M. K. (1991). The Big Five personality dimensions and job performance: A meta-analysis. *Personnel Psychology, 44,* 1–26.

Barrick, M. R., Stewart, G. L., Neubert, M. J., & Mount, M. K. (1998). Relating member ability and personality to work-team processes and team effectiveness. *Journal of Applied Psychology, 83,* 377–391.

Barrick, M. R., Stewart, G. L., & Piotrowski, M. (2002). Personality and job performance: Test of the mediating effects of motivation among sales representatives. *Journal of Applied Psychology, 87,* 43–51.

Beal, D. J., Cohen, R. R., Burke, M. J., McLendon, C. L. (2003). Cohesion and performance in groups: A meta-analytic clarification of construct relations. *Journal of Applied Psychology, 88,* 989–1004.

Beidel, E., & Magnuson, S. (2011, August). Government, military face severe shortage of cybersecurity experts. *National Defense.* Retrieved from http://www.nationaldefensemagazine.org/archive/2011/August/Pages/Government,MilitaryFaceSevereShortageOfCybersecurityExperts.aspx

Bell, S. T. (2007). Deep-level composition variables as predictors of team performance: A meta-analysis. *Journal of Applied Psychology, 92,* 595–615.

Boardman, J., & Sauser, B. (2008). *Systems thinking: Coping with 21st century problems.* Boca Raton, FL: CRC Press.

Cacioppo, J. T., Petty, R. E. (1982). The need for cognition. *Journal of Personality and Social Psychology, 42,* 116–131.

Caldwell, B. S. (2005). Multi-team dynamics and distribution expertise in mission operations. *Aviation, Space, and Environmental Medicine, 76*(6, Suppl.), B145–B153.

Cannon-Bowers, J. A., Tannenbaum, S. I., Salas, E., Volpe, C. E. (1995). Defining competencies and establishing team training requirements. In R. Guzzo & E. Salas (Eds.), *Team effectiveness and decision making in organizations* (pp. 333–380). San Francisco: Jossey-Bass.

Cattell, R. B. (1963). Theory of fluid and crystallized intelligence: A critical experiment. *Journal of Educational Psychology, 54,* 1–22.

Chen, G., Gully, S. M., Whiteman, J. A., & Kilcullen, R. N. (2000). Examination of relationships among trait-like individual differences, state-like individual differences, and learning performance. *Journal of Applied Psychology, 85,* 835–847.

Costa, P. T., & McCrae, R. R. (1992). *NEO PI-R professional manual.* Odessa, FL: Psychological Assessment Resources.

Davison, R. B., Hollenbeck, J. R., Barnes, C. M., Sleesman, D. J., & Ilgen, D. R. (2012). Coordinated action in multiteam systems. *Journal of Applied Psychology, 87,* 808–824.

DeChurch, L. A. & Marks, M. A. (2006). Leadership in multiteam systems. *Journal of Applied Psychology, 91,* 311–326.

Dudley, N. M., Orvis, K. A., Lebiecki, J. E., & Cortina, J. M. (2006). A meta-analytic investigation of conscientiousness in the prediction of job performance: Examining the intercorrelations and the incremental validity of narrow traits. *Journal of Applied Psychology, 9,* 40–57.

Eby, L. T., & Dobbins, G. H. (1997). Collectivistic orientation in teams: An individual and group-level analysis. *Journal of Organizational Behavior, 18*, 275–295.

Eyob, E. (1994). Managing the motivation of information technology staff for higher organizational productive and employee job satisfaction. *Journal of International Information Management, 3*(1), Article 3. Retrieved from http://scholarworks.lib.csusb.edu/jiim/vol3/iss1/3

Fiedler, F. E. (1967). *A theory of leadership effectiveness*. New York: McGraw-Hill.

Fleischhauer, M., Enge, S., Brocke, B., Ullrich, J., Strobel, A., & Strobel, A. (2010). Same or different? Clarifying the relationship of need for cognition to personality and intelligence. *Personality and Social Psychology Bulletin, 36*, 82–96.

Furnham, A., Swami, V., Arteche, A., & Chamorro-Premuzic, T. (2008). Cognitive ability, learning approaches and personality correlates of general knowledge. *Educational Psychology, 28*, 427–437.

Goldstein, F. C., & Levin, H. S. (1987). Disorders of reasoning and problem-solving ability. In M. Meier, A. Benton, & L. Diller (Eds.), *Neuropsychological rehabilitation* (pp. 327–344). New York: Guilford Press.

Goodman, P. S., Ravlin, E. C., & Schminke, M. (1987). Understanding groups in organizations. In B. M. Staw & L. L., Cummings (Eds.), *Research in organizational behavior* (Vol. 9, pp. 121–173). Greenwich, CT: JAI Press.

Gottfredson, L. S. (2002). Where and why g matters: Not a mystery. *Human Performance, 15*, 25–46.

Gould, J. (2013, April 15). Cyber soldiers: Army set to load up 2 new enlisted MOSs. *Army Times, 1*, 8–19.

Hambrick, D. Z., & Engle, R. W. (2003). The role of working memory in problem solving. In J. E. Davidson & R. J. Sternberg (Eds.), *The psychology of problem solving* (pp. 176–206). Cambridge, England: Cambridge University Press.

Heggestad, E. D., & Kanfer, R. (2000). Individual differences in trait motivation: development of the motivational trait questionnaire. *International Journal of Educational Research, 33*, 751–776.

Hinsz, V. B., & Betts, K. R. (2011). Conflict in multipleteam situations. In S. J. Zacarro, M. A. Marks, & L. A. DeChurch (Eds.), *Multiteam systems: An organization form for dynamic and complex environments* (pp. 289–321). New York: Routledge.

Hough, L. M., & Schneider, R. J. (1996). Personality traits, taxonomies, and applications in organizations. In K. R. Murphy (Ed.), *Individual differences and behavior in organizations* (pp. 31–88). San Francisco: Jossey-Bass.

House, R. J. (1971). A path goal theory of leader effectiveness. *Administrative Science Quarterly, 16*, 321–339.

Ingersoll, G. (2013, May 28). REPORT: Chinese hackers stole plans for dozens of critical US weapons. *Business Insider*. Retrieved from http://www.businessinsider.com/china-hacked-us-military-weapons-systems-2013-5

Kanfer, R. (1990). Motivation theory and industrial and organizational psychology. In M. D. Dunnette & L. Hough (Eds.), *Handbook of industrial and organizational psychology* (2nd ed., Vol. 1, pp. 75–170). Palo Alto, CA: Consulting Psychologists Press.

Kanfer, R. (1992). Work motivation: New directions in theory and research. In C. L. Cooper & I. T. Robertson (Eds.), *International review of industrial and organizational psychology* (Vol. 7, pp. 1–53). New York: Wiley.

Landy, F. J., & Conte, J. M. (2004). *Work in the 21st century: An introduction to industrial and organizational psychology*. Boston: McGraw-Hill.

LePine, J. A., Colquitt, J. A., & Erez, A. (2006). Adaptability to changing task contexts: Effects of general cognitive ability, conscientiousness, and openness to experience. *Personnel Psychology, 53*, 563–593.

Lewis, K. (2004). Knowledge and performance in knowledge-worker teams: A longitudinal study of transactive memory systems. *Management Science, 50*, 1519–1533.

Lewis, K., Lange, D., & Gillis, L. (2005). Transactive memory systems, learning, and learning transfer. *Organization Science, 16*, 581–598.

Libicki, M. C., Senty, D., & Pollack, J. (2014). *Hackers wanted: An examination of the cybersecurity labor market.* Santa Monica, CA: RAND Corporation.

McClelland, D. C. (1987). *Human motivation.* Cambridge, England: Cambridge University Press.

McCrae, R. R., & Costa, P. T. (1987). Validation of the five-factor model of personality across instruments and observers. *Journal of Personality and Social Psychology, 52*, 81–90.

Marks, M. A., DeChurch, L. A., Mathieu, J. E., Panzer, F. J., & Alonso, A. (2005). Teamwork in multiteam systems. *Journal of Applied Psychology, 90*, 964–971.

Marks, M. A., Mathieu, J. E., & Zaccaro, S. J. (2001). A temporally based framework and taxonomy of team processes. *Academy of Management Review, 26*, 356–376.

Mathieu, J. E., Heffner, T. S., Goodwin, G. F., Cannon-Bowers, J. A., & Salas, E. (2005). Scaling the quality of teammates' mental models: Equifinality and normative comparison. *Journal of Organizational Behavior, 26*, 37–56.

Mathieu, J. E., Marks, M. A., & Zaccaro, S. J. (2001). Multiteam systems. In N. Anderson, D. Ones, H. Kepir Sinangil, & C. Viswesvaran (Eds.), *Handbook of industrial, work, and organizational psychology: Vol. 2. Organizational psychology* (pp. 289–312). London: Sage.

Mathieu, J. E., Maynard, M. T., Rapp, T., & Gilson, L. (2008). Team effectiveness 1997–2007: A review of recent advancements and a glimpse into the future. *Journal of Management, 34*, 410–476.

Moriya, J., & Tanno, Y. (2008). Relationships between negative emotionality and attentional control in effortful control. *Personality and Individual Differences, 44*, 1348–1355.

Moynihan, D. P. (2007). *From forest fires to Hurricane Katrina: Case studies of incident command systems.* Retrieved from http://www.businessofgovernment.org/report/forest-fires-hurrican-katrina-case-studies-incident-command-systems

Murase, T., Carter, D. R., DeChurch, L. A., & Marks, M. A. (2014). Mind the gap: The effect of leadership on collective cognition in multiteam systems. *The Leadership Quarterly.* Advance online publication. http://dx.doi.org/10.1016/j.leaqua.2014.06.003

Murase, T., Jiménez, M. J., Sanz, E., Resick, C. J., & DeChurch, L. A. (2011). Leadership and collective cognition. In E. Salas, S. Fiore, & M. Letsky (Eds.), *Theories of team cognition: Cross-disciplinary perspectives* (pp. 117–144). New York: Routledge.

National Initiative for Cybersecurity Education. (2012a). *The national cybersecurity workforce framework.* Retrieved from http://csrc.nist.gov/nice/framework/

National Initiative for Cybersecurity Education. (2012b). *The national cybersecurity workforce framework: Interactive how-to and implementation guide.* Retrieved from http://csrc.nist.gov/nice/framework/

National Research Council. (2002). *Cybersecurity today and tomorrow: Pay now or pay later.* Washington, DC: National Academies Press.

Orvis, K. & Zaccaro, S. J. (2008). Optimizing teams for virtual collaboration. In J. Nemiro, M. Beyerlein, L. Bradley, & S. Beyerlein (Ed.), *The handbook of high performance virtual teams: A toolkit for collaborating across boundaries* (pp. 243–262). San Francisco: Jossey-Bass.

Peeters, M. A. G., van Tuijl, H. F. J. M., Rutte, C. G., & Reymen, I. M. M. J. (2006). Personality and team performance: A meta-analysis. *European Journal of Personality, 20,* 377–396.

Pretz, J. E., Naples, A. J., & Sternberg, R. J. (2003). Recognizing, defining, and representing problems. In J. E. Davidson & R. J. Sternberg (Eds.), *The psychology of problem solving* (pp. 3–30). Cambridge, England: Cambridge University Press.

Pulakos, E. D., Arad, S., Donovan, M. A., & Plamondon, K. E. (2000). Adaptability in the workplace: Development of a taxonomy of adaptive performance. *Journal of Applied Psychology, 85,* 612–624.

Rajivan, P., Champion, M., Cooke, N. J., Jariwala, S., Dube, G., & Buchanan, V. (2010). Effects of teamwork versus group work on signal detection in cyber defense teams. In D. D. Schmorrow & C. M. Fidopiastis (Eds.), *Foundations of augmented cognition.* (pp. 172–180). Berlin, Germany: Springer.

Richmond, B. (1993). Systems thinking: Critical thinking skills for the 1990s and beyond. *Systems Dynamics Review, 9,* 113–133.

Richwine, L. (2014, December 9). Sony's hacking scandal could cost the company $100 million. *Business Insider.* Retrieved from http://www.businessinsider.com/sonys-hacking-scandal-could-cost-the-company-100-million-2014-12

Rulke, D. L., & Rau, D. (2000). Investigating the encoding process of transactive memory development in group training. *Group & Organization Management, 25,* 373–396.

Sarter, N. B., & Woods, D. D. (1991). Situation awareness: A critical but ill-defined phenomenon. *International Journal of Aviation Psychology, 1,* 45–57.

Schmidt, F. L., & Hunter, J. E. (1998). The validity and utility of selection methods in personnel psychology: Practical and theoretical implications of 85 years of research findings. *Psychological Bulletin, 124,* 262–274.

Schmitt, N., Cortina, J. M., Ingerick, M. J., & Wiechmann, D. (2003). Personnel selection and employee performance. In W. C. Borman, D. R. Ilgen, & R. J. Klimoski (Eds.), *Handbook of psychology: Vol. 12. Industrial and organizational psychology* (pp. 77–105). Hoboken, NJ: Wiley.

Spiro, R. J., & Jehng, J. (1990). Cognitive flexibility and hypertext: Theory and technology for the nonlinear and multidimensional traversal of complex subject matter. In D. Nix & R. Spiro (Eds.), *Cognition, education, and multimedia: Exploring ideas in high technology* (pp. 163–205). Hillsdale, NJ: Erlbaum.

Squires, A., Wade, J., Dominick, P., & Gelosh, D. (2011, April). *Building a competency taxonomy to guide experience acceleration of lead program systems engineers.* Paper presented at the Ninth Annual Conference on Systems Engineering Research (CSER), Redondo Beach, CA.

Sterman, J. D. (2002). All models are wrong: Reflections on becoming a systems scientist. *System Dynamics Review, 18,* 501–531.

Sternstein, A. (2013, March 19). *Pentagon plans to deploy more than 100 cyber teams by late 2015.* Retrieved from http://www.nextgov.com/defense/2013/03/pentagon-plans-deploy-more-100-cyber-teams-late-2015/61948/

Taylor, H. C., & Russell, J. T. (1939). The relationship of validity coefficients to the practical effectiveness of tests in selection. *Journal of Applied Psychology, 23,* 565–578.

Thompson, E. R. (2008). Development and validation of an international English Big-Five mini-markers. *Personality and Individual Differences, 45,* 542–548.

Tribbey, C. (2014, December 22). *Experts: Lessons to be learned from Sony cyber attack.* Retrieved from http://www.cdsaonline.org/latest-news/experts-lessons-to-be-learned-from-sony-cyber-attack-cdsa/

Trippe, D. M., Moriarty, K. O., Russell, T. L, Carretta, T. R., & Beatty, A. S. (2014). Development of an information and communications technology literacy test for military enlisted technical training qualification. *Military Psychology, 26,* 182–198.

U.S. Department of Defense. (2013, December 4). *Department of Defense cyberspace workforce strategy.* Retrieved from http://dodcio.defense.gov/Portals/0/Documents/DoD%20 Cyberspace%20Workforce%20Strategy_signed(final).pdf

Wegner, D. M. (1987). Transactive memory: A contemporary analysis of the group mind. In B. Mullen & G. R. Goethals (Eds.), *Theories of group behavior* (pp. 185–208). New York: Springer.

Zaccaro, S. J., Chen, T. R., Winslow, C. J., & Hargrove, A. K. (2014, June 22). *Understanding cyber security incident response teams (CSIRTs) as multiteam systems (MTSs).* Paper presented at the annual meeting of Forum of Incident Response and Security Teams (FIRST), Boston, MA.

Zaccaro, S. J., & DiRosa, G. A. (2012). The process of team staffing: A review of relevant studies. In G. P. Hodgkinson & J. K. Ford (Eds.), *International review of industrial and organizational psychology 2012* (Vol. 27, pp. 197–229). Chichester, England: Wiley.

Zaccaro, S. J., Kemp, C., & Bader, P. (2004). Leader traits and attributes. In J. Antonakis, A. T. Cianciolo, & R. J. Sternberg (Eds.), *The nature of leadership* (pp. 101–123). Thousand Oaks, CA: Sage.

9

SELECTION AND STAFFING OF CYBER SECURITY POSITIONS

Rose Mueller-Hanson and Maya Garza

Introduction

A chronic shortage in the quantity and quality of cyber security professionals represents what many experts consider to be a national security crisis. Security threats are evolving at an unprecedented rate as cyber crime syndicates, "hactivists," and nation-states launch persistent and increasingly sophisticated attacks to commit fraud, espionage, acts of vengeance, and terrorism. The cyber threat has shifted rapidly to web-based applications that cannot be protected by a secure perimeter, thereby exposing confidential personal, financial, and health data stored on critical enterprise systems.

President Obama asserted that the "cyber threat is one of the most serious economic and national security challenges we face as a nation" (Aldridge & Raduege, 2010). This statement has been echoed by most, if not all, government agencies and critical infrastructure organizations. In a recent report, the Homeland Security Advisory Council (2012) noted a 200 percent increase in cyber attacks, including many on organizations that had not previously been targets.

The threat is not just to government data, however. Personal financial and health information is also at risk, as is critical national infrastructure (energy, water, roadways, etc.). Recent distributed denial-of-service attacks on major U.S. banks, which were publicized in advance by a previously unknown Islamist group calling itself "Qassam Cyberbrigades," provide stark justification for increasing concern (Nakashima, 2014). Systems that are part of everyday life are now open to attack as a result of our continuously more connected world. For example, hackers recently took over electronic freeway billboards in California and reported bogus warnings to drivers (Sternstein, 2014). Although this incident seems largely innocuous, it is a demonstration of how simple technology, often taken for granted, may be open to attack, and can potentially cause public distress and panic on a mass scale.

Effective cyber security professionals are essential to helping organizations prevent, identify, and respond to cyber threats (e.g., identify flaws in highway notification sign–configuration software before its released, quickly determine a fix once an attack has been identified). The cost of failure in such roles may be quite significant, resulting in situations such as compromised financial data (e.g., from hackers accessing U.S. financial banks), hijacked power plants, diverted airplanes, and so on. Selection is, therefore, paramount to identifying individuals who can be appropriately trained to perform the tasks required for cyber security or who already possess the key skills to be effective. The costs are very high for training entry-level individuals to be fully equipped to serve in these roles and address the challenges presented by cyber threats. Given the size of the investment, identifying individuals who will successfully complete training and continue on to be productive employees is essential.

The Challenge of Selecting for Cyber Roles

There is widespread concern over the acute lack of talent available to fill critical cyber security roles, and this gap is only expected to increase. By some estimates up to an additional 50,000 cyber security professionals will be needed in the near future (Fitzpatrick, 2012). Both government and industry leaders have noted that the fierce competition for cyber talent is resulting in difficulties in filling key positions (e.g., Homeland Security Advisory Council, 2012). At the same time, the effort and expense required to replace a bad hire is high. Therefore, selecting for cyber roles requires a delicate balance of not constricting the applicant pool too much with an overly rigorous process while being selective about who is hired so as not to waste time and money on people who will ultimately not work out.

Numerous cyber security experts have observed that a lack of critical skills is at the root of this staffing challenge. According to Frost & Sullivan's (2011) ISC^2 Global Information Security Workforce Study, a lack of skills has made many cyber security professionals unqualified to adequately secure organizations from threats posed by social media, cloud computing, mobile devices, and software applications. Although organizations are spending billions on new technology to increase security, policy experts have noted that hiring people with the right knowledge, skills, and abilities (KSAs) to implement expensive new technologies is necessary for success (Center for Strategic and International Studies, 2010).

The challenge for selection is not as simple as identifying individuals who have the right skills, however. Technology keeps advancing, and so does the sophistication of attacks. The skills needed to address current challenges and technology are evolving rapidly. The pace of change is too fast for anyone to even be able to predict with much accuracy what will be needed in the near future.

Therefore, cyber security professionals must not only possess the skills needed today, they must also have the ability to learn and adapt quickly to new threats and technology requirements. Further, the dynamic nature of many cyber security roles also requires a look beyond typical between-persons predictors of performance, specifically focusing on within-person variability that may require a more nuanced examination of the work context and individual difference variables that may affect successful performance in a constantly shifting environment. Often, within-person variability is treated as error in studies of performance, but as Dalal, Bhave, and Fiset (2014) asserted, extant theories of within-person performance variability all converge on one common conclusion: job performance is dynamic rather than static. Combined with the fact that cyber security is a highly dynamic field, with many roles requiring varying levels of activity within a given day, understanding potential within-person variability in performance may have large implications for selection considerations.

Despite the obvious importance of staffing for cyber security roles, little research exits on the topic of selection for these roles. Both the perceived skill shortage and the shifting nature of the relevant threats suggest that a traditional selection approach may not be sufficient for filling the gap. For example, in hiring entry-level cyber security professionals, attributes such as agility, adaptability, and a learning mindset may be much more critical for long-term success than specific technical knowledge. This is not to say that technical knowledge is unimportant; rather, that it is necessary but not sufficient for cyber roles.

Traditional approaches to selecting for information technology (IT) professionals have tended to focus on assessing technical knowledge and skills. A key question that must still be answered, however, is whether selecting for cyber roles is distinct from selecting for broad IT roles (i.e., because of the need for foundational computer science understanding and expertise). As mentioned, little research exists to offer a definitive answer to this question. Yet, we contend that the approach *must* be different because of some of the unique knowledge and skills that are required, as well as the less "technical" responsibilities that are essential for success. To explore this area further, we offer a number of ideas as to why and how selection must be different and testable hypotheses for researchers to explore further.

An additional consideration when exploring the unique nature of cyber security work is that of a multilevel view. That is, in many instances, cyber security professionals are not lone agents. They must not only perform their individual duties but also contribute to larger team goals. Specifically, many cyber security professionals work in teams, and the work of the individuals in the team is highly interdependent. In turn, these teams must then interact with other parts of the organization, resulting in a complex system of multiple teams that must coordinate and collaborate within and among diverse groups. Therefore, selection practices must take into account not only individual performance but also team and multiteam performance.

To appropriately address the key considerations of staffing, selection, and classification for cyber security roles, in the sections that follow, we first describe the work of cyber security professionals from individual and team perspectives. Then, we describe the attributes necessary to perform this work effectively. Finally, we discuss selection methods most likely to predict success in individual and team roles. We conclude with a discussion of potential directions for future research.

Cyber Security Work Defined

The first step in any selection effort is to define the work for a given role. However, cyber security work is diverse and includes not one role but many. Moreover, the work of cyber security professionals overlaps with and yet is distinct from more general IT work. Therefore, although some of what we know about IT work could generalize to cyber security work, we need to consider the unique tasks performed by cyber professionals when choosing the right selection approach.

To help facilitate cyber security workforce planning and professional development efforts, the National Initiative for Cybersecurity Education (NICE) conducted a comprehensive workforce assessment to define the functions and roles that fall within the cyber security domain. As a partnership between the federal government, academia, and the public sector, the NICE team developed the National Cybersecurity Workforce Framework (hereafter, *Framework*; National Initiative for Cybersecurity Careers and Studies, 2014), which provides a taxonomy of cyber work to include major functions and roles; the critical tasks performed in each role; and the KSAs required to perform these tasks effectively. The Framework identifies seven categories, or functional areas (e.g., operate and maintain, protect and defend) and 31 roles that are all part of the cyber security profession. These roles span the spectrum of cyber security responsibility, from systems security architecture to computer network defense and cyber threat analysis.

The Framework provides a good starting point upon which to base choices about selection methods. It also illustrates the diversity of cyber security work and the need to assess the most relevant KSAs needed for a given role. A detailed examination of selection requirements for specific cyber security roles is beyond the scope of this chapter. However, we can make some assumptions about requirements that apply broadly to cyber security work by thinking about successful performance in terms of three broad categories: task performance, contextual performance, and adaptive performance.

Task Performance

Task performance entails carrying out the specific technical activities relevant to a given cyber security role. For example, in the role of vulnerability assessment and management, the Framework defines several tasks, such as the following:

- Analyze site/enterprise Computer Network Defense policies and configurations and evaluate compliance with regulations and enterprise directives.

- Assist with the selection of cost-effective security controls to mitigate risk (e.g., protection of information, systems, and processes).
- Conduct and/or support authorized penetration testing on enterprise network assets.
- Conduct required reviews as appropriate within environment (e.g., Technical Surveillance Countermeasure Reviews ..., TEMPEST countermeasure reviews). (National Initiative for Cybersecurity Careers and Studies, 2014)

Performing these tasks successfully is critical to effective job performance overall for a given role, and the task performance for one role may look very different from the requirements for other roles.

Successfully performing the core tasks for a given role is necessary but not sufficient for overall effective job performance. Also important are the supporting behaviors that contribute to the overall context of the work environment. For example, to be successful, most employees need to communicate and collaborate effectively, keeping others informed of their progress and helping coworkers when needed. These activities have been termed *contextual performance* (Borman & Motowidlo, 1993, 1997) to distinguish supporting activities from technical work.

Contextual Performance

Unlike task performance, which will vary with each job, successful contextual performance can be defined more similarly across jobs. Contextual performance is essential to success in cyber security roles, because cyber professionals must be able to communicate proactively with a vast array of stakeholders in other disciplines and with business leaders across the organization. Often these communications require the cyber professional to translate highly technical terms into language that non-technical stakeholders can understand and act upon. In addition, given the highly specialized nature of many cyber roles, it is imperative for cyber professionals to work together and leverage knowledge from each other to work more effectively in a team environment.

Adaptive Performance

In addition to task and contextual performance, a third type of performance has been identified as critical for many roles: *adaptive performance* (Hesketh & Neal, 1999). Adaptive performance has been defined in numerous ways, but a common theme across definitions involves making an effective change in response to an altered situation. Adaptive performance includes several components: awareness of the environment to know when a change is needed, actual behavior change in response to this awareness, evaluation of feedback from the environment, and future adjustments to ensure an effective result.

Pulakos, Arad, Donovan, and Plamondon (2000) developed a model of adaptive performance with eight distinctive dimensions:

- handling emergencies;
- handling work stress;
- solving problems creatively;
- dealing with uncertain situations;
- learning work tasks, technologies, and procedures;
- interpersonal adaptability;
- cultural adaptability; and
- physically oriented adaptability.

Of the eight dimensions, the first six are most relevant to cyber professionals across a variety of roles. For example, a cyber attack is an emergency situation that is highly stressful for all involved. Therefore, handling emergencies and work stress effectively is critical for cyber professionals. In addition, cyber work is characterized by *wicked problems*—problems that are highly complex, ambiguous, and hard to solve (Lowenstein & Na, 2011). Solving these problems requires creativity and the ability to deal with the inherent uncertainty that can stem from a lack of prior experience and established methods for handling emerging threats. As mentioned previously, cyber systems and the nature of threats are constantly changing, making learning new work tasks, technologies, and procedures important. Finally, cyber professionals must effectively communicate their concerns to others and work effectively with diverse stakeholders, making interpersonal adaptability (and, in some cases, cultural adaptability) critical to success.

Defining the Work of Cyber Teams

Given the highly specialized nature of many cyber security roles, cyber professionals are increasingly working in team environments in which the members of a team each bring unique knowledge and skills. Team members must work effectively together, leverage knowledge from each other, and share information both within and outside of the team. In their seminal chapter on teams and work groups, Kozlowski and Bell (2003) described the changing nature of work; the emergence and criticality of teams; and the various aspects of team formation, functioning, and effectiveness critical for organizational success. Most organizational competency models include some type of a "teamwork" or "collaboration" competency as essential for success, and effective interpersonal skills are often required for all employees in all roles.

Despite the importance of teams in many lines of work, disagreement remains about the relative importance of working in teams versus working individually. For example, Stanard, Thordson, McCloskey, and Vincent (2001) found that many analysts do not see the value or potential to coordinate and do not see the larger picture of how their role fits with others. Anecdotally, many professionals in the IT or computer science domains (feeder pools into cyber security) are well equipped to work independently, yet they are not always expected to and may not be equipped to work effectively in interdependent teams. For example, computer network defenders and cyber threat analysts must monitor, connect, and analyze large quantities of data in order to identify patterns that might correspond to potential cyber attacks. Because cyber attacks evolve rapidly, this work must be performed under significant time pressure, requiring analysis of large amounts of data. As a result, these professionals may experience cognitive overload. To improve speed and accuracy, organizations are moving to a team-based structure in which the cyber defenders and/or analysts work together on different levels of the required tasks and use their domain-specific knowledge and expertise. Yet these teams frequently do not work well together or come together effectively. Rajivan et al. (2013) argued that organizational structure and reward mechanisms may contribute to poor team performance in addition to the cognitive overload and overall uncertainty inherent in cyber roles, yet more research is needed to fully understand the barriers to effective team performance and how selection practices may help to address this challenge.

Recently, the U.S. government and other organizations have sponsored team-based cyber competitions with the goal of training the next generation of cyber warriors and identifying potential job candidates. Many of the competitions place participants in a team-based environment to solve real-world cyber challenges. Typically, formal education may not prepare students for these types of competitions or for working in a team environment. Mauer, Stackpole, and Johnson (2012) developed a course curriculum to mimic the team-based cyber competition sponsored by the National Collegiate Cyber Defense Competition. They found that the training not only improved students' technical skills but that their teamwork skills also improved. They also found that the students' understanding of the *value* of teamwork increased. An observational study also found that some groups of individuals working in a cyber coopetition were more able to coalesce as a team and perform effectively when communication and coordination were present (Jariwala, Champion, Rajivan, & Cooke, 2012).

Cyber Security Attributes and Selection Methods

The multifaceted nature of most cyber roles requires that cyber professionals possess a diverse array of attributes. A successful candidate will have the KSAs to perform the technical aspects of his or her role effectively, skill in collaborating and communicating with colleagues, the capacity to learn and adapt to rapidly evolving technology and threats, and the ability to maintain high levels of performance in the face of a demanding and dynamic environment. In addition, with the difficulty of finding cyber professionals and the high cost of replacing them, a successful selection strategy will identify candidates who are more likely to be committed to their work and the organization and, therefore, less likely to turn over.

In considering specific selection strategies and methods, it may be essential to consider the nature of cyber security work and whether between-persons predictors are sufficient when selecting for certain roles. Working within the cyberspace requires managing the interplay of human cognition, technology, and organizational constraints. Often, personnel are challenged to effectively monitor, connect, and analyze large quantities of data in order to identify patterns that might correspond to potential cyber attacks (Boyce et al., 2011; D'Amico & Whitley, 2008). And, because cyber attacks evolve rapidly, this work must be performed under significant time pressure, requiring analysis of large amounts of data. As a result, these cyber security professionals may experience cognitive overload (Salas, Cooke, & Rosen, 2008), affecting their performance over time. In this example, the work situation has a strong impact on the job performance of the individual (Johns, 2006). And to the extent that the work situation varies, so will the performance. As another example of the influence of within-person variability on performance, the familiarity an analyst has with certain data patterns or types of attacks might affect his or her performance in some situations and not others. Because cyber security is an evolving field with highly dynamic threats, it may not be possible to always be at peak performance.

As Dalal et al., (2014) noted, typical selection approaches are based on the notion that performance is stable across time. In their extensive review of within-person variability of job performance, they summarized several theories that suggest not only that performance is variable but that the validities of the predictor variables may change over time. Yet little has been done in the cyber security space to uncover the vast variability of task requirements in cyber security roles and how performance does or may change over time. In selecting cyber security professionals, therefore, it is critical to review the job tasks and characteristics to determine not just the predictors of static performance but also predictors of performance in the varying situations that may be faced by the employee. This includes variability in the job itself and variability in how the employee may react across situations and throughout the day (e.g., changes in mood, motivation, cognitive capacity).

Given the lack of specific research on predicting success in cyber roles, in this section, we offer several hypotheses about relevant attributes necessary for success in each of the broad performance domains presented previously: task performance, contextual performance, and adaptive performance. Figure 9.1 provides an illustration of hypothesized predictors and their relationships with each other and each type of performance. For example, general cognitive ability predicts one's ability to acquire technical knowledge and skills, which in turn predicts technical performance. Although technical knowledge and skills are easier to develop than general cognitive ability, organizations must decide how feasible

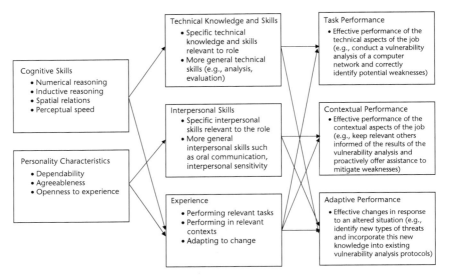

FIGURE 9.1 Hypothesized Predictors of Individual Cyber Security Job Performance

training these skills is for new employees and, therefore, the level of knowledge and skill required upon entry. For each set of attributes, we also discuss common methods of selection. A summary of these methods is provided in Table 9.1. Each category of predictors and associated selection methods are discussed in more detail in the following.

Cognitive Ability

Cognitive ability has been shown to be a strong predictor of performance across a variety of jobs (e.g., Hunter & Hunter, 1984). As such, it will likely be a good predictor of success in cyber security and other technology-focused jobs. For example, Witt and Burke (2002) found a .36 correlation between a test of general cognitive ability and technical proficiency for IT professionals, and Darcy and Ma (2005) found support for a relationship between grade point average and programming skills. Therefore, to the extent that most cyber security roles require a sound IT foundation, assessments of general cognitive abilities are likely to be useful in predicting who will be most likely to acquire job-relevant knowledge and skills and, therefore, have successful task performance.

Well-developed tests of general cognitive ability are plentiful, inexpensive, and easy to administer through online platforms. As such, they can be especially useful as a first step in screening a large number of applicants to identify the candidates who are most likely to succeed. One significant downside to using cognitive ability as a predictor of performance is the tendency for members of some ethnic groups to score lower than others on these tests, resulting in lower

TABLE 9.1 Selection Approaches for Cyber Security Predictors

Assessment type	Attributes measured	Advantages	Disadvantages
Credentials: May include degrees, certifications, and certificates	Knowledge and skills	• Easy to assess and verify possession of credentials	• Difficult to judge quality of credentials • Validity for predicting success uncertain
Cognitive ability test: Typically multiple-choice items with right or wrong answers; questions may be presented using verbal language or images, such as patterns	Cognitive abilities such as general intelligence, reasoning, and critical thinking or specific abilities like reading, verbal intelligence, spatial intelligence, or math	• Usually inexpensive • Quick and easy to administer • Objective and consistent • Good predictors of future job success across a variety of roles	• May result in adverse impact for minorities • Candidates sometimes object when tests do not appear directly relevant to the job
Personality assessment: Typically presented as statements with forced choice or Likert-type scales (e.g., level of agreement with each statement)	Traits such as extraversion, conscientiousness, risk taking, and so forth that tend to be stable in adulthood	• Inexpensive • Quick and easy to administer • Minimal or no adverse impact • Modest prediction of future job success	• Self-report, potential for faking • Candidates sometimes object when tests do not appear directly relevant to the job
Situational judgment tests: Realistic, scenario-based measures, generally in a multiple-choice format, that ask the respondent to choose from a list of alternative actions; scenarios may be presented as text only, or text with pictures, video, or other media	Decision making on job-specific tasks, which provides an indication of knowledge, skills, abilities, and experiences	• Appears job relevant and therefore more acceptable to test takers • Can measure a variety of competencies • Can be used as a learning tool when detailed feedback is provided on incorrect responses	• Some potential for adverse impact when reading requirements are high • Multiple-choice versions limit complexity of possible responses • Measures judgment only and not actual behavior

(Continued)

TABLE 9.1 (Continued)

Assessment type	Attributes measured	Advantages	Disadvantages
Structured interviews: Consistent questions and structured scoring guidelines applied to all participants to enable direct comparisons among individuals	Motives/interests, knowledge, skills, and/or experiences	• Minimal adverse impact • Can be tailored to each job as needed • More valid and fair than unstructured interviews	• Some managers resist using structured interviews • Time-consuming to develop questions and scoring guidelines
Résumé/reference checks: Participants provide a record of past experiences and accomplishments via a résumé that can be verified with reference checks	Past experiences, education, credentials	• Generally accepted by applicants • Résumés can be reviewed quickly, and review can be automated	• Experiences need verification to ensure accuracy • Reference checks can be time-consuming to conduct • Many organizations resist providing references for fear of litigation
Simulations: Simulates the job environment by providing complex situations that call for a complex set of behavioral responses; observation and scoring is typically performed by trained assessors; delivery can be in person or automated	Knowledge, skills, abilities, and experiences; may predict future behavior	• Especially powerful for predicting potential, because it allows for participants to demonstrate competencies in situations that they may not have yet experienced • Perceived as realistic and job relevant, therefore more acceptable to applicants	• Expensive and time-consuming to develop and administer

selection rates for these groups (Schmidt, 2002). In addition, applicants sometimes react negatively to tests of cognitive ability when the job relevance of the test is not clear to them. Therefore, cognitive ability is best used as a predictor for positions in which little prerequisite specific knowledge, skills, or experience is required upon entry and the new employee is expected to acquire this knowledge on the job through employer-sponsored training or experience (e.g., for military roles in which individuals are training for new cyber roles, and the knowledge is unique to that context and highly specialized). In these situations, organizations are seeking to predict who will most readily acquire and be able to apply necessary knowledge and skills.

Personality

As in the case of cognitive ability, empirical research on personality characteristics as predictors of job performance has been limited to general IT professionals and has not addressed cyber security roles specifically. For example, Witt and Burke (2002) found a −.23 correlation between agreeableness and technical proficiency for IT professionals (reinforcing the unfortunate reputation of IT professionals for lack of interpersonal skills). However, this finding may not apply to cyber roles, in which collaboration is becoming increasingly important.

The lack of specific research on the relationship between specific personality characteristics and effective performance in cyber security roles requires that we posit some hypotheses about which characteristics might be most relevant given what we know from broader research. Because cyber roles often require high attention to detail, we can posit that conscientiousness—and specifically the facets of competence (completing tasks successfully), dutifulness (following rules), and deliberation (avoiding mistakes)—could be useful indicators of potential success. Also, given the increasing need for effective communication and collaboration behaviors, we can hypothesize that aspects of extraversion (specifically assertiveness) and agreeableness (specifically trust) will be important in taking the initiative to reach out proactively to others and developing effective working relationships. Finally, a certain amount of openness to experience and flexibility may be an important indicator of those who will be curious and willing to try new approaches and adapt to change.

Similar to cognitive ability tests, personality assessments tend to be inexpensive and plentiful. They can be administered online and are also useful for screening large numbers of applicants in an efficient manner. Unlike cognitive ability tests, personality assessments do not tend to have adverse impacts on test takers, making them a good choice as a supplement to cognitive ability tests. However, their appropriateness for selection can vary, so it is important to select a personality assessment that has been validated for use in selection. It is also important to match the attributes being assessed with the requirements of the job. Unlike cognitive ability, some personality characteristics are more relevant for some jobs than others (Barrick & Mount, 1991).

Knowledge and Skills

As demonstrated by the Framework, the diverse array of work tasks for cyber professionals has a correspondingly diverse array of technical knowledge and skills required to perform these tasks effectively. Some of the knowledge areas and skills overlap with those of general IT professionals (e.g., network operations), whereas others are unique to cyber security. For example, a cyber risk analyst needs core technical skills plus cyber risk management and evaluation skills. The Framework provides a good starting point for differentiating the technical skills necessary to be effective in various cyber roles, though more specific definition will likely be needed for the staffing of individual positions.

KSAs may also help to regulate the impact of within-person variability in performance. People high in these areas may be more familiar with a large number of various cyber situations and, therefore, be more able to respond in an automatic way across a variety of situations. The situations for these highly knowledgeable and skilled people are less complex than they are for less knowledgeable people; therefore, the expected within-person variability that may come from handling many different types of situations may be reduced (Johnson, Change, & Lord, 2006). KSAs, therefore, may not only be useful as predictors of success—they may also be helpful as means of ensuring consistently effective performance across multiple situations.

As described elsewhere throughout this chapter, in addition to technical knowledge and skills, a variety of nontechnical skills are likely important for cyber security roles, especially for individuals working in teams. Although the required skills will vary by role, common requirements are likely to include oral communication, information sharing, perspective taking, interpersonal sensitivity, and a host of others.

Assessment of knowledge and skills can be accomplished in a variety of ways. Some of the most effective are situational judgment tests (SJTs), structured interviews, and simulations. SJTs present a situation and a variety of options for responding. Although these tests are time-consuming to develop, SJT administration and scoring can be automated, making them a good choice for large applicant pools. SJTs are generally good predictors of job performance, though it is not always clear what they are measuring. Structured interviews can be labor-intensive to develop and administer, but they tend to be well-received by applicants and are a valid way to predict job performance (Campion, Palmer, & Campion, 1997). Simulations are perhaps the most difficult to develop and administer (with the exception of some online simulations); however, they can be highly predictive of job performance if they provide high-fidelity representations of the work to be performed.

One significant source of controversy in the selection of cyber security professionals is the value of certifications and other credentials as a means of ensuring technical knowledge and skill. Credentials such as specific college degrees, certifications, and certificate programs are often cited as minimum qualifications for cyber security roles. However, there has been a proliferation of cyber security certifications and certificates from which to choose. A simple online search for "cyber security certification programs" yields thousands of results ranging from university-based programs to programs offered by private training organizations. Such a vast array of options makes it difficult to judge the quality of any specific credential for a specific cyber role, and many experts have questioned the value of these credentials (Wilson, 2012). Organizations wishing to require specific credentials should carefully consider whether the credential, by itself, can be justified as job relevant and if requiring possession of the credential is a reliable way of identifying qualified candidates.

Experience

Experience can be a useful predictor of successful job performance, especially when organizations need new employees to quickly perform effectively in their new roles with little to no training. Experience can include both technical and nontechnical activities. For example, past successful performance of technical activities is a reasonable way to predict future successful performance of those same activities. Likewise, experience successfully adapting to change and handling emergency situations can predict future success in such situations (Pulakos et al., 2002).

Past experience can be measured in résumés, reference checks, and structured interviews. Résumés are notoriously inaccurate but are usually required upon initial application and can be a useful way to screen out applicants without requisite experience. Reference checks can help to verify the claims in résumés. As described earlier, structured interviews can be highly effective predictors of performance. Questions that assess experience often begin with "Tell me about a time when you had to …" as contrasted with hypothetical questions that ask applicants to imagine a specific scenario.

Selection Method Considerations

In addition to using the right selection methods to measure the right attributes, organizations must consider several other factors when designing a selection approach. The first consideration is whether candidates are expected to possess desired attributes upon hire or if the organization is planning to provide training so that new employees can develop the attributes on the job. Assessment of more stable attributes is most useful when a subject has not yet had an opportunity to gain the knowledge, skills, or experiences required for effective behavior in a new role. Therefore, cognitive ability and personality assessments are most appropriate when narrowing a large pool of applicants at entry into the organization, especially when specialized knowledge and skills are expected to be learned on the job.

Related to the topic of selecting for the attributes necessary upon entry is the consideration of the potential within-person variability in performance that may be expected in the given role. Dalal et al. (2014) stated that the existence of within-person variability suggests that selection must manage not only initial levels of expected performance but also long-term performance trends and patterns of momentary levels of performance. To do so well, however, requires the organization to think critically about how job characteristics fluctuate (and potentially affect individual performance variability) and the primary timeframe of performance that is of most value.

A second area of consideration in designing a selection approach is the resources available to the organization to conduct assessment. Considerations of this sort include the time and costs required to develop and validate selection instruments and the time and costs required to administer them. Standardized assessments—such as personality inventories, cognitive ability tests, and SJTs— can be easily administered and scored online, minimizing costs and time requirements. Many well-developed instruments of this type can be purchased off the shelf, minimizing development and validation costs. As such, these assessments can be useful as a first step in a multiple-hurdle selection system. More time-intensive procedures, such as structured interviews and simulations, can then be used to make final selection decisions. These methods also tend to take more time to develop and validate if the organization desires custom assessments. However, technology-enabled interviews and simulations are now becoming more widely used.

A third consideration is applicant reactions to assessments and any potential for adverse impact. In general, applicants are more accepting of assessments that seem to be job relevant (e.g., technical interview questions) than assessments that do not appear to relate to the target job (e.g., general personality and cognitive ability measures). Applicant reactions are especially important to attend to for roles like cyber security in which many organizations are competing for talent. Similarly, organizations need diverse workforces, and assessments that result in adverse impact will reduce the diversity of the applicant pool. Assessments that have a high *cognitive load*—that is, assessments that require a high degree of cognitive skill, such as SJTs—may tend to have adverse impact on certain ethnic groups. In addition, minimum qualifications, such as a degree in computer science, will likely reduce the number of women who are eligible to apply for a position.

In sum, organizations must consider a variety of factors when designing selection systems for cyber security professionals. In general, organizations can improve their chances of success by (1) ensuring that the selection process is based on a thorough analysis of job requirements, (2) ensuring that all selection measures are valid for predicting job performance, (3) using measures with the lowest potential for adverse impact, and (4) gathering feedback on the assessment process to ensure that applicants have positive reactions.

Team and Multiteam Staffing

Our main focus thus far has been on selection for individual roles. However, staffing for cyber security roles requires a multilevel perspective to include staffing for teams and sets of teams, or *multiteams*. The nature of cyber security work often requires *cross-functional* teams—that is, teams whose members have complementary skills and must work together to meet a common goal (Katzenbach & Smith, 1993). The collective set of KSAs of team members has a significant impact on team performance, surpassing the simple sum of the capabilities of individual team members (Kozlowski & Ilgen, 2006). Therefore, effective team staffing is not simply about selecting individuals with specific skills; it is also about selecting people who will work well together and effectively leverage their collective skills in alignment with contextual needs.

Zaccaro and DiRosa (2012) provided a framework for team staffing that builds off of well-accepted models for staffing for individual roles. This model includes consideration of both the KSAs necessary for task performance and effective teamwork and how each team member fits within the group and how all team members work together. Another consideration is the duration that the team is expected to work together. Finally, the nature of the candidate pool must be considered—will candidates come from inside or outside the organization or potentially from both sources? These considerations suggest adjustments to the traditional concept of selection that are relevant for teams. Zaccaro and DiRosa noted that first it is important to identify relevant tasks and the attributes that team members will need to succeed. Then candidates should be recruited and assessed with these attributes in mind so that the best-fitting mix of candidates is selected for the team.

Beyond individual teams, Mathieu, Marks, and Zaccaro (2001) define *multiteam systems* (MTSs) as organizational structures in which multiple teams work independently toward shared goals. MTSs are most relevant when problems are especially complex and a diverse array of specialized knowledge is needed to generate innovative solutions. Although research in this area is still emerging, a growing body of evidence indicates that effective leadership is essential for these teams to succeed. Such leadership needs to bring different groups together, redirect competition toward the achievement of shared goals, and drive collaboration.

Carter, DeChurch, and Zaccaro (2014) demonstrated that team structure affects the level of innovation in MTSs in a variety of ways:

- Direction setting is best accomplished by a central leader within each team.
- Responsibility for motivation and inspiration of the team should be shared among multiple team members.
- Responsibility for leading coordination across teams should be shared by relatively few leaders from different teams, each with connections to various subgroups.

Although this body of research has not yet been applied to cyber security MTSs in particular, we can surmise that the complex problem sets such teams deal with might benefit from these findings. In a selection context, therefore, it will be important to consider selection at three levels of analysis.

The first consideration is the capabilities that an individual needs to fill a given role (e.g., technical skills unique to the role). Beyond specific technical skills, team members must also possess skills that will make them more likely to work effectively in a team setting, such as the willingness to share information and work collaboratively with others. A variety of measures have been developed and validated for use in assessing these teamwork attributes. For example, Stevens and Campion (1999) developed an SJT that evaluates a variety of teamwork skills, and others have used interviews and biodata assessments as well (e.g., Morgeson, Reider, & Campion, 2005). Although these strategies may be more or less feasible for organizations, given specific contexts, assessment of teamwork skills in addition to technical skills is important for successful team staffing.

The second consideration is the set of capabilities that the team collectively needs across members. For example, a team that conducts penetration testing may need individuals with in-depth knowledge of different systems to allow for more comprehensive and thorough testing. No one individual will be an expert on every system, so the team collectively needs to ensure that each set of specialized knowledge and skills is represented. In addition, the team will collectively need a diverse array of nontechnical skills, such as networking skills to liaise effectively with other teams to share information, analysis skills to evaluate risks, business acumen to identify potential business impacts of risks, communication skills to discuss findings with organizational leaders in an easily understood manner, and persuasion skills to convince stakeholders to take preventative action when needed.

Although not every team member needs to possess all of these skills, collectively, the team will need to accomplish these tasks. In addition, the team will need one or more leaders to provide direction and help keep team members engaged and focused. Therefore, when filling team roles, the different technical and nontechnical skills needed on the team need to be considered at both the individual and the team level, because there are a number of configurations that might result in an effective team. For example, if four key skills are needed on a team of two people, Person A may have Skills 1 and 2, whereas Person B has Skills 3 and 4; however, it could work equally well for Person A to have Skills 1 and 3 and Person B to have Skills 2 and 4. As long as all the skills are covered, the combinations of skills in people may matter less. Therefore, team staffing decisions are difficult in isolation and must take into account the team configuration as a whole.

Simply selecting the highest scoring candidates on team assessments is not sufficient—the mix of team members is critical (Hollenbeck, DeRue, & Guzzo, 2004; Klimoski & Zukin, 1999). Zaccaro and DiRosa (2012) noted three distinct patterns of team composition. The first is team homogeneity, which refers to how similar team members are to each other (e.g., similar levels of high cognitive ability or teamwork skills). According to a meta-analysis by Bowers, Pharmer, and Salas (2000), team homogeneity is not necessary for high performance except in potentially narrow circumstances. Therefore, although team members might initially find it easier to work with others more similar to them, such similarity is not necessary for high performance. The second is team diversity, which is the extent to which team members have different characteristics and backgrounds. It is often assumed that greater diversity in teams yields more creative and innovative thinking. As Zaccaro and DiRosa noted in their review, the research on this question has yielded mixed results, with the strongest evidence for diversity of functional area and educational background from the meta-analysis by Bell, Villado, Lukasik, Belau, and Briggs (2011). This analysis showed small positive results between functional and educational background diversity and team creativity and innovation and overall team performance.

The third pattern reflects the extent to which team members complement one another's knowledge and skills. This is a complex concept and one on which much more research is needed. Given the already challenging task of finding enough qualified cyber professionals to fill critical roles, it may be difficult to select for both individual characteristics and team composition at the same time. Moreover, it may be difficult to properly assess the extent to which team members complement each other until they actually work together. It is our view that a good first step is selecting for the right mix of knowledge and skills at the individual level, considering functional diversity where appropriate. Evaluation of how well team members complement each other may be best accomplished once the team is actively working together. Any gaps identified can then be addressed through training or potentially by supplementing the team.

The third consideration is the set of capabilities that MTSs collectively need across teams but not within each team (e.g., at least two of the team leaders must be well-connected in the organization and with other teams to facilitate coordination of efforts across and beyond teams; however, not all team leaders need to have this capability). As in the case of the foregoing example, staffing for MTSs is difficult to accomplish in isolation and must be informed by consideration of the system configuration as a whole. Individual teams can be well-constructed and work well together, but this does not guarantee that they will work effectively across teams.

Summary and Future Research Directions

The goal of selection is to predict which candidates are most likely to be successful in a given role. Classic selection practice calls for organizations to clearly define the work performed in the target role and the attributes (KSA, experiences, and other characteristics) required to perform this work successfully.

Armed with this knowledge, organizations can then choose the right assessments to measure these attributes in a reliable and cost-effective way.

In this chapter, we have described cyber security work as a diverse field covering multiple specialties and roles. We have also described the complex nature of organizational structures in which cyber security work is performed—individually, in teams, and in MTSs. Consequently, the attributes needed for successful performance in these roles vary widely, and selection in this context is complex.

Although the model presented in this chapter is a useful place to start building an effective selection program, several questions remain that require further exploration and research. In this section, we discuss a few of the most critical questions and propose some approaches for addressing them:

1. Are the attributes important for cyber security roles distinct from the attributes needed for more general IT roles? Although we have hypothesized several differences, research on this topic has yet to be conducted. There are a number of likely differences, so we suggest prioritizing those likely to have the largest distinctions. Aside from specific technical knowledge and skills, we believe that key distinctions might include business acumen, analysis, communication, and collaboration—if not for all individuals on a team, at least for the team as a whole. Research on this question would help organizations better focus their selection efforts on the attributes that matter most—especially when selecting employees from a typical feeder pool of more general IT occupations.

2. Which of these important attributes are needed at hire and which might be developed over time? As shown in our hypothetical model, key cognitive abilities and personality traits are harder to develop than skills that are more proximal to performance. Therefore, we would suggest that these attributes are more important at hire, especially for entry-level roles, than are other attributes. This assertion remains to be tested, although past research suggests that they are effective predictors for a wide variety of jobs (e.g., Barrick & Mount, 1991; Schmitt & Hunter, 1998). A more interesting issue, perhaps, is what types of skills are more important at hire and which are more easily developed on the job. For example, is it more important for new employees to possess specific technical knowledge and skills, or is it more important for them to possess broader analysis, critical thinking, and interpersonal skills? If the latter set is more important, this would potentially open up opportunities to more candidates for cyber roles and help to alleviate the current skills gaps.

3. What is the extent of within-person variability on job performance in cyber roles, and are some roles more prone to the influence of within-person variability? The dynamic and demanding nature of many cyber jobs suggests that within-person variability is likely. However, the lack of research on cyber security job performance warrants a closer look at this possibility.

Dalal et al. (2014) offered several theories that may help to understand within-person variability and implications on selection approaches to manage the impact. Additional work needs to be done to better understand the potential for performance fluctuation and how to best manage it using valid selection techniques.

4. What is the value of the various credentials and certifications that are available to prediction of success in cyber roles? A myriad of certification programs and other credentials exist for cyber knowledge and skills. As noted earlier, experts have hotly debated the value of certificates and other certifications. Obtaining these credentials is time-consuming and expensive. Research on their actual value as predictors of success is sorely needed so that organizations can make better decisions about whether and how to include these credentials as minimum qualifications for cyber security roles. As part of this work, it would be useful to create a taxonomy of credential characteristics (e.g., whether they include assessments and the validity of these assessments, whether they require practical experience), because they all differ in rigor and focus. Such a taxonomy would be useful in generalizing conclusions from research beyond a single credential. In addition, consistent standards of quality would help organizations make better choices about which credentials are relevant.

5. Do requirements for teamwork in the cyber profession differ from teamwork requirements in other professions? A related question is this: Do characteristics that make one an effective cyber security individual contributor support or detract from the ability to function effectively as a team member? As organizations balance the need to select for individual roles with the need to form teams with a collective set of skills, these questions will be increasingly important to answer.

Addressing these questions will require a significant amount of research from diverse fields. At the same time, improving selection for cyber security professionals has the potential to provide a significant amount of value to our national security. Not only would this research improve organizations' ability to counter cyber threats, it could potentially help high-quality candidates find meaningful and important work.

REFERENCES

Aldridge, S. C., & Raduege, H. D., Jr. (2010, August 30). Build an army of cyber warriors. *The Baltimore Sun*. Retrieved from http://articles.baltimoresun.com/2010-08-30/news/bs-ed-cyber-soldiers-20100830_1_cyber-security-cyber-warriors-cyber-threat

Barrick, M. R., & Mount, M. K. (1991). The Big Five personality dimensions in job performance: A meta-analysis. *Personnel Psychology*, 44, 1–26.

Bell, S. T., Villado, A. J., Lukasik, M. A., Belau, L., & Briggs, A. L. (2011). Getting specific about demographic diversity variable and team performance relationships: A meta-analysis. *Journal of Management*, 37, 709–743.

Borman, W. C., & Motowidlo, S. J. (1993). Expanding the criterion domain to include elements of contextual performance. In N. Schmitt & W. C. Borman (Eds.), *Personality selection* (pp. 71–98). San Francisco: Jossey-Bass.

Borman, W. C., & Motowidlo, S. J. (1997). Task performance and contextual performance: The meaning for personnel selection research. *Human Performance, 10*, 99–109.

Bowers, C. A., Pharmer, J. A., & Salas, E. (2000). When member homogeneity is needed in work teams: A meta-analysis. *Small Group Research, 31*, 305–327.

Boyce, M. W., Duma, K. M., Hettinger, L. J., Malone, T. B., Wilson, D. P., & Lockett-Reynolds, J. (2011). Human performance in cybersecurity. *Proceedings of the Human Factors and Ergonomics Society Annual Meeting, 55*, 1115–1119.

Campion, M. A., Palmer, D. K., & Campion, J. E. (1997). A review of structure in the selection interview. *Personnel Psychology, 50*, 655–702.

Carter, D. R., DeChurch, L. A., & Zaccaro, S. J. (2014). Impact of leadership network structure on the creative output of cross-functional multiteam systems. *Proceedings of the Academy of Management Proceedings, 2014*(1), 1577–1582.

Center for Strategic and International Studies. (2010, July). *A human capital crisis in cybersecurity: Technical proficiency matter: A white paper of the CSIS Commission on Cybersecurity for the 44th Presidency*. Retrieved from http://csis.org/files/publication/100720_Lewis_HumanCapital_WEB_BlkWhteVersion.pdf

Dalal, R. S., Bhave, D. P., & Fiset, J. (2014). Within-person variability in job performance. A theoretical review and research agenda. *Journal of Management, 40*, 1396–1436.

D'Amico, A., & Whitley, K. (2008). The real work of computer network defense analysts. In J. R. Goodall, G. Conti, & K.-L. Ma (Eds.), *VizSEC 2007: Proceedings of the Workshop on Visualization for Computer Security* (pp. 19–37). New York: Springer

Darcy, D., & Ma, M. (2005) Exploring individual characteristics and programming performance: Implications for programmer selection. In *Proceedings of the 38th Hawaii International Conference on System Sciences, 2005*. Retrieved from http://www.computer.org/csdl/proceedings/hicss/2005/2268/09/22680314a.pdf

Fitzpatrick, A. (2012, May 29). Cybersecurity experts needed to meet growing demand. *The Washington Post*. Retrieved from http://www.washingtonpost.com/business/economy/cybersecurity-experts-needed-to-meet-growing-demand/2012/05/29/gJQAtev1yU_story.html

Frost & Sullivan. (2001). *ISC² Global Information Security Workforce Study*. Retrieved from https://www.isc2cares.org/industryresearch/GISWS/

Hesketh, B., & Neal, A. (1999). Technology and performance. In D. R. Ilgen & E. D. Pulakos (Eds.), *The changing nature of performance: Implications for staffing, motivation, and development* (pp. 21–55). San Francisco: Jossey-Bass.

Hollenbeck, J., DeRue, D., & Guzzo, R. (2004). Bridging the gap between I/O research and HR practice: Improving team composition, team training, and team task design. *Human Resource Management, 43*, 353–366.

Homeland Security Advisory Council. (2012, Fall). *CyberSkills Task Force report*. Retrieved from http://www.dhs.gov/sites/default/files/publications/HSAC%20CyberSkills%20Report%20-%20Final.pdf

Hunter, J. E., & Hunter, R. F. (1984). Validity and utility of alternate predictors of performance. *Psychological Bulletin, 96*, 72–98.

Jariwala, S., Champion, M., Rajivan, P., & Cooke, N. J. (2012). Influence of team communications and coordination on the performance of teams at the iCTF competition. *Proceedings of the Human Factors and Ergonomics Society, 56*, 458–462.

Johns, G. (2006). The essential impact of context on organizational behavior. *Academy of Management Review, 31*, 386–408.

Johnson, R. E., Change, C., H., & Lord, R. G. (2006). Moving from cognition to behavior: What the research says. *Psychological Bulletin, 132*, 381–415.

Katzenbach, J., & Smith, D. (1993). *The wisdom of teams: Creating the high-performance organization*. Boston: Harvard Business School Press.

Klimoski, R. J., & Zukin, L. B. 1999. Selection and staffing for team effectiveness. In E. Sundstrom & Associates (Eds.), *Supporting work team effectiveness: Best management practices for fostering high performance* (pp. 63–91). San Francisco: Jossey-Bass.

Kozlowski, S. W. J., & Bell, B. S. (2003). Work groups and teams in organizations. In W. C. Borman, D. R. Ilgen, & R. J. Klimoski (Eds.), *Handbook of psychology: Vol. 12. Industrial and organizational Psychology* (pp. 333–375). Hoboken, NJ: Wiley.

Kozlowski, S. W. J., & Ilgen, D. R. (2006). Enhancing the effectiveness of work groups and teams. *Psychological Science in the Public Interest, 7*, 77–124.

Lowenstein, D., & Na, R. (2011, June 21). *Cyber security: Wicked problems, messes and metaphors*. Retrieved from http://www.zdnet.com/news/cyber-security-wicked-problems-messes-and-metaphors/6250342

Mathieu, J. E., Marks, M. A., & Zaccaro, S. J. (2001). Multiteam systems. In N. Anderson, D. Ones, H. Kepir Sinangil, & C. Viswesvaran (Eds.), *Handbook of industrial, work, and organizational Psychology: Vol. 2. Organizational psychology* (pp. 289–312). London: Sage.

Mauer, B., Stockpole, W., & Johnson, D. (2012). *Developing small team-based cyber security exercises*. Retrieved from http://scholarworks.rit.edu/other/301

Morgeson, F. P., Reider, M. H., & Campion, M. A. (2005). Selecting individuals in team settings: The importance of social skills, personality characteristics, and teamwork knowledge. *Personnel Psychology, 58*, 583–611.

Nakashima, E. (2014, April 11). U.S. rallied multinational response to 2012 cyberattack on American banks. *The Washington Post*. Retrieved from http://www.washingtonpost.com/world/national-security/us-rallied-multi-nation-response-to-2012-cyberattack-on-american-banks/2014/04/11/7c1fbb12-b45c-11e3-8cb6-284052554d74_story.html

National Initiative for Cybersecurity Careers and Studies. (2014). *National cybersecurity workforce framework*. Retrieved from http://niccs.us-cert.gov/training/national-cybersecurity-workforce-framework

Pulakos, E. D., Arad, S., Donovan, M. A., & Plamondon, K. E. (2000). Adaptability in the workplace: Development of a taxonomy of adaptive performance. *Journal of Applied Psychology, 85*, 612–624.

Pulakos, E. D., Schmitt, N., Dorsey, D., Arad, S., Borman, W., & Hedge, J. (2002). Predicting adaptive performance: Further tests of a model of adaptability. *Human Performance, 15*, 299–323.

Rajivan, P., Champion, M., Cooke, N. J., Jariwala, S., Dube, S., & Buchanan, V. (2013). Effects of teamwork versus group work on signal detection in cyber defense teams. In D. D. Schmorrow & C. M. Fidopiastis (Eds.), *Foundations of augmented cognition: 7th International Conference, AC 2013, held as part of HCI International 2013, Las Vegas, NV, USA, July 21–26, 2013. Proceedings* (pp. 172–180). New York: Springer.

Salas, E., Cooke, N. J., & Rosen, M. A. (2008). On teams, teamwork, and team performance: Discoveries and developments. *Human Factors, 50*, 540–547.

Schmidt, F. L. (2002). The role of general cognitive ability and job performance: Why there cannot be a debate. *Human Performance, 15*, 187–210.

Schmidt, F. L., & Hunter, J. E. (1998). The validity and utility of selection methods in personnel psychology: Practical and theoretical implications of 85 years of research findings. *Psychological Bulletin, 124*, 262–274.

Stanard, T., Thordson, M., McCloskey, M., & Vincent, P. (2001). *Cognitive task analysis and work-centered support system recommendations for a deployed network operations support center (NOSC-D)*. Wright-Patterson Air Force Base, OH: Air Force Research Laboratory.

Sternstein, A. (2014, June 5). Flaw lets hackers control electronic highway billboards. *Nextgov Newsletter*. Retrieved from http://www.nextgov.com/cybersecurity/2014/06/flaw-lets-hackers-control-electronic-highway-billboards/85849/?oref=ng-channeltopstory

Stevens, M. J., & Campion, M. A. (1999). Staffing work teams: Development and validation of a selection test for teamwork settings. *Journal of Management, 25*, 207–228.

Wilson, T. (2012, September 11). Security skills shortage creates opportunities for enterprises, professionals. *InformationWeek Dark Reading*. Retrieved from http://www.darkreading.com/security-skills-shortage-creates-opportunities-for-enterprises-professionals/d/d-id/1138345

Witt, L. A., & Burke, L. A. (2002). Selecting high-performing IT professionals. *Journal of End User Computing, 14*, 37–50.

Zaccaro, S. J., & DiRosa, G. A. (2012). The processes of team staffing: A review of relevant studies. In G. P. Hodgkinson & J. K. Ford. (Eds.), *International review of industrial and organizational psychology* (Vol. 27, pp. 197–229). London: Wiley.

10
TRAINING CYBER SECURITY PERSONNEL[1]

Bradley J. Brummel, John Hale, and Matthew J. Mol

Introduction

Organizational cyber security is an evolving field that needs to constantly adapt to meet the demands of the latest threats. This means that cyber security personnel must be continually developing their knowledge, skills, and abilities to meet this challenge. One cyber security instructor claimed that his students needed to be like MacGyver—able to solve any problem with whatever resource is available. He also claimed that these students needed to be a combination of Jesus and Einstein—archetypes of both virtue and intelligence. Although these are evocative descriptions, the reality is that organizations need to be able to hire and train normal people with human capabilities and virtues to work to achieve their cyber security goals. In fact, all organization members have some role to play in the cyber security posture of an organization; in effect, all employees can be considered cyber security personnel. However, most employees need to spend most of their time on tasks other than cyber security. These employees need to be trained to fulfill their cyber security roles as well as their primary work roles if the organization hopes to be successful while maintaining a strong cyber security posture.

Cyber security professionals have explicitly told us that training employees to adopt secure computing behaviors does not work. However, research across a wide variety of content areas and methods has overwhelmingly shown that training *does* work (Aguinis & Kraiger 2009; Eminağaoğlu, Uçar, & Eren, 2009; Salas, Tannenbaum, Kraiger, & Smith-Jentsch, 2012). But the research also shows that the way in which training is designed, delivered, and implemented has a large influence on whether or not it is effective (Salas et al., 2012). It is likely that most organizational training of cyber security personnel has not been designed to be as effective as it could be. This chapter incorporates what industrial and organizational (I-O) psychology knows about effective training design to suggest a strategic approach to training organizational employees across multiple roles for a strong cyber security posture. This perspective focuses on who needs what competencies to accomplish their tasks within the organization for effective cyber security. Specifically, any approach to effectively training all employees on cyber security requires documentation of the ways in which each role influences the cyber security of the organization. In this chapter, we adapt the National Institute of Standards and Technology (NIST) approach to cyber security training, focusing on performance requirements for different organizational roles (Wilson, de Zafra, Pitcher, Tressler, & Ippolito, 1998; Wilson & Hash, 2003). This approach suggests different training content and methods as well as different objectives for cyber security awareness, training, and education for each role within the organization.

The chapter begins with an overview of cyber security roles and how these roles support the security architecture of an organization. Next, we describe how training should be designed on the basis of needs analysis leading to specific training objectives for employees in each role within the system. This includes approaches for evaluating whether the training objectives were achieved and making strategic decisions about future training approaches from the evaluation. We include a checklist summarizing the steps in this design and evaluation process. Then we describe some of the current methods used to train cyber security personnel in different roles. We include evidence about the effectiveness of these approaches and potential limitations of each of them. Following this review of methods, we discuss some of the individual differences in employees that can influence the success of cyber security training. We also discuss some of an organization's options for handling situations when training fails to reach objectives for cyber security. We conclude with a forward-looking vision for effective training that meets the evolving cyber security needs of modern organizations.

Cyber Security Roles and Security Architecture

Cyber security personnel are those who execute critical security functions on an information system. These functions influence anyone in the organization with access to a computer or a network. (In modern organizations, this includes virtually every employee.) Although all employees may have some role in the cyber security of their organization, the nature of these roles can be very different. Cyber security competencies can run the gamut from awareness to literacy to programming to business-process skills. These competencies can focus on skills necessary to mitigate technical risks, capacity to design policies and governance, or specific practices needed to achieve regulatory compliance. In fact, one of the first steps in evaluating and improving an organization's cyber security posture is to define these roles within the security architecture. Once these roles and their expectations are defined, it is possible to evaluate who needs what type of training to ensure the cyber security of the broader system.

Although there are many potential ways to distinguish these roles depending on the organization, for this chapter we have chosen to categorize employees into four broad roles that differentiate their functions within an organization's cyber security architecture. These roles are labeled *users, administrators, engineers*, and *executives*. We also include a section on the overall *organization* role for the purpose of showing how these individual roles interact to influence the organization's cyber security. In the following sections we describe these roles including the job tasks that they need to accomplish and the competencies the people in them should have. These descriptions are summarized in Table 10.1 along with typical training and tools for these roles that are discussed later in the chapter.

Users

Users include most of an organization's employees. People with this role are unlikely to have any specific expectation or knowledge of their responsibilities in cyber security. Users are those who ultimately drive the operation of the organization's computer applications. Accordingly, they must be aware of relevant cyber security issues, policies, and threats. They must also be able to execute or engage user-level security practices and controls prescribed by organizational policy. This typically requires some literacy of computer security concepts, terms and definitions. Users also need to apply protections embedded within applications. They, for example, may be required to use an application feature that encrypts documents for storage or communication. They may also be required to perform password maintenance periodically, calling for them to construct and rotate strong passwords. In all cases, it is imperative that users understand the "why" of security and how the practices they are required to perform address security policy and compliance concerns.

Administrators

System administrators ensure the secure operation of fielded systems. They install, configure, manage, and maintain applications and information services over organizational systems and networks. This is likely to be the largest group of employees that would typically be considered cyber security personnel. This role requires fluency and proficiency with commercial and open-source security technologies such as firewalls, security tokens, and network security appliances. In addition, administrators should demonstrate a familiarity with sound security architecture practices and the configuration of security controls in operating systems and applications. Essentially, they require many of the same knowledge bases as engineers, but their knowledge can be less specialized. They also require knowledge of administration and management. The reasoning-focused skills and

TABLE 10.1 Cyber Security Training by Organizational Role

Role	Description	Role tasks/competencies	Common training methods	Tools to assist performance
User	Any member of the organization who has access to the network	• Computer security literacy • Operating applications safely • Knowledge of security policies • Compliance with security policies	• Required employee training • E-mails from the information technology department • Self-phishing • Simulations and competition-based trainings	• Warnings • Limited access
Administrator	• Ensures the secure operation of fielded systems • Configures, manages, and maintains organizational systems and networks	• Firewall and network appliance installation and management • Network security architecture • Secure operating system configuration • Patch management	• Formal degree programs • Online degrees and certifications • Conferences and professional meetings • Self-development • Simulations and competition-Bbased trainings	• Technical security controls • Network architecture
Engineer	Develops and implements hardware and software for an information system to support organizational mission	• Security requirements engineering • System design and architecture • Secure and defensive programming • System integration • Testing and validation	• Formal degree programs • Conferences and professional meetings • Self-development	• Security architecture • Software security analysis tools • Security application programming interfaces and libraries
Executive	An organization leader who shapes and enforces organizational security requirements	• Computer security fundamentals • Laws, regulations, and policies • Organizational risk management • Organizational security programs	• Online degrees and certifications • Simulations and competition-based trainings	• Policies and procedures • Checklist for training design

abilities required in this role mirror those of engineers closely as well but with an increased emphasis on arranging actions and ideas according to a desired pattern or set of rules.

Engineers

Engineers include hardware and software developers charged with developing and implementing an information system to support organizational mission fulfillment. Although an organization may include other employees with engineering roles, these employees would likely be users in terms of their cyber security roles. For both of these positions, it is imperative that engineers stay current with technological advances, which is difficult in such a quickly evolving field. In addition to the initiative required to stay current, engineers also need to be able to pay attention to small details and be critical thinkers. All of these demands also require a relatively high level of intelligence. Engineers typically have at least an associate's or bachelor's degree in computer science or a related field.

Software developers of secure information systems must be trained in defensive coding practices and the sound integration of security technologies such as encryption and access control. Software developers require a strong knowledge base in computers, digital logic, and mathematics. They must be capable of complex problem-solving, programming, and systems analysis. As such, they are also highly reliant on deductive and inductive reasoning and should be sensitive to potential problems.

Hardware and systems engineers must understand and account for performance and integration issues associated with security solutions implemented at the software level. Like software developers, they require a strong knowledge base regarding computers and digital systems, but they also need a background in engineering, technology, and design. The skills that hardware engineers need to have include critical thinking, reading comprehension, and active listening. They also need to be capable of deductive and inductive reasoning; have strong oral comprehension; and, like software developers, be sensitive to the potential for problems. Working as part of a team, developers and engineers must be trained to operate within a methodology that integrates system engineering and security engineering processes (Hansche, 2005). Companion processes include requirements development, system design and implementation, and testing.

Executives

Executives shape and enforce organizational security requirements. Although this role may be taken on by members of an organization's C-suite leadership, it may also be distributed to employees at other levels in the organizational structure. However, given the importance of cyber security in the modern organization, a vice president of cyber security or chief cyber security officer may be a desirable position for an organization to have. To shape and enforce the security requirements, executives must understand the influence of regulation, law, and policy. Such understanding relies on an awareness of information assurance fundamentals, the value of information assets and services managed by the organization, and the prevailing threat landscape. Information assurance fundamentals include the core properties of cyber security—confidentiality, integrity, and availability—along with the services designed to preserve these properties. This understanding must be combined with that of the differential security requirements associated with information and applications managed by an organization. Knowledge of the operational environment, including prospective threat agents, is also needed to fully appreciate cyber security risks posed to an organization. Ultimately, executives must conceive of cyber security as a risk-management process that balances exposure to achieve mission fulfillment with security controls designed to safeguard organizational interests.

Organizations

An organization's cyber security posture is only effective when all of these roles work together. The technical aspects of an organizational cyber security program are directed by administrators who install and operate enterprise-level security controls developed by engineers that protect networks and computer systems. These activities are supported by executives, who provide resources and establish organizational cyber security policies reflecting mission and compliance requirements. Ultimately, however, the security fate of an organization rests in the hands of the end user. End users must adhere to acceptable use policies, engage application-level security controls, and exercise best practices for secure computing to preserve the confidentiality, integrity, and availability of computer resources. Any disconnect in this web of interdependencies will result in an organizational failure to achieve security objectives.

Training Design for Cyber Security Personnel

Training involves planned, systematic activities that are designed to promote the acquisition of knowledge, skills, and attitudes relevant for organizational performance (Salas et al., 2012). This performance is often broken down into specific tasks or individual competencies. Training exists because there is a perceived need for employees to perform these tasks or have these competencies to maintain an organization's cyber security posture. Often a breach, intrusion, or other cyber security event is used as the impetus to enact a new training program or revise an old training procedure. However, these reactionary changes in training are only effective if they are designed to respond to the correct issues with employee performance. This requires development of training objectives that fit the tasks and competencies required of the employees' roles within the cyber security architecture.

For example, an organization might set a goal of having zero compromises due to employee responses to phishing in a given year. It might also try to have zero violations of media and software copyrights on its network or set other goals related to malware, virus-detection updates, and a whole host of other noble cyber security outcomes. When these goals are not achieved, the organization is likely to initiate training of some sort. Unfortunately, these organizational cyber security goals do not directly translate into useful training objectives, because they do not dictate what learning should occur by people in which roles through which method of training. As mentioned in the Introduction, training effectiveness is determined by the design, delivery, and implementation of the training. In the following subsections, we summarize some of what is known about designing training to be effective. This includes choosing the right training objectives and evaluating whether each training activity was successful. This section concludes with a checklist of the necessary steps for effective cyber security training design.

Role-Specific Training Objectives

One of the biggest advances in the understanding of what makes training effective has been the finding that all training should start with training objectives that specify desired changes in the employees being trained (Campbell & Kuncel, 2001). This means that training is primarily focused on individual learning. However, these changes in individual knowledge, skills, or attitudes can result in both team- and individual-level performance improvements in tasks and competencies that change the security posture of an organization. Training design that ignores the steps by which the larger team goals—and, in turn, the organization's cyber security goals—are achieved through individual employee behaviors is likely to fail by focusing on the wrong training objectives and methods.

Categorizing employees by their roles within the cyber security architecture is an important first step in coming up with appropriate training objectives. These roles allow for differentiation between required tasks and competencies described previously and listed in Table 10.1. This process is called *job analysis* or *competency modeling* in I-O psychology. For this chapter, we have described some general roles with tasks and competencies related to cyber security, but each individual organization should conduct this process on the basis of its goals and needs. The determination of task and competencies should align with training areas relevant to the specific cyber security architecture. Training individuals not only on their own tasks and competencies but also on other team members' tasks and competencies can facilitate synergistic gains through team coordination while mitigating potential weaknesses that could result from an individual's failings (Marks, Sabella, Burke, & Zaccaro, 2002). NIST reports (Wilson et al., 1998; Wilson & Hash, 2003) suggest differentiating between beginning, intermediate, and advanced knowledge levels for each training area. The training area is dictated by what the role requires—for example, with users, this could mean password management or familiarity with the acceptable use policy of the organization. Beginning knowledge means trainees have achieved learning objectives characterized by terms like *research*, *know*, and *identify* within a training area. Intermediate knowledge means trainees have learned to *analyze*, *understand*, and *apply* within the training area. Advanced knowledge means trainees have learned to *interpret*, *approve*, *decide*, and *issue* within the training area (Wilson, et al., 1998).

Once the organization has determined what level of knowledge someone in a specific role within the organization needs to have in a training area, it can determine what the organizational training needs are through a training needs analysis. This analysis involves systematically measuring gaps in employee performance rather than inferring them on the basis of violations of organizational policy. A specific issue might only be relevant for some employees within a specific role within the organization. If this is the case, then it would be inefficient and potentially counterproductive to send all employees to training related to that violation.

After the specific training needs have been determined, an organization can write training objectives that target the specific knowledge, skills, and attitudes that need to change to fix the performance gaps that are identified. For example, an organization may discover that its users cannot identify phishing attempts (using online deceit for the purpose of obtaining private information). This would lead to training specifically designed to improve user skill at distinguishing legitimate web requests from phishing attempts. Ideally, this training would be designed on the basis of the features of web communications that are visible to users (Staggs et al., 2014). The training objective would be something like this: *Users will be able to distinguish legitimate web requests from phishing attempts.* The advantage of this type of learning objective is that it informs the choice of training method as well as the choice of the most appropriate questions to answer in training evaluation. Some training methods are more effective than others, depending on the objectives and situational constraints of the training (Day, Blair, Daniels, Kligyte, & Mumford, 2006). We discuss some of the most common methods for training cyber security personnel later in the chapter, but next we discuss the important step of training evaluation.

Training Evaluation

One of the most important parts of cyber security training that I-O psychologists can help organizations with is training evaluation. Without evaluation, there is no way to know if the current training is effective. However, training evaluation is complicated, and it takes a substantial effort to do it in a way that results in useful information for strategic decision making. Because of this, training evaluation is rarely conducted. When it is done, there is a tendency to focus on less useful but easy-to-measure criteria (Alliger, Tannenbaum, Bennett, Traver, & Shotland, 1997).

No evaluation can answer every possible question about what a training could have accomplished, so careful thought must be given to which questions are most important to answer given limited resources. In this section, we review some of the most relevant issues for making these choices about training evaluation.

The most common approach to training evaluation is Kirkpatrick's (1994) four-level model. These levels are *reactions, learning, behavior,* and *results.* The logic of this approach is that when employees react positively to training, they are more likely to learn the material. If they learn the material, then they are more likely to change their behavior (performance) on the job. If their performance on the job improves, then the organization is likely to see improvements in its cyber security and return on its investment in training. Favorable reactions to training are typically divided into positive affective responses to the training, such as liking the trainer or the design, and believing that the training was worthwhile (Alliger et al., 1997). The characteristics that lead to positive reactions to training are varied, and they may or may not be relevant for decisions about training (Sitzmann, Brown, Casper, Ely, & Zimmerman, 2008). These reactions can be measured using self-report surveys from trainees at the end of training. Often, training evaluation stops at this level. However, training is unlikely to be considered effective from an organizational perspective if it only amounts to an enjoyable experience for employees. Learning includes any changes in knowledge, skill, behavioral choice, or attitude that result from training. These changes can be measured by tests at the end of training or through simulated emergency exercises (Grance et al., 2006). However, it is sometimes necessary to retest employees after some time to see if they have retained changes over time. Unfortunately, even when employees demonstrate changes, they may fail to apply these new competencies on the job. Behavior, or *transfer,* involves measuring whether employees are applying their training on the job. Employees can fail to use their new knowledge, skills, and abilities for a variety of reasons, from a lack of supervisor support to a lack of confidence. Training can be described as effective if employees are changing their on-the-job behavior in desired directions, but organizations may also want to consider the relative benefit of a training given the resources put into the program. Results compare the value of the change in employee behavior with the cost of the training. If a cheaper training method appeared to be as or more effective, the organization might prefer that option even if the current program had been demonstrated to be effective.

These levels have proven to be useful for organizing research on the effectiveness of training and documenting what types of evaluation are most frequently undertaken (Alliger, et al., 1997). The levels are also useful in determining exactly what a training evaluation is actually saying about the usefulness of training when making strategic decisions. However, there are different approaches to organizing training evaluation. Other scholars (Kraiger, 2002) have pointed out that Kirkpatrick's classic approach to training evaluation may be deficient in that it does not cover all relevant questions about training, and it is not necessary for employees to like a training for them to change their behavior as a result of the training. Kraiger presented an approach in which training evaluators choose which questions they are hoping to answer about changes to learners, training content and design, and organizational payoffs. Regardless of the framework chosen for training evaluation, it is important to know what questions about the effectiveness of training you are hoping to answer in order to choose appropriate methods for measuring those outcomes. These questions should be tied to the training objectives and provide the information necessary for the organization to determine whether the training is accomplishing its goals.

Like most fields, the field of cyber security has been relatively unsystematic in its evaluation of training effectiveness, though the NIST has provided some good advice for training evaluation that is similar to what we have described here (Wilson & Hash, 2003). Organizations often fail to see a direct payoff from a specific training program, even though the larger literature is clear about the benefits of training that is well designed (Aguinis & Kraiger, 2009; Salas et al., 2012). For example, researchers have shown that knowledge of phishing alone does not yield behavioral change (Kumaraguru et al., 2009). The failure may not be in the content of the training but in the application to behaviors on the job. Professionals designing training for all cyber security roles should "close the loop" on their training offerings by asking appropriate evaluation questions and using appropriate measurement methods to answer those questions. This information allows for more effective decision making, feedback, and design of cyber security training. As we review some of the current approaches to cyber security training in the following section of this chapter, we include what is known about the effectiveness of these approaches as well as some suggestions for important evaluation questions that should be investigated. Following that discussion, we cover what to do when more or different training does not seem to be the best solution for performance issues within the cyber security architecture.

Checklist for Cyber Security Training Design

In an effort to tie all of this work together, we have provided a checklist of the steps an organization should take to strategically approach designing and evaluating training for a strong organizational cyber security posture (see Table 10.2).

Current Cyber Security Training Methods

It seems obvious that professionals involved in training design and implementation would choose their training methods on the basis of the learning objectives for the training. However, there is a tendency to construct training without stated learning objectives or to purchase training packages that are cheap, popular, or easy to acquire. Training methods include on-the-job training, formal classroom training, online certifications, simulations, and experiential learning.

TABLE 10.2 Checklist for Cyber Security Training Design

Step	Description
1. Security architecture	Determine the specific cyber security roles for all employees within the organization.
2. Job analysis/competency model	Detail the cyber security tasks and competencies for each cyber security role.
3. Training needs analysis	Measure the degree to which employees in each role are currently performing these task and have these competencies.
4. Training objectives	Write objectives that target specific knowledge, skill, and attitude levels aligned with tasks and competencies.
5. Training method	Choose methods appropriate for the training objectives, and conduct the training.
6. Training evaluation	Choose all of the questions to be answered in evaluation, and measure whether the training is effective.
7. Strategic decision making	Use evaluation results to adapt training, or move to nontraining solutions.

The content of cyber security training should focus on the development of the competencies discussed in the earlier section on cyber security roles. In the rest of this section we provide examples of some of various approaches that are currently being used to teach cyber security competencies to employees in user, administrator, engineer, and executive roles. Where possible, we discuss what is known about the effectiveness of these approaches.

Formal Degree Programs

Formal degree programs in cyber security have grown out of traditional computer science programs at universities. More common at the undergraduate level are certificate programs and other forms of curricular specializations within computer science, information technology (IT), or management of information systems degree programs. As such, specialized cyber security content is folded into the elective components of degree programs. Students in such programs pursue a more general track in cyber security, which entails more fundamental principles and stresses less operational proficiency with specific technologies and solutions. Undergraduates in these cyber security specializations will study the foundations of cryptography and of network security, among other topics. The emphasis is on principles and applications as opposed to training on vendor-specific solutions. This form of education is most critical for engineers, for whom the historically targeted skill sets for computer science and IT majors have revolved around software development (i.e., programming) and the construction of information systems. System administrators commonly emerge from these programs as well, heavily invested in the technology background required for their job functions.

At the graduate level, universities have started master's-level degree programs in cyber security and digital forensics, which offer a more targeted educational experience and greater specialization in professional skill development. In a master's-level digital forensics program, students are expected to have the requisite background in computer science and IT, so they, can focus their attention on mastering forensic processes and on familiarizing themselves with the dominant tools of the trade. Capstone experiences and realistic labs and exercises may involve having students work through a virtual "crime scene." Administrators seeking technological specializations in niche areas of cyber security (e.g., network security, digital forensics) may identify graduate programs that afford them the opportunity to pursue such specializations. Similarly, executives may enroll in graduate degree programs that emphasize specializations in organizational cyber security management.

Given the intensity of this level of training through educational institutions, some groups have distinguished between *training* and *education* in cyber security, with training being limited to programs offered by the organization that do not confer formal degrees (Wilson & Hash, 2003). Other methods of training are more common for users and for the continued training of administrators, engineers, and executives. However, a strong organizational cyber security posture probably requires at least some personnel in some roles to have formal degrees that are closely related to cyber security.

Online Degrees and Certifications

The market for professionals with cyber security skills has driven the demand for educational opportunities and credentials obtainable outside of a mainstream university experience. For-profit and not-for-profit institutions have responded to this demand by developing online and distance learning offerings in the cyber security space. Students can pursue certificates, along with undergraduate and graduate degrees, entirely over the Internet. Online programs tend to offer more specialized educational pathways in areas such as critical infrastructure protection, disaster response planning, and homeland security. These programs cater to career professionals and, accordingly, blend technical with managerial content. These kinds of programs may appeal to either administrators or executives, depending on the orientation of the training (technical vs. business). In some cases, an online program may appeal to both training constituencies, bridging a gap between technology and business processes.

On the technical side, online programs challenge students to not only master fundamental concepts but also apply practical security functions and operate security applications. Students may develop their own programs to define security controls, or they may engage security tools to implement a segment of a network security architecture. Programming exercises are rarer in these programs as compared with more traditional university degree programs. The focus is on teaching administrators and cyber security personnel to use security tools to protect a system. Increasingly common is the use of virtual environments in which to simulate cyber attack scenarios.

Online programs also incorporate the "soft side" of cyber security—business and managerial processes that often drive the implementation of technical controls. Common managerial program elements include cyber security policy development, ethics, governance and compliance issues, and disaster recovery planning. Skills and knowledge in these areas are vital to fulfillment of job functions by executives and managers playing cyber security roles within an organization.

Conferences and Professional Meetings

Many organizations invest in sending employees to conferences and professional meetings as a way to keep skills and training current. A range of such venues exists in the field of cyber security. Conferences and workshops can expose participants to the latest technologies and security solutions as well as the burning issues and topics of the day. Many offer parallel sessions and tracks comprising tutorials or workshops designed to instill specific skills for selected topics, such as access control solutions for mainframe computing systems. These kinds of conferences attract not only academics and researchers but engineers and administrators as well. Establishing travel to conferences and meetings as a component of a training program helps administrators to maintain a current and relevant cyber security knowledge base.

Each event takes on its own flavor, depending on the nature of the primary sponsoring organization. Conferences run by academics focus on research developments, emerging issues, and next-generation technologies. Papers presented by researchers demonstrate previously unknown vulnerabilities in information systems and present theoretical results with practical applications to open challenges in the field. Those operated by the federal government may integrate some of these aspects but more commonly are dominated by best practices and cyber security technology standards. The NIST, for example, advances standards in computer security such as the Security Content Automation Protocol initiative through the support of frequent workshops and meetings (Barrett, Johnson, Mell, Quinn, & Scarfone, 2009). Conferences and professional meetings organized by the private sector routinely showcase vendor-specific technology solutions.

Professional meetings dedicated to standards, governance, or compliance issues may draw interest from executives who wish to understand regulatory implications for their organization. In some cases, such meetings offer an opportunity for not only heightened awareness or training on a topic but also influence.

Required Employee Training

Many organizations have cyber security training as part of their onboarding process, and some require recertification every year. This kind of training is geared for the end user, or for the operator of information systems, and is provided either in a lecture format or through an online program. This training typically takes less than an hour and requires employees to pass a knowledge test at the end of the program. Most such programs simply present knowledge about what is expected of employees within the organization and organizational policies, but some may include practice in things like creating a strong password. This training has taken its place next to sexual harassment and ethics training as required elements of organizational membership. These types of trainings are generally effective at conveying some knowledge about a topic. However, employees may respond cynically to the training, believing that it is simply there to be documented to allow the organization to blame employees for any violations of policy. Organizations would be wise to not only measure the knowledge gains from such trainings but to also track employee sentiment around the value of these kinds of trainings, especially if recertification is required yearly.

E-Mails from the IT Department

When cyber security administrators notice higher than normal occurrences of a specific type of phishing attempt, inappropriate network behavior, or a vulnerability to a new virus or malware, they will often send out a blanket e-mail to all users to warn them about the issue. This approach could be useful to the degree that employees actually read the e-mail, understand the contents, believe that it applies to their cyber security behavior, and are competent to change their behavior in line with the vulnerability. When any of these conditions is not met, the information provided in the e-mail will fail to cause the desired behavior change. The tone of the e-mail, the manner in which the threat is explained, and the timing of it all factor in to its effectiveness. Ironically, a good many phishing attempts are disguised as e-mails from an organization's IT department. The ultimate effect of this phenomenon is an erosion of employee trust in and sensitivity to such e-mails, legitimate or otherwise.

Self-Phishing

Some organizations take an experiential approach to training employees in a user role not to respond to phishing attempts. This is typically done by allowing the cyber security professionals to send tailored phishing e-mails to the organization's employees. If an employee responds to the phishing attempt, they are directed to a webpage informing them that they have just been phished by the company.

This often includes information on how to avoid falling prey to phishing attempts in the future. This approach has the benefit of targeting training toward employees who are falling for phishing attempts. When done correctly, it has been shown to decrease phishing success and to be favorably received by trainees (Kumaraguru et al., 2009). However, some organizations do not allow this because they worry about the potential influence it might have on employee attitudes. The tone of feedback and its timing are critical for a positive training outcome in a self-phishing campaign. If handled incorrectly, this training technique could lead to a backlash from employees. Moreover, care must be taken to ensure that the exercise does not escape the intended bounds of the organization. E-mails may be forwarded by employees to family and friends, allowing phishing attempts to meet with unexpected (and undesired) success.

Simulations and Competition-Based Training

Computer simulations can be highly immersive training tools (Cannon-Bowers & Cannon, 2010) that put administrators and executives in realistic cyber attack and defend scenarios. In some cases, the intent of a simulation is to stress the efficient operation of technical security controls; in other cases, the execution of management-level plans is brought to the fore. Learning objectives for administrators may include greater proficiency with specific technologies, familiarity with policies and procedures, and the evaluation of security-related plans—incident handling, disaster recovery, and business continuity, to name a few.

High-level simulations aimed at executives are commonly referred to as *tabletop exercises* and are mainly used to raise awareness of potential threats and risks, to identify gaps in planning, and to exercise the decision-making process in realistic scenarios. These simulations allow executives to understand the safety, business continuity, and recovery-of-operations implications of a cyber security intrusion event. More technology-oriented simulations are targeted toward system and network administrators and embrace virtual computing environments that permit the operation and evaluation of security solutions and products. Some simulations are targeted at average users and stress cyber security awareness (Cone, Irvine, Thompson, & Nguyen, 2007); however, such simulations are uncommon.

Where metrics and scoring systems are introduced, simulations take on the characteristics of competition-based training. In some cases, such as capture-the-flag competitions, teams of individuals go head to head to achieve specific cyber security-related tasks. These tasks may involve identifying and exploiting (or remediating) exposures in systems. Others may involve supporting organizational mission and required IT services in the presence of adverse circumstances. It is important to align any scoring system or simulation metric with identified learning objectives.

Self-Development

The advent of open courseware has opened new doors of opportunity for self-directed learning. Entire classes on all manner of topics—including computer and network security—can be found online, offered by prominent institutions of higher learning. Universities, academic and professional societies, and government agencies maintain vast digital libraries of articles and documents on the full spectrum of cyber security topics. Although some libraries require subscriptions or memberships, many are open and freely available. The web itself is a rich resource of knowledge on the topic. Social networks and social media outlets bring together learning communities in a powerful way to cooperatively develop, share, and consume instructional content. Self-development in cyber security is most commonly approached by administrators and executives with core security functions that are viewed as their primary job responsibilities. Conti, Caroland, Cook, and Taylor (2011) described a plan for self-development of cyber security personnel in the military that includes readings, conferences, and videos.

The Role of Individual Differences in Training Design and Success

The previous sections have provided an overview of how cyber security training is currently done and how we feel that it should be evaluated. However, it is important to note that even training shown to be effective overall will not be equally effective for everyone. A comprehensive approach to training would include some consideration of the people who are not learning in the chosen training system and provide them with other options. These options might be other methods of training delivery or adaptive designs to meet these people's specific needs. In addition, some employees might need to change their attitudes toward cyber security before they are motivated to learn. There is a substantial body of literature on individual differences that influence the success of training (e.g., Fleishman & Mumford, 1989; Snow & Lohman, 1984). These differences can influence whether employees learn during training and whether they transfer that learning to the job. For example, self-efficacy, goal orientation, and motivation to learn have all been shown to influence learning in training (Salas et al., 2012). In addition, employee age, experience, ability, and motivation can all influence the transfer of training (Blume, Ford, Baldwin, & Huang, 2010).

Cyber security training has some unique aspects that may require organizations to adapt their training for some employees. Any time training involves computer technology, age and computer experience are important to examine. There are substantial differences in the ways in which different generations interact with computers. For instance, older people have been found to perceive less risk in loss of data confidentiality than do young adults (Byrne et al., 2012) and, therefore, may benefit from awareness training. Gender also plays a role in risky online behavior. Milne, Labrecque, and Cromer (2009) found that males are more likely than females to engage in risky behavior online. People possessing certain personality traits such as extraversion are more likely to violate cyber security policies, whereas people possessing a higher openness to experience and emotional instability are less likely to do so (McBride, Carter, & Warkentin, 2012). Employees with higher levels of organizational commitment complete more information security behaviors (Stanton, Stam, Guzman, & Caldera, 2003). People with cultural traits such as individualism have been linked with increased abuse of access to information assets (Lowry, Posey, Roberts, & Bennett, 2013). This knowledge allows for the targeting of employees who are less likely to comply with policy for additional training. Also, one could target whole departments that tend to have high levels of a trait for training. For instance, people in sales tend to possess higher levels of extraversion and are therefore at risk for policy violation. Providing more extensive training and education of policy infractions for the sales department might be beneficial.

When Training Fails

Once an organization follows all the steps to adequately design, evaluate, and adapt training to its employees, it can make an informed decision as to whether some behaviors needed to maintain an effective cyber security posture require other solutions. These other solutions can vary from tools installed on specific users' computers to spatial access control to removing an employee from the organization. This section reviews some of the currently available solutions when training has failed.

System Tools for Mitigating Cyber Security Threats

Tools for mitigating cyber security threats can be categorized as either preventive or detective controls. Preventive controls primarily work to minimize the likelihood of a successful attack, whereas detective controls seek to identify compromises in the hopes of minimizing impact. Antivirus software is a preventive control that identifies patterns in computer viruses in the hopes of preventing their execution on hosts. Similarly, firewalls scan network traffic for malicious content in order to selectively deny communication to internal networks.

Alerts and warning boxes may be triggered by systems, focusing user attention on present security concerns such as suspicious web pages or downloads. Other user-centric tools deal with password management, requiring that user passwords be changed periodically and/or that they possess a certain composition or strength.

One tool/control type that enjoys a special relationship to training is audit. Computer security audit tools track user and system actions in cyber space. These tools support the core security property of nonrepudiation, guaranteeing the attribution of online behavior. That is, every action taken by a user may be unambiguously attributed to him or her. As such, audit trails provide a window into user behavior. A robust audit capability is an integral component for developing an understanding of behavioral gaps of cyber security personnel. Correspondingly, it is also a powerful tool for illuminating the effectiveness of cyber security training. Using audit data and logs to track changes in user and group behavior over time can be associated with training encounters to measure the impact of specific kinds of training. The ability to distill raw audit information into meaningful measures is one key to success in this regard.

Organizational Tools for Mitigating Cyber Security Threats

In addition to system-level tools that comprise security controls over individual computers and employees, organizations can benefit from environmental enablers of security. A security program is more than the sum of its parts and greater than its collection of technologies, policies, and procedures. Principally, we can conceive of information architecture and organizational culture as defining elements of a security posture. Both are reified by specific programmatic components in the form of technical, operational, and managerial controls, but each is influenced and nurtured by external forces.

An information architecture establishes what data are stored, transmitted, and processed by an enterprise and for what purpose. It also defines zones of interaction, rules of engagement, and communication patterns between operational units in an organization. From the security perspective, characterizing what information is needed to fulfill organizational mission is the first step to understanding risk. A lean organization that reduces its data footprint and constrains access on a need-to-know basis has taken important first steps in simplifying its set of security concerns. Concomitantly, establishing a network architecture that intelligently partitions operational units and controls interfaces promotes the effective deployment of technical controls. Operational zones are also natural delineators for policy and training specialization. Human resource zones and accounting zones may have different security requirements and, therefore, fall under unique policies. It follows that employees may require different training on the basis of their positions within the organization as to what to keep confidential and the methods for doing so. Employees operating out of sales or working in the field may likewise need training that is distinct from what is needed by employees in accounting. In these ways, a sound information architecture can help guide the development of a security program.

Far less tangible, yet no less vital, is an organization's security culture. A security culture includes the habits and attitudes of employees about information security. It affects their willingness to respect information security policies, to accept and adopt security controls, and to maintain the vigilance needed to protect organizational data. Culture begins with an awareness of and an appreciation for cyber risks. Knowing the "why" of security is an essential motivator for its practice in the real world. A mature security culture nurtures a training climate that not only raises awareness but also translates awareness and appreciation into habit and behavior, permeating the day-to-day operations of an organization. Without it, even the most well-designed enterprise security solution is doomed to fail. A security control—be it an application-level encryption tool or an authentication solution—viewed as a hassle or a hindrance by an employee may be circumvented, rendering it worse than useless (worse, because, at the organizational level, the presumption is that it is being used!). Organizations with a robust security culture identify problems early and seek opportunities to improve cyber security. In these organizations, training programs are put in place to address new threats and the cyber security implications of emerging technologies. Such organizations do not wait to become victims before educating employees on potential cyber hazards. Those without such a culture are relegated to a reactionary posture, at best competent to handle only yesterday's attack.

When to Remove the Internal Threat

At some point, an employee may be considered an insider threat to cyber security due to incompetent security behavior. We believe that organizations that are concerned about their overall cyber security posture should include core security competencies in their performance management systems and remove employees who do not maintain the required standards. By making bad security behavior equivalent to violations like stealing, harassment, and unethical behavior, an organization can make a statement about its impact and eliminate it from its organizational culture.

A central issue is defining the threshold and terms for removing an employee as a security threat. Here, audit, logging, and measurement of a system and network's security are essential. An organization must be able to track user actions online to catch infractions and identify unsafe behavior. Once this capability is in place, the organization can determine what is most sensible for it. A few factors to keep in mind when deciding to remove an employee for cyber security infractions are the costs of recruiting, selecting, and providing onboarding for a new employee as well as the costs associated with leaving a position vacant while going through all of the aforementioned procedures. The losses incurred through the cyber security infractions must outweigh the costs of removal and replacement. In addition, there are potential costs to a system in which employees believe that they are constantly being monitored for mistakes. If the approach is not communicated carefully or feels controlling, it could decrease employee performance, satisfaction, and trust (Douthitt & Aiello, 2001; Stanton, 2000).

The Future of Cyber Security Training

Cyber security training must evolve to meet the ever-changing needs of cyber security personnel. Effective training is a pillar of any organization's cyber security program. As new information technologies emerge, the cyber attack vulnerabilities of organizations adopting these technologies also expand. Training must respond not only to these changes but also to the growing sophistication of the cyber adversary.

The ability to adapt training begins with a sound organizational cyber security architecture that details the requirements of employees in every job role. Without the type of processes that we have described in this chapter, organizations will jump from training fad to training fad without achieving their training goals. Optimistically, the future of cyber security training will be characterized by a global maturation process in which organizations follow these processes and incorporate strategic and adaptive training methods to achieve their objectives.

The future modalities of cyber security training will be increasingly dynamic and interactive. Training programs will continue to gradually move away from passive learning methods to offer more engaging and immersive content. The past decade has seen the rise of competitive games that invest participants intellectually and emotionally in mastering concepts, techniques, and technologies. Where competitive games have been largely the dominion of capture-the-flag contests for administrators, they will expand into settings designed to train and educate end users and executives alike. Future games aimed at users and executives could at once raise awareness of the importance of "security hygiene" for information resources and systems and challenge them to gain proficiency with end-point security controls (e.g., user-level encryption, password management, permission setting).

The coming years will also see an increase in the development of targeted and personalized training for cyber security. Targeted training recognizes organization-specific weaknesses in cyber security and promotes a program designed specifically to meet them (e.g., focusing awareness campaigns on spear-phishing tactics that have been effective against a particular business unit). In addition, there is great potential for personalized training as the neuroscience and psychology of cyber trust becomes better understood. For example, we are currently using eye-tracking technology to examine novice and expert approaches to determining the trustworthiness of potential phishing attempts. Additionally, we are working with neuroscience researchers examining the neural pathways activated when people are presented with phishing attempts. For deployment within an organization, personalized training also relies on a mature cyber security program capable of instrumenting the human as well as the network. The ability to profile employees and categorize them in terms of cyber trust decision-making tendencies affords the opportunity to design and deliver custom training to optimize learning for the individual.

Mobile training platforms will deliver cyber security training where it has not gone before. These training programs will adopt shorter and more focused sessions to harmonize with mobile use and engagement patterns. Moreover, training that emphasizes the security of mobile devices that bridge home and work use will become an essential part of an organization's cyber security training portfolio.

With respect to formal degree programs, these will continue to evolve and mature as the common view of the standard body of knowledge for the field converges. More specialized education pathways will be cultivated—degrees and certificate programs in niche areas such as security engineering, critical infrastructure protection, cyber physical system security, and electronic discovery may become standard fare at colleges and universities. Cyber security training is truly in its adolescence, and it will be interesting to see where it goes as it matures.

Conclusion

In this chapter, we have argued that cyber security training is necessary for an organization to maintain a strong cyber security posture. We have also talked about how to tell if a specific approach to training is working and what to do if it is not working. We ended the chapter with our vision for the work that needs to be done to improve cyber security training if there is to be any hope of having cyber secure organizations in the future. Next time one of your organization's cyber security personnel says that training doesn't work, please respond with, "Our current training may not be working, but training can work if it is done correctly. We need to call our friendly neighborhood I-O psychologist and fix the training!"

Note

1 This work was sponsored in part by the Air Force Office of Scientific Research (AFOSR), under award number FA9550-12-1-0457. Any opinions, findings, and conclusions or recommendations expressed in this publication are those of the authors and do not necessarily reflect the views of the AFOSR.

References

Aguinis, H., & Kraiger, K. (2009). Benefits of training and development for individuals and teams, organizations, and society. *Annual Review of Psychology, 60,* 451–474.

Alliger, G. M., Tannenbaum, S. I., Bennett, W., Traver, H., & Shotland, A. (1997). A meta-analysis of the relations among training criteria. *Personnel Psychology, 50,* 341–358.

Barrett, M., Johnson, C., Mell, P., Quinn, S., & Scarfone, K. (2009, May). *Guide to adopting and using the Security Content Automation Protocol (SCAP)* (Special Publication No. 800-117, Draft). Gaithersburg, MD: National Institute of Standards and Technology, U.S. Department of Commerce.

Blume, B. D., Ford, J. K., Baldwin, T. T., & Huang, J. L. (2010). Transfer of training: A meta-analytic review. *Journal of Management, 36*, 1065–1105.

Byrne, Z., Weidert, J., Liff, J., Horvath, M., Smith, C., Howe, A., & Ray, I. (2012, April). *Perceptions of internet threats: Behavioral intent to click again.* Poster session presented at the 27th Annual Conference of the Society for Industrial and Organizational Psychology, San Diego, CA.

Campbell, J. P., & Kuncel, N. R. (2001). Individual and team training. In N. A. Anderson, D. S. Ones, H. Kepir Sinangil, & C. Viswesvaran (Eds.), *Handbook of industrial, work, and organizational psychology: Vol. 1. Personnel psychology* (pp. 278–312). London: Sage.

Cannon-Bowers, J., & Bowers, C. (2010). Synthetic learning environments: On developing a science of simulation, games, and virtual worlds for training. In S. W. J. Koslowski & E. Salas (Eds.), *Learning, training, and development in organizations* (pp. 229–261). New York: Routledge.

Cone, B. D., Irvine, C. E., Thompson, M. F., & Nguyen, T. D. (2007). A video game for cyber security training and awareness. *Computers & Security, 26*, 63–72.

Conti, G., Caroland, J., Cook, T., & Taylor, H. (2011). *Self-development for cyber warriors.* West Point, NY: Military Academy.

Day, E. A., Blair, C., Daniels, S., Kligyte, V., & Mumford, M. D. (2006). Linking instructional objectives to the design of instructional environments: The integrative design matrix. *Human Resource Management Review, 16*, 376–395.

Douthitt, E. A., & Aiello, J. R. (2001). The role of participation and control in the effects of computer monitoring on fairness perceptions, task satisfaction, and performance. *Journal of Applied Psychology, 86*, 867–874.

Eminağaoğlu, M., Uçar, E., & Eren, . (2009). The positive outcomes of information security awareness training in companies—A case study. *Information Security Technical Report, 14*, 223–229.

Fleishman, E. A., & Mumford, M. D. (1989). Abilities as causes of individual differences in skill acquisition. *Human Performance, 2*, 201–223.

Grance, T., Nolan, T., Burke, K., Dudley, R., White, G., & Good, T. (2006). *Guide to test, training, and exercise programs for IT plans and capabilities: Recommendations of the National Institute of Standards and Technology* (Special Publication No. 800-84). Gaithersburg, MD: National Institute of Standards and Technology, U.S. Department of Commerce

Hansche, S. (2005). *Official (ISC)² guide to the CISSP-ISSEP CBK.* Boca Raton, FL: Auerbach.

Kirkpatrick, D. L. (1994). *Evaluating training programs: The four levels.* San Francisco: Berrett-Koehler.

Kraiger, K. (2002). Decision-based evaluation. In K. Kraiger (Ed.), *Creating, implementing, and managing effective training and development: State-of-the-art lessons for practice* (pp. 331–376). San Francisco: Jossey-Bass.

Kumaraguru, P., Cranshaw, J., Acquisti, A., Cranor, L., Hong, J., Blair, M. A., & Pham, T. (2009). *School of phish: A real-world evaluation of anti-phishing training.* Retrieved from http://www.cs.cmu.edu/~jasonh/publications/soups2009-school-of-phish-final.pdf

Lowry, P. B., Posey, C., Roberts, T. L., & Bennett, R. J. (2014). Is your banker leaking your personal information? The roles of ethics and individual-level cultural characteristics in predicting organizational computer abuse. *Journal of Business Ethics, 121*, 385–401.

McBride, M., Carter, L., & Warkinten, M. (2012, September). *Exploring the role of individual employee characteristics and personality on employee compliance with cyber security policies.* Retrieved from http://sites.duke.edu/ihss/files/2011/12/CyberSecurityFinalReport-Final_mcbride-2012.pdf

Marks, M. A., Sabella, M. J., Burke, C. S., & Zaccaro, S. J. (2002). The impact of cross-training on team effectiveness. *Journal of Applied Psychology, 87,* 3–13.

Milne, G. R., Labrecque, L. I., & Cromer, C. (2009). Toward an understanding of the online consumer's risky behavior and protection practices. *Journal of Consumer Affairs, 43,* 449–473.

Salas, E., Tannenbaum, S. I., Kraiger, K., & Smith-Jentsch, K. A. (2012). The science of training and development in organizations: What matters in practice. *Psychological Science in the Public Interest, 13,* 74–101.

Sitzmann, T., Brown, K. G., Casper, W. J., Ely, K., & Zimmerman, R. D. (2008). A review and meta-analysis of the nomological network of trainee reactions. *Journal of Applied Psychology, 93,* 280–295.

Snow, R. E., & Lohman, D. F. (1984). Toward a theory of cognitive aptitude for learning from instruction. *Journal of Educational Psychology, 76,* 347–376.

Staggs, J., Beyer, R., Mol, M., Fisher, M., Brummel, B., & Hale, J. (2014). A perceptual taxonomy of contextual cues for cyber trust. *Journal of the Colloquium for Information System Security Education (CISSE), 2,* 152–169.

Stanton, J. M. (2000). Reactions to employee performance monitoring: Framework, review, and research directions. *Human Performance, 13,* 85–113.

Stanton, J. M., Stam, K. R., Guzman, I., & Caldera, C. (2003). Examining the linkage between organizational commitment and information security. In *IEEE International Conference on Systems, Man, and Cybernetics, 2003* (Vol. 3, pp. 2501–2506). New York: Institute of Electrical and Electronics Engineers.

Wilson, M., de Zafra, D. E., Pitcher, S. I., Tressler, J. D., & Ippolito, J. B. (1998, April). *Information technology security training requirements: A role- and performance-based model* (Special Publication No. 800-16). Gaithersburg, MD: National Institute of Standards and Technology, U.S. Department of Commerce.

Wilson, M., & Hash, J. (2003, October). *Building an information technology security awareness and training program* (Special Publication No. 800-50). Gaithersburg, MD: National Institute of Standards and Technology, U.S. Department of Commerce.

11

DESIGNING MEANINGFUL, HEALTHY, AND EFFECTIVE CYBER SECURITY WORK

Sharon K. Parker, Carolyn J. Winslow, and Lois E. Tetrick

> Work design is a high-priority issue for public policy makers, private commercial interests, and individual workers. Perhaps no other area of organization science has had such a profound impact on practice.
>
> (Sinha & Van de Ven, 2005, p. 389)

The foregoing observation reflects a great deal of well-established theory and evidence that work design "matters," not only for individuals and their health and well-being, but for the effective functioning of organizations and even societies. As we discuss in this chapter, work design can affect individuals' sense of meaning, creativity, performance, desire to stay within an organization, likelihood of experiencing musculoskeletal problems, and more. At the same time, work design can affect how well members of a team share their knowledge, the quality of products made or services delivered, and the level of innovation in an organization. At the societal level, work design can also be critical: For example, in the context of cyber security, if poor work design causes poor performance that leads to undetected threats, there can be catastrophic consequences for national security. Miner (2003) analyzed theories of organizational behavior and rated work design theory as one of the small set of theories in this field that are simultaneously theoretically important, valid, and useful.

The importance of work design theoretically and practically means it is crucial that we attend to this topic, especially as work and its nature shift as a result of changes in technology, society, and the economy. Cyber security is an example of a relatively new type of work that has emerged in recent times, and it is crucial that we fully understand the work design options and challenges within this context. Organizations increasingly include cyber security operations, in which a group of people have the responsibility of monitoring and defending an organization against cyber attack (Zimmerman, 2014). Typical tasks of those working in a cyber security incident response team (CSIRT) include detecting, analyzing, responding to, reporting on, and preventing cyber security incidents. As noted by Zimmerman (2014), "people and process issues are increasingly the primary impediment to effective computer network defense" (p. 6).

In this chapter, we outline current work design theory and evidence and then apply this existing body of knowledge to cyber security work roles. We consider the design of cyber security work from a motivation and performance perspective; from a health and safety perspective; and, finally, from a learning perspective. We draw on interviews conducted with team leaders and analysts working in CSIRTs by two of this chapter's authors and their colleagues, as described in Chen et al. (2014) and Tetrick et al. (2014). Specifically, interviews and focus groups were conducted with 117 analysts and managers representing 45 CSIRTs in government and private industry in the United States and Europe assessing work design issues and their relation to CSIRT effectiveness. In the final sections of the chapter, we propose implications of our analysis. In addition to the practical implications that flow from applying what is already known about work design, we highlight how considering work design from a cyber security perspective shows ways that work design theory can, and should, be extended to maintain its contemporary relevance. We conclude with future research directions.

Before we begin, it is important to clarify what we mean by work design. *Work design* refers to "the content and organization of one's work tasks, activities, relationships and responsibilities" (Parker, 2014, p. 662). Applied to cyber security, example work design decisions that might be made when designing the role of a cyber security analyst include answers to the following: Which activities should be grouped together to form a meaningful cyber security job? Which decisions should be made by Tier 1 analysts and which by their supervisors? Should individual cyber security jobs be grouped together into a team, and, if so, how? What level of vigilance activity is reasonable, and what level might overwhelm analysts' cognitive resources? Can the activities in the job be organized in a way that minimizes strain to the musculoskeletal system? Work design decisions such as these are often reflected in individuals' perceptions of work characteristics, such as job autonomy, job variety, work load, and social support.

Throughout this discussion, we use the term *work design* instead of the narrower term *job design* (Morgeson & Campion, 2003; Parker & Wall, 1998) to convey that employees not only carry out set tasks in a fixed job but sometimes engage in emergent, social, and self-initiated activities within flexible roles. It is also important to consider that work design is part of, but distinct from, the larger system of leadership and organization design. For example, one could ask how much support a cyber security analyst should receive from his or her manager. Support provided by a manager is an aspect of leadership that can shape work design and interact with it to influence outcomes. In contrast, support that arises as a result of the organization of tasks—such as the grouping of individual jobs into a team structure—is a work design issue.

Designing Motivating Work

Here, we review theory and evidence regarding how to design motivating and meaningful work that, in turn, can enhance performance outcomes. We then consider the design of motivating cyber security jobs.

History of and Theory on Motivational Work Design

Arising from the Industrial Revolution, and influenced by Smith's (1776) concept of the *division of labor* as well as Taylor's (1911) notion of *scientific management*, the dominant approach to factory work design was that managers carried out "mental" work, such as decision making, whereas operators' jobs were highly simplified and repetitive so that individuals could be trained quickly and cost-effectively (Davis, 1966). An early approach to redesigning these alienating jobs emerged from analyses of coal mining. Scholars concluded that both social and technical elements should be considered when designing work, rather than focusing solely on technical aspects (Trist & Bamforth, 1951). The sociotechnical principles arising from this approach included that work be reasonably demanding and provide variety, allow learning, include an area of autonomous decision making, offer social support, be of social relevance, and lead to a desirable future (Cherns, 1987). When applied to groups, these criteria resulted in autonomous work groups, or what has come to be known as *self-managing teams*.

At the same time as these group work design experiments were occurring, experiments focused on redesigning individual jobs began to emerge. These redesign efforts to increase the motivational quality of work included job rotation (rotating people from one job to another), job enlargement (expanding the content of jobs to include additional tasks), and job enrichment (e.g., increasing employees' autonomy over the planning and execution of their own work). In addition, quality circles in which teams of employees worked offline to address quality issues became popular. The ideas in these types of redesign, especially job enrichment, were consolidated into the job characteristics model (JCM), introduced by Hackman and Oldham (1976), which ultimately became perhaps the most influential model of motivational work design, as we describe next.

The JCM proposes that work should be designed to have five core job characteristics (skill variety, autonomy, feedback, task significance, and task identity), which then engender various psychological states (individuals' experiencing meaning, feeling responsible for their outcomes, and understanding the results of their efforts) and, in turn, enhance employee motivation, job satisfaction, and performance and reduce turnover. The model has not been immune to criticism (e.g., Salancik & Pfeffer, 1978), but the overarching idea from the model that job characteristics affect attitudinal outcomes is now well established. In 2007, in a meta-analysis of 259 studies, Humphrey, Nahrgang, and Morgeson (2007) found that all or most of the five core work characteristics predict job satisfaction, growth satisfaction and internal work motivation, organizational commitment, coworker satisfaction, burnout, and role perceptions, with experienced meaning being the most important mediating critical psychological state. Longitudinal and quasi-experimental studies also support these meta-analyses (see Parker, 2014, for a review), such as a study by Griffin (1991) that found that job enrichment led to an increase in bank tellers' job satisfaction and commitment. When it comes to performance and behavioral outcomes, findings from meta-analyses have shown clear links between work characteristics and subjective job performance (Fried & Ferris, 1987; Humphrey et al., 2007), with job autonomy also being associated with higher objective performance (Humphrey et al., 2007). Although performance benefits are not always demonstrated, several quasi-experimental and longitudinal studies have shown positive performance effects of motivating work characteristics (e.g., Birdi et al., 2008, who showed that devolving authority to individuals or teams was associated with greater performance).

Although exceptionally dominant when it comes to considering which characteristics of work are motivating, the JCM has been both critiqued and extended. Morgeson and Humphrey (2006) proposed an integrative conceptualization of work design, and, in their elaborated model of job characteristics, Parker, Wall, and Cordery (2001) advocated an expanded set of work characteristics beyond the JCM's five (e.g., social work characteristics, such as interdependence, and different forms of autonomy, such as autonomy over working hours), elaborated outcomes (e.g., customer satisfaction, work–home conflict, innovation), suggested new mechanisms beyond critical psychological states (e.g., learning, fast responses), expanded moderators (e.g., the importance of uncertainty in enhancing the value of enriched work characteristics), and highlighted the need to consider antecedents of work characteristics (both individual influences, such as personality, and broader influences, like technology and national culture).

Whereas the JCM focuses on designing work that is experienced as intrinsically motivating, in an approach referred to as *relational work design*, Grant and colleagues focused on designing work that fuels prosocial motivation. That is, when jobs are structured to provide employees with contact with beneficiaries (such as connecting lifeguards with families whose children have been saved from drowning), employees empathize, identify with, and take the perspective of these beneficiaries and, thereby, develop stronger affective commitment towards them, which in turn encourages effort, persistence, and helping behavior (Grant, 2007). Several studies have supported this relational perspective (e.g., Grant, 2008; Grant et al., 2007; Turner, Hadas-Halperin, & Raveh, 2008).

Why Motivation Matters in Cyber Security Work

In regard to cyber security jobs, the design of motivating work is important from at least two perspectives. First, turnover in the context of skill shortages appears to be a major challenge within the industry. Evans and Reeder (2010) argued that the low supply of cyber security practitioners, combined with relatively high turnover, has created a "human capital crisis" in the sector. Turnover and the resulting skills gaps can cause potential security breaches and data loss (Stanton, Stam, Guzman, & Caldera, 2003). The problem is unlikely to go away given that the global demand for cyber security practitioners is increasing, yet the pool of applicants remains limited. The challenges created by turnover, combined with a skill shortage, highlight the importance of work designs that motivate individuals to stay in work.

Second, from a performance perspective, it is quite obvious that high performance is crucial—not only from an individual, team, or organizational perspective—but from a societal perspective as well. Cyber attacks on information systems are becoming more frequent and more complex, causing not only financial consequences for organizations, but also security threats. Our interviews reveal the importance of a high level of commitment for employees to carry out threat detection effectively. For instance:

> A passion and an interest for this type of work is a must. If someone were to come by and take a look at our shop and watch these guys in action, you'd see them staring at this glass looking through code that looks incredibly tedious and boring. It's nothing but hexadecimal code over and over and over again. And you have to say to yourself, how can you possibly look at that for more than five minutes? But the passion comes from ... solving a puzzle, or figuring out how, even if it's malicious, you can certainly respect when you find something that's done in a clever and unique fashion and actually get excited about it.

Importantly, effective performance appears to require a high level of persistence, in some cases, sustained over the very long term:

> We have people who are not afraid of like spending a long time trying to figure out the hard problems. People who are ... persistent.
> We had some data that we were seeing randomly from outside the United States, had no idea what it was. And we worked that for almost eight months until we corrected it and finally figured out what it was.

Proactive behavior, or self-initiating improvements in the situation or one's self (Parker, Williams, & Turner, 2006), also appears important, especially as cyber security is a dynamic type of work with frequent change: "Everyone in my group maintains their expertise by constantly studying, being part of the Listservs, answering questions as well as asking them." Work design is an important potential lever for enhancing cyber security analysts' motivation and, in turn, their performance including their persistence and proactivity.

Motivating Work Design in Cyber Security Jobs

We are unaware of any research on the topic of cyber security analysis work design to date. However, our interview-based evidence suggests that there are some positive features of work design and some challenges. We first describe the traditional five job characteristics and then consider other elements of work design that are likely to be important.

On the basis of our interviews, *skill variety*—or the degree to which a job requires a variety of activities that involve the use of different skills (Hackman & Oldham, 1976)—appears to vary greatly, both within and between teams. A typical structure within a CSIRT is a tiered triage structure (Zimmerman, 2014). Tier 1 analysts are at the front line and are devoted to real-time inspection of alerts as well as other routine tasks. If an alert reaches a predefined threshold, it is escalated to Tier 2 analysts, typically more experienced, who then investigate the event in more depth. As Tier 2 and higher analysts are not engaging in real-time monitoring, they tend to have more time available, and potentially more skill variety, and part of their role is to gather further information (e.g., cyber intelligence) and liaise with relevant parties (system owners, individuals engaged in physical security, law enforcement officers, etc.). But this structure means that there is likely to be quite a lot of repetitive work for the Tier 1 analysts (those at the front line), so skill variety can be limited. Zimmerman, for example, warned that the strategy of having staff too tightly pigeonholed into one role is likely to result in increased turnover.

Nevertheless, it is possible that there are work design strategies that could increase skill variety for analysts at the lowest tier, such as greater participation in improvement activities. For example, it appears that Tier 1 analysts can attempt to alleviate some repetitiveness through the creation of tools that automatically do work for them:

> Well, day in and day out, for something as simple as auditing logs, we have gigs [i.e., gigabytes] and gigs of logs. We don't want to manually have to go through them. So maybe I'll write a script or something that'll search for key words. That's essentially what a lot of the tools are—automating processes.

This quote suggests that the analysts—at least in this case—have the autonomy to decide to write a script to improve their work. *Job autonomy* refers to the job providing substantial freedom, independence, and discretion in regard to work schedules and work methods (Hackman & Oldham, 1976). On weekends and at night, autonomy can also be high because management is not present. Other evidence, however, suggests that analysts sometimes lack autonomy over their work methods: "Off the top of my head, we have heard of instances where the analyst makes a recommendation to solve the issue but does not have the authority to actually take corrective action." In part, autonomy might be compromised by the high level of interdependence among tasks, which in some cases is accompanied by bureaucratic processes:

> One of the things in working with large companies, a lot of times when we need to make a change and we need to make an implementation, it doesn't mean that we can pick up the phone and go, "Hey, can you do this for me?" It means that we have to follow a process, we have to fill out forms .... But we're not going to see the completion for weeks, because the paperwork got submitted like within the last day. And it takes like three weeks for another team to do it. So you can't just expect immediate results.

Work method autonomy and decision-making autonomy both tend to be more important predictors of job satisfaction than autonomy over the timing of one's work (Humphrey et al., 2007), and there is evidence that job satisfaction can in turn affect job performance (Judge, Thoresen, Bono, & Patton, 2001). Moreover, because autonomy promotes self-efficacy and a strong sense of ownership or felt responsibility, it has been identified as an especially important work characteristic for fueling persistence and proactivity (e.g., Parker et al., 2006). To the extent that these behaviors are critical for effective performance, job autonomy is likely to be a key work design issue. As we discuss later, autonomy also might be important from the perspectives of both health and learning, suggesting that this aspect of work deserves especially close attention when designing cyber security jobs.

The JCM identifies the importance of *feedback*, or how much carrying out the job results in clear and direct information about performance effectiveness for the incumbent (Hackman & Oldham, 1976). For cyber security analysts involved in detecting risks, it can be very difficult to know when the job has been performed well and when it has not. Consequently, with a lack of feedback from the task itself, cyber security analysts often rely heavily on feedback from clients, other teams, or managers. In our interviews, such feedback was often pointed to as lacking, even when risks or threats had been detected. For example, a team leader observed: "The feedback actually so far has been quite poor.... I would like to be able to give team feedback, at the absolute minimum. I think where there are specific roles that are employed, individual feedback would be great." Consistent with this point, another team leader noted the following about staff: "They also do not always learn whether the action was taken and it worked, taken but it didn't work, or the action was not taken." Similarly, when an analyst hands off a potential threat to more senior analysts, it seems there is little feedback, discussion, or follow-up: "Historically, it's been more on the lines of you turn the ticket over and it's never seen again. You don't get any input whatsoever." Likewise, when speaking of an individual on another team to whom a team member passes information, a team member noted, "And we would like to have this feedback loop where he comes back to us and says: 'By the way, this case is now closed, great detection done'; but it's not there."

Sometimes the feedback exists, but it can appear to be somewhat arbitrary and untimely:

> We make our recommendation to X [executive leader], "Hey, you should take these actions." And then it's on them to approve or just let it drop. Frequently … we'll make our recommendation … . Maybe they'll do something on it. Maybe they won't. And then a week later, they're in a frenzy because, "It's on Fox. It's on CNN. It's the end of the world." And they come ask us. And—yeah, we blocked it, so we cover ourselves that way.

Ultimately, inconsistent or inadequate feedback on one's job performance is demotivating and, as we highlight later, potentially impedes learning.

Task identity is high when a job requires completion of a whole and identifiable piece of work, from beginning to end (Hackman & Oldham, 1976). A cyber security worker is often one individual in one team within a very large multiteam system, which means that task identity can be low. Consistent with this notion, one individual observed the following in relation to a product that teams collectively developed: "We configured it. Another team shipped, and then the contractors are going to be racking it." The relatively low task identity might be compounded by the long-term nature of the work: "For a lot of the things that we do, we do something now, but we won't see the fruit for weeks, months down the road." A lack of feedback, such as when a threat is escalated, is also likely to diminish analysts' perception of task identity.

Task significance refers to the job having a substantial impact on the lives or work of other people in the organization or beyond (Hackman & Oldham, 1976). It is clear that cyber security work has the potential to be seen as highly significant, especially in government contexts in which individuals are protecting national institutions and agencies, such as the military. For example, one individual commented:

> I want to protect this network. At the end of the day, we're not protecting just X. We're stopping our network from being hacked, which would affect our guys in uniform. So at the end of the day, we're taking care of them … . Customer satisfaction is important to us definitely. That's what our service is here for, to protect the network and, ultimately, customer service.

Sometimes the sense of task significance is fueled by the leader. For example, one manager expects the following of employees: "I need two things from you. I need passion, and I need loyalty. You have to realize where you are. This is [a very well-known agency]." Nevertheless, it is clear that, in some contexts, cyber security work is less likely to feel important, and the "big picture" consequences of the work may get lost in the day-to-day work. This limited perception of the overarching consequences of the work might be exacerbated when individuals do not get feedback on their efforts or experience relatively low task identity and long-term outcomes in some cases. It is possible that relational work design, in which analysts are proactively connected with the beneficiaries of their jobs, might have some impact, such as if clients occasionally met with analysts to give them powerful examples of the effects of their work.

A further set of important work characteristics are those concerned with the social elements of work. Although not part of the original JCM, many work design scholars have argued that work is inherently social and, therefore, that social work characteristics can be as important as intrinsic work design features.

One social characteristic that has been identified as important is interdependence, or the extent to which individuals need to cooperate with others to achieve their work goals (Kiggundu, 1983). In particular, *interdependence* shapes the work design decisions that should be made in regard to team working. Team work does not make sense if team members have low task interdependence, as indeed was demonstrated by Langfred (2005): Teams with high task interdependence performed better with high levels of team autonomy, whereas low-interdependence teams performed better with high levels of individual autonomy (see also Burke et al., 2006; Sprigg, Christine, Jackson, & Parker 2000). To the extent that cyber security analysts have work that is interdependent, teamwork makes sense. Being physically co-located appears to support such teamwork, as does face-to-face communication: "We're working right next to the cube next to them. That's how close we are to each other as far as the team goes." Nevertheless, the high task significance of cyber security can also mean that if one individual is ill, that individual needs to be isolated so that the rest of the team is protected.

Zimmerman's (2014) discussion of what sorts of organizational designs are likely to be most effective is informative in terms of interdependence. He strongly advocated that all of the functions of cyber security should be consolidated within a single organization so as to ensure effective coordination. For example, if Tier 1 analysts are not in the same organization as Tier 2 analysts, then this organizational structure can slow down follow-up and mean that a Tier 1 analyst does not get feedback. In essence, the argument is that interdependent functions should be housed within a single organization.

In terms of what structure works best within an organization, Zimmerman (2014) advocated a strongly function-based structure with traditional management hierarchies (e.g., there is a Tier 1 unit with a Tier 1 leader, there is a Tier 2 unit with a Tier 2 leader). It is an interesting question as to whether other sorts of organizational structures might make sense in these organizations, which in turn might allow for enhanced work designs. For example, analogous to a product-based structure in other organizations, perhaps the work could be structured by client or threat type, and perhaps analysts from different tiers could work together as an autonomous unit to deal with particular threats. In fact, there are examples of such structures across the CSIRTs we interviewed. The effectiveness of the various organizational structures needs further exploration.

Social support is a key social work characteristic that helps individuals to feel connected in the workplace. For example, Humphrey et al. (2007) reported that the social characteristics of work were less important for predicting internal work motivation, yet they were especially important for predicting organizational commitment and turnover intentions, most likely because of their impact on individuals' need for connection and belonging. Social support has also been identified as a resource that protects individuals from job strain, as we discuss later. Social support was identified in our interviews as an important feature of good cyber security work:

> We all have to have each other's back.
> A lot of it has to do with people … . We have a great bunch of people that works on our team … . A lot of us could leave and work outside and probably make more money, but it's not the issue. The issue is that we enjoy working with each other. So, to find somebody to fit like a glove on your team, that's hard to do. But most of all, it's important to have individuals who have the mindset to be on this team.

In sum, although there is likely to be considerable variation across teams, organizational contexts, and levels, a positive motivational feature of cyber security work design is that the work has high task significance. Some analysts' jobs also have skill variety, autonomy, task identity, and feedback from the job, although our interviews suggest that these motivating features can also be lacking. From a social perspective, these jobs are likely to have at least some interdependence, but whether this is taken into consideration (e.g., when creating the boundaries for teams) is unknown. Altogether, there appears to be considerable potential for improving the motivational design of cyber security work, which might be essential for attracting and retaining individuals. Table 11.1 summarizes key work design principles and example ways that they might be applied within cyber security jobs.

Designing Healthy and Safe Work

A further critical perspective is to look at the design of work through the lens of health and safety. As we discuss in this section, work design can affect employees' mental health (e.g., anxiety, depression, well-being) as well as their physical health (e.g., safety, musculoskeletal outcomes, cardiovascular disease, obesity).

TABLE 11.1 Evidence-Based Work Design Principles and Their Potential Application within Cyber Security Work

Work design principle	Example ways to achieve the principle within cyber security
Design cyber security work roles so that analysts (especially Tier 1 analysts) have a variety of tasks and use a range of skills.	• Include a varied set of interdependent tasks that use a range of skills within each work role. • Involve cyber security analysts in improvement activities, such as developing automation tools. • Consider a job-rotation scheme.
Design cyber security work roles so that analysts have the opportunity to develop new skills and increase their situational awareness.	• Identify opportunities for employees to learn new skills while they are doing their work (e.g., through engagement in problem-solving, through autonomy to take corrective action). • Use periods of low demand for training and development. • Ensure that analysts interact with others with whom their work is interdependent to promote learning and situational awareness.
Arrange cyber security work roles so that analysts can influence their own work situation, working methods, and pace of work.	• Remove unnecessary bureaucracy that limits analysts' discretion. • Allow analysts to influence—and, if possible, control—the scheduling of tasks and their work methods. • Give analysts the opportunity to take corrective action/address problems when they occur. • Identify decisions currently made by more senior analysts and/or supervisors that could be made by lower level analysts. • Involve analysts in quality control, in the design/improvement of work procedures, and in other decisions that affect their work.
Design cyber security work roles so that employees obtain timely feedback about their work.	• Ensure that higher level analysts provide regular feedback to lower level analysts, such as follow-up feedback when Tier 1 analysts make recommendations regarding potential threats. • As far as possible, design tasks so that analysts receive timely feedback from the work itself.
Seek ways to build task significance (perception that one is doing something important) and task identity (sense that one is doing a "whole" job).	• Group an analyst's tasks into a meaningful job that promotes understanding of the whole work process. • Make clear the connections between individual analysts' tasks and the "bigger picture." • Ensure that client/customer feedback is shared with analysts. • Communicate long-term outcomes with analysts. • Have clients/customers meet directly with analysts so that analysts can appreciate the value of their work.

(Continued)

Designing Work in Cyber Security 251

TABLE 11.1 (Continued)

Work design principle	Example ways to achieve the principle within cyber security
Design work so that interdependent tasks are combined into one job and interdependent roles are combined into one team.	• Create an organizational structure in which interdependent analysts work together. For example, consider client-based organizational structures (all analysts serving a particular client working together) rather than functional structures as a way to manage work interdependencies among analysts. • Locate interdependent analysts together as much as possible.
If analysts' work as a team, ensure good work design at the team level.	• Ensure that the team includes a meaningful and logical set of interdependent tasks that involves a balance between less and more desirable tasks and that there are clear boundaries. • Ensure that the team has clear and challenging performance goals and that it gets feedback on its performance. • As far as possible, empower the team to plan and manage all aspects of its work, including planning, scheduling, and organizing rest breaks. • Give the team responsibility for managing its own resources, and minimally specify work methods. • Increase the skill level of employees to allow flexible responses to uncertainties and the capacity to cope with peak demands. • Ensure that systems for training, selection, and payment align with teamwork, and ensure that the team is trained in teamwork skills.
Ensure that analysts have social support.	• Structure the physical work environment so that analysts have sufficient social contact with others. • Create a positive and supportive work environment.
Design work to guard against excessive workload.	• Monitor workloads to ensure that they remain reasonable. • Ensure that employees have as much job autonomy and social support as possible (as this can mitigate the effects of demands), especially during peak periods.
Ensure that analysts have clear roles and responsibilities.	• Communicate regularly with analysts about work expectations. • Provide regular and clear feedback.

(Continued)

TABLE 11.1 (Continued)

Work design principle	Example ways to achieve the principle within cyber security
Ensure moderate levels of cognitive demands that are not so high as to cause strain or so low as to cause excess boredom.	• If a large number of tasks are highly monotonous, try to redesign work to increase variety and allow some opportunity for more complex problem-solving. • Ensure that there are sufficient work breaks. • Provide job autonomy, especially control over work methods, as much as possible. • During low periods, provide opportunities for skill development and engagement in improvement activities.
Design work to allow for postural variety and the avoidance of excess sitting.	• Ensure good ergonomic design of work stations (considering lighting, seating, avoidance of noise, etc.) and allowance for individual differences in height and so forth. • Design opportunities to rotate from sitting to nonsitting tasks. • Ensure adequate rest breaks. • Encourage, and provide opportunities for, employees to engage in physical exercise.

Theory Related to the Design of Healthy and Safe Work

The most dominant work design model relevant to health is the job demands–control model of strain (Karasek, 1979), which was initially extended to include social support (the demand–control–support model; Karasek & Theorell, 1990) and has now been extended to the job demands–resources model (Bakker & Demerouti, 2007). The former model proposes that high job demands, low job control, and low social support cause psychological strain and, in the long term, stress-related illnesses such as cardiovascular disease. More specifically, the model proposes that high job demands cause strain when also accompanied by low decision latitude (i.e., low job control and low skill discretion), but if demands occur in the presence of high decision latitude, then strain will not occur. Instead, an active job results in feelings of mastery and self-confidence that, in turn, enable a person to cope with further job demands, promoting further learning, in a positive spiral (Karasek & Theorell, 1990). A similar buffering role is proposed for social support and other such resources.

We have already highlighted the importance of autonomy for motivation, but it is also important from a health perspective. In a review of longitudinal studies, de Lange, Taris, Kompier, Houtman, and Bongers (2003) reported that just under half of the studies they examined linked job control (or job autonomy) to subsequent health outcomes, showing that control can reduce job strain, albeit not for all individuals or in all situations. Similarly, there is clear evidence that social support from supervisors and peers improves employees' health and well-being (de Lange et al., 2003; Van der Doef & Maes, 1999). The idea that control "buffers" the effects of demands has had mixed evidence: The buffering effect has been by and large supported in laboratory studies (e.g., Karasek, 1979) but inconsistently supported in field studies (e.g., de Lange et al., 2003). Applied to social support, the evidence appears a little more consistent, with several studies showing that social support mitigates the effects of demands in the workplace (Bakker, Demerouti, & Euwema, 2005; Viswesvaran, Sanchez, & Fisher, 1999).

In terms of the direct effects of demands, the evidence is quite clear: Excess demands cause strain. In their meta-analysis, for example, Lee and Ashforth (1996) reported that work load and work pressure predict depersonalization and emotional exhaustion. Likewise, in 19 longitudinal studies, de Lange et al. (2003) reported that two thirds of the studies showed negative effects of job demands, especially for psychological well-being and sickness/absence. High demands and low control together also have been shown to affect cardiovascular disease in a series of rigorous studies (Belkic, Landsbergis, Schnall, & Baker 2004), likely because of these work characteristics' effects on psychological strain, hypertension, and physical risk factors (e.g., smoking), which in turn increase the likelihood of heart disease. Excess job demands also can reduce safety (Nahrang, Morgeson, & Hofmann, 2011).

In recent times, scholars have advocated a distinction between challenge demands that entail an opportunity for development (e.g., time pressure, responsibility) and hindrance demands that create obstacles to achievement and growth (e.g., role ambiguity, job insecurity, constraints; Cavanaugh, Boswell, Roehling, & Boudreau, 2000). Whereas both types of demands can cause strain, meta-analyses suggest that hindrance demands are associated with turnover and withdrawal, whereas challenge demands can be positive for motivation and, hence, performance (Crawford, LePine, & Rich, 2010; Le Pine, Podsakoff, & LePine, 2005; Podsakoff, LePine, & LePine, 2007).

Application to Cyber Security Work

With respect to cyber security work, in the context in which we conducted our analysis, a feature of the work appears to be the perhaps sporadic occurrence of *excess workload*. Importantly, this high workload appears to be inconsistent, depending on external challenges:

> As far as volume ... it's a wave. One week we'll be super busy. We'll have botnets coming through, spam e-mails, phishing e-mail attempts. And the next [week], you won't even see that.
>
> For example, I've seen up to over 1,000 e-mails that came in that we were evaluating. And then next week we're down to about 10. So it all depends on the threat level for that week.

Sometimes a fast pace of work, or *time pressure*, is crucial because analysts need to able to reduce a potential threat before it escalates:

> Speed is a factor definitely. Timing is very important in this—in this arena. Accuracy as far as ensuring that the threat is not false positive, and taking it forward from there.
>
> Mitigating the threat before it gets further into the network. That's one area of the speed. The second is being able to access the system that's infected before it's no longer available. Understand that most of our work is remote. So, if a system's offline, we can't do anything with it.

The extent to which (fluctuating) excess work load and time pressure cause strain for cyber security analysts is currently unknown, but research and theory suggest that the effects will depend on the extent of these variables, whether individuals have control over their work and can therefore mitigate the demands, how much support exists in the environment, whether these variables are perceived to be a hindrance or a challenge, and the personality of the job incumbents.

Scholars have also considered cognitive demands arising from one's job. Focusing on main effects, Humphrey et al. (2007), in their meta-analysis, reported that *information processing*, the extent to which a job necessitates focusing on information and its management, has a positive overall association with job satisfaction. This is likely because information processing is associated with solving novel and complex problems that can be intrinsically motivating. Nevertheless, there was a rather low number of studies addressing information processing in the meta-analysis, so any conclusion is premature. Earlier research suggested that cognitive demands likely interact with other work characteristics. Thus, an early study by Martin and Wall (1989) showed that for shopfloor workers, attentional demands (high degrees of attention and focus required in the job) caused psychological strain, but only when *cost responsibility* (a perceived high cost of error) was also high. It seems that having to be highly vigilant, with a heavy penalty if a mistake is made, can induce strain. Evidence from the ergonomics domain also suggests that it can be both more effortful and more stressful to maintain attention when tasks are intellectually unchallenging or monotonous (e.g., Robertson & O'Connell, 2010). Strain, fatigue, and performance detriments can occur over time, partly as a result of the high degree of self-regulation required to sustain attention in a demanding yet not intrinsically interesting task (Langner, Steinborn, Chatterjee, Sturm, & Willmes, 2010). Conversely, when tasks are more cognitively challenging, although still demanding of attention, they do not necessarily cause strain or fatigue and can even involve "flow" experiences (Csikszentmihalyi, 1988).

As with other demands, the effects of cognitive demands also might depend on the level of job control: Wall and Jackson (1995) considered the interaction between job control and two cognitive demands: *monitoring demands*, the extent of passive monitoring, and *problem-solving demands*, the extent of active cognitive processing to prevent or solve problems. They found that these demands were associated with lower job satisfaction and higher depression, but this effect was buffered if method autonomy was also high. Thus, consistent with the demand–control model, it appeared that control mitigated the potentially stressful effects of these demands.

It is clear from our interviews that cyber security jobs often have high cognitive demands, with high degrees of attentional demand and problem-solving demands. Most CSIRTs need to process vast amounts of security-related data. The cost of error, or cost responsibility, is also high. This configuration of work characteristics might be a combination that induces strain. This comment from an interview suggests both high cognitive demand and high cost of error: "If one person is … not focused, [and] I'm looking at something, [but] he's looking at something else, and then Client C goes down, and that third person who's not focused could have been watching it." Our interviews also suggest that the effect of high attentional demand might depend partly on individuals' personal levels of commitment to the work, with those individuals who are most committed to their work putting in the greatest attentional effort.

In quiet periods, some managers noted that the demands can be so low as to induce boredom. At such times, managers encouraged their employees to use the downtime to catch up on cyber security–relevant current events and maintain their expertise: "It's probably five hours a week they spend reading journals, or looking at the Listservs, or seeing the online training that comes." The extent to which these periods of low demand cause dissatisfaction or even strain potentially depend on individual differences, such as how conscientious or proactive an individual is.

This brief analysis suggests that a deeper understanding of the mental health effects of high levels of cognitive demand in cyber security work is required. Our analysis suggests the importance of individuals' experiencing their work as intrinsically interesting, which is shaped partly by person factors (e.g., interest, skill, personality characteristics like resilience) but also by the motivating work design factors discussed earlier (task variety, task identity, etc.). In other words, high cognitive demands in a cyber security job are not necessarily stressful, and can be motivating, consistent with the idea of a *challenge demand*. However cognitive demands might induce strain when the cost of error is high, when the task is uninteresting, and/or when job control is low.

A further issue to explore is whether individuals adapt to sustained high levels of cognitive demands. The theory of learned industriousness (Eisenberger, 1992) suggests that individuals learn what level of effort is required in a situation, with this learning then transferring across tasks, such that over time, they can develop greater industriousness and increase their capacity to deal with high demands. Likewise, adaptation-level theory (Helson, 1964) suggests that individuals adaptively develop internal norms as a result of their experience, which then serve as internal reference points that guide their behavior, such that they can adapt to high demands. Consistent with these theories, Converse and DeShon (2009) showed that exposure to two demanding tasks led to positive adaption effects, whereas exposure to one demanding task resulted in depletion.

A final type of demand that appears relevant to cyber security work is the level of *physical demands* associated with long periods of sitting and monitoring computer screens. Many of the cyber security job advertisements that we reviewed mentioned that applicants should be have the "physical capacity to sit for extended periods of time." Shifts can be as long as 12 hours, and much of that time can be spent sitting. Job rotation is often considered a way to alleviate the physical demands of work, but if the rotation involves moving from one computer-oriented task to the next, little might be gained from this strategy. Improved ergonomic design—such as desks that one can raise and lower, enabling a combination of standing and sitting—is likely to be important. Reducing work hours, reconfiguring shift structures, exploring other forms of rotation, and embedding regular rest breaks into a shift, are obvious work design strategies to consider for preventing the musculoskeletal disorders associated with excess sedentary work. Table 11.1 summarizes some of the recommendations that flow from designing healthy work.

Designing Work for Learning and Development

In a practitioner-oriented article, Assante and Tobey (2011) argued that, with increasing asymmetric and interconnected security threats becoming the norm, the standard approach for achieving the development of expertise—thousands of hours of practice—becomes a less useful strategy. These authors made several recommendations to promote the skill acquisition needed, such as using simulation forms of training. Interestingly, they did not consider the potential role of work design. Yet recent theory and evidence suggests that in the complex and unpredictable environments that characterize many cyber security situations, high levels of job autonomy (likely in combination with feedback) might be a vehicle for accelerating skill development. This theoretical perspective—that good work design promotes learning, knowledge sharing, and cognitive development (Parker, 2014)—has been much more neglected than the motivational and health work design perspectives discussed earlier. Given issues around skill development within the cyber security context, looking at work design as a vehicle for development makes a good deal of sense.

Several scholars have argued that work designs affect learning-related outcomes and even long-term development, although this perspective is far from mainstream. Frese and Zapf (1994), for example, drew on German action theory to argue that lower levels of job control and lower job complexity impede employee learning. Job control allows individuals to choose strategies to deal with a situation, which generates feedback that prompts learning. Job complexity means that tasks must be regulated at the highest intellectual level, and over time, with practice, new skills become routinized, freeing up capacity for learning yet more skills. Wall and Jackson (1995) argued that when individuals control variances at the source, enabled by autonomy, they learn what works and thereby develop more elaborated mental models. They also can observe cause and effect and so learn to anticipate and prevent problems, a type of learning. Field studies support these ideas linking work design and anticipatory levels (e.g., Leach, Wall, & Jackson, 2003), and other studies have linked job autonomy to reports of systemic understanding (Parker & Axtell, 2001) and job rotation to increased self-reported business knowledge (Campion, Cheraskin, & Stevens, 1994). When individuals are better able to control their attention via psychological flexibility, the learning effects of work design are even stronger (Bond & Flaxman, 2006).

Such learning-related benefits of work design might explain why evidence suggests that enriched job designs, and especially high job autonomy, are most beneficial for performance in dynamic and uncertain operating environments (e.g., Cordery, Morrison, Wright, & Wall, 2010; Wall, Cordery & Clegg, 2002). In the words of Wall et al. (2002),

> Operational uncertainty represents a lack of understanding about cause and effect, or action and outcome, within the system … . Where such uncertainty is high, knowledge is incomplete and problem solving requirements are high. Thus there is both the opportunity to empower employees, in terms of giving them important areas of decision making, and [there is] scope for learning. (pp. 159–160)

There is also some evidence that such learning effects can accumulate over time, resulting in cognitive development such as increased cognitive complexity. Schooler, Mulatu, and Oates (2004) reported that, controlling for prior levels of these variables assessed 20 years earlier, complex work with low supervision predicted employees' later intellectual flexibility. Parker (2014) summarized further promising evidence in this vein and recommended more systematic enquiry into this topic.

How cyber security work design helps or hinders learning and cognitive development is currently unknown, although Zimmerman's (2014) discussion of what sorts of organizational designs are likely to be most effective is informative. As mentioned earlier, he strongly advocated that all of the functions of cyber security be consolidated within a single organization so as to ensure effective coordination. (For example, if Tier 1 analysts are not in the same organization as Tier 2 analysts, this structure can slow down follow-up and mean that a Tier 1 analyst does not get feedback.) Although not using this terminology, Zimmerman's arguments relate to a proper consideration of the interdependencies within a system. We concur with this recommendation to create organizational structures and work designs that capture key interdependences. However, we go beyond

Zimmerman to suggest that such a strategy not only promotes coordination but is also important for fostering learning.

In a related vein, work design might affect the development of situational awareness among cyber security agents—that is, analysts' understanding of the environment in which they operate. A pilot, for example, needs to be aware of an array of factors (what he or she can see outside the window, instruments, etc.), synthesize those factors and make meaning from them, and then act on that basis. Zimmerman (2014) argued that situational awareness is just as important among analysts—maybe even more so, because the analyst's job is "more complex due to the size and complexity of the 'cyber'" (p. 25). Analysts need to maintain awareness over the broad scope of network, mission, and threat, and work can be configured in ways that either help or hinder this situational awareness development (Brandon & Hollingshead, 2004; Ellis, 2003).

Finally, it is possible that, over the longer term, good work design helps one to develop one's personality and identity (e.g., optimism, resilience, learning orientation), with these attributes, in turn, promoting deeper engagement in one's work, enhanced ability to deal with setbacks, and accelerated acquisition of knowledge and skill. For example, Parker (1998) argued that having enriched work designs promotes the development of self-efficacy because individuals have greater opportunity for challenge and mastery experiences. Several studies support the effect of work design on self-efficacy. One might imagine that, accumulated over time, such processes result in more profound change (Parker, 2014). Recently, for example, Li, Fay, Frese, Harms, and Gao (2014) showed that job control and job demands promotes the longer term development of proactive personality. Consequently, it might be possible to configure cyber security work in a way that maximizes not only cognitive development but also personality and identity development, which in turn have multiple spin-off positive consequences for motivation, health, innovation, and performance. The most likely work design features for promoting such development are job autonomy and having reasonably challenging job demands, work characteristics that we have already identified as important from a motivational and health perspective (see Table 11.1).

Conclusions and Future Directions

In this chapter, we first discussed the potential for improving the motivating features of cyber security work design. Our interviews suggested that whereas analysts' jobs are characterized by high task significance, the motivating features of skill variety, autonomy, task identity, and feedback from the job can be lacking, along with several social elements of work (i.e., interdependence and social support). Second, we considered the design of cyber security work from a health and safety perspective, discussing the role of inconsistent and excessive work load, time pressure, and cognitive and physical demands. Third, we described how cyber security work might be specifically designed to facilitate learning and development, including long-term development that can arise from cumulative short-term effects. Relatedly, we discussed how work design might affect situational awareness, identity, and subsequently, the acquisition of relevant knowledge and skills. We conclude this chapter by discussing some theoretical and practical implications, as well as future directions for research.

Theoretical Implications and Future Directions

Given that there has been limited empirical research on the topic of work design for cyber security, essentially all of the topics that have been discussed thus far in this chapter lend themselves well to future research endeavors. More generally, we suspect that many different factors will shape the work design of those involved in cyber security work and should therefore be accounted for in future cyber security work design research. These factors include organization size, whether the CSIRT is part of the organization it serves or external to it, whether the security capability is distributed (and pulled together when required) or centralized, and the level of authority/discretion in the CSIRT (e.g., whether the CSIRT makes recommendations that might or might not be followed or has full authority to dictate changes). In addition, researchers should consider how work design issues change as a function of the type of team one is a member of—for example, whether one is a Tier 1 analyst (e.g., engaged in real-time monitoring and triaging) versus a Tier 2 analyst (e.g., evaluating malware or forensics). It might be, for example, that forensics team members work less interdependently, and do not face inconsistent or excessive time pressure, compared with Tier 1 analysts.

In addition to these general recommendations, we have also identified several areas for future cyber security work design research that were not explicitly mentioned in our interviews and described earlier. First, it would be worth investigating whether some analysts who face time pressure and initially experience stress subsequently habituate or adapt to the stress so that it is no longer stressful. Indeed, psychophysiology research demonstrates that repeated exposure to the same psychological stressor, or a set of similar stressors, results in significant attenuation of cardiovascular reactivity (e.g., al'Absi et al., 1997; Kelsey, Soderlund, & Arthur, 2004). This idea has yet to be examined in a work context, but it stands to reason that similar effects could be observed among workers who are repeatedly exposed to stressors. If this phenomenon can be replicated in the workplace, research should be devoted to understanding the role of work design as a contributing factor. For example, as discussed earlier, high cognitive demands on the job might induce strain when the cost of error is high, when the task is uninteresting, and/or when job control is low.

Second, research on contagion has demonstrated that individuals can transmit their moods to others when others observe an individual's public display (Hatfield, Cacioppo, & Rapson, 1994). According to this line of research, emotional contagion takes place in two separate stages. During Stage 1, observers unintentionally mimic the emotional expressions of others; in Stage 2, mimicking of facial and vocal behaviors leads to actual experiencing of the emotions associated with those behaviors. For example, Totterdell (2000) demonstrated that individual professional athletes' positive moods were related to positive group affective tone, as well as subjective individual athletic performance. Relatedly, it might be that not only do team members transmit their moods to other team members but also that team managers transmit their emotions to team members. Indeed, a handful of empirical studies has shown that leader affect can be contagious. For example, at least two recent studies concluded that individual followers led by leaders in a positive mood experienced more positive affect than individual followers led by leaders in a negative mood (Bono & Ilies, 2006; Sy, Côté, & Saavedra, 2005). As such, one potential area for future research would involve examining whether this phenomenon occurs in cyber security work teams; factors that affect its occurrence; its implications for group outcomes; and how work design might be used to, for example, facilitate the transfer of positive moods and deter the transfer of negative ones.

Third, cyber security is an excellent example of a context in which work must be designed in such a way that it addresses simultaneously the goals of control and flexibility. Parker (2014) argued that this is an important new direction for work design research more generally, and we see it as crucial here. On the one hand, allowing individuals job autonomy enables them to deal with problems at the source, resulting in faster and more effective problem-solving in situations of high operational uncertainty (Cordery et al., 2010). Autonomy also fosters motivation, engagement, creativity, and proactivity (e.g., Parker et al., 2006), all of which support flexible and agile individual responses. On the other hand, although job autonomy promotes flexible outcomes like creativity and motivation, autonomy can also create challenges of coordination at the team or organizational level (Lanaj, Hollenbeck, Ilgen, Barnes, & Harmon, 2013). In other words, there can be a tension between granting individuals autonomy and coordinating individual action into a coherent whole. Adler and Chen (2011) discussed this issue in the context of large-scale collaborations like the design of a new aircraft: The tasks are uncertain and novel, requiring the agility that is prompted by autonomy; yet, at the same time, the tasks are complex and interdependent, requiring control and coordination. We see this as a critical tension in the context of cyber security. For all the reasons we have already outlined, job autonomy is likely to foster improved individual health, well-being, motivation, learning, and performance. Yet cyber analysts work in teams, and effective coordination is vital for success. What are the best ways to achieve coordination (a form of control) and the benefits of autonomy? We see this as an intriguing and important direction for research in the future.

Practical Implications

Although we have outlined new directions for research, in fact we already know quite a lot about which types of work designs are healthy and motivating.

TABLE 11.2 Principles for the Process of Work Design and/or Work Redesign

Process principle

- Secure the commitment of leaders and other key stakeholders (e.g., union representatives).
- Ensure that work design is included in relevant policies (e.g., health and safety policies) and business plans.
- Assess work design risks/opportunities by assessing work characteristics (from interviews, confidential surveys, observations, etc.) and by collecting/analyzing other relevant data (e.g., assessing worker demographics; absenteeism levels; turnover; medical data such as levels of musculoskeletal complaints, etc). Involve analysts in the monitoring of work design risks and the collection of relevant data.
- Establish a representative internal steering group to manage the process of work design and to ensure that objectives are reached. Involve appropriate experts to inform the steering group (organizational psychologists, ergonomists, safety experts, researchers, etc.) and learn from other organizations. Ensure that analysts are meaningfully and actively involved in every step of the process.
- Allocate resources to the design/redesign process (e.g., budget, training, time).
- Conduct a gap analysis comparing the current reality against the ideal, and then develop an action plan to close this gap. Ensure that the plan includes principles of effective change management. Adopt a holistic, system-level approach that considers technology, organizational culture, structure, and so on.
- Recognize that any work redesign will affect multiple stakeholders, all of whom should be represented in the process of design/redesign. For example, any move to self-managing teams will require a significant change in supervisory roles.
- Systematically evaluate the effects of any work redesign.
- Take steps to build improved work design into the system in a sustainable way (e.g., have it as part of strategic planning, align reward/training/recruitment systems).
- Regularly monitor work design and associated outcomes, reevaluating and updating policies and practices as required.

Consequently, we recommend that managers (and other stakeholders who have the opportunity to shape work design in cyber security) actively seek to diagnose the quality of work design, and, where appropriate, take steps to redesign the work. A highly participatory process is strongly recommended, because it is the individuals doing the work who have the local knowledge to make sensible decisions. Continual monitoring and evaluation of work redesign is then important to determine whether a change is achieving its intended benefits, whether there are any unintended negative consequences, and what the next steps should be. Detailed guidance for the process of work redesign comes from various national government bodies, such as the U.S. National Institute for Occupational Safety and Health, as well as from the research literature on work design (e.g., Clegg, 2000; Parker & Wall, 1998) and change management more generally (e.g., Kotter, 2006).[1] Table 11.2 summarizes key recommendations for managing the process of work design and work redesign.

It is also worth considering the potential impact of bottom-up forms of improving work design through, for example, job crafting: "changes that employees make to balance their job demands and job resources with their personal abilities and needs" (Tims, Bakker, & Derks, 2012, p. 174). Consistent with other positive psychology intervention activities, job crafting entails changes that are initiated by employees themselves and is suggested for use by all employees, even those who occupy jobs characterized by low levels of autonomy (Wrzesniewski & Dutton, 2001). Further, Tims et al. proposed that job crafting consists of four types of activities: (1) decreasing hindering job demands, (2) increasing challenging job demands, (3) increasing structural job resources, and (4) increasing social resources. Given that it is said to act as a mechanism for achieving balance between work demands and resources, job crafting could be a fruitful avenue for work design interventions for cyber security workers facing high demands and low resources.

NOTE

1 Readers are additionally encouraged to refer to the following websites for practical guidelines on how to design healthy and motivating work: http://www.cdc.gov/niosh/topics/workorg/, http://www.ccohs.ca/oshanswers/hsprograms/job_design.html, and https://www.osha.gov/dsg/topics/safetyhealth/resources.html.

REFERENCES

Adler, P. S., & Chen, C. X. (2011). Combining creativity and control: Understanding individual motivation in large scale collaborative creativity. *Accounting, Organizations, and Society, 36*, 63–85.

al'Absi, M., Bongard, S., Buchanan, T., Pincomb, G. A., Licinio, J., & Lovallo, W. R. (1997). Cardiovascular and neuroendocrine adjustment to public speaking and mental arithmetic stressors. *Psychophysiology, 34*, 266–275.

Assante, M. J., & Tobey, D. H. (2011, January/February). Enhancing the cybersecurity workforce. *IT Professional, 13*(1), 12–15.

Bakker, A. B., & Demerouti, E. (2007). The job demands–resources model: State of the art. *Journal of Managerial Psychology, 22*, 309–328.

Bakker, A. B., Demerouti, E., & Euwema, M. C. (2005). Job resources buffer the impact of job demands on burnout. *Journal of Occupational Health Psychology, 10*, 170–180.

Belkic, K. L., Landsbergin, P. A., Schnall, P. L., & Baker, D. (2004). Is job strain a major source of cardiovascular disease risk? *Scandinavian Journal of Work, Environment & Health, 30*, 85–128.

Birdi, K., Clegg, C., Patterson, M., Robinson, A., Stride, C. B., Wall, T. D., & Wood, S. J. (2008). The impact of human resource and operational management practices on company productivity: A longitudinal study. *Personnel Psychology, 61*, 467–501.

Bond, F. W., & Flaxman, P. E. (2006). The ability of psychological flexibility and job control to predict learning, job performance, and mental health. *Journal of Organizational Behavior Management, 26*, 113–130.

Bono, J. E., & Ilies, R. (2006). Charisma, positive emotions, and mood contagion. *The Leadership Quarterly, 17*, 317–334.

Brandon, D. P., & Hollingshead, A. B. (2004). Transactive memory systems in organizations: Matching tasks, expertise, and people. *Organization Science, 15*, 633–644.

Burke, C. S., Stagl, K. C., Klein, C., Goodwin, G. F., Salas, E., & Halpin, S. M. (2006). What type of leadership behaviors are functional in teams? A meta-analysis. *The Leadership Quarterly, 17*, 288–307.

Campion, M. A., Cheraskin, L., & Steven, M. J. (1994). Career-related antecedents and outcomes of job rotation. *Academy of Management Journal, 37*, 1518–1542.

Cavanaugh, M., Boswell, W., Roehling, M., & Boudreau, J. (2000). An empirical examination of self-reported work stress among U.S. managers. *Journal of Applied Psychology, 85*, 65–74.

Chen, T. R., Shore, D. B., Zaccaro, S. J., Dalal, R. S., Tetrick, L. E., & Gorab, A. K. (2014, September/October). An organizational psychology perspective to examining computer security incident response teams. *IEEE Security & Privacy, 12*(5), 61–67.

Cherns, A. (1987). Principles of sociotechnical design revisited. *Human Relations, 40*, 153–162.

Clegg, C. W. (2000). Sociotechnical principles for system design. *Applied Ergonomics, 31*, 463–477.

Converse, P. D., & DeShon, R. P. (2009). A tale of two tasks: Reversing the self-regulatory resource depletion effect. *Journal of Applied Psychology, 94*, 1318–1324.

Cordery, J. L., Morrison, D., Wright, B. M., & Wall, T. D. (2010). The impact of autonomy and task uncertainty on team performance: A longitudinal field study. *Journal of Organizational Behavior, 31*, 240–258.

Crawford, E. R., LePine, J. A., & Rich, B. L. (2010). Linking job demands and resources to employee engagement and burnout: A theoretical extension and meta-analytic test. *Journal of Applied Psychology, 95*, 834–848.

Csikszentmihalyi, M. (1988). The flow experience and its significance for human psychology. In M. Csikszentmihalyi, & I. S. Csikszentmihalyi (Eds.), *Optimal experience: Psychological studies of flow in consciousness* (pp. 15–35), Cambridge, England: Cambridge University Press.

Davis, L. E. (1966). The design of jobs. *Industrial Relations: A Journal of Economy and Society, 6*, 21–45.

de Lange, A. H., Taris, T. W., Kompier, M. A., Houtman, I., & Bongers, P. M. (2003). "The very best of the millennium": Longitudinal research and the demand–control–(support) model. *Journal of Occupational Health Psychology, 8*, 282–305.

Eisenberger, R. (1992). Learned industriousness. *Psychological Review, 99*, 248–267.

Ellis, A.P.J. (2003). The effects of acute stressors on transactive memory and shared mental models in temporary project teams: An information processing approach. *Dissertation Abstracts International: Section B. Sciences and Engineering, 64*(5), 2425.

Evans, K., & Reeder, F. (2010, November). *A human capital crisis in cybersecurity: Technical proficiency matters: A report of the CSIS Commission on Cybersecurity for the 44th Presidency.* Retrieved from http://csis.org/files/publication/101111_Evans_HumanCapital_Web.pdf

Frese, M., & Zapf, D. (1994). Action as the core of work psychology: A German approach. In M. D. Dunnette, H. C. Triandis, & L. M. Hough (Eds.), *Handbook of industrial and organizational psychology* (pp. 271–340). Palo Alto, CA: Consulting Psychologists Press.

Fried, Y., & Ferris, G. R. (1987). The validity of the job characteristics model: A review and meta-analysis. *Personnel Psychology, 40*, 287–322.

Grant, A. M. (2007). Relational job design and the motivation to make a prosocial difference. *Academy of Management Review, 32*, 393–417.

Grant, A. M. (2008). The significance of task significance: Job performance effects, relational mechanisms, and boundary conditions. *Journal of Applied Psychology, 93*, 108–124.

Grant, A. M., Campbell, E. M., Chen, G., Cottone, K., Lapedis, D., & Lee, K. (2007). Impact and the art of motivation maintenance: The effects of contact with beneficiaries on persistence behavior. *Organizational Behavior and Human Decision Processes, 103*, 53–67.

Griffin, R. W. (1991). Effects of work redesign on employee perceptions, attitudes, and behaviors: A long-term investigation. *Academy of Management Journal, 34*, 425–435.

Hackman, J. R., & Oldham, G. R. (1976). Motivation through the design of work: Test of a theory. *Organizational Behaviour and Human Performance, 16*, 250–279.

Hatfield, E., Cacioppo, J. T., & Rapson, R. L. (1994). *Emotional contagion*. New York: Cambridge University Press.

Helson, H. (1964). *Adaptation-level theory*. Oxford, England: Harper & Row.

Humphrey, S. E., Nahrgang, J. D., & Morgeson, F. P. (2007). Integrating motivational, social, and contextual work design features: A meta-analytic summary and theoretical extension of the work design literature. *Journal of Applied Psychology, 92*, 1332–1356.

Judge, T. A., Thoresen, C. J., Bono, J. E., & Patton, G. K. (2001). The job satisfaction–job performance relationship: A qualitative and quantitative review. *Psychological Bulletin, 127*, 376–407.

Karasek, R. A. (1979). Job demands, job decision latitude, and mental strain: Implications for job redesign. *Administrative Science Quarterly, 24*, 285–308.

Karasek, R. A., & Theorell, T. (1990). *Healthy work: stress, productivity, and the reconstruction of working life*. New York: Basic Books.

Kelsey, R. M., Soderlund, K., & Arthur, C. M. (2004). Cardiovascular reactivity and adaptation to recurrent psychological stress: Replication and extension. *Psychophysiology, 41*, 924–934.

Kiggundu, M. N. (1983). Task interdependence and job design: Test of a theory. *Organizational Behaviour and Human Performance, 31*, 145–172.

Kotter, J. P. (2006). Leading change: Why transformation efforts fail. In J. V. Gallos (Ed.), *Organization development: A Jossey-Bass reader* (pp. 239–251). San Francisco: Jossey-Bass.

Lanaj, K., Hollenbeck, J., Ilgen, D., Barnes, C., & Harmon, S. (2013). The double-edged sword of decentralized planning in multiteam systems. *Academy of Management Journal, 56*, 735–757.

Langfred, C. W. (2005). Autonomy and performance in teams: The multilevel moderating effect of task interdependence. *Journal of Management, 31*, 513–529.

Langner, R., Steinborn, M. B., Chatterjee, A., Sturm, W., & Willmes, K. (2010). Mental fatigue and temporal preparation in simple reaction-time performance. *Acta Psychologica, 133*, 64–72.

Leach, D. J., Wall, T. D., & Jackson, P. R. (2003). The effect of empowerment on job knowledge: An empirical test involving operators of complex technology. *Journal of Occupational and Organizational Psychology, 76*, 27–52.

Lee, R. T., & Ashforth, B. E. (1996). A meta-analytic examination of the correlates of the three dimensions of job burnout. *Journal of Applied Psychology, 81*, 123–133.

LePine, J. A., Podsakoff, N. P., & LePine, M. A. (2005). A meta-analytic test of the challenge stressor–hindrance stressor framework: An explanation for inconsistent relationships among stressors and performance. *Academy of Management Journal, 48*, 764–775.

Lewis, J. A. (2010, July). *A human capital crisis in cybersecurity: Technical proficiency matters* [White paper]. Retrieved from http://csis.org/files/publication/100720_Lewis_HumanCapital_WEB_BlkWhteVersion.pdf

Li, W.-D., Fay, D., Frese, M., Harms, P. D., & Gao, X. Y. (2014). Reciprocal relationship between proactive personality and work characteristics: A latent change score approach. *Journal of Applied Psychology, 99*, 948–965.

Martin, R., & Wall, T. D. (1989). Attentional demand and cost responsibility as stressors in shopfloor jobs. *Academy of Management Journal, 32*, 69–86.

Miner, J. B. (2003). The rated importance, scientific validity, and practical usefulness of organizational behavior theories: A quantitative review. *Academy of Management Learning and Education, 2*, 250–268.

Morgeson, F. P., & Campion, M. A. (2003). Work design. In W. C. Borman, D. R. Ilgen, & R. J. Klimoski (Eds.), *Handbook of psychology: Vol. 12. Industrial and organizational psychology* (pp. 423–452). Hoboken, NJ: Wiley.

Morgeson, F. P., & Humphrey, S. E. (2006). The Work Design Questionnaire (WDQ): Developing and validating a comprehensive measure for assessing job design and the nature of work. *Journal of Applied Psychology, 91*, 1321–1339.

Nahrgang, J. D., Morgeson, F. P., & Hofmann, D. A. (2011). A meta-analytic investigation of the link between job demands, job resources, burnout, engagement, and safety outcomes. *Journal of Applied Psychology, 96*, 71–94.

Parker, S. K. (1998). Enhancing role breadth self-efficacy: The roles of job enrichment and other organizational interventions. *Journal of Applied Psychology, 83*, 835–852.

Parker, S. K. (2014). Beyond motivation: Job and work design for development, health, ambidexterity, and more. *Annual Review of Psychology, 65*, 661–691.

Parker, S. K., & Axtell, C. M. (2001). Seeing another viewpoint: Antecedents and outcomes of employee perspective taking. *Academy of Management Journal, 44*, 1085–1100.

Parker, S. K., & Wall, T. (1998). *Job and work design: Organizing work to promote well-being and effectiveness*. London: Sage.

Parker, S. K., Wall, T. D., & Cordery, J. L. (2001). Future work design research and practice: Towards an elaborated model of work design. *Journal of Occupational and Organizational Psychology, 74*, 413–440.

Parker, S. K., Williams, H., & Turner, N. (2006). Modeling the antecedents of proactive behavior at work. *Journal of Applied Psychology, 91*, 636–652.

Podsakoff, N. P., LePine, J. A., & LePine, M. A. (2007). Differential challenge stressor–hindrance stressor relationships with job attitudes, turnover intentions, turnover, and withdrawal behavior: A meta-analysis. *Journal of Applied Psychology, 92*, 438–454.

Robertson, I. H., & O'Connell, R. (2010). Vigilant attention. In A. C. Nobre & J. T. Coull (Eds.), *Attention and time* (pp. 79–88). New York: Oxford University Press.

Salancik, G. R., & Pfeffer, J. (1978). Uncertainty, secrecy, and the choice of similar others. *Social Psychology, 41*, 246–255.

Schooler, C., Mulatu, M. S., & Oates, G. (2004). Occupational self-direction, intellectual functioning, and self-directed orientation in older workers: Findings and implications for individuals and societies. *American Journal of Sociology, 110*, 161–197.

Sinha, K. K., & Van de Ven, A. H. (2005). Designing work within and between organizations. *Organization Science, 16*, 389–408.

Smith, A. (1776). *The wealth of nations*. London: W. Strahan and T. Cadell.

Sprigg, C. A., Christine, A., Jackson, P. R., & Parker, S. K. (2000). Production teamworking: The importance of interdependence and autonomy for employee strain and satisfaction. *Human Relations, 53*, 1519–1543.

Stanton, J. M., Stam, K. R., Guzman, I., & Caldera, C. (2003, October). *Examining the linkage between organizational commitment and information security*. Paper presented at the IEEE International Conference on Systems, Man, and Cybernetics, Washington, DC.

Sy, T., Côté, S., & Saavedra, R. (2005). The contagious leader: Impact of the leader's mood on the mood of group members, group affective tone, and group processes. *Journal of Applied Psychology, 90*, 295–305.

Taylor, F. W. (1911). *The principles of scientific management*. New York: Harper & Brothers.

Tetrick, L. E., Dalal, R. S., Zaccaro, S. J., Steinke, J. A., Hargrove, A., & Winslow, C. J. (2014). *Enhancing the effectiveness of cyber security teams*. Poster session presented at the Department of Homeland Security, Science and Technology, Cyber Security Division, Research and Development Showcase and Technical Workshop, Washington, DC.

Tims, M., Bakker, A. B., & Derks, D. (2012). Development and validation of the job crafting scale. *Journal of Vocational Behavior, 80*, 173–186.

Totterdell, P. (2000). Catching moods and hitting runs: Mood linkage and subjective performance in professional sport teams. *Journal of Applied Psychology, 85*, 848–859.

Trist, E. L., & Bamforth, K. W. (1951). Some social and psychological consequences of the longwall method of coal-getting. *Human Relations, 4*, 3–38.

Turner, Y. N., Hadas-Halperin, I., & Raveh, D. (2008, November). *Patient photos spur radiologist empathy and eye for detail*. Paper presented at the 94th Scientific Assembly and Annual Meeting of the Radiological Society of North America, Chicago, IL.

Van der Doef, M., & Maes, S. (1999). The job demand–control(–support) model and psychological well-being: A review of 20 years of empirical research. *Work Stress, 13*, 87–114.

Viswesvaran, C., Sanchez, J. I., & Fisher, J. (1999). The role of social support in the process of work stress: A meta-analysis. *Journal of Vocational Behavior, 54*, 314–334.

Wall, T. D., Cordery, J. L., Clegg, C. W. (2002). Empowerment, performance, and operational uncertainty: A theoretical integration. *Applied Psychology, 51*, 146–169.

Wall, T. D., & Jackson, P. R. (1995). New manufacturing initiatives and shopfloor work design. In A. Howard (Ed.), *The changing nature of work* (pp. 139–174). San Francisco: Jossey-Bass.

Wrzesniewski, A., & Dutton, J. E. (2001). Crafting a job: Revisioning employees as active crafters of their work. *Academy of Management Review, 26*, 179–201.

Zimmerman, C. (2014). *Ten strategies of a world-class cybersecurity operations center*. Bedford, MA: MITRE Corporation.

12

FACTORS INFLUENCING THE HUMAN–TECHNOLOGY INTERFACE FOR EFFECTIVE CYBER SECURITY PERFORMANCE[1]

Michael D. Coovert, Rachel Dreibelbis, and Randy Borum

Overview

To develop an interface for effective cyber security, one must think about broader issues than a traditional graphical user interface (GUI). As such, this chapter outlines a series of issues focusing on the behavior of individuals when interacting with information devices and systems. After a brief introduction, we begin by defining cyber security from the end user's perspective. We highlight behaviors related to the security, compliance, risk, and damage of an organization's information system. We then move to a discussion of the interaction of humans and technology from a cyber security point of view, touching on system complexity, trust in information technology (IT), and the perspective taken by some who believe that effective cyber security behaviors interfere with one's ability to perform a job. As many jobs are now computer mediated, with individuals working in virtual teams, we consider issues associated with trust in virtual teams. We argue that we must be able to quantify the latent growth and decline of trust in individuals if we are to effectively model the nature of trust between individuals, technology, and systems. Then, we consider vigilance and how it affects cyber security IT professionals. We note the importance of cognitive load and alarm fatigue in influencing cyber security behavior and offer some points toward balancing technology and human solutions. The final two sections stress the importance of social engineering through the use of cyber intelligence and cyber counterintelligence in the human–technology interface.

Introduction

As organizations continue to move their information to systems that operate via the Internet and wireless networks, information systems (IS) security becomes essential. Instead of fear over the physical loss of files, organizations must now defend themselves from cyber attacks and digital loss. This loss is not just a weightless concern but is in fact a very real occurrence. Moreover, independent surveys in the United States and the United Kingdom found that nearly half of the responding organizations reported some sort of information security incident (Department for Business Enterprise and Regulation Reform, 2008; Richardson, 2010). The rapid rate of change in technology and the increasing numbers of cyber threats to organizations make it difficult to quantify and anticipate the risks that organizations face (Pfleeger & Caputo, 2012). Although organizations continue to invest in increasingly advanced security systems to protect themselves from threats, these systems are only as safe as the weakest points within them.

It is now acknowledged that employees within the organization pose a major threat to information security. Previous research has shown that insider threats are in fact the largest source of threat to an organization's information security (Ernst & Young, 2008; Hu, Dinev, Hart, & Cooke, 2012; Stanton, Stam, Mastrangelo, & Jolton, 2005) and that the majority of information security breaches result from actions taken by employees (Computer Security Institute Computer Crime and Security Survey, as cited by Hu et al., 2012). A more recent survey conducted in the United Kingdom indicated that 36 percent of the worst security breaches were caused by inadvertent human error (Department for Business, Innovation and Skills, 2013). For the majority of this chapter, the term *employees* refers to end users, who use an organization's IS to carry out daily business duties. IT employees, who are responsible for developing and maintaining the IS within the organization, are not included in that definition. Because IT employees' jobs involve protecting and maintaining the information systems, their knowledge base is much larger, and their motivations for harming the system might be different because they have a higher level of expertise than the average end user. Due to their limited technical knowledge, end users are often viewed as more of a liability than IT employees (Guo, Yuan, Archer, & Connelly, 2011). However, it should be noted that IT workers still have a significant influence on a company's cyber security, and part of this chapter discusses that perspective. Because end users' behaviors can cause such a large threat to an organization's information, it is important to not only study the antecedents of their computer behaviors but also to understand how these employees interact with technology in the workplace. Doing so can help us better understand how to implement IT solutions to protect organizations from both external and internal threats.

A common and recommended method for organizations to protect against internal threats is to implement security policies. Although this method might clarify expected behaviors and consequences for employees regarding IS assets, these policies, like any set of rules, do not guarantee that employees will act in a desired manner (Guo et al., 2011). One survey found that many employees allow others to use their computers, despite knowing that this might compromise the security of the information on their computers (Dubie, 2007). Much past research has focused on policy compliance (i.e., Hu et al., 2012). However, because rule following and rule breaking are different behaviors (Tyler & Blader, 2005), these studies do not explain why employees knowingly break the rules. Past research has suggested that factors such as organizational norms, security awareness, motivation, top management, and organizational culture affect an employee's propensity to engage in actions that could either protect an organization's digital information or put it at risk (Guo, 2013; Guo et al., 2011; Hu et al., 2012; Padayachee, 2012), but it is less clear whether internal or external sources are the primary influence on these behaviors.

Stepping away from employee behavior for just a moment, we consider the most appropriate course of action for organizations seeking to protect their information from cyber attacks. Given that the insider threat is of considerable concern, security policies are not enough, and we need to consider the role of actual technological systems in the equation of cyber security at work. History suggests that locking down data within a secure cyber vault might not be enough to provide the security that companies require. As companies implement increasingly secure and complex technological systems to protect their data, we certainly need to consider how that technology interacts with the human side of those organizations. As stressed by Borum and colleagues (Borum, 2014; Borum, Felker, & Kern, 2014; Mattern, Felker, Borum, & Bamford, 2014), organizations need to be proactive and analyze the cyber threat surface from strategic, operational, and tactical levels.

What is Cyber Security from an End User's Point of View?

Before discussing the role that technology plays in interacting with employee behavior, it is important to consider the various cyber behaviors that employees engage in at work. Though past research attempted to look at the antecedents of cyber security behaviors, disagreement exists about the conceptualization of cyber security–related behaviors (Guo, 2013). Various studies have focused on positive intentions and behaviors, such as policy compliance (e.g., Bulgurcu, Cavusoglu, & Benbasat, 2010; Herath & Rao, 2009; Hu et al., 2012; Vance, Siponen, & Pahnila, 2012), whereas others (e.g., D'Arcy, Hovav, & Galletta, 2009; Guo et al., 2011; Straub, 1990) have focused on negative behaviors, such as computer abuse. However, these studies all treated these behaviors as either side of a single coin (Guo, 2013). Guo suggested that this approach is less than ideal, because the factors that explain security policy compliance are not necessarily the same as those factors that explain security policy violations and abuse of systems.

Recognizing the variety of classifications for cyber security behaviors, Guo (2013) sought to redefine information security behaviors to facilitate the development of future studies with a more consistent dependent variable conceptualization. Four dimensions are used to classify cyber behaviors: *intentionality* (whether an employee's behavior is intentional or unintentional), *motive* (whether an employee's behavior is malicious or nonmalicious), *expertise* (the degree of IS knowledge and skills that an employee needs in order to perform the behavior in question), and *job relatedness* (whether an employee's behavior is related to his or her job). Using these dimensions, Guo conceptualized security-related behavior into four broad categories: security assurance behaviors (SABs), security compliance behaviors (SCBs), security risk behaviors (SRBs), and security-damaging behaviors (SDBs). These four types of behavior are distinct and should be considered separately when exploring different traits to explain each type of behavior (Guo, 2013). Whereas organizations seek to prevent SRBs and SDBs, they should promote SABs as these are the behaviors that can actively help protect an organization from harm. Exploring the factors that influence attitudes and intentions of these behaviors is crucial to organizations that wish to create an environment in which SCBs and SABs are the norm.

SABs (Security Assurance Behaviors)

SABs are "active behaviors by an individual who has clear motive to protect the organization's information systems" (Guo, 2013, p. 248). These types of behaviors involve "effortful action" and are not generally required by the organization. Guo stated that a high level of expertise is needed to perform these actions, although that might not necessarily be the case. For example, although identifying and reporting a virus might require a high level of knowledge about computers and how to detect a virus, setting strong passwords and changing them frequently requires only working knowledge of computer use, or merely the ability to follow steps from a help card. Because of the motivation to protect the organization, these behaviors might have some relationship to organization-directed organizational citizenship behaviors, similar in nature to those discussed by Organ (1988).

SCBs (Security Compliance Behaviors)

SCBs are defined as "behaviors that are in line with organizational security policies" (Guo, 2013, p. 248). These behaviors are considered the norm and can be seen as "employees doing what they are expected to do or not do what they are expected not to do" (Guo, 2013, p. 249). Unlike SABs, these behaviors might be a result of action or inaction. Employees might either actively refrain from a prohibited behavior or follow organizational policy by simply not engaging in any risk or prohibited behavior. In addition, employees might do something without information security in mind, but these actions might still be in line with policy. Researchers tend to focus on antecedents of these behaviors. Padayachee (2012) identified extrinsic and intrinsic motivational factors that contributed to compliant behaviors. However, it should be noted that although personality is relevant in these motivations, because certain traits might contribute to a sense of personal conduct, they were not considered in that taxonomy. More research should examine those personality traits that might contribute to SCBs.

Herath and Rao (2009) looked at antecedents of policy-compliance intentions and found that penalties (severity and certainty), social pressures (normative beliefs and peer behavior), and perceived effectiveness of compliance all predicted employee intentions to comply with IS security policies. In addition, it is important for employees to feel like their actions make a difference in the overall security of the company. Vance et al. (2012) stressed the importance of looking at past behavior when evaluating motivation behind compliance behaviors.

SRBs (Security Risk Behaviors)

SRBs are "behavior[s] that may put the organization's information security at risk" and behaviors in which employees "do what they are expected not to do" (Guo, 2013, pp. 248–249). These behaviors do not necessarily emerge from a motive to intentionally harm the organization, but they have the potential to cause damage nonetheless. These behaviors can involve any level of expertise. Examples include writing down a password and sticking it on the computer (low expertise) or copying confidential data to another hard drive (moderate expertise). These behaviors are also similar to Guo et al.'s (2011) conceptualization of nonmalicious security violations (NSMVs). These authors examined antecedents of NSMV attitudes and intentions and found that intentions to violate security measures were predicted by relative job performance advantage. In other words, if the act of engaging in SRBs was seen as a means to help improve productivity, employees were more likely to engage in those behaviors (Guo et al., 2011).

SDBs (Security Damaging Behaviors)

SDBs are behaviors that will cause direct damage to the organization's IS and involve employees doing what they are prohibited from doing (Guo, 2013, pp. 248–249). By their nature, SDBs are violations, and those who commit them can be subject to punishment under government law, not just company policy. The primary difference between SRBs and SDBs is consequence. Where SRBs have the potential to cause harm to the organization, SDBs will cause direct damage. Guo stated that these behaviors require a high level of expertise, and these behaviors are similar to Stanton et al.'s (2005) intentional destruction category of behavior. SDBs have potential similarities to Robinson and Bennett's (1995) classification of property deviance as a form of counterproductive work behavior.

For the purposes of this chapter, we use these four categories to classify cyber behaviors when discussing unique technology solutions to either encourage or discourage these behaviors.

What Is the Interaction between Humans and Technology?

Taking lessons learned from the experiences of companies like Target, Neiman Marcus, Marriott, and Michaels (just to name a few), organizations are jumping on board to increase cyber security policies and tighten the technologies behind those policies. Many technologies are available to help accomplish these goals, but their focus is to mitigate outside threats and come in the form of firewalls, data encryption, and intrusion-detection systems (Colwill, 2009). Although these solutions are reasonable and potentially helpful, these systems often cause frustration among employees (Pfleeger & Caputo, 2012). Workers have perceived these measures as obstacles for several reasons. First, employees can be overwhelmed with the new security measures because of a lack of information on how they operate (Albrechtsen, 2007, Pfleeger & Caputo, 2012). Second, individuals may place too much trust in the system, thus attributing all information security responsibility to IT professionals (Albrechtsen, 2007). Lastly, employees often view this type of security as an obstacle to completing their own jobs and override it altogether (Pfleeger & Caputo, 2012). To mitigate these effects, employees need to be taught responsible use of a system, given the tools they need to act responsibly, and then trusted to behave responsibly in regard to the system (Pfleeger & Caputo, 2012).

Complex IT Systems Can Overwhelm Employees

When organizations implement complex security infrastructures, it may cause confusion among employees about how to interact with those systems. If employees encounter systems on their computer that include complex firewalls, multi-step log-in processes, and locked-down e-mail, they can become frustrated with the system and seek ways around the security measures. Further, a qualitative study on employees' views of information security at their organization revealed that although they had some awareness of information security and its importance, they did not necessarily know how their individual actions contributed to security on a regular basis (Albrechtsen, 2007). If employees believe that a system is so complex that their actions do not make a difference, they will be less likely to engage in assurance and compliance behaviors because they will not know how to do so. As discussed later in this chapter, the design of security systems is just as important as the level of security provided. There must be a balance between functionality and security as well as an interface that makes the system easy to use for all employees. In addition, employees should be made aware of simple, effective actions that they can take to help protect their data and how these actions are directly related to the security of the company. Social engineering is one major thrust in this direction. Typically, social engineering has been utilized by hackers to apply psychological pressure and manipulation in order to exert information or to get an individual to perform some action on behalf of the hacker. But organizations can use social engineering strategies in order to train employees on how to avoid being manipulated by hackers. We discuss this more in the final section of the chapter.

Excessive Trust in IT Systems

Employee trust has long been viewed as an integral part of an organization's culture and infrastructure, and it has important implications for employee behavior. Trust has been studied in varied contexts within organizations, including interpersonal trust, trust in organizations, and trust in technology. It is important to note that trust in technology and trust toward individuals are different (Costa, Roe, & Taillieu, 2001; J. D. Lee & See, 2004). Employees' trust in their organization and technological systems both play important roles in how they carry out cyber security behaviors. Those with a high level of trust in their organization's information security systems and the IT professionals behind them might not see a need to engage in SABs, or they might even engage in risky behaviors because they rely too heavily on the security structure put in place by the organization. Trust typically consists of two elements: anticipation of positive behavior from others (Costa, 2003; Lewicki & Bunker, 1995, 1996) and willingness to assume vulnerability (Costa, 2003; Mayer, Davis, & Schoorman, 1995).

In giving trust, an individual becomes subject to risk and uncertainty by assuming that the trustee will alleviate negative outcomes through their behaviors (McAllister, 1995). Another conception of trust is as "a willingness to be vulnerable to the actions of another party based on the expectation that the other will perform a particular action important to the trustor, irrespective of the ability to monitor or control that other party" (Mayer et al., 1995, p. 712). Trust is also linked to organizational culture, even in organizations that rely heavily on technology (Alston & Tippet, 2009). Thus, when employees perceive that their company's system is completely "locked down," they do not necessarily view their own shortcuts as causing harm to their organization. For example, if an employee believes that the IT department is completely responsible for protecting the system against viruses obtained via e-mail, he or she may be more likely to click on or respond to spam e-mail—an SRB. Although the security system might be able to defend against consequences from such an action, these sorts of vulnerabilities can be avoided if employees are warned of the implications of their actions.

Work Interference

> Information security is not my job. I have to concentrate on my own working tasks, and trust that the security system is in place. Information

security is not something I should think about. How much should a user actually think about information security? It is not possible to be too cautious—it must be possible for us to carry out our work smoothly.

(Bank employee, as quoted in Albrechtsen, 2007, p. 281)

Such views by employees are not uncommon. Perhaps one of the most unexplored reasons for employee cyber misbehavior is the idea that employees perceive that security measures actually interfere with their ability to perform their job. Known as *relative advantage for job performance*, this is defined as "the extent to which users expect their actions to help them do their job" (Guo et al., 2011, p. 212). Because cyber security is often not the primary objective in task performance, employees see it as an obstacle preventing them from getting their job done (Besnard & Arief, 2004). This attitude indicates that employees place task performance above information security and, thus, consult with their leaders about whether it is fruitful to sacrifice task performance for the sake of security (Guo et al., 2011). In addition, Post and Kagan (2007) found that employees perceived increases in information security policies and practices as having increased interference with their job responsibilities. Because employees can view cyber security as an interference with their task performance, they may be more likely to ignore security policies, make a conscious decision to engage in an SRB, and justify their action by viewing the behavior as a necessity in order to do their job. Qualitative research has supported this notion as well, with employees mentioning that one of the greatest problems in information security is the balance between security and functionality, noting that a very strict IT system prevents them from completing actual work tasks, and blaming poor information security behavior on this interference (Albrechtsen, 2007).

A common example of the real-world implications of this effect are password changes. Studies have found that when faced with a mandatory password change, employees intentionally delayed the change and viewed the requirement as an unnecessary interruption to their workday. Despite the fact that employees are aware of the implications of a password breach, this awareness does not seem to affect their attitudes toward security behavior (Albrechtsen, 2007). Further, employees with a high level of technical competence view these mandatory changes as an insult to their abilities to protect their work and the system. These views might result in overall negative attitudes toward information security systems at work and perpetuate the problem (Pfleeger & Caputo, 2012), resulting in SRBs.

Should We Consider Trust in Virtual Teams?

Trust is a central construct in all of human endeavors; common examples include individuals working in a team and individuals relying on technology for sources of input to their jobs. In each of these situations, trust plays a pivotal role.

Whereas reviews of trust in automation exist (J. D. Lee & See, 2004), no current state-of-the-art typology frames the theoretical understanding of trust development in individuals. Further, nearly everything we know of trust is based on face-to-face interactions, and very little is known about trust development in virtual teams (Coovert, Pavlova Miller, Bennett, Arvan, & Coovert, 2013). As we stated earlier, it is important to note that trust in technology and trust toward individuals are different (Costa et al., 2001; J. D. Lee & See, 2004).

Prior to addressing trust in virtual teams, we consider broader issues. For example, there are variations in the underlying facets of the trust construct. The literature contains several models that describe trust (e.g., Costa et al., 2001; McAllister, 1995; Sitkin & Roth, 1993; Smith & Barclay, 1997) and assume it to be a relatively unchanging construct. Rashid and Edmondson (2011) discussed risky trust in high-stakes environments but made no claim as to its development.

Generally, trust is investigated as either a one-factor construct (Blomqvist, 2002) or a multifaceted construct (Cook & Wall, 1980; McAllister, 1995; Smith & Barclay, 1997; Webber 2008). The multifaceted view of trust is more prevalent. Cook and Wall (1980) proposed that one trust component is "faith in the trustworthy intentions of others" and that the other one is "confidence in the ability of others, yielding aspirations of capability and reliability" (p. 40). Henttonen and Blomqvist (2005) distinguished between four distinct trust components—behavior, goodwill (morality and positive intentions), capability (technological, business, and cooperation), and self-reference (clear identity and decision-making skills). Lewicki, McAllister, and Bies (1998) hypothesized a three-faceted view—calculus-based trust, knowledge-based trust, and identity-based trust.

McAllister (1995) proposed the most widely investigated model, and it contains two factors: cognition-based trust and affect-based trust. Unlike the models already mentioned, McAllister's model focuses not on differences in perceptions and behaviors but on the mechanisms involved in the development of trust. McAllister (1995) conceptualized trust as "the extent to which a person is confident in, and willing to act on the basis of, the words, actions and decisions of another" (p. 25). Cognition-based trust is generally derived from knowledge possessed about the entity to be trusted; affect-based trust captures the emotional ties between the one trusting and the one being trusted. Empirical investigation of the model confirmed this two-factor structure. Further, each factor has a distinct association with various antecedents and outcomes. Reliable peer performance, cultural and ethnic similarity, and professional credentials are identified as unique factors that facilitate the development of cognition-based trust. Cognition-based trust, in turn, has a direct influence on control-based monitoring and defensive behaviors and is related to manager performance. Affect-based trust, however, is uniquely predicted by interaction frequency and citizenship behaviors. Affect-based trust was found to influence citizenship behaviors as well as need-based monitoring. Need-based monitoring and citizenship behaviors then affected both peer and manager performance. Results also revealed that a certain level of cognition-based trust needs to be achieved in order for affect-based trust to develop (McAllister, 1995). Thus, individuals working in computer-mediated teams develop cognitive-based trust derived from knowledge of the other individuals in the team and affect-based trust from the frequency of interactions with others. Because one's knowledge of others in the team (cognitive trust) surely changes over time, and affective trust develops through interaction frequency, we argue that trust toward others and trust in technology needs to be modeled as an evolving construct that changes in levels over time.

Dynamic Trust

Over the last of decade, a more realistic perspective of the nature of trust has developed (Levin, Whitener, & Cross, 2006; Serva, Fuller, & Mayer, 2005; Wilson, Straus, & McEvily, 2006). This perspective views trust as a dynamic within-person process that changes over time. Unfortunately, these early studies used statistical tools that were unable to correctly address critical issues such as the estimation and removal of error variance and how to correctly handle change scores with both latent and measured variables. In addition, virtually all of the models that explain trust development focus on traditional, face-to-face teams and, therefore, do not take into account the challenges facing virtual teams.

For virtual teams, two theories have been widely used to explain change in levels of trust over time: the time, interaction, and performance theory (McGrath, 1991) and social information processing theory (Walther, 1992). These are general models and examine multiple aspects of teams, with trust often playing a secondary role. More recently, Webber (2008) introduced the idea of swift trust and its development in teams. Here, preliminary levels of trust influence the development of cognitively based trust, which comprises two separate facets, each of which develops independently. Our preliminary work (Coovert et al., 2013; Grichanik, Coovert, & Bennett, 2014; Pavlova, Coovert, & Bennett, 2013) has examined, among other things, the role of cognitive trust in distributed teams and how it evolves over time.

If trust is dynamic and changes over time, what model best reflects this change? A case for trust being both linear and nonlinear is seen in the literature. For example, proponents of dispositional trust argue that ample evidence exists that people differ considerably in their general predispositions to trust others (Gurtman, 1992; Sorrentino, Holmes, Hanna, & Sharp, 1995). These authors argue for different initial levels of trust for individuals and seemingly different growth rates—a random-effects model. Random-effects models (Bauer, 2011) are incorporated within latent change score (LCS) models (McArdle, 2009). As linear models are a special case of random effects, both models are capable of being statistically evaluated.

We believe that the appropriate way to study trust is over time. Although a few researchers have studied change in this fashion, the results need to be carefully considered, because the LCS methodology for examining within-person change in trust has only recently been fully developed. Although we do not claim that all prior research is problematic, we do believe it is appropriate to carefully consider existing claims and the state of the theory. Perhaps Nannestad (2008) captured it best: "The question of trust is a huge puzzle that is not even near solution" (p. 432). In order to answer the question and develop solutions, we must begin with the appropriate methodological tools, such as LCS (for details, see Coovert et al., 2013).

Only once we understand the latent growth (decline) of trust over time will we be able to accurately model its relationship with the various aspects of cyber security, such as trust in technology, systems, and those with whom people interact both within and outside of the organization. As trust changes over time, we are likely to see initial SRBs give way to SCBs and SABs. For situations in which negative information leads to a decline in or lack of trust, it is not unreasonable to expect the reemergence of SRBs and, perhaps, even SDBs. With a better understanding of the importance of modeling the changing nature of trust over time, we now consider the role of vigilance for those who work in cyber security.

Is Vigilance an Issue for Cyber Security IT Workers?

Although the previous sections focused on end-user behaviors, it is also important to consider the role that IT professionals play in the security of an organization's information. Within an organization, the IT and security professionals are responsible for the protection, maintenance, and monitoring of all technological systems. From a cyber security perspective, these professionals must protect the systems not only from outsider attacks but also from insider threats. Because insider threats can result from both malicious (SDBs) and nonmalicious (SRBs) actions on the part of employees, IT professionals must be especially vigilant in detecting threats from multiple sources. In order to protect against insider threats, it is recommended that, at a minimum, security teams should include encryption technologies; access control; minimum privilege thresholds; and monitoring, auditing, and reporting systems (Colwill, 2009). Even with these technical controls in place, IT professionals should keep in mind that a checklist of security features is not enough to ensure data safety and, rather, seek to balance these controls with human factors. We address this further in the What Is Cyber Counterintelligence and the Human–Technology Interface? section.

As demonstrated with end users, even the best set of security measures are only as good as the humans monitoring them, and this statement applies equally to IT professionals. If the humans monitoring the system fail to detect a threat, the technological system can only do so much to protect the company's data. In fact, this is not an uncommon occurrence. The data breach of a major retail company might never have occurred if the company's security team had responded to the multiple warnings and notifications regarding the presence of malware in the system (Riley, Elgin, Lawrence, & Matlack, 2014). In fact, the breach could have been stopped without human intervention; however, the security team had disabled the system's ability to automatically delete malware threats (Riley et al., 2014). Although this is just one example of how human mistakes can result in major security breaches and widespread consequences, it exemplifies the need to explore the idea of vigilance in security teams of IT professionals.

Vigilance refers to the "ability of organisms to maintain their focus of attention and remain alert to stimuli over prolonged periods of time" (Warm, Parasuraman, & Matthews, 2008, p. 433). In terms of IT security, this means that the employees who are monitoring the systems are pouring over multitudes of data for long periods of time but must maintain focus at all times in order to catch anomalies or warnings in the system. Though it was previously thought that this sort of task required little mental effort, more recent research has determined that vigilance entails a very high workload and is highly stressful (Warm et al., 2008). This could result in fewer SABs and SCBs. In addition, vigilance tasks like monitoring for threats to a security system or pouring over network activity logs are exacting, capacity-draining assignments that consume cognitive resources, often leading to performance decrements over time (Warm et al., 2008). Because vigilance does tend to decrease over time due to cognitive exhaustion, the chances of security professionals detecting threats also decreases (Warm et al., 2008). By using eye-based cues, one study designed a system that was able to detect the moment when individuals began to experience decreased levels of vigilance during a threat-detection task (Langhals, Burgoon, & Nunamaker, 2013). Designing a feedback system that can alert individuals of their decreased vigilance would help them maintain high levels of cognitive readiness (Langhals et al., 2013). The feedback system or other automated approach for alerting must be carefully designed to minimize false positives as alert fatigue (the propensity for ignoring alerts) has been well documented in other areas, such as medicine (Baker, 2009; Barton, 2011; Isaac et al., 2009; Lin et al., 2008). Thus, we need to develop an understanding of the effects that disruptions and information attacks have on security systems, understand the information and decisions that cyber professionals need to make when dealing with these attacks, and explore technological systems that help to monitor and improve vigilance and situational awareness in these professionals. These efforts can reduce the errors made by those who serve as the main protectors of companies' security systems. By minimizing cognitive overload resulting from vigilance, we ensure maximization of the likelihood of SCBs and SABs while minimizing SRBs.

Should There Be a Balance Between Technology and Human Solutions?

We believe that the human element is central to cyber security operations and must remain in place as opposed to being engineered or programmed out of the system. The challenge is in how we balance the human and technological approaches to cyber security. Current research points to a blended approach for helping end users, IT professionals, and the technology protecting their information to interact in such a way to maximize information security. More specifically, systems need to balance technology-based control of human behavior and comprehensive education and training for system users. First, systems need to provide enough security to protect against outsider *and* insider threats, both intentional and unintentional, without trying to completely control employee behavior. Second, employees need to be aware that the system cannot protect against every threat and that their actions still contribute to the overall security of the company. When employees are provided with information about easy and effective behaviors they can engage in to help protect the organization's information security, their attitudes toward the system may become increasingly positive, resulting in increased SABs and SCBs. Third, both IT professionals and system designers need to be aware that information security is not a primary focus for employees and strive to keep employees' information security workload low in order to minimize the chances that they will engage in SRBs to make their jobs easier. Table 12.1 offers some tips for achieving these objectives.

How Can Cyber Intelligence Improve Cyber Security Performance?

Cyber security performance is highly sensitive to context. Deploying more security measures, by itself, does not necessarily make a system more secure. What drives security performance is a dynamic, adaptive, risk-based defense posture in which an organization's valued assets are aligned with prioritized threats (specified threats, not threats "in general") and available resources (Chabinsky, 2010;

TABLE 12.1 Recommendations for Achieving Balance between Individuals and Technology

Recommendation

- Design systems that are secure but usable for end users.
- Expect information breaches to come from unintentional employee behaviors more often than from malicious attacks.
- Make employees aware of the system in place and how they help protect it.
- Trust employees to perform basic security behaviors, but reinforce assurance and compliance behaviors to enhance commitment and ownership.
- Understand that employees might view security behaviors as things that distract from their actual jobs.
- Provide information technology professionals with the tools they need to remain vigilant and protect the system from outsider and insider threats.

Hutchins, Cloppert, & Amin, 2011; Maisey, 2014). Intelligence—or actionable knowledge/insights—is what enables an enterprise to realize that objective (Borum, 2014; Borum et al., 2014; Maisey, 2014).

Cyber intelligence is the process and the product of monitoring and analyzing the capabilities, intentions, and activities of potential adversaries and competitors, as they evolve, in the cyber domain (Borum et al., 2014; Mattern, Felker, Borum, & Bamford, 2014). It is concerned with people and technology and the interactions between them. Too often, cyber threats are viewed as only a "technical" challenge. But system attacks, intrusions, and exploits are perpetrated by people, not machines. Malicious actors and hacking crews have intentions, motivations, objectives, knowledge, and capabilities that guide their actions (Chiesa, Ducci, & Ciappi, 2008; Kirwan & Power, 2013). As in any planned and targeted criminal activity, attackers engage in a range of behaviors while they are contemplating, planning, preparing and executing an intrusion or attack in the cyber domain (Arkin, 2002a, 2002b). Instead of thinking about cyber attacks as "events," it might be more useful to consider them as processes or the end results of processes of planning and preparation. That approach implies a need to assess and understand potential adversaries, maintain situational awareness, and consider how the internal and external features of the operating environment might affect an adversary's actions and objectives (Borum et al., 2014; Enrici, Ancilli & Lioy, 2010; Lafrance, 2004).

One popular approach to understanding and investigating pre-cyber attack behaviors is the Cyber Kill Chain, an intelligence-driven approach to network defense introduced by the Lockheed Martin Computer Incident Response Team (Hutchins et al., 2011). Within this model, *kill chain* simply describes the progression of activity that a threat actor/vector must follow to produce a malicious effect. The chain begins after the malicious actor has penetrated the defended network long enough to log a discernible pattern of activity. By following the network behavior, an analyst can discern potential points at which the attacker could be interrupted or thwarted (Gupta & Joshi, 2012).

Ultimately, however, cyber security should seek to *prevent* intrusions *before* they occur (N. Lee, 2013), so cyber defenders must be willing to extend the scope of collection on preattack behaviors beyond their own networks. Network activity data can be combined with other information about potential adversaries and the threat environment to help security personnel get "left of the hack." With a broader intelligence aperture, the security team can better identify what types of malicious actors (or even specific actors) might target their system; what those actors' capabilities and intentions might be; what they might hope to gain from intruding on the system; and perhaps even when, where, and how malicious actors might attempt an attack (Klaus, 2013; Mattern et al., 2014). It is important to note that these insights do not come principally from profiling demographic or purported psychological characteristics of hackers in general but from analysis of case-specific information (Chiesa et al., 2008).

Intelligence-led efforts can initiate a nontrivial shift from a (technical) threat-based cyber defense posture to an adversary-based cyber defense posture. By identifying and acting on early, preattack behaviors, security personnel can push an adversary into a reactive posture, which can lengthen security personnel's time to action and impose additional costs. As with "target hardening" efforts in physical security, when a malicious actor—particularly an opportunistic one—becomes frustrated, has to work harder, or expend more resources to circumvent an intended victim's defenses, the actor may shift interest to a different target.

There are other, broader informational advantages to using cyber intelligence to guide cyber defense. Although an intelligence-driven defense is generally more robust, it also supports decision making across the organization. The on-the-network (tactical) fight is only one component of cyber security. The Intelligence and National Security Alliance's Cyber Intelligence Task Force uses a common three-part framework to describe the different levels at which actionable knowledge influences decisions and activities within an enterprise. The three overlapping levels are *strategic, operational, and tactical.* The defining features of each level are based on the intended consumer, decision requirements, timeframe, adversary characterization, collection scope, and methods. The strategic level focuses on setting an organization's mission, direction, and objectives and developing a plan for how those objectives will be achieved. The operational level focuses on enabling and sustaining day-to-day operations and output, including logistics by looking internally at the organization's operations and collateral partners and externally at risks and threats. Finally, the tactical level focuses on the technical/logical tactics, techniques, and procedures used to target the system/organization. Effective cyber security works from the premise that defense is not a one-size-fits all activity. An organization's most valued assets and those with the greatest business impact should have the greatest level of protection. Addressing all three levels, security operations can then support executives to make informed investments and develop or deploy countermeasures to effectively defend those high-priority assets.

Now that we have an understanding of the role of cyber intelligence in cyber security, we move to cyber counterintelligence and the role it can play in cyber security.

What Is Cyber Counterintelligence and the Human–Technology Interface?

The discipline of counterintelligence is concerned with protecting secrets and valued assets (Duvenage & von Solms, 2013). In the language of information assurance, its focus is on the "C" element of the C–I–A triad (confidentiality, integrity, and availability). Whitten and Tygar (1999) outlined five "problematic properties of security" that pose inherent challenges for protecting asset confidentiality in computer systems:

- *The unmotivated user property*: When interacting with a system, the user's primary goal is to efficiently "use" that system to accomplish his or her intended objective. Security, at best, is a secondary consideration.
- *The abstraction property*: Users of computer systems are unfamiliar with the policies, regulations, and principles that govern access control. Permissions, to them, are abstract and nontransparent.
- *The lack of feedback property*: Most computer systems are designed to perform a user's intended task. Feedback for the user is getting what he or she wants from the perspective of task accomplishment. The system is not designed to provide the user with security-related feedback on his or her behavior.
- *The barn door property*: If valued information is left unprotected, even accidentally, that information is presumed to be compromised and is to be treated accordingly. Protecting the information after the fact is like "locking the barn door after the horse is gone."
- *The weakest link property*: The overall security of a networked system is only as strong as the weakest component in that system.

The perspective from social engineering is that it is often much easier to get an individual to do something on your behalf than it is to hack software or hardware. This "weakest link" property in most "secure" systems is the human user or employee. Cyber attackers know this vulnerability, perhaps even better than the defenders. Kevin Mitnick, a convicted computer hacker/fraudster and now president of his own security firm, offered this sobering assessment:

> A company can spend hundreds of thousands of dollars on firewalls, intrusion detection systems and encryption and other security technologies, but if an attacker can call one trusted person within the company, and that person complies, and if the attacker gets in, then all that money spent on technology is essentially wasted. (CNN, 2005)

For cyber defense, this raises a need to worry not only about the malicious or disgruntled insider but also the well-intentioned, helpful, inadvertent insider (Greitzer et al., 2014).

Human vulnerability poses an incredibly vexing security (and counterintelligence) problem. Effective cyber security strategies need to better account for users. This should be addressed in two ways: (1) an increased focus on usable security and (2) user inoculation against interpersonal manipulation in what are called *social engineering* attacks. With guidance for enhancing usable security,

Sasse and Flechais (2005) conceptualized secure systems as "sociotechnical" systems with three components: product (user requirements for security policies and mechanisms), process (involving the user in system design and requirements), and panorama (creating a positive security climate within the organization). Addressing these points requires some sweeping revisions throughout the typical security supply chain, but those actions are necessary to modify the behavior of employees who are either unable or unwilling to behave in a way that security policies require.

Enhancing usable security in the human–technology interface is a key step, but personnel also must be equipped to deflect the lure of social engineering. Social engineering attacks use the devices and stratagems of interpersonal influence and persuasion to manipulate a person to take specific actions or provide specific information (Mann, 2012; Tetri & Vuorinen, 2013; Townsend, 2010). These attack methods are widely used and highly effective. And if you believe that only the "gullible" are victims (social psychologists would call that belief the *illusion of invulnerability*), think again (Downs, Holbrook, & Cranor, 2006). A Treasury Inspector General's security audit showed that a third of Internal Revenue Service managers gave out their user name and password access over the phone to unknown individuals posing as IT help desk personnel. That was a 50 percent improvement from a similar test four years earlier (Treasury Inspector General for Tax Administration, 2005).

Through social engineering, malicious actors can access assets and technology without typing even a single line of code. Neither the attack nor the defense necessarily relies on technology; they rely on modification of behavior. Technology can enable these attacks, of course. *Phishing* is a commonly used tactic in which a malicious actor uses artifice to send an e-mail message that prompts the recipient to open a file or click a link, which then infects the machine, and possibly the network, with software that might destroy or steal the user's information or even control the system itself (Hong, 2012; Jakobsson & Myers, 2006). Some e-mail phishing attacks are very rudimentary, such as the well-known Nigerian "419" scams (named after the relevant fraud section of the Nigerian Criminal Code) in which people are asked to provide their financial or banking information to "help" an important person in expectation of receiving a substantial monetary reward. Other phishing schemes are increasingly sophisticated, using a bank's own graphics and e-mail format to add credibility and getting the recipients to provide their access credentials under the guise of "logging in" to solve a problem, such as a freeze ostensibly being put on their account (Tetri & Vuorinen, 2013). Clearly, these scams rely on individuals who are trusting in nature and want to assist the individual requesting help. This emphasizes our call to understand the nature of trust in computer-mediated communications, especially when the individuals do not know one another.

It is users' decisions and actions under these circumstances that determine a system's security. There is no "silver bullet" solution to inoculating users against phishing and social engineering, and nearly all experts recommend a multilayered approach, including training (Khonji, Iraqi, & Jones, 2013; Luo, Brody, Seazzu, & Burd, 2011; Peltier, 2006; Purkait, 2012; Yue & Wang, 2008). In addition to informing employees about security policies (and their rationales), an organization also might provide inoculation training for social engineering and illegitimate persuasion. By discussing case studies and examples, employees can become more aware of, and sensitized to, the tactics of social engineers, the kinds of content they might be most likely to seek, and how social engineers can use that information (Kumaraguru, Sheng, Acquisti, Cranor, & Hong, 2010; Sheng, Holbrook, Kumaraguru, Cranor, & Downs, 2010). Learning to spot a social engineering attack is a good first step. By using scenarios and interactive exercises, users learn to respond to manipulative approaches and receive immediate feedback. These training principles are not dissimilar to those used in resistance-to-persuasion studies (Sagarin, Cialdini, Rice, & Serna, 2002; Scheeres, Mills, & Grimaila, 2008).

Hadnagy (2010) recommended several steps that an organization can take to mitigate its social engineering risk:

- *Create a "personal security culture"*: Employees investigate and reflect on the information about themselves that they make publically available and its potential for misuse by others.
- *Understand the value of the information being requested*: By thinking through the ways in which a social engineer could use their available personal information ("Where are you from?") or information they might disclose ("Who currently maintains your heating, ventilating, and air-conditioning system?"). For exploitation, employees become more difficult targets for elicitation.
- *Keep software updated*: Many cyber exploits occur through known system vulnerabilities that have been subsequently been "patched." If the attacker knows that you are using an outdated version of an application, he or she has a good starting point to penetrate the system.
- *Develop scripts*: It might be helpful to provide a written outline for employees to guide their responses in foreseeable, difficult situations. This would include what questions to ask, what information to gather to verify a caller's identity, and how to follow up in documenting or reporting a suspicious query.
- *Conduct social engineering audits*: Sometimes the best way to identify a specific vulnerability is to test the system. According to Hadnagy (2010), "a social engineering audit is where a security professional is hired to test the people, policies, and physical perimeter of a company by simulating the same attacks that a malicious social engineer would use" (p. 348).

Summary

There is no such a thing as a truly effective GUI or human–computer interface when it comes to cyber security. This chapter has argued there are many factors and motives influencing individuals' behavior related to cyber security in the workplace. Many of these factors—such as SABs and SCBs, trust in teammates, trust in technology, vigilance, and principles from social engineering—are macro factors and go well beyond what can be designed in the typical user interface. It is true that technology can address some of the problems—for example, an embedded agent that monitors a worker's fatigue or the number of false alarms associated with alerts—but because the behavioral space of individuals is so dense and complex, it would not be possible to have a traditional interface that is effective for all cyber security. Rather, our perspective is that one needs to consider a systems approach to designing such an interface, and it would operate at the organizational level. The system has strategic, operational, and tactical levels (Borum, 2014). Think broadly in terms of social engineering and develop policies, procedures, and trainings that focus on the nature of effective and ineffective cyber security behaviors for employees and the motivations and tactics utilized by hackers to gain access to our IS.

Note

1 This work was supported in part by Contract PO-JN42903 to Michael D. Coovert. The statements here reflect the views of the authors and should not be considered those of the U.S. Department of Defense.

References

Albrechtsen, E. (2007). A qualitative study of users' view on information security. *Computers & Security*, 26, 276–289.

Alston, F., & Tippett, D. (2009). Does a technology-driven organization's culture influence the trust employees have in their managers? *Engineering Management Journal*, 21(2), 3–10.

Arkin, O. (2002a). Tracing hackers: Part 1. *Computer Fraud & Security*, 2002(4), 12–17.

Arkin, O. (2002b). Tracing hackers: Part 2: A concept for tracing and profiling malicious computer attackers. *Computer Fraud & Security*, 2002(5), 8–11.

Baker, D. E. (2009). Medication alert fatigue: The potential for compromised patient safety. *Hospital Pharmacy*, 44, 460–461.

Barton, A. J. (2011). Alert fatigue: Implications for the clinical nurse specialist. *Clinical Nurse Specialist*, 25, 218–219.

Bauer, D. J. (2011). Evaluating individual differences in psychological processes. *Current Directions in Psychological Science*, 20, 115–118.

Besnard, D., & Arief, B. (2004). Computer security impaired by legitimate users. *Computers & Security*, 23, 253–264.

Blomqvist, K. (2002). *Partnering in the dynamic environment: The role of trust in asymmetric technology partnership formation* (Doctoral dissertation). Retrieved from http://urn.fi/URN:ISBN:978-952-214-598-7

Borum, R. (2014). Getting "left of the hack": Honing your cyber intelligence can thwart intruders. *InfoSecurity Professional*, 7(5), 25–29.

Borum, R., Felker, J., & Kern, S. (2014). Cyber intelligence operations: More than just 1s and 0s. *Proceedings of the Marine Safety and Security Council: The U.S. Coast Guard Journal of Safety and Security at Sea*, 71(4), 65–68.

Bulgurcu, B., Cavusoglu, H., & Benbasat, I. (2010). Information security policy compliance: An empirical study of rationality-based beliefs and information security awareness. *MIS Quarterly, 34,* 523–548.

Chabinsky, S. R. (2010). Cybersecurity strategy: A primer for policy makers and those on the front line. *Journal of National Security Law & Policy, 4,* 27–39.

Chiesa, R., Ducci, S., & Ciappi, S. (2008). *Profiling hackers: The science of criminal profiling as applied to the world of hacking.* Boca Raton, FL: CRC Press.

CNN. (2005, October 13). *A convicted hacker debunks some myths.* Retrieved from http://www.cnn.com/2005/TECH/internet/10/07/kevin.mitnick.cnna/

Colwill, C. (2009). Human factors in information security: The insider threat—Who can you trust these days? *Information Security Technical Report, 14,* 186–196.

Cook, J., & Wall, T. (1980). New work attitude measures of trust, organizational commitment and personal need non-fulfillment. *Journal of Occupational and Organizational Psychology, 53,* 39–52.

Coovert, M. D., Pavlova Miller, E. E., Bennett, W., Arvan, M., & Coovert, D. (2013, December). A quantitative assessment of the impact of team effectiveness on changes in individual trust. In *Proceedings from Interservice/Industry Training, Simulation and Education* (pp. 1945–1954). Orlando, FL: Interservice/Industry Training, Simulation and Education.

Costa, A. C. (2003). Work team trust and effectiveness. *Personnel Review, 32,* 605–622.

Costa, A. C., Roe, R. A., & Taillieu, T. (2001). Trust within teams: The relation with performance effectiveness. *European Journal of Work and Organizational Psychology, 10,* 225–244.

D'Arcy, J., Hovav, A., & Galletta, D. (2009). User awareness of security countermeasures and its impact on information systems misuse: a deterrence approach. *Information Systems Research, 20,* 79–98.

Department for Business, Enterprise and Regulation Reform. (2008). *Information security breaches survey 2008.* Retrieved from http://www.bis.gov.uk/file45714.pdf

Department for Business, Innovation and Skills. (2013). *2013 information security breaches survey: Technical report.* Retrieved from https://www.gov.uk/government/uploads/system/uploads/attachment_data/file/200455/bis-13-p184-2013-information-security-breaches-survey-technical-report.pdf

Downs, J. S., Holbrook, M. B., & Cranor, L. F. (2006). Decision strategies and susceptibility to phishing. In *Proceedings of the Second Symposium on Usable Privacy and Security* (pp. 79–90). New York: Association for Computing Machinery.

Dubie, D. (2007). End users behaving badly. *Network World.* Retrieved from http://www.networkworld.com/slideshows/2007/121007-end-users-behaving-badly.html

Duvenage, P., & von Solms, S. (2013). The case for cyber counterintelligence. In *2013 International Conference on Adaptive Science and Technology (ICAST)* (pp. 1–8). New York: Institute of Electrical and Electronics Engineers.

Enrici, I., Ancilli, M., & Lioy, A. (2010, May). A psychological approach to information technology security. In T. Pardela & B. Wilamowski (Eds.), *3rd International Conference on Human System Interaction (HSI)* (pp. 459–466). New York: Institute of Electrical and Electronics Engineers.

Ernst & Young. (2008). *Moving beyond compliance: Ernst & Young 2008 global information security survey.* Retrieved from http://www.ncc.co.uk/article/?articleid=15619

Greitzer, F. L., Strozer, J. R., Cohen, S., Moore, A. P., Mundie, D., & Cowley, J. (2014). Analysis of unintentional insider threats deriving from social engineering exploits. In *2014 IEEE Security and Privacy Workshops (SPW)* (pp. 236–250). New York: Institute of Electrical and Electronics Engineers.

Grichanik, M., Coovert, M. D., & Bennett, W. (2014, May). The effects of collaborative critical thinking training on monitoring, trust development, and effectiveness in virtual teams. In M. Prewett (Chair), *Strategies for improving virtual team processes and emergent states*. Symposium conducted at the meeting of the Society for Industrial and Organizational Psychology, Honolulu, HI.

Guo, K. H. (2013). Security related behavior in using information systems in the workplace: A review and synthesis. *Computers & Security, 32*, 242–251.

Guo, K. H., Yuan, Y., Archer, N. P., & Connelly, C. E. (2011). Understanding nonmalicious security violations in the workplace: A composite behavior model. *Journal of Management Information Systems, 28*, 203–236.

Gupta, K., & Joshi, J. (2012). Methodological and operational deliberations in cyber attack and cyber exploitation. *International Journal of Advanced Research in Computer Science and Software Engineering, 2*(11), 385–389.

Gurtman, M. B. (1992). Trust, distrust, and interpersonal problems: A circumplex analysis. *Journal of Personality and Social Psychology, 62*, 989–1002.

Hadnagy, C. (2010). *Social engineering: The art of human hacking*. Hoboken, NJ: Wiley.

Henttonen, K., & Blomqvist, K. (2005). Managing distance in a global virtual team: The evolution of trust through technology-mediated relational communication. *Strategic Change, 14*, 107–119.

Herath, T., & Rao, H. R. (2009). Encouraging information security behaviors in organizations: Role of penalties, pressures and perceived effectiveness. *Decision Support Systems, 47*, 154–165.

Hong, J. (2012, January). The state of phishing attacks. *Communications of the ACM, 55*(1), 74–81.

Hu, Q., Dinev, T., Hart, P., & Cooke, D. (2012). Managing employee compliance with information security policies: The critical role of top management and organizational culture. *Decision Sciences, 43*, 615–659.

Hutchins, E. M., Cloppert, M. J., & Amin, R. M. (2011). Intelligence-driven computer network defense informed by analysis of adversary campaigns and intrusion kill chains. In J. J. Ryan (Ed.), *Leading issues in information warfare and security research* (pp. 80–86). Reading, England: Academic Publishing International.

Isaac, T., Weissman, J. S., Davis, R. B., Massagli, M., Cyrulik, A., Sands, D. Z., & Weingart, S. N. (2009). Overrides of medicine alerts in ambulatory care. *Archives of Internal Medicine, 169*, 305–311.

Jakobsson, M., & Myers, S. (Eds.). (2006). *Phishing and countermeasures: understanding the increasing problem of electronic identity theft*. New York: Wiley.

Khonji, M., Iraqi, Y., & Jones, A. (2013). Phishing detection: A literature survey. *IEEE Communications Surveys & Tutorials, 15*, 2091–2121.

Kirwan, G., & Power, A. (2013). *Cybercrime: The psychology of online offenders*. Cambridge, England: Cambridge University Press.

Klaus, J. (2013). Understanding and overcoming cyber-security anti-patterns. *Computer Networks, 57*, 2206–2211.

Kumaraguru, P., Sheng, S., Acquisti, A., Cranor, L. F., & Hong, J. (2010). Teaching Johnny not to fall for phish. *ACM Transactions on Internet Technology, 10*(2), Article 7.

Lafrance, Y. (2004). *Psychology: A precious security tool*. Retrieved from http://www.zma.es/SecurityEssentials_5/psychology-precious-security-tool/default.pdf

Langhals, B. T., Burgoon, J. K., & Nunamaker, J. F. (2013). Using eye-based psychophysiological cues to enhance screener vigilance. *Journal of Cognitive Engineering and Decision Making, 7*, 83–95.

Lee, J. D., & See, K. A. (2004). Trust in automation: Designing for appropriate reliance. *Human Factors, 46*, 50–80.

Lee, N. (2013). *Counterterrorism and cybersecurity*. New York: Springer

Levin, D. Z., Whitener, E. M., & Cross, R. (2006). Perceived trustworthiness of knowledge sources: The moderating impact of relationship length. *Journal of Applied Psychology, 91*, 1163–1171.

Lewicki, R. J., & Bunker, B. B. (1995). Trust in relationships: A model of trust development and decline. In B. B. Bunker & J. Z. Rubin (Eds.), *Conflict, cooperation, and justice: Essays inspired by the work of Morton Deutsch* (pp. 133–173). San Francisco: Jossey-Bass.

Lewicki, R. J., & Bunker, B. B. (1996). Developing and maintaining trust in work relationships. In R. M. Kramer & T. R. Tyler (Eds.), *Trust in organizations: Frontiers of theory and research* (pp. 114–139). Thousand Oaks, CA: Sage.

Lewicki, R. J., McAllister, D. J., & Bies, R. J. (1998). Trust and distrust: New relationships and realities. *Academy of Management Review, 23*, 438–458.

Lin, C. P., Payne, T. H., Nichol, W. P., Hoey, P. J. Anderson, C. L., & Gennari, J. H. (2008). Evaluating clinical decision support systems: Monitoring CPOE order check override rates in the Department of Veterans Affairs' computerized patient record system. *Journal of the American Medical Informatics Association, 15*, 620–626.

Luo, X., Brody, R., Seazzu, A., & Burd, S. (2011). Social engineering: The neglected human factor for information security management. *Information Resources Management Journal, 24*(3), 1–8.

McAllister, D. J. (1995). Affect- and cognitive-based trust as foundations for interpersonal cooperation in organizations. *Academy of Management Journal, 38*, 24–59.

McArdle, J. J. (2009). Latent variable modeling of differences and changes with longitudinal data. *Annual Review of Psychology, 60*, 577–605.

McGrath, J. E. (1991). Time, interaction, and performance (TIP): A theory of groups. *Small Group Research, 22*, 147–174.

Maisey, M. (2014). Moving to analysis-led cyber-security. *Network Security, 2014*(5), 5–12.

Mann, M. I. (2012). *Hacking the human: Social engineering techniques and security countermeasures*. Burlington, VT: Gower.

Mattern, T., Felker, J., Borum, R., & Bamford, G. (2014). Operational levels of cyber intelligence. *International Journal of Intelligence and CounterIntelligence, 27*, 702–719.

Mayer, R. C., Davis, J. H., & Schoorman, F. D. (1995). An integrative model of organizational trust. *Academy of Management Review, 20*, 709–734.

Nannestad, P. (2008). What have we learned about generalized trust, if anything? *Annual Review of Political Science, 11*, 413–436.

Organ, D. W. (1988). *Organizational citizenship behavior: The good soldier syndrome*. Lanham, MD: Lexington Books.

Padayachee, K. (2012). Taxonomy of compliant information security behavior. *Computers & Security, 31*, 673–680.

Pavlova, E., Coovert, M. D., & Bennett, W. (2013). Trust development in computer-mediated teams: A latent change score model. *Multivariate Behavioral Research, 48*, 166–167.

Peltier, T. R. (2006). Social engineering: Concepts and solutions. *Information Systems Security, 15*(5), 13–21.

Pfleeger, S. L., & Caputo, D. D. (2012). Leveraging behavioral science to mitigate cyber-security risk. *Computers & Security, 31*, 597–611.

Post, G. V., & Kagan, A. (2007). Evaluating information security tradeoffs: Restricting access can interfere with user tasks. *Computers & Security, 26*, 229–237.

Purkait, S. (2012). Phishing counter measures and their effectiveness—Literature review. *Information Management and Computer Security, 20,* 382–420.
Rashid, F., & Edmondson, A. C. (2011, February 16). *Risky trust: How multi-entity teams develop trust in a high risk endeavor* (Working Paper 11-089). Cambridge, MA: Harvard Business School.
Richardson, R. (2010). *CSI computer crime and security survey.* New York: Computer Security Institute.
Riley, M., Elgin, B., Lawrence, D., & Matlack, C. (2014). Missed alarms and 40 million stolen credit card numbers: How Target blew it. *Bloomberg Businessweek.* Retrieved from http://www.businessweek.com/articles/2014-03-13/target-missed-alarms-in-epic-hack-of-credit-card-data#p2
Robinson, S. L., & Bennett, R. J. (1995). A typology of deviant workplace behaviors: A multidimensional scaling study. *Academy of Management Journal, 38,* 555–572.
Sagarin, B. J., Cialdini, R. B., Rice, W. E., & Serna, S. B. (2002). Dispelling the illusion of invulnerability: The motivations and mechanisms of resistance to persuasion. *Journal of Personality and Social Psychology, 83,* 526–541.
Sasse, M., & Flechais, I. (2005). Usable security: Why do we need it? How do we get it? In L. F. Cranor & S. Garfinkel (Eds.), *Security and usability: Designing secure systems that people can use* (pp. 13–30). Sebastopol, CA: O'Reilly Media.
Scheeres, J., Mills, R., & Grimaila, M. (2008). Establishing the human firewall: Improving resistance to social engineering attacks. In L. Armistead (Ed.), *Proceedings of the 3rd International Conference on Information Warfare and Security* (pp. 325–334). Reading, England: Academic Publishing Limited.
Serva, M. A., Fuller, M. A., & Mayer, R. C. (2005). The reciprocal nature of trust: A longitudinal study of interacting teams. *Journal of Organizational Behavior, 26,* 625–648.
Sheng, S., Holbrook, M., Kumaraguru, P., Cranor, L. F., & Downs, J. (2010, April). Who falls for phish? A demographic analysis of phishing susceptibility and effectiveness of interventions. In *Proceedings of the SIGCHI Conference on Human Factors in Computing Systems* (pp. 373–382). New York: Association for Computing Machinery.
Sitkin, S. B., & Roth, N. L. (1993). Explaining the limited effectiveness of legalistic "remedies" for trust/distrust. *Organization Science, 4,* 367–392.
Smith, J. B., & Barclay, D. W. (1997). The effect of organizational differences and trusting on the effectiveness of selling partner relationships. *Journal of Marketing, 61,* 3–21.
Sorrentino, R. M., Holmes, J. G., Hanna, S. E., & Sharp, A. (1995). Uncertainty orientation and trust in close relationships: Individual differences in cognitive styles. *Journal of Personality and Social Psychology, 68,* 314–327.
Stanton, J. M., Stam, K. R., Mastrangelo, P., & Jolton, J. (2005). Analysis of end user security behaviors. *Computers & Security, 24,* 124–133.
Straub, D. W., Jr. (1990). Effective IS security: An empirical study. *Information Systems Research, 1,* 255–276.
Tetri, P., & Vuorinen, J. (2013). Dissecting social engineering. *Behaviour & Information Technology, 32,* 1014–1023.
Townsend, K. (2010, September 27). The art of social engineering. *Infosecurity, 7*(4), 32–35.
Treasury Inspector General for Tax Administration. (2005, March 15). *While progress has been made, managers and employees are still susceptible to social engineering techniques* (Reference No. 2005-20-042). Washington, DC: U.S. Department of the Treasury.
Tyler, T. R., & Blader, S. L. (2005). Can businesses effectively regulate employee conduct? The antecedents of rule following in work settings. *Academy of Management Journal, 48,* 1143–1158.

Vance, A., Siponen, M., & Pahnila, S. (2012). Motivating IS security compliance: Insights from habit and protection motivation theory. *Information & Management, 49,* 190–198.

Walther, J. B. (1992). Interpersonal effects in computer-mediated interaction: A relational perspective. *Communication Research, 19,* 52–90.

Warm, J. S., Parasuraman, R., & Matthews, G. (2008). Vigilance requires hard mental work and is stressful. *Human Factors, 50,* 433–441.

Webber, S. S. (2008). Development of cognitive and affective trust in teams. *Small Group Research, 39,* 746–769.

Whitten, A., & Tygar, J. D. (1999). Why Johnny can't encrypt: A usability evaluation of PGP 5.0. In *Proceedings of the 8th Conference on USENIX Security Symposium* (Vol. 8, p. 14). Berkeley, CA: USENIX Association.

Wilson, J. M., Straus, S. G., & McEvily, B. (2006). All in due time: The development of trust in computer-mediated and face-to-face teams. *Organization Behavior and Human Decision Processes, 99,* 16–33.

Yue, C., & Wang, H. (2008). Anti-phishing in offense and defense. In *Annual Computer Security Applications Conference, 2008.* (pp. 345–354). New York: Institute of Electrical and Electronics Engineers.

13

TECHNOLOGICAL SOLUTIONS FOR IMPROVING PERFORMANCE OF CYBER SECURITY ANALYSTS[1]

Massimiliano Albanese and Sushil Jajodia

Introduction

Our society is becoming increasingly dependent on complex information and communication technology (ICT) infrastructures for a wide range of critical functions and missions. As a consequence, financial institutions, power distribution networks, national security, and mass transit—to name just a few—are exposed to a wide range of potentially devastating cyber attacks designed to leverage the inherent weaknesses of such complex systems. The threats we are constantly facing in today's complex cyberspace include the risk of massive data losses or data leaks, theft of intellectual property, credit card breaches, denial of service, identity theft, and threats to our privacy. In addition, the widespread integration of ICT into physical systems—such as the power grid, air traffic control, manufacturing, and so on—has created a whole new class of threats with the potential of causing catastrophic disruptions of critical infrastructures and devastating economic consequences.

On one side, attackers can exploit weaknesses in network configurations as well as unpatched vulnerabilities to incrementally penetrate a network and compromise critical systems. On the other side, due to the growing number and sophistication of high-profile cyber attacks, cyber security analysts need to continuously examine large amounts of security alerts and monitoring data generated by a multitude of sensors in order to detect attacks in a timely manner and enable effective response and mitigation efforts. However—given the inherent complexity of the problem—manual analysis is labor-intensive and prone to error, and it distracts the analyst from capturing the "big picture" of the cyber situation. In most current solutions, human analysts are heavily involved in every phase of the monitoring and response process. This represents a major factor in limiting the performance of security analysts, who find themselves spending an incredible amount of time looking at details that, ideally, an automated tool should have analyzed. To address current limitations, we should move from a *human-in-the-loop* approach to a *human-on-the-loop* approach in which human analysts have the responsibility of overseeing automated processes and validating the results of automated analysis of monitoring data.

This chapter explores, from a conceptual point of view, several classes of technological solutions that can automate some of the most time-consuming and tedious tasks an analyst would otherwise need to perform manually. These and similar tools have the potential to address some of the factors that limit the performance of cyber security analysts.

The chapter is organized as follows. The "Assessing Technological Solutions" section discusses the factors limiting the performance of cyber security analysts and suggests criteria and metrics that can be adopted for assessing technological solutions aimed at overcoming such limitations. The next section provides an overview of the state of the art in cyber defense technology. This is followed by a section discussing in more detail some representative technologies—namely, tools for gaining cyber situational awareness, zero-day analysis, and network hardening. The final section discusses what additional capabilities we need to develop in the future and gives some concluding remarks.

Assessing Technological Solutions

As security threats evolve, new security tools and technologies are devised to counter newer generations of cyber attacks and mitigate their impact. In recent years, the research community has been particularly active in attempting to establish the foundations of the cyber security discipline and develop more effective defenses based on a better understanding of cyberspace dynamics. Of particular note are a multitude of interdisciplinary approaches aimed at understanding and modeling the complex relationships between the systems being defended, malicious actors attempting to breach such systems, and security analysts attempting to identify intrusions as they occur.

Researchers across disciplines have investigated the role that humans play in a complex defense system comprising several classes of tools and technologies. Such studies have involved, among other aspects, team cognition and coordination, situational (or situation) awareness, mental models, and human–computer interaction (Cooke, Champion, Rajivan, & Jariwala, 2013; Cooke, Gorman, Myers, & Duran, 2013). As a result, several metrics have been defined to assess and quantify the performance of cyber security analysts and to study how performance can benefit from the introduction of automated tools. In practice, such metrics can be used to evaluate and compare the performance of analysts in preautomation and postautomation scenarios. Intuitively, we expect performance to improve with automation, and, in fact, the lesson learned from such efforts is that when *properly* designed, automated security analysis tools can greatly enhance an analyst's performance with respect to multiple evaluation metrics. Without getting into the details of the many available metrics, at a very high level, three major metrics should be considered—namely, throughput, false alarm rate, and missed detection rate. The *throughput* is a measure of the amount of work completed in a certain amount of time. With respect to this metric, the performance of an analyst is clearly limited in the sense that there is an intrinsic limit on the amount of information a human being can process in a given amount of time, although such a limit may vary from subject to subject. The *false alarm rate* is the percentage of alarms that do not correspond to actual intrusions, whereas the *missed detection rate* is the percentage of actual intrusions that are not detected. There is an intrinsic tradeoff between these two rates: A decrease in missed detections typically leads to an increase in false alarms, and vice versa. These metrics can be used to assess the performance of an analyst, but they can also be used to analyze the performance of tools as well as any combination of tools and manual analysis. When used to assess the performance of a human analyst, such metrics may be affected by the analyst's subjective perception of risk. A more conservative analyst, who would err on the side of caution, might want to minimize the risk of missed detections, which in turn may lead to identifying as potentially *malicious* events that are instead benign. A less conservative analyst might flag fewer events as suspicious. This can certainly reduce the number of false alarms, but, at the same time, more intrusive events may go undetected.

In order to assess new defense tools or technologies, we should evaluate the performance of an analyst with respect to these three metrics before and after the introduction of such tools and technologies. In addition to these quantifiable performance attributes, other factors should be considered, such as improved user experience and reduced frustration, but looking at the automation of security analysis from this perspective goes beyond the scope of this chapter.

State of the Art

As defenders, we now have access to a wide range of security tools and technologies (e.g., intrusion detection and prevention systems, firewalls, antivirus software), security standards, training resources, vulnerability databases (e.g., NVD [National Institute of Standards and Technology {NIST}, n.d.], CVE [MITRE Corporation, n.d.]), best practices, and catalogues of security controls (e.g., Cloud Security Alliance, n.d.; NIST, 2013) as well as countless security checklists, benchmarks, and recommendations. To help us understand current threats and stay ahead in the security game, we have seen the emergence of threat information feeds, reports (e.g., Symantec's Internet Security Threat Report [Symantec Corporation, 2014], Mandiant's APT1 report [Mandiant, 2013]), tools (e.g., Nessus, Wireshark), standards, and threat-sharing schemes. And to pull all of this together, we are surrounded by security requirements (e.g., FIPS 200; NIST,

2006), risk management frameworks (e.g., NIST, 2010), compliance regimes, regulatory mandates, and so forth. Therefore, there is certainly no shortage of information available to security practitioners on how they should secure their infrastructure.

However, without well-defined processes to integrate all this knowledge in a consistent and coherent manner, all of these resources may have the undesired consequence of introducing competing options, priorities, opinions, and claims that can paralyze or distract an enterprise from taking critical actions. In the last decade, threats have evolved dramatically, malicious actors have become smarter and more persistent, advanced persistent threats have emerged, and users have become more mobile. Data are now distributed across multiple platforms and locations, many of which are not within the physical control sphere of an organization. With more reliance on cloud computing platforms, data and applications are becoming more distributed, thus progressively eroding the traditional notion of security perimeter.

Representative Technologies

In this section, we briefly survey some of the classes of tools and technologies that are available to help security analysts streamline their jobs and improve their performance. First, we discuss *cyber situational awareness*, a broad term used to refer to a set of capabilities aimed at gaining a full understanding of the cyber landscape of an enterprise and using this knowledge to protect the enterprise from current and future threats. Although cyber situational awareness is not a technology per se, a number of tools and technologies have been developed to automate the process of acquiring and acting upon situational awareness. Second, we discuss *topological vulnerability analysis*, an approach to modeling the interdependencies among network elements and their vulnerabilities. Third, we present a brief overview of *zero-day analysis*, a term that refers to the capability of assessing the impact of unknown vulnerabilities. Last, we briefly discuss *network hardening*, which refers to the capability of systematically altering a network's configuration to prevent attackers from reaching well-defined targets.

Cyber Situational Awareness

Today, when a security incident occurs, the top three questions security administrators would ask are, in essence, these: What happened? Why did it happen? What should I do? Answers to the first two questions form the core of cyber situational awareness. Whether the last question can be satisfactorily answered is greatly dependent upon the specific cyber situational awareness capabilities of an enterprise.

Situational awareness has been studied from a number of different perspectives. Whereas, on one side, computer scientists have traditionally looked at a wide range of very technical aspects, on the other side, psychologists have examined the role of human analysts—both as individuals and as teams—in complex collaborative environments in which human factors play a critical role in terms of both developing theoretical perspectives and metrics and developing guidelines for system, training, and procedure design (Salmon, 2007; St. John & Smallman, 2008). More recently, a multidisciplinary group of leading researchers in cyber security, cognitive science, and decision science have elaborated on the fundamental challenges facing the research community and identified promising solution paths (Jajodia, Liu, Swarup, & Wang, 2010). At an abstract level, such solution paths imply an understanding of the behavior and motifs of adversaries (i.e., knowledge of *them*), detailed knowledge of the assets being defended (i.e., knowledge of *us*), and the development of technical solutions that take all these elements—both technical and nontechnical—into account. A variety of computer and network security research topics belong to or touch the scope of cyber situational awareness. However, the cyber situational awareness capabilities of an enterprise are still very limited for several reasons, including, but not limited to the following:

- *Inaccurate and incomplete vulnerability analysis, intrusion detection, and forensics*: Most organizations do not devote enough resources to cyber defense. As a consequence, their ability to identify vulnerabilities and detect intrusions in a timely manner is often very limited.
- *Lack of capability to monitor certain microscopic system or attack behaviors*: When security solutions are deployed, organizations tend to focus on capturing macroscopic events and may miss many important details.
- *Limited capability to transform information into actionable intelligence*: Information relevant to cyber defense may originate from multiple sources. Without reliable processes in place to distill and integrate information from multiple and diverse sources, an enterprise may not be able to gain actionable intelligence to inform security-related decisions.
- *Limited capability to handle uncertainty*: Many information sources may be intrinsically uncertain, and enterprises often lack adequate models and tools to properly handle uncertain information and make decisions under uncertainty.

Without losing generality, cyber situational awareness can be viewed as a three-phase process: (1) situation perception, (2) situation comprehension, and (3) situation projection. *Perception* provides information about the status, attributes, and dynamics of relevant elements within the environment. *Comprehension* of the situation encompasses how human subjects combine, interpret, store, and retain information. *Projection* of the elements of the environment (current situation) into the near future encompasses the ability to make predictions on the basis of the knowledge acquired through perception and comprehension.

Situational awareness is gained by a system, which is usually the system being threatened by random or organized cyber attacks.

Several definitions of cyber situational awareness have been proposed in the literature. Endsley (1995) provides a general definition of *situational awareness* (SA) in dynamic environments: "Situation awareness is the perception of the elements of the environment within a volume of time and space, the comprehension of their meaning, and the projection of their status in the near future" (p. 36). Endsley (1995) also differentiates between situational awareness—which he defines as "a state of knowledge"—and situation assessment—which he defines as the "process of achieving, acquiring, or maintaining situation awareness" (p. 36). This distinction becomes extremely important when trying to apply computer automation to situational awareness. Because situational awareness is "a state of knowledge," it is a cognitive process and resides primarily in the minds of human analysts, whereas situation assessment—being a process or set of processes—lends itself to automated techniques. Another definition of situational awareness is provided by Alberts, Garstka, Hayes, and Signori (2001):

> When the term situational awareness is used, it describes the awareness of a situation that exists in part or all of the battlespace at a particular point in time. In some instances, information on the trajectory of events that preceded the current situation may be of interest, as well as insight into how the situation is likely to unfold. The components of a situation include missions and constraints on missions (e.g., Rules of Engagement), capabilities and intentions of relevant forces, and key attributes of the environment. (p. 120)

The Army Field Manual 1-02 (September 2004) defines situational awareness as follows:

> Knowledge and understanding of the current situation which promotes timely, relevant and accurate assessment of friendly, competitive and other operations within the battlespace in order to facilitate decision making. An informational perspective and skill that fosters an ability to determine quickly the context and relevance of events that are unfolding. (p. 1-171)

There are many other definitions available for situation awareness, but the ones described here seem to be or are becoming widely accepted.

The goal of current research in this area is to explore ways to elevate the cyber situational awareness capabilities of an enterprise to the next level by measures such as developing holistic cyber situational awareness approaches and evolving existing system designs into new systems that can achieve self-awareness.

Topological Vulnerability Analysis

Situational awareness, as defined in the previous section, implies knowledge and understanding of both the defender and the attacker. In turn, this implies knowledge and understanding of all of the weaknesses existing in the computing infrastructure we aim to defend. By their very nature, security concerns on networks are highly interdependent. Each machine's susceptibility to attack depends on the vulnerabilities of other machines in the network. Attackers can combine vulnerabilities in unexpected ways, allowing them to incrementally penetrate a network and compromise critical systems. To protect our critical infrastructure networks, we must understand not only our individual system vulnerabilities but also their interdependencies. Although we cannot predict the origin and timing of attacks, we can reduce their impact by knowing the possible attack paths through our networks. We need to transform raw security data into roadmaps that let us proactively prepare for attacks, manage vulnerability risks, and have real-time situational awareness. We cannot rely on manual processes and mental models. We need automated tools to analyze and visualize vulnerability dependencies and attack paths so that we can understand our overall security posture, providing context over the full security life cycle.

A viable approach to such full-context security is topological vulnerability analysis (TVA; Jajodia & Noel, 2010). TVA monitors the state of network assets, maintains models of network vulnerabilities and residual risk, and combines these to produce models that convey the impact of individual and combined vulnerabilities on the overall security posture. The core element of this tool is an attack graph showing all possible ways an attacker can penetrate the network. This approach provides a unique new capability, transforming raw security data into a roadmap that lets one proactively prepare for attacks, manage vulnerability risks, and have real-time situational awareness. It supports both offensive (e.g., penetration testing) and defensive (e.g., network hardening) applications. The mapping of attack paths through a network via TVA provides a concrete understanding of how individual and combined vulnerabilities affect overall network security. For example, we can (1) determine whether risk-mitigating efforts have a significant impact on overall security, (2) determine how much a new vulnerability will affect overall security, and (3) analyze how changes to individual machines may increase overall risk to the enterprise.

This approach has been implemented as a security tool—CAULDRON (Jajodia, Noel, Kalapa, Albanese, & Williams, 2011)—that transforms raw security data into a model of all possible network attack paths. In the development of this tool, several technical challenges have been addressed, including the design of appropriate models, efficient model population, effective visualizations and decision support tools, and the development of scalable mathematical representations and algorithms. The result is a working software tool that offers truly unique capabilities.

TVA looks at vulnerabilities and their protective measures within the context of overall network security by modeling their interdependencies via attack graphs. Figure 13.1 shows a simplified attack graph[2] for a network of three machines (referred to as Machines 0, 1, and 2, respectively). Rectangles represent vulnerabilities that an attacker may exploit, whereas ovals represent security conditions that are either required to exploit a vulnerability (preconditions) or created as the result of an exploit (postconditions). Purple ovals represent initial conditions, which depend on the initial configuration of the system, whereas blue ovals represent intermediate conditions created as the result of an exploit. In this example, the attacker's objective is to gain administrative privileges on Machine 2, a condition denoted as **root(2)**. In practice, to prevent the attacker from reaching a given security condition, the defender has to prevent exploitation of all vulnerabilities that have that condition as a postcondition. For instance, in the example of Figure 13.1, one could prevent the attacker from gaining user privileges on Machine 1, denoted as **user(1)**, by preventing exploitation of both **rsh(0,1)** and **sshd_bof(0,1)**.[3] Conversely, to prevent exploitation of a vulnerability, at least one precondition must be disabled. For instance, in the example of Figure 13.1, one could prevent the attacker from exploiting **rsh(1,2)** by disabling either **trust(2,1)** or **user(1)**.

The analysis of attack graphs provides alternative sets of protective measures that guarantee the safety of critical systems. For instance, in the example of Figure 13.1, one could prevent the attacker from reaching the target security condition **root(2)** by disabling one of the following two sets of initial conditions:

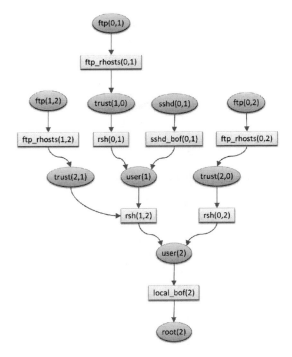

FIGURE 13.1 Example of Attack Graph

- **ftp(0,2)** and **ftp(1,2)** or
- **ftp(0,2)**, **ftp(0,1)**, and **sshd(0,1)**.

Through this unique new capability, administrators are able to determine the best sets of protective measures that should be applied in their environment. In fact, each set of protective measures may have a different cost or impact, and administrators can choose the best option with respect to any of these variables.

Still, we must understand that not all attacks can be averted in advance, and there must usually remain some residual vulnerability even after reasonable protective measures have been applied. We then rely on intrusion detection techniques to identify actual attack instances. But the detection process needs to be tied to residual vulnerabilities, especially ones that lie on paths to critical network resources discovered by TVA. Tools such as Snort (https://www.snort.org/) can analyze network traffic and identify attempts to exploit unpatched vulnerabilities in real time, thus enabling timely response and mitigation efforts. Once attacks are detected, comprehensive capabilities are needed to react to them. TVA can reduce the impact of attacks by providing knowledge of the possible vulnerability paths through the network. TVA attack graphs can be used to correlate and aggregate network attack events, across platforms as well as across a network. These attack graphs also provide the necessary context for optimal response to ongoing attacks.

In conclusion, topological analysis of vulnerabilities plays an important role in gaining situational awareness and, more specifically, what we earlier termed *knowledge of us*. Without automated tools such as CAULDRON, human analysts would be required to manually perform vulnerability analysis, and this would be an extremely tedious and error-prone task. From the example of Figure 13.1, it is clear that even a relatively small network may result in a large and complex attack graph. With the introduction of automated tools such as CAULDRON, the role of the analyst shifts toward higher level tasks: Instead of trying to analyze and correlate individual vulnerabilities, analysts have in front of them a clear picture of existing vulnerability paths; instead of trying to manually map alerts to possible vulnerability exploits, analysts are required to validate the findings of the tool and drill down as needed (Albanese, Jajodia, Pugliese, & Subrahmanian, 2011; Albanese, Pugliese, & Subrahmanian, 2013). The revised role of human analysts—while not changing their ultimate mandate and responsibilities—will require that they are properly trained to use and benefit from the new automated tools. Most likely, because their productivity is expected to increase as a result of automating the most repetitive and time-consuming tasks, fewer analysts will be required to monitor a given infrastructure.

Zero-Day Analysis

As stated earlier, attackers can leverage complex interdependencies among network configurations and vulnerabilities to penetrate seemingly well-guarded networks. Besides well-known weaknesses, attackers may leverage unknown (zero-day) vulnerabilities, which even developers are not aware of. In-depth analysis of network vulnerabilities must consider attacker exploits not merely in isolation but in combination. Attack graphs reveal such threats by enumerating potential paths that attackers can take to penetrate networks. This helps to determine whether a given set of network-hardening measures provides safety to given critical assets. However, attack graphs can only provide qualitative results (i.e., secure or insecure), and this renders resulting hardening recommendations ineffective or far from optimal.

To address these limitations, traditional efforts on network security metrics typically assign numeric scores to vulnerabilities as their relative exploitability or likelihood, on the basis of known facts about each vulnerability. However, this approach is clearly not applicable to zero-day vulnerabilities due to the lack of prior knowledge or experience. In fact, a major criticism of existing efforts on security metrics is that zero-day vulnerabilities are unmeasurable due to the less predictable nature of both the process of introducing software flaws and that of discovering and exploiting vulnerabilities (McHugh, 2006). Recent work addresses the above limitations by proposing a security metric for zero-day vulnerabilities—namely, k-zero-day safety (Wang, Jajodia, Singhal, & Noel, 2010). Intuitively, the metric is based on the number of distinct zero-day vulnerabilities that are needed to compromise a given network asset. A larger such number indicates relatively more security, because it will be less likely to have a larger number of different unknown vulnerabilities all available at the same time, applicable to the same network, and exploitable by the same attacker. However, as shown in Wang et al., the problem of computing the exact value of k is intractable. Moreover, Wang et al. assume the existence of a complete attack graph, but, unfortunately, generating attack graphs for large networks is usually not feasible in practice (Noel & Jajodia, 2004). These facts comprise a major limitation in applying this metric or any other similar metric based on attack graphs.

Albanese, Jajodia, Singhal, and Wang (2013) propose a set of efficient solutions to address this limitation and enable zero-day analysis of practical importance to be applied to networks of realistic sizes. This approach—which combines on-demand attack graph generation with the evaluation of k-zero-day safety—starts from the problem of deciding whether a given network asset is at least k-zero-day safe for a given value of k (Wang et al., 2010), meaning that it satisfies some baseline security requirements: In other words, in order to penetrate a system, an attacker must be able to exploit at least a relatively high number of zero-day vulnerabilities. Second, it identifies an upper bound on the value of k, which intuitively corresponds to the maximum security level that can be achieved with respect to this metric. Finally, if k is large enough, we can assume that the system is sufficiently secure with respect to zero-day attacks. Otherwise, we can compute the exact value of k by efficiently reusing the partial attack graph computed in previous steps.

In conclusion, similarly to what we discuss at the end of the next section, the capability presented in this section is critical to gaining situational awareness and can be achieved either manually or automatically. However, given the uncertain nature of zero-day vulnerabilities, the results of manual analysis could be more prone to subjective interpretation than any other capability we discuss in this chapter. At the same time, because automated analysis relies on assumptions about the existence of zero-day vulnerabilities, complete reliance on automated tools may not be the best option for this capability, and a human-in-the-loop solution may provide the most benefits. In fact, the solution presented in Albanese, Jajodia, et al. (2013) can be seen as a decision-support system in which human analysts can play a role in the overall workflow.

Network Hardening

As discussed earlier, attack graphs reveal threats by enumerating potential paths that attackers can take to penetrate networks. Attack graph analysis can be extended to automatically generate recommendations for hardening networks, which consists in changing network configurations in such a way as to make a network resilient to certain attacks and prevent attackers from reaching certain goals. One must consider combinations of network conditions to harden, which has a corresponding impact on removing paths from the attack graph. For instance, in the section on TVA, we discussed how one could prevent the attacker from reaching the target security condition **root(2)** in the example of Figure 13.1, and we identified two possible hardening solutions. Further, one can generate hardening solutions that are optimal with respect to some notion of cost. Such hardening solutions prevent the attack from succeeding, while minimizing the associated costs. However, the general solution to optimal network hardening scales exponentially as the number of hardening options itself scales exponentially with the size of the attack graph.

In applying network hardening to realistic network environments, it is crucial that the algorithms are able to scale. Progress has been made in reducing the complexity of attack graph manipulation so that it scales quadratically—or linearly within defined security zones (Noel & Jajodia, 2004). However, many approaches for generating hardening recommendations search for exact solutions (Wang et al., 2010), which represents an intractable problem. Another limitation of most work in this area is the assumption that network conditions are hardened independently. This assumption does not hold true in real network environments. Realistically, network administrators can take actions that affect vulnerabilities across a network, such as pushing patches out to many systems at once. Further, the same hardening result may be obtained through more than one action.

Overall, to provide realistic recommendations, the hardening strategy proposed in Albanese, Jajodia, & Noel (2012) takes such factors into account and removes the assumption of independent hardening actions. Albanese et al. (2012) define a network-hardening strategy as a set of allowable atomic actions that administrators can take (e.g., shutting down an file transfer protocol server, blacklisting certain Internet Protocol addresses) and that involve hardening multiple network conditions. A formal cost model is introduced to account for the impact of these hardening actions. Each hardening action has a cost in terms of both implementation and loss of productivity (e.g., when hardening requires shutting down a vulnerable service). This model allows the definition of hardening costs that accurately reflect realistic network environments. Because computation of the minimum-cost hardening solution is intractable, Albanese et al. (2012) introduce an approximation algorithm for optimal hardening. This algorithm finds near-optimal solutions while scaling almost linearly—for certain values of the parameters—with the size of the attack graph, which the authors validate experimentally. Finally, theoretical analysis shows that there is a theoretical upper bound for the worst-case approximation ratio, whereas experimental results show that, in practice, the approximation ratio is much lower than such a bound—that is, the solutions found using this approach are not far, in terms of cost, from the optimal solution.

In conclusion, automated analysis of network-hardening options can greatly improve the performance of a security analyst by providing a timely list of recommended strategies to prevent attackers from compromising the target system while, at the same time, minimizing the cost for the defender. The analyst will then be responsible solely for validating the recommended strategies and selecting the ones that appear to be the most effective in meeting not only quantitative but also qualitative requirements. For instance, automated analysis may conclude that the most cost-effective hardening solution is one that requires—among other things—temporary shutdown of the server hosting the company's website. Although this website may not be running any revenue-generating services, the potential impact on the company's reputation may make this solution less attractive, and a human analyst looking at the results of the automated tools may opt for the second-best solution after taking into account factors that the tools were not able to capture.

Conclusions and Future Directions

In this chapter, we have provided an overview of the state of the art in cyber defense and discussed the role that humans play in the security equation as well as factors limiting their performance. We have analyzed several representative technologies that are available to facilitate analysis of security events and reduce the workload for security analysts. The technologies discussed in this chapter are directly related to the research experience of the authors, but they are representative of several significant research efforts the scientific community has undertaken in recent years. Findings in such critical research areas have proven to have the potential to greatly enhance the performance of cyber analysts, but more work needs to be done to achieve more ambitious objectives. One such objective, and probably the most ambitious, is that of achieving the capability of designing systems that can autonomously (i.e., without human intervention) gain complete awareness of a cyber situation, respond to current intrusions, and adapt to prevent or mitigate future threats.

NOTES

1 The work of Sushil Jajodia and Massimiliano Albanese on this chapter was supported in part by the Army Research Office under awards W911NF-13-1-0421, W911NF-09-1-0525, and W911NF-13-1-0317 and by the Office of Naval Research under awards N00014-12-1-0461 and N00014-13-1-0703.
2 For ease of presentation, we have only included paths that are relevant to achieving root privileges on Machine 2. The complete attack graph would include additional conditions, vulnerabilities, and paths.
3 Understanding of the exact meaning of **rsh(0,1)** and **sshd_bof(0,1)** is not required to gain a general understanding of the notion of attack graph.

REFERENCES

Albanese, M., Jajodia, S., Pugliese, A., & Subrahmanian, V. S. (2011). Scalable analysis of attack scenarios. In V. Atluri & C. Diaz (Eds.), *Proceedings of the 16th European Conference on Research in Computer Security* (pp. 416–433). Berlin, Germany: Springer-Verlag.

Albanese, M., Jajodia, S., & Noel, S. (2012). Time-efficient and cost-effective network hardening using attack graphs. In *Proceedings of the 2012 42nd Annual IEEE/IFIP International Conference on Dependable Systems and Networks* (pp. 1–12). Washington, DC: IEEE Computer Society.

Albanese, M., Jajodia, S., Singhal, A., & Wang, L. (2013). An efficient approach to assessing the risk of zero-day vulnerabilities. In M. S. Obaidat & J. Filipe (Eds.), *E-Business and Telecommunications International Joint Conference, ICETE 2013, Reykjavik, Iceland, July 29–31, 2013, revised selected papers* (pp. 322–340). Berlin, Germany: Springer-Verlag.

Albanese, M., Pugliese, A., & Subrahmanian, V. S. (2013). Fast activity detection: Indexing for temporal stochastic automaton-based activity models. *IEEE Transactions on Knowledge and Data Engineering, 25*, 360–373.

Alberts, D. S., Garstka, J. J., Hayes, R. E., & Signori, D. A. (2001). *Understanding information age warfare*. Washington, DC: Command and Control Research Program.

Cloud Security Alliance. (n.d.). Cloud Controls Matrix (Version 3.0) [Computer software]. Retrieved from https://cloudsecurityalliance.org/research/ccm/

Cooke, N. J., Champion, M., Rajivan, P., & Jariwala, S. (2013). Cyber situation awareness and teamwork. *EAI Endorsed Transactions on Security and Safety, 13*(2), e5. http://dx.doi.org/10.4108/trans.sesa.01-06.2013.e5

Cooke, N. J., Gorman, J. C., Myers, C. W., & Duran, J. L. (2013). Interactive team cognition. *Cognitive Science, 37*, 255–285.

Endsley, M. (1995). Toward a theory of situation awareness in dynamic systems. *Human Factors Journal, 37*, 32–64.

Jajodia, S., Liu, P., Swarup, V., & Wang C. (Eds.). (2010). *Cyber situational awareness: Issues and research*. New York: Springer.

Jajodia, S., & Noel, S. (2010). Topological vulnerability analysis. In S. Jajodia, P. Liu, V. Swarup, & C. Wang (Eds.), *Cyber situational awareness: Issues and research* (pp. 139–154). New York: Springer.

Jajodia, S., Noel, S., Kalapa, P., Albanese, M., & Williams, J. (2011). Cauldron: Mission-centric cyber situational awareness with defense in depth. In *Proceedings of the Military Communications Conference, 2011* (pp. 1339–1344). New York: Institute of Electrical and Electronics Engineers.

McHugh, J. (2006). Quality of protection: Measuring the unmeasurable? In *Proceedings of the 2nd ACM Workshop on Quality of Protection* (pp. 1–2). New York: Association for Computing Machinery.

Mandiant. (2013). *APT1: Exposing one of China's cyber espionage units.* Retrieved from http://intelreport.mandiant.com/

MITRE Corporation. (n.d.). *Common vulnerabilities and exposures.* Retrieved from http://cve.mitre.org/

National Institute of Standards and Technology. (2006, March). *Minimum security requirements for federal information and information systems* (Federal Information Processing Standards Publication No. 200). Gaithersburg, MD: NIST.

National Institute of Standards and Technology. (2010, February). *Guide for applying the risk management framework to federal information systems: A security life cycle approach* (Special Publication No. 800-37, Revision 1). Gaithersburg, MD: NIST.

National Institute of Standards and Technology. (2013, April 30). *Security and privacy controls for federal information systems and organizations* (Special Publication No. 800-53, Revision 4). Gaithersburg, MD: NIST.

National Institute of Standards and Technology. (n.d.). *National vulnerability database.* Retrieved from http://nvd.nist.gov/

Noel, S., & Jajodia, S. (2004). Managing attack graph complexity through visual hierarchical aggregation. In *Proceedings of the ACM CCS Workshop on Visualization and Data Mining for Computer Security* (pp. 109–118). New York: Association for Computing Machinery.

Salmon, P. M., Stanton, N. A., Jenkins, D. P., Walker, G. H., Young, M. S., & Aujla, A. (2007). What really is going on? Review, critique and extension of situation awareness theory. In D. Harris (Ed.), *Engineering psychology and cognitive ergonomics* (pp. 407–416). New York: Springer.

St. John, M., & Smallman, H. S. (2008). Staying up to speed: Four design principles for maintaining and recovering situation awareness. *Journal of Cognitive Engineering and Decision Making, 2,* 118–139.

Symantec Corporation. (2014). *Internet security threat report 2014* (Vol. 19). Retrieved from http://www.symantec.com/content/en/us/enterprise/other_resources/b-istr_main_report_v19_21291018.en-us.pdf

Wang, L, Jajodia, S., Singhal, A., & Noel, S. (2011). k-zero day safety: Measuring the security risk of networks against unknown vulnerabilities. In *Proceedings of the 15th European Symposium on Research in Computer Security* (pp. 573–587). Berlin, Germany: Springer-Verlag.

14
CONCLUSIONS AND DIRECTIONS FOR FUTURE RESEARCH

Lois E. Tetrick, Reeshad S. Dalal, Stephen J. Zaccaro, and Julie A. Steinke

> Cyber security risks pose some of the most serious economic and national security challenges of the 21st century.
>
> (*Cyberspace Policy Review*, 2009, p. iii)

Cyber security is a rapidly evolving field accompanying the widespread growth in the use of digital technologies, including the Internet, in communications, commerce, finance, critical infrastructure, medicine and health care, national security, and global relations. In fact, there is not agreement as to whether cyber security is a single word or two words, as is evident in any literature search. Even so, digital technologies affect most, if not all, areas of individual and organizational life, and with these advances come increasing risks to individuals, organizations, and societies through intentional and unintentional threats to the security of these systems and the information and assets included in them.

The purpose of this volume was to bring an interdisciplinary perspective to our understanding of cyber security work, with the recognition that the cyber security field involves human–computer interaction and that much cyber security work is being conducted by individuals and teams working together with the use of sophisticated tools to promote the security of cyberspace and prevent the exploitation of system vulnerabilities. The chapters in this volume were written by experts in cyber technology and organizational psychology to reflect the joint perspectives, contributions, and challenges inherent in the complexity of cyber security.

Overview of Cyber Security Work

Cyber security analysts are involved in complex knowledge work, as described in several chapters in this volume. In Chapter 2, Zaccaro, Hargrove, Chen,

Repchick, and McCausland present a taxonomy based on an integration of prior frameworks, such as National Institute of Standards and Technology, National Initiative for Cybersecurity Education (2012), the literature on teams, and newly obtained data. This taxonomy translates major functions that cyber security analysts perform into specific tasks that delineate cognitive and behavior activities distinguishing between processes and outcomes. Paralleling this Jose, LaPort, and Trippe (Chapter 8) translate what is known about cyber security work into knowledge, skills, abilities, and other characteristics required of the human analyst to be effective. Both of these chapters provide perspectives based on the human operator working individually or in a team environment and also teams working in a multiteam system. Paralleling these two chapters, Bhatt, Horne, Sandaramurthy, and Zomlot (Chapter 3) and Albanese and Jajodia (Chapter 13) provide rich descriptions of the more technical aspects of cyber security work. What is clear from these general descriptions of cyber security work is that it is complex, dynamic, and with considerable uncertainty that is aided by technology.

Specific Psychosocial Challenges

In this environment, with the tight coupling of human performance and information processing with digital technological systems, several psychosocial challenges are identified. One such challenge is the need for cyber security analysts to be creative, not only in the reactive sense of responding to incidents that may harm the integrity of an organization and its clients' data and other assets but also in the proactive sense of preventing intrusions into systems. The creative problem-solving literature—as referred to by Steinke, Fletcher, Niu, and Tetrick (Chapter 6)—may provide some insights and guidance for cyber security work; however, the constant job demand to be creative may create some unintended negative consequences, as suggested by Steinke et al. and by Parker, Winslow, and Tetrick (Chapter 11).

This dynamic aspect of the cyber security work environment with many work design pressures (noted by Parker et al., Chapter 11) may also relate to counterproductive work behavior and possibly insider threat, especially when one considers that insider threat may take the form of unintentional behaviors as well as intentional attempts to harm or dismantle a cyber system (see Dalal & Gorab, Chapter 5).

A third aspect of cyber security work that is not necessarily unique to such work but is surprisingly understudied in the literature on teams is that of escalation. As Dalal, Bolunmez, Tomassetti, and Sheng (Chapter 4) observe, there are several potential models to describe the decision-making process whereby an individual analyst or a team may decide to hand off an incident to another individual or team. The medical team literature indicates that this is one possible point at which errors are more likely to occur, and given the cyber security work environment, it is posited that this may also be a weak point in cyber security work (see Dalal et al., Chapter 4).

These are just a few of the psychosocial characteristics of cyber security work. The individual chapters provide much more fine-grained analyses. What is apparent is that to understand cyber security work and to improve the effectiveness of cyber security analysts, it is important to consider dynamics of the psychosocial environment as well as the technical environment.

Approaches to Improving Cyber Security Work

Technical Solutions

The domain of human–computer interactions has long been faced with the question of how to allocate functions to humans and to computer systems. This tension is also apparent in cyber security work, with a recognition that many cyber security threats arise from end users; this can be through a lack of knowledge and understanding of the need for cyber security practices and policies, lack of adequate usability of such practices and policies, simple human errors, or intentional malicious behaviors (see Coovert, Dreibelbis, & Borum, Chapter 12). These pressures on the cyber security system encourage experts in cyber technology to aspire to eliminate the human from the system (as Albanese & Jajodia discuss in Chapter 13). Certainly, some automated solutions have improved cyber security, but the ultimate elimination of threat by eliminating the end user has been elusive.

Bhatt et al. (Chapter 3) suggest that adaptive case management may offer a more optimal solution. In this approach, technology is designed to be adaptive to cyber security analysts' needs; the approach seeks to maximize the benefits of digital technology for storage and processing of information by automating the repetitive aspects of analysts' work yet adhering to the evidence-based principles of work design described by Parker et al. (Chapter 11).

Albanese and Jajodia (Chapter 13) offer a different perspective in what they call the *human-on-the loop* approach, in which cyber security analysts are responsible for overseeing an automated system, and they offer several performance metrics for such a system. Advances in threat vulnerability analyses may lead to better situational awareness through technology, removing the human analyst from the most time-consuming and tedious tasks.

Technical solutions can be useful, though there are several factors to consider. As Coovert et al. (Chapter 12) discuss, complex technical solutions may overwhelm analysts and end users, and they may require a level of trust in digital solutions that is not shared by various stakeholders. Therefore, Coovert et al. argue for the need to maintain balance between technology and the human cyber security analyst, using technological solutions as well as psychosocial solutions to enhance the effectiveness of cyber security.

Psychosocial Solutions

Several approaches for promoting the effectiveness of cyber security personnel have been offered in the traditional work and organizational psychology field.

Four of these that are reflected in this volume are selection and staffing, training, work design, and leadership.

Perhaps one of the most traditional psychosocial solutions is to select people for cyber security positions with the requisite knowledge, skills, and abilities and to place these individuals in the best positions and teams given their knowledge, skills, and abilities. Mueller-Hanson and Darza (Chapter 9) provide a description of the various selection techniques and the relative advantages and disadvantages of each. Given, as Mueller-Hanson and Darza observe, that there is currently a shortage of skilled cyber security analysts, an alternative to selection might be to provide training, as described by Brummel, Hale, and Mol (Chapter 10). To use either approach, it is important to consider the characteristics of the individuals who will most likely be successful in this work environments (see Jose et al., Chapter 8).

To complement the discussion of selection and training, Parker et al. (Chapter 11) provide a description of evidence-based principles for designing jobs and several examples of the application of these principles as well as examples that do not appear to be consistent with these principles. In many instances, the designs of cyber security incident response teams have followed traditional information technology (IT) designs without sufficient consideration of differences between cyber security analytic work and IT work (see Mueller-Hanson & Garza, Chapter 9). If there are differences in analysts' work, there are likewise important implications for leadership. As Klimoski and Murray (Chapter 7) assert, the chief information security officer must inspire cyber security personnel and end users to be creative in protecting an organization's assets and manage an acceptable level of risk to the organization.

One common theme among the chapters is the importance of growth and development in the cyber security domain. The dynamic nature of digital technologies—with new applications, hardware, and other technologies rapidly emerging—may be challenging in and of itself, and to maintain competent and motivated personnel, opportunities for growth and development in this turbulent organizational function are critical.

Future Research Directions

Each chapter identifies gaps in our knowledge and important future research directions, and we do not repeat these here. Rather, we conclude the volume with some research questions that we believe draw on both technological and psychological solutions.

Cyber Security as a Multilevel Phenomenon

When industrial and organizational psychologists think of multilevel phenomena, we need to think about the individual level, the team level, and the organizational level (Kozlowski & Klein, 2000). Cyber security work suggests at least two more levels. First, in addition to the organizational level, it appears that many cyber security response teams are embedded in multiteam systems. These multiteam systems may reside within a single organization, or they may actually span across organizations. Further, cyber security incident response teams may vary depending on the type of organization (e.g., commercial enterprise, governmental agency, enterprise coordinated among multiple organizations/agencies) and the types of functions that they perform—that is, do they focus on malware, threats, and vulnerabilities, for example? These differences in function and type of organization raise questions as to whether and, if so, how these contextual factors fundamentally alter the processes and structures of the multiteam systems.

The second level that we suggest might be added to our current notion of multilevel phenomena is the technological systems that are an important component of the cyber security environment. There is a long history of considering the human–computer interaction in human factors, cognitive sciences, and organizational sciences (Wickens, 1992), but much of this work has focused on the individual human operator and the technology. With continuing advances in digital technologies, including mobile devices, it may be informative to conceptualize a more integrative systems approach in which individuals, teams, multiteam systems, organizations, and multiple organizations interact with the technological system. This perspective potentially would expand the continuing question of what aspects of cyber security work are best performed by people and what is best carried out by digital technologies.

Collaboration and Decision Making in Cyber Security

The involvement of teams and multiteam systems in cyber security work implies a need for collaboration among cyber security analysts. To fully understand the implications of this, research is needed to better understand when and how cyber security analysts decide to engage another analyst or other analysts to resolve a potential incident. A corollary to this is the question of cyber security analysts and teams that decide to simply hand off an incident to another individual, team, or organization rather than work collaboratively. Are there certain factors relative to the incident or organizational policies and practices that may prove more effective? It may be that the literature on knowledge sharing can inform our understanding of collaboration although research in the complex, dynamic cyber security environment has not yet been conducted.

Once we better understand the dynamics of individual and team decision making and collaboration, the logical next step would be to design training programs for cyber security analysts to foster a collaborative environment. Much cyber security incident response team training seems to be done in competitions and other simulation exercises. Future research might consider how best to integrate into these forms of training the development of effective teamwork and collaboration skills.

Work Design Considerations for Effective Cyber Security Performance

Consistently throughout the chapters in this volume, cyber security work is described as complex, dynamic knowledge work. This poses a number of questions for future research. How do work design factors affect vigilance, teamwork, and core cyber security performance? There is a considerable body of work on the factors of work design that promote resilience, performance, and well-being in the general industrial and organizational psychology literature (Parker, 2014). However, much of this research has been conducted only at the individual level of analysis, and relatively few studies have included professionals in technological fields. Further, research has tended to take a "main effects" approach rather than a configural, interactional approach. Therefore, future research needs to consider the joint effects of various work design and contextual factors.

The literature on work design tends to take a relatively static approach. Future research in the cyber security field needs to consider temporal dynamics. Cyber security analysts appear to be under considerable time pressure, at least intermittently. This raises the questions of whether analysts may habituate to such time pressure, whether the effect of this time pressure is cumulative, and what might be the best practices to facilitate analysts' recovery from chronic and acute stressors?

A fundamental question inherent in these issues is how cyber security analysts and cyber security incident response teams' job performance should be assessed. In one sense, cyber security work can be viewed as essentially a search for support of the null hypothesis—that is, if a cyber security analyst performs perfectly, no incidents occur! Others would argue that this is unrealistic and that performance needs to be defined in a multidimensional view that takes into account such factors as time to resolve an incident and number of incidents handled. However, these dimensions are, at least partially, contaminated by other factors such as opportunity and the presence of automated tools.

Summary

The intent of this volume was to offer ways in which cyber technology and organizational psychology can contribute to the effectiveness of cyber security analysts and teams. Its chapters provide a rich description of this domain, although several questions remain for future research, and we have only included some of these in the foregoing discussion. To advance our understanding of cyber security and enhance the effectiveness of cyber security analysts, incident response teams, multiteam systems, and organizations integrated with technological systems, more research is needed.

References

Cyberspace Policy Review: Assuring a Trusted and Resilient Information and Communications Infrastructure. (2009. May). Retrieved from http://www.whitehouse.gov/assets/documents/Cyberspace_Policy_Review_final.pdf

Kozlowski, S. W. J., & Klein, K. J. (2000). A multilevel approach to theory and research in organizations: Contextual, temporal, and emergent processes. In K. J. Klein & S. W. J. Kozlowski (Eds.), *Multilevel theory, research, and methods in organizations: Foundations, extensions, and new directions* (pp. 3–90). San Francisco: Jossey-Bass.

National Institute of Standards and Technology, National Initiative for Cybersecurity Education. (2013). *National cybersecurity workforce framework.* Retrieved from Retrieved from http://csrc.nist.gov/nice/framework/

Parker, S. K. (2014). Beyond motivation: Job and work design for development, health, ambidexterity, and more. *Annual Review of Psychology, 65,* 661–691.

Wickens, C. D. (1992). *Engineering psychology and human performance* (2nd ed.). New York: HarperCollins.

INDEX

Note: 'N' after a page number indicates a note; 'f' indicates a figure; 't' indicates a table.

ACM (adaptive case management): and CTA (cognitive task analysis) 70–71; overview of 69–70; vs. process model approach 56, 69
Acquisti, A. xxvii
Adams A. xxv
adaptive case management (ACM). *See* ACM (adaptive case management)
adaptation-level theory 255–256
adaptive performance: and creativity 199; defined 4, 19–20, 198; in incident response 19–20, 38–39; model of 25, 199; required in IT field 4–5. *See also* cognitive load; cyber security work; performance
adaptive readiness, defined 5
Adler, P. S. 260
administrators: role of, in cyber security 219, 221, 222; training of 220t
after-action reviews 38–39, 65, 122, 126–127, 128
agreeableness 182, 205
Ahmad, A. 2–3, 68
Albanese, M. 291, 300, 301, 302
Alberts, C. 35, 65, 68
Alberts, D. S. 296
alert fatigue 279
Alexander, Keith 13
Amabile, T M. 117, 118, 120
Amos, B. 159, 161
Anderson, N. 117, 121, 130

Anthony, D. xxvii
Arad, S. 20, 199
ARCSIGHT software 2
Ariely, D. 129
Army Field Manual 296
Ashforth, B. E. 253
Assante, M. J. 256
assessments, in hiring process 206–208
asset management systems 62
attack graphs 297–299, 298f, 300, 301
audits 233–234, 284
automated strategies: and employee performance 292–293, 302; overview of 2; SIEM (security incident and event management) system 59; topological vulnerability analysis (TVA) 299
autonomy 245–246, 252–253, 255, 257, 260
Avolio, B. J. 161

Baard, S. K. 4, 19–20
Bader, P. 171
Bailey, J. 67
Bakker, A. B. 262
Barrick, M. R. 182
Basadur, M. 120
Beal, D. J. 183
behavioral processes 35, 36, 37, 270–271. *See also* counterproductive work behavior
Bélanger, F. xxvi

Belau, L. 211
Bell, B. S. 199
Bell, S. T. 181, 211
Bennett, R. J. 95, 271
Betts, K. R. 186
Bhatt, S. 56
Bhave, D. P. 196
Bies, R. J. 275
'black hat' research 42
Bledow, R. 121
Blomqvist, K. 275
Bolumnez, B. 74
Bongers, P. M. 252
boredom 255
Borum, R. 3, 267, 269
Bowers, C. A. 211
Boyd, John 66
BPM (business process management) 65
brainstorming 126, 127
Briggs, A. L. 211
Bronk, H. 18
Brummel, B. J. 217
Bulford, C. 94
Burke, C. S. 25
Burke, L. A. 202, 205
business process management (BPM). *See* BPM (business process management)
Byrne, C. D. 38

Campion, M. A. 210
Cannon-Bowers, J. A. 182
Caputo, D. D. xxv, xxvi, xxvii, 3, 14, 76
Caroland, J. 232
Carter, D. R. 209
case management systems 61
Casper, C. 155–156
Castelfranchi, C. xxvii
CAULDRON 297, 299
CERT Coordination Center 57
Chen, B. X. xxv
Chen, C. X. 260
Chen, T. 1–2
Chen, T. R. 4, 13, 241
Chertoff, Michael 185
Cichonski, P. 24
CISO (chief information security officer): competencies required for 152–155, 153f, 158–162; as cyber educator 141–142; evolution of capabilities 154, 154f; functional requirements of 149–152; functions of 145–146; leadership style 143; reporting relationships 146–147; role of, in organizations 138–142, 156–158; technology investment strategy 155–156, 156f. *See also* executive leaders
Citrix 153
Clapper, James 93
cognitive attributes: and motivation 178; as predictor of performance 202, 205; problem-solving skills 179–180; required for cyber security work 172–174, 202f
cognitive bias 113
cognitive load: and ACM (adaptive case management) 70; of cyber security work 4, 5; and employee well-being 254; of hiring assessments 208; reduced, by automated technology 2; and teams 182. *See also* adaptive performance
cognitive processes: in creative problem-solving 19, 123; demands of, in cyber security work 255; development of 257; monitoring vs. problem-solving demands 254–255; in reactive performance processes 35, 36, 37; shared mental models 47–48; situational awareness 296; used for incident response 18–19, 21–22
cognitive task analysis (CTA). *See* CTA (cognitive task analysis)
cohesion 183
collectivism 181
Collignon, S. xxv
communication 21, 22, 36–37, 305; "chain" communication in hierarchical organizations 81–82, failure 69; protocols 63–64
competencies, of CISO 152–155, 153f, 158–162
competency modeling 223
complexity leadership 137
compositional attributes 187
confidence 80–81, 84, 161
conscientiousness 174, 176–177, 182, 205
contextual performance 198
Conti, G. 232
Conti, R. 117
Converse, P. D. 256
Cook, J. 275
Cook, T. 232
Coon, H. 117
Coovert, M. D. 3, 267
Cordery, J. L. 243
cost responsibility 254, 255
counterintelligence. *See* cyber counterintelligence

counterproductive work behavior: case studies 103–104; defined 95–97; detection of 98–100; interventions 104–105; motives 102–103; predictors of 97–98; and SDBs (security-damaging behaviors) 271; severity of 101–102; terminology 100–101; and unintentional behavior 102. *See also* end users; insider threat
Coyle, C. 118
creative problem-solving: and after-action reviews 127; autonomous vs. directed resourcing 126; brainstorming 126, 127; cognitive processes required for 19, 123; and incident response 123–128, 123f; process models 119–122; as proximal attribute 179–180; and security personnel 114, 121–123
creativity: and adaptive performance 199; aspects of 118; defined 116–117; and ethics 129; and flow 129–130; in hackers 114, 130–131; in incident response 19; and innovation 117; limitations of 128–129; Osborn model of 118; and personality 119, 128; process flows as obstacles to 68; process models 118, 119–122; in security personnel 111, 113–116, 177–178; and staff training 156–157; in teams 120–121, 126, 130
credentials 206–207, 213
credibility 161–162
Csikszentmihalyi, M. 117, 254
CSIRTs (cyber security incident response teams): after-action reviews 39; and cognitive load 182; cognitive processes 47–48; cohesion of 183; compositional attributes 187; contextual attributes of 182–184; defined 15, 18, 19, 56; and escalation 85; expansion of 14; in incident response planning 35–37; infrastructure planning 40–41; interdependence, with other teams 185; interpersonal interactions 39–40; mental models 47–48, 184, 186; and mitigation solutions 37–38; and MTSs (multiteam systems) 22–24, 23f; multi-level 15, 20–23; as multiteam system 185; overview of 57; performance outcomes 45–48, 46t, 86; performance requirements of 18–23; and personality 182; proactive performance processes 40–44; reactive performance processes 25, 35–40; structure 43–44; transactive memory 183–184; transportable attributes of 181–182; well-being 48. *See also* incident response taxonomy; MTSs (multiteam systems); SOCs (Security Operations Centers)
CTA (cognitive task analysis), and ACM (adaptive case management) 70–71
culture 234–235, 272
Cushenbery, L. 126, 130
cyber breaches/threats: changing nature of xxv; consequences of 4, 122, 167, 194–195, 268; financial costs 13, 167; and human failure 278–279; increase in 1, 57, 291; at IRS 283; Marconi's telegraph 57; mitigation solutions 233–235; Morris's worm 57; Nigerian '419' scams 283; phishing 230–231, 236, 283; and U.S. Department of Defense 168. *See also* incident response; insider threat
cyber competitions 200
cyber counterintelligence 281–284
cyber intelligence 279–281
Cyber Kill Chain 280
cyber security: automated strategies 2, 59, 292–293, 299, 302; blended, with human solutions 279–280, 280t; challenges of 282; domain framework 112; effective methods xxvi; end users' role in 219, 222, 268–269; executive leaders' role in 135–136; human element of 2–4; infrastructure planning 40–41; maturity levels, by industry 148, 149f; as obstacle to user productivity xxvi, 3, 139, 272, 274; performance enhancement model 5–6, 6f; prevention, as aim of 280; preventive vs. detective controls 233–234; and trust mechanisms xxvii. *See also* automated strategies; psychosocial strategies
cyber security behaviors 270–271. *See also* counterproductive work behavior
cyber security performance, elements of successful outcomes 4
cyber security personnel: administrators 219, 221, 222; attributes of 112–113, 200–202, 203–204t; autonomy of 245–246, 252–253; cognitive attributes 172–174, 202, 202f, 205; creativity in 111, 113–116, 177–178; as CSIRT members 113; end users as 219, 222; engineers 221, 222; executive leaders as 221–222; and hackers 114–115, 115f; hiring challenges 195–197;

KSAs (knowledge, skills, and abilities) required for 175–176t, 195–196, 200; motivational attributes 178; multistage model of performance 172f; personality attributes 174, 176–178, 202f, 205; problem-solving skills 114, 121–123, 179–180; shortage of 167, 188, 194, 195, 244; social skills 180; and SOCs (Security Operations Centers) 59–60; technical knowledge 179, 180, 202f; turnover 64, 68, 244, 245, 253; work experience 207. *See also* CISO (chief information security officer); CSIRTs (cyber security incident response teams); end users; MTSs (multiteam systems)

cyber security work: adaptive performance 4–5, 19–20, 25, 38–39, 198–199; categories of 170t; contextual performance 198; defined 169–170, 197–200; feedback in 246–247; motivation's role in 244–249; National Cybersecurity Workforce Framework 197; overview of 305–307; as sedentary 256; skill variety in 245; task identity 247; task performance 197–198; task significance 247–248; work design principles applied to 244–249, 250–252t

Dalal, R. S. ,1, 74, 84, 92, 196, 201, 208, 213, 305
Darcy, D. 202
Davenport, T. H. 69
DeChurch, L. A. 25, 209
decision-making structures: escalation 78f; heuristics in 78–79; individual 76, 78–79; judge-advisor system 76, 79, 88; non-escalation 77f; teams 76, 79. *See also* escalation
de Lange, A. H. 252, 253
Deloitte Risk Intelligence Enterprise framework 139–140, 140f
Derks, D. 262
DeShon, R. P. 256
developmental attributes 187
DeVore, C. J. 95
DiRosa, G. A. 209, 210–211
distal attributes 172–178
Donovan, M. A 199
Donovan, M. A. 20
Doraiswamy, P. 75
Dorofee, A. 65, 79
Drachsler, H. 18
Dreibelbis, R. 3, 267

Earnest, L. xxv
Edmondson, A. C. 275
emotional contagion 259–260
employee performance: adaptive performance 4–5, 19–20, 25, 38–39, 198–199; and automated strategies 292–293, 302; cognitive ability as predictor of 202, 205; contextual performance 198; criticality of 244; effect of work characteristics on 243; escalation and CSIRTs 85–86; experience as predictor of 207; incident response performance processes 17f; KSAs (knowledge, skills, and abilities) as predictor of 206–207; limitations on 291–292; metrics for evaluating 292–293; multistage model of 172f; outcomes 45–48, 46t, 86; personality as predictor of 205; within-person variability of 196, 206, 208, 212–213; predictors of 201–202, 202f; proactive processes 24–25, 40–44; reactive processes 25, 35–40; requirements for CSIRT workers 18–23; task performance 197–198; variability of 201

employee selection. *See* hiring
Endsley, M. R. 35, 36, 37, 296
end users: role of, in cyber security 219, 222, 268–269; security technology seen as obstacle xxvi, 3, 139, 235, 274; training of 220t; as 'weakest links' 282. *See also* counterproductive work behavior; insider threat
Enget, K. xxv
engineers 220t, 221, 222
Erez, M. 121
ergonomic design 256
escalation: and 'chain' communication in hierarchical organizations 81–82; decision-making structures 76, 76–79, 78f; defined 74; and impression management 80–81; as iterative 85; models 59, 60f, 61; outcomes 82–83, 85–88; and personnel confidence 80–81; and reactive performance 85–86; timing of 84–85. *See also* decision-making structures
escalation reports 83–84
ethics 129, 162, 230
European Network and Information Security Agency 80, 81, 82
Evans, K. 244

executive leaders: CISO role 138–142; 'enabling leadership' in 137–138; role of, in cyber security 135–136, 221–222; technology investment strategy 155–156, 156f; titles related to outcomes 147, 147f; training of 220t. *See also* CISO (chief information security officer)
extraversion 205

fade out phenomenon 105
Falcone, R. xxvii
false alarm rates 293
false-negative alerts 63
false-positive alerts 62–63
Farr, J. 121
Farr, J. L. 117
Fay, D. 258
FBI 14
feedback 246–247
financial costs: of cyber crime 13, 167; spending per employee by industry 148, 149f
Fiore, S. M. 21
Firestien, R. L. 118
FIRST (Forum of Incident Response and Security Teams) 14
Fiset, J. 196
Fitzgerald, T. 147
Flechais, I. xxvii, 283
Fleishman, E. A. 16
Fletcher, L. 111
flexibility 173
flow 129–130, 254
fluid intelligence 173, 178, 180
forecasting 37–38
Fox, S. 96
Frese, M. 121, 256, 258

Gao, X. Y. 258
Garstka, J. J. 296
Garza, M. 194
Gino, F. 129
Girotra, K. 126
Global Information Security Workforce Study 195
Gorab, A. K. 92
Grant, A. M. 243
Greenberg, J. 98
Greitzer, F. L. 100
Griffin, R. W. 243
groupthink 79
Gruys, M. L. 95

Guilford, J. P. 116, 118, 119, 120
Guo, K. H. 269, 270, 271, 274

Haber, E. 67
hackers and hacking: creativity in 114, 130–131; and cyber intelligence 280; and flow 129–130; interactive cycle of, with security personnel 114–115, 115f; 'red teaming' 124; and social engineering 272; Sony Corporation 167, 168. *See also* cyber breaches/threats
Hackman, J. R. 242
Hadgkiss, J. 2–3
Hadnagy, C. 284
Hakkaja, M. 18
Hale, J. 217
Hall, D. T. 161
Handoff 21, 74–75, 129–30
Hannah, S. T. 161
hardening actions 301–302
Hargrove, A. K. 1–2, 13
Harms, P. D. 161, 258
Hayes, R. E. 296
Hennessey, B. A. 118
Henttonen, K. 275
Herath, T. 271
Hermida, R. 84
Herron, M. 117
heuristics 78–79
Hewlett-Packard 64
Hinsz, V. B. 21, 186
hiring: assessments used in 206–208; challenges of 195–197; and credentials 206–207, 213; and personnel attributes 200–207; selection criteria 201, 203–204t; and team dynamics 196, 209–211. *See also* performance
Hollenbeck, G. P. 161
Homeland Security Advisory Council 194
honeypots 99, 106n4
Horne, W. 56
Houtman, I. 252
Humphrey, S. E. 243, 249, 254
Hunker, J. 94
Hunter, S. T. 119, 126, 130

Ilgen, D. R. 21
impression management 80–81
incident response: adaptive performance in 19–20; after-action reviews 38–39; case management systems 61; cognitive processes used 18–19, 21–22; and creative

problem-solving 123–128, 123f; creativity in 19; escalation models 59, 60f, 61; forecasting 37–38; generic performance processes 17f; individual level 20; as knowledge work 18–20, 21; and mental models 67; mitigation solutions 37–38, 233–235; and MTSs (multiteam systems) 22–24, 23f, 35–37, 38; multi-level 20–23; phases of 122; team level 20–21

incident response taxonomy 26–34t; applications 48–49; construction of 23–25; performance outcomes 45–48, 46t; preliminary validation 44–45; proactive performance processes 24–25, 40–44; reactive performance processes 25, 35–40. *See also* CSIRTs (cyber security incident response teams)

Industrial/Organization (I/O) psychology, performance enhancement model 5–6, 6f

information architecture 234
information processing 254
information sharing 76, 79, 127, 185–186, 206
Information Technology Infrastructure Library (ITIL). *See* ITIL (Information Technology Infrastructure Library)
infrastructure planning 40–41
innovation: and creativity 117; defined 117; and security personnel 113–116. *See also* creativity
innovative ambidexterity 121
input interdependence 185
insider threat: consequences of 92–93; defined 94–95; and electronic monitoring of employees 99–100; and end users xxv, 235, 268–269, 282; motives 102–103. *See also* counterproductive work behavior; cyber breaches/threats
intelligence 280. *See also* cyber intelligence
interdependence 185, 248, 297
Internal Revenue Service (IRS) 283
interpersonal interactions: emotional contagion 259–260; and relational work design 243; and social skills 180; social support 249, 253; in teams 39–40, 128, 248
interviews 206
intrusion detection 299
ITIL (Information Technology Infrastructure Library) 65, 67
IT Policy Compliance Group 162

Jackson, P. R. 254, 257
Jajodia, S. 291, 300, 301
jangle fallacy 100
Jarvis, D. 152
JCM (job characteristics model) 242–243
Jehng, J. 173
Jervis, S. 13
job analysis 223
job characteristics model (JCM) 242–243
job crafting 262
job demands-control model 252
job design. *See* work design
Johnson, D. 200
Jose, I. 167

Kagan, A. 274
Kahneman, D. 142
Kandogan, E. 67
Karyda, M. 94
Kemp, C. 171
kill chains 280
Killcrece, G. 65, 79
Kiountouzis, E. 94
Kirkpatrick, D. L. 225
Klimoski, R. J. 135, 159, 161
knowledge, skills, and abilities (KSAs). *See* KSAs (knowledge, skills, and abilities)
knowledge work 18–20, 21, 47
Kokolakis, S. 94
Kompier, M. A. 252
Kozlowski, S. W. J 199
Kozlowski, S. W. J. 4, 19–20, 21
Kraiger, K. 226
Krause, M. 147
KSAs (knowledge, skills, and abilities): as component of psychosocial strategy 2; as predictor of performance 206–207; required for cyber security work 175–176t, 179, 180, 195–196, 200. *See also* training
k-zero-day safety 300

Lakhani, K. R. 129
Langfred, C. W. 248
Lant, T. 21
LaPort, K. 167
Lasswell, H. D. 79
Lazenby, J. 117
leadership: coordination of, among teams 186; development of 158–162; 'three C' rubric 159–162; value of, for organizations 162–163
learned industriousness, theory of 255

learning 256–258. *See also* training
Lee, R. T. 253
'lessons learned' reviews. *See* after-action reviews
Lester, P. B. 161
Lewicki, R. J. 275
Li, W.-D. 258
linkage attributes 187
Lovejoy, K. 152
Lukasik, M. A. 211

Ma, M. 202
MacCrimmon, K. 148
Maglio, P. P. 67
Manzey, D. H. 3
Marion, R. 137–138
Marks, M. A. 22, 25, 39, 209
Martin, R. 254
Masucci, C. 118
Mathieu, J. E. 22, 185, 209
Matthews, G. 279
Matthews, M. D. 4
Mauer, B. 200
Mayer, R. C. 272
McAllister, D. J. 275
McCausland, T. 1–2, 13
McCloskey, M. 199–200
memory, transactive 47, 183–184
memory, working 173–174, 180
mental models: and creative problem-solving 127; and incident response 67; shared, in teams 47–48, 184, 186; and work design 257
Meyer, R. D. 84
Miner, J. B. 240
minority groups 202, 208
missed detection rates 293
mitigation solutions 37–38. *See also* incident response
Mitnick, Kevin 282
Mol, M. J. 217
Morgeson, F. P. 243
Morris, Robert 57
motivation: and cyber security work 244–249; in security personnel 178; and work design 242–243
MTSs (multiteam systems) 23f; CSIRTs (cyber security incident response teams) as 185; defined 22–23, 185, 209; hiring for work in 209–211; as multilevel phenomenon 309. *See also* CSIRTs (cyber security incident response teams); incident response taxonomy; teams
Mueller-Hanson, R. 194

Mulatu, M. S. 257
Mumford, M. D. 25, 38, 119, 120, 127
Murase, T. 186
Murray, J. 135

Nahrgang, J. D. 243
Nannestad, P. 277
National Cybersecurity Workforce Framework 197
National Initiative for Cybersecurity Education (NICE) 112, 169, 197
National Institute of Standards Technology (NIST) 112, 144–145
Negangard, E. xxv
network hardening 301–302
NICE. *See* National Initiative for Cybersecurity Education (NICE)
Nigerian '419' scams 283
NIST. *See* National Institute of Standards Technology (NIST)
Niu, Q. 111
Noel, S. 301
NSMVs (nonmalicious security violations) 271

Oates, G. 257
Obama, Barack 13, 194
Oldham, G. R. 242
openness/intellectance 177
Organ, D. W. 270
organizations: 'chain' communication in hierarchical 81–82; culture of, and trust 272; enterprise scale 147–148; life cycles of 148; products/services 148–149; security culture of 234–235; security training in, by role 220t; structure of 248–249; and uncertainty 137–138. *See also* executive leaders
Orvis, K. 181
Osborn, A. F. 117–118, 120
Osorno, M. 35
outcome interdependence 185

Padayachee, K. 270–271
Paller, Allen 160
Parasuraman, R. 3, 279
Parker, S. K. 240, 241, 243, 257, 258, 260
Parnes, S. J. 120
passwords, changing xxv, 274
Paulus, P. B. 120
Peeters, M.A.G. 182
performance. *See* employee performance
performance adaptation. *See* adaptive performance

performance enhancement model 5–6, 6f
personality: attributes required for cyber security work 174, 176–178, 202f; and creativity 119, 128; defined 174; as predictor of performance 205; and teams 182; and work design 258
Pfleeger, S. L. xxvii; on human element of cyber security 14; on insider threat 94; on pace of technology change xxv; on terminology 101; on users' mistrust of security technology 3; on value of psychosocial approach xxvi, 76
Pharmer, J. A. 211
phishing 230–231, 236, 283. *See also* cyber breaches/threats
physical demands 256
Plamondon, K. E. 20, 199
policy compliance 268–269, 271
Post, G. V. 274
postmortems. *See* after-action reviews
Predd, J. B. 94
privacy management 141
proactive performance processes. *See* incident response taxonomy; process model approach
problem-solving skills. *See* creative problem-solving
process interdependence 185
process model approach: vs. ACM (adaptive case management) 56, 69; benefits of 63–64; and BPM (business process management) 65; for creative problem-solving 119–122; CSIRT models 56; limitations of 68; models 65–67, 66f; prescriptive vs. descriptive 65; proactive 24–25, 40–44; reactive 25, 35–40, 85–86; in Security Operations Centers (SOCs) 63–68. *See also* incident response taxonomy
productivity: security technology seen as obstacle to xxvi, 3, 139, 235, 272, 274; and SRBs (security risk behaviors) 271
proximal attributes 178–180
psychology: 2, 14, 65, 92, 98, 103–104, 218, 223, 310; cybertrust 236; I/O: 5–6; organizational 76–77, 80, 92; personnel 187; positive 262.
psychosocial strategies: benefits of xxvi; overview of 2; research in xxvii–xxviii
Puccio, G. J. 118
Pugliese, A. 300
Pulakos, E. D. 20, 199

Qassam Cyberbrigades 194
Quaintance, M. K. 16

Rajivan, P. 182, 200
Rao, H. R. 271
Rashid, F. 275
reactive performance processes. *See* incident response taxonomy; process model approach
'red teaming' 124
Reeder, F. 244
Reinhardt, W. 18, 19, 21
Rench, T. A. 4, 19–20
Repchick, K. M. 1–2, 13
reports 38
research: 26–34t, 42, 75–76, 97–100, 127; 'black hat' 42; cyber security 14–15; psychology 97, 98; in psychosocial strats xxvii–xxviii; team dynamics 21, 129; in trust 275–277; on work design 259–60
resistance behavior xxv
response teams. *See* CSIRTs (cyber security incident response teams)
Reymen, I. M. M. J. 182
Rhodes, M. 118, 127
risk management: CISO role in 138–142; and company life cycle 148; and company product/service offerings 148–149; Deloitte Risk Intelligence Enterprise framework 139–140, 140f; and enterprise scale 147–148; and leadership titles vs. outcomes 147; National Institute of Standards Technology (NIST) Risk Management Framework 144–145, 144f; PricewaterhouseCoopers Cyber Security Risk Management Model 143–144, 143f; and privacy management 141; of social engineering attacks 284; and technology investment strategy 155–156
Robinson, S. L. 95, 271
Rosen, M. A. 21
Ruefle, R. 65, 79
Ruighaver, A. B. 2–3, 68
Rutte, C. G. 182

SABs (security assurance behaviors) 270
Sackett, P. R. 95
Salas, E. 21, 211
Salazar, M. 21
SAs (security analysts). *See* cyber security personnel
Sasse, M. 283

Sasse, M. A. xxv, xxvii, xxvii–xxviii
SCBs (security compliance behaviors) 270–271
Schmidt, B. 18
Schooler, C. 257
SDBs (security-damaging behaviors) 270, 271
security incident and event management (SIEM) systems. *See* SIEM (security incident and event management) system
Security Operations Centers (SOCs). *See* SOCs (Security Operations Centers)
Shaw, E. D. 93
Shedden, P. 68
Sheng, Z. 74
Shipman, A. S. 38
Shiv, P. 75
SIEM (security incident and event management) system: false-negative alerts 63; false-positive alerts 62–63; and SOCs (Security Operations Centers) 59
Signori, D. A. 296
Silowash, G. J. 92
simulations 206, 231
Sinha, K. K. 240
situational awareness 35, 180, 258, 294–296
situational judgment tests (SJTs) 206
skill variety 245
Sloep, P. 18
Smith, A. 242
Snort 299
social capital 162
social engineering 271–272, 282–284
social skills 180. *See also* interpersonal interactions
social support 249, 253
socio-technical systems xxvii
SOCs (Security Operations Centers): challenges of 62–63, 67; as CSIRT 57–58; functions of 58–62; process flows in 63–68
Sony Corporation 13, 167, 168
Spector, P. E. 96
Spiro, R. J. 173
SRBs (security risk behaviors) 270, 271
staffing. *See* hiring
Stanard, T. 199–200
Standbury, W. 148
Stanton, J. M. 271
Steinke, J. A. 1, 111, 305
Stevens, M. J. 210
Stewart, J. 152, 158
Stockpole, W. 200

Subrahmanian, V. S. 300
Sundaramurthy, S. 56
systems thinking 173–174, 180

tacit knowledge 69, 70
talent management 167–169, 187–188
Taris, T. W. 252
task identity 247
task performance 197–198. *See* performance
task significance 247–248
taxonomy 16–17. *See also* incident response taxonomy
Taylor, F. W. 242
Taylor, H. 232
teams: collectivism 181; composition of 210–211; creativity in 120–121, 126, 130; and decision making 309; defined 21; hiring for work in 196, 209–211; interpersonal interactions 39–40, 43–44, 128, 248; overview of 199–200; and personality 182; self-managing 242; virtual, and dynamic trust 276–277. *See also* CSIRTs (cyber security incident response teams); MTSs (multiteam systems)
technical knowledge. *See* KSAs (knowledge, skills, and abilities)
Terwiesch, C. 126
Tetrick, L. E. 1, 111, 240, 305
Theoharidou, M. 94
Thomassetti, A. J. 74
Thorbruegge, M. 18
Thordson, M. 199–200
throughput 293
time pressure 254, 310
Tims, M. 262
Tobey, D. H. 256
topological vulnerability analysis (TVA). *See* TVA (topological vulnerability analysis)
Totterdell, P. 260
training: alternatives to 233–235; conferences 229; and creativity 156–157; design of 222–226, 227t, 309; effectiveness of 217–218, 225–226; e-mails 230; evaluation of 224–226; future of 236–237; and individual differences 232–233; job analysis/competency modeling 223; methods 226–232; mobile 237; online programs 228–229; by organizational role 220t; and process flows 64; self-development

232; self-phishing 230–231; simulations 231; and social engineering attacks 284; university programs 227–228; and work design 256–258. *See also* KSAs (knowledge, skills, and abilities)
trait affect 177–178
transformation process 137
Tribbey, C. 168
Tripp, D. M. 167
trust: affect-based 275–276; cognition-based 275–276; and cyber security xxvii; dynamic, and virtual teams 276–277; and executive leadership 138; research in 275–277; and social engineering attacks 283–284; and team interpersonal interactions 39–40, 44; in technology vs. individuals 272, 275
turnover 64, 68, 244, 245, 253
TVA (topological vulnerability analysis) 297–299
Tversky, A. 142
Tygar, J. D. 282

Ulrich, K. T. 126
uncertainty 137
U.S. Department of Defense 168
users. *See* end users

Vance, A. 271
Van de Ven, A. H. 240
van Tuijl, H.F.J.M. 182
van Zadelhoff, M. 152, 154–155
vigilance 278
Villado, A. J. 211
Vincent, P. 199–200
Vogelgesang, G. R. 161
von Winterfeldt, D. 83
vulnerabilities: testing for 42–43; TVA (topological vulnerability analysis) 297–299; zero-day analysis 299–301

Wall, T. 275
Wall, T. D. 243, 254, 257
Wallas, G. 119
Wang, L. 300
Warm, J. S. 279
Webber, S. S. 276
Wehrung, D. 148
Weis, E. 4
well-being 48, 249, 252–256
West, M. A. 117
West-Brown, M. 15
West-Brown, M. J. 74
Whitten, A. 282
Winslow, C. J. 240
Witt, L. A. 202, 205
Wolf, R. G. 129
work design: and cyber security work 244–249, 250–252t; defined 241–242; effectiveness of 310; and employee well-being 249, 252–256; future research 259–260; and job crafting 262; learning-related benefits of 256–258; motivational 242–249; and personality 258; principles for 261t; relational 243; and situational awareness 258; value of 240–241
work experience 207
workload requirements 171t; and cognitive exhaustion 279; and cost responsibility 254, 255; excess 253–254

Yukl, G. 161

Zaccaro, S. J. 1–2, 4–5, 22, 25, 171, 181, 209, 210–211
Zajicek, M. 65, 79
Zapf, D. 256
zero-day analysis 299–301
Zimmerman, C. 241, 245, 248, 257, 258
Zomlot, L. 56